BOCONNOC

BOCONNOC

THE HISTORY OF A CORNISH ESTATE

CATHERINE LORIGAN

The
History
Press

For Elizabeth, Clare and Sarah and in memory of Anthony.

And for Andrew, who suggested that I write this book.

First published 2017

The History Press
The Mill, Brimscombe Port
Stroud, Gloucestershire, GL5 2QG
www.thehistorypress.co.uk

British Library Cataloguing in Publication Data.
A catalogue record for this book is available from the British Library.

ISBN 978 0 7509 6773 0

Typesetting and origination by The History Press
Printed and bound by CPI (Group) UK Ltd

CONTENTS

ABOUT THE AUTHOR

Born in London, Catherine Lorigan has degrees from the universities of Birmingham, Oxford and Exeter. Her love of Cornwall began during her teenage years and has led to its history becoming the focus of her research interests. The author of three books on the county, her first encapsulated the dual themes of the social and economic history of the village of Delabole. Based on her PhD thesis, this book was awarded the Holyer an Gof trophy in 2008 by the Cornish Gorsedh for the best book published about Cornwall in the previous year. Delabole was followed by Connections, which drew together a number of interlinking aspects of the history of North Cornwall. Boconnoc is her third book.

When not visiting or writing about Cornwall, Catherine spends her time studying Renaissance music, playing the viol (an early music instrument) in consorts with friends, and singing.

ACKNOWLEDGEMENTS

To the following I extend my thanks:

In Cornwall: Elizabeth, Clare and Sarah Fortescue; Angela Broome at the Courtenay Library, Royal Institution of Cornwall; the staff at the Cornish Studies Library, Redruth; the staff at the Cornwall Record Office, Truro; Christine and Colin Edwards; Andrew Foot; Paul Holden; Dan Mallet; Jim Matthews; Michael Swift; Carole Vivian.

In England: The archivists of: Balliol College, Oxford; Charterhouse; Christ Church, Oxford; the Coldstream Guards; the College of Arms; Harrow School; the Inner Temple; Lincoln's Inn; the Sir John Soane's Museum, London; Mary Beal; Kildare Bourke-Borrowes; the staff at the British Library; the staff at Christie's; Mildred Cookson, Trustee of the Mills Archive; the Countess of Arran; the staff at the Devon Record Office; Frances Dodds; the staff at the Hampshire Record Office; Bryan Lorigan; the staff at the National Trust Picture Library; the staff at the Picture Gallery and Library, Christ Church, Oxford; Anna McEvoy, Stowe Restoration Trust; Ann Stuart; Jim Sutton; Emma Trelawny-Vernon; The Weiss Gallery, London; Min Wood.

In Australia: Caitlyn Lehmann; Philip Payton.

In Ireland: Sharon Carroll, Cultural & Heritage Administrator, Irish Georgian Society; Aisling Dunne, Archivist, Irish Architectural Archive; the staff at Harold's Cross/Mount Jerome cemetery, Dublin; Brian Lynch.

In Italy: Ugo Valdrè.

ABBREVIATIONS
AND CURRENCY

BL   British Library
BRO   Berkshire Record Office
CRO   Cornwall Record Office
DRO   Devon Record Office
HES   Historic Environment Service (Cornwall)
HRO   Hampshire Record Office
NPG   National Portrait Gallery
RIC   Royal Institution of Cornwall
TNA   The National Archives (formerly the Public Record Office)

CURRENCY

Prior to decimalisation in February 1971, 12 pence (*d*) = 1 shilling (*s*)
20 shillings (*s*) = £1
There were 240 pence (*d*) in £1

LIST OF FIGURES
AND PLATES

FIGURES

16. Gamekeepers at Boconnoc: reproduced by permission of Historic England (Commander R. Phillimore Collection).

17. Frontispiece, To Dear Papa from his loving children, L.S.A.F. (Annie) & H.E.F. (Harriet), drawing of Boconnoc church tower: Phillimore Papers, HRO, 115M88, F6/2.

18. Plan of Boconnoc church, *c.* 1835 by Arthur Tatham: CRO, P/12/2/3, reproduced courtesy of the Cornwall Record Office.

19. Reverend Arthur Tatham: Phillimore Papers, HRO, 115M88/P24.

20. The Fowey ferry in the 1950s: photograph courtesy of Jim Matthews.

21. Detail of the engraving of the harbour of Fowey by Willem Schellinks, 1662: © Österreichische Nationalbibliothek, Vienna (*see* colour section).

PLATES

1. Portrait of Sir Reginald Mohun and Dorothy Chudleigh – English School *c.* 1604: © The Weiss Gallery, London.

2. Seal showing Richard Symonds in profile: 'Symonds' Essex Vol. 2. Reproduced by permission of the Kings, Heralds and Pursuivants of Arms, College of Arms.

3. Portrait of Anne, Lady Grenville by John Hoppner (1758–1810): © Christie's Images Limited 2009.

4. Portrait of William Wyndham, Lord Grenville in the robes of the Chancellor of the University of Oxford by William Owen: by permission of the Governing Body of Christ Church, Oxford.

5. An undated painting of George Grenville Fortescue's grave with the white cross in Algiers; Phillimore Papers, Hampshire Record Office (HRO), 115M88/F5/5.

6. Memorial in Christ Church Cathedral, Oxford, south aisle, southwest corner. The inscription reads: 'In Pious Memory of George Grenville Fortescue of Boconnoc in the county of Cornwall and one time a Student of this House, whose body, when he had been snatched away by a sudden death, lies in Algeria among the Africans.' His friends commissioned a stained-glass window which was installed above the memorial. The window, by William Wailes, dated 1858, shows the Crucifixion and two scenes from the life of Christ.

7. Grave of Annie Moore (née Fortescue) in Harold's Cross/Mount Jerome cemetery, Dublin. The inscription reads: Louisa Susan Anne Moore, Daughter of the Honble George and Lady Louisa Fortescue and wife of William Westby Moore Esqre, Born Novr 14th 1833, Married June 25th 1863, Died March 31st 1864. To her dearly loved memory her sorrowing husband Inscribes this stone. Psalm XXIII.

8. Detail of the tithe map of Boconnoc parish, 1838: CRO, TM/12. Reproduced courtesy of the Cornwall Record Office.

9. Detail of Henry VIII's map of coastal fortifications showing 'Boconnocke': BL, Cotton Augustus I.i.38. Reproduced by permission of the British Library.

10. Detail of the map, 'Draft of the East Commons' showing 'Boconack Howse': CRO, AD644. Reproduced courtesy of the Cornwall Record Office.

11. Drawing of an arch for Boconnoc, Cornwall by Thomas Pitt, 1st Lord Camelford: © Sir John Soane's Museum, London.

12. Detail of a map by I. Black, *c.* 1761–71: CRO, F/3/14/11. Reproduced courtesy of the Cornwall Record Office.

13. Boconnoc House, 2016.

14. The staircase at Boconnoc: © Boconnoc estate.

15. Painting on the staircase at Boconnoc.

16. Detail of painting on the staircase at Boconnoc: © Min Wood.

17. Stowe House, Buckinghamshire.

18. The Menagerie, Stowe House, Buckinghamshire.

19. *The Dance of the Hours*, by Vincenzo Valdrè, Music Room at Stowe House, Buckinghamshire. Reproduced by permission of the Stowe House Preservation Trust.

20. Plan of manors in Cornwall owned by Lord and Lady Grenville: CRO, F/4/78/6, nineteenth century. Reproduced courtesy of the Cornwall Record Office.

21. Portrait of Sir Reginald Mohun in later life, *c.* 1620s: reproduced courtesy of Emma Trelawny-Vernon.

22. The stream in Valley Crucis, holiday sketchbook of LSAF (Louisa Susan Anne Fortescue – Annie), Boconnoc, August 1856: HRO, Phillimore papers, 115M88/D3.

23. The entrance to the Bath House.

24. Interior of the Bath House.

25. The Dovecote.

26. The wheel-headed wayside cross in Boconnoc churchyard.

27. The font in Boconnoc church, fifteenth century. From a drawing book owned by Harriet Buller, mother of Harriet Trelawny.

28. The Carminow brass plate in Menheniot church: see Edwin Hadlow Wise Dunkin, *Monumental Brasses of Cornwall*, London, p. 87.

29. The harbour of Fowey, Willem Schellinks, 1662 , the ferry, bottom right: © Österreichische Nationalbibliothek, Vienna, Z85032805.

30. Boconnoc House and church, 2016: © the author.

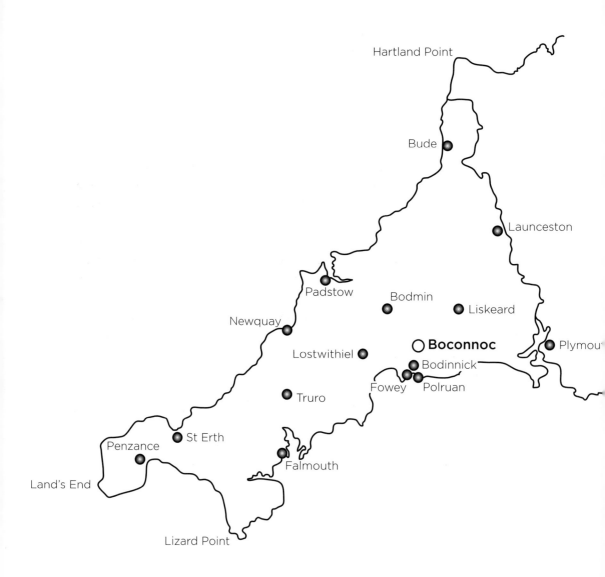

Hartland Point

Bude

Launceston

Padstow

Bodmin

Liskeard

Newquay

Boconnoc

Lostwithiel

Bodinnick

Plymou

Fowey   Polruan

Truro

St Erth

Penzance

Falmouth

Land's End

Lizard Point

CORNWALL

FOREWORD

In 1967 F.E. Halliday, best known for his 1953 edition of Richard Carew's *Survey of Cornwall*, produced a volume entitled *A Cornish Chronicle*, an account of the Carew family of Antony from the time of the Spanish Armada to the Civil War. It is a good book but for me one of its most memorable passages is that which describes the location of Boconnoc, the Cornish house and estate. 'One of the most delectable – and inaccessible – regions of Cornwall,' wrote Halliday, 'is the country defined on the north by the upper waters of the Fowey where it cuts the southern slope of Bodmin Moor, on the west by its lower reaches as it turns abruptly at Lanhydrock and slides below the Black Prince's castle at Restormel, on the east by the Looe River, and on the south by the sea.' As Halliday mused, it is 'virtually an island carved out of the country by rivers', the 'kingdom of Mark and Isolde and magical Celtic names', its geographic extent encompassing much of the old Hundred of West Wivel, 'an almost perfect square, its sides eight miles long, with the little towns of Fowey, Lostwithiel, Liskeard and Looe at the four corners'. And, Halliday added: 'Near the middle of this square is Boconnoc.' As a description of Boconnoc's situation, Halliday's sketch can hardly be bettered. But his brief depiction of the locality also hints at the area's seeming impenetrability, its mysterious detachment from the rest of Cornwall. Even today that sense of entering a hidden land is apparent, as the motorist negotiates the narrow high-hedged lanes before suddenly, and often unexpectedly, encountering the 300-acre estate that is Boconnoc. A.L. Rowse and John Betjeman were both enchanted by Boconnoc, the former by its romantic Civil War associations, the latter by its gardens and deer park and house and church. Countless others have been similarly intrigued. Now that the once ruinous house has been happily restored – a venue for all kinds of events, from book launches to wedding ceremonies and receptions, the gardens open periodically to visitors – it presents a more welcoming and public face to the world at large. But it retains its almost elusive atmosphere, deep in its insular position in one of the least known parts of Cornwall.

In this fine study, Catherine Lorigan sheds much light on this remarkable and hitherto often shadowy estate, encouraging us to get to know it better, and allowing us to understand its place in the wider history of Cornwall. Already well known for her *Delabole:*

The History of the Slate Quarry and the Making of its Village Community, published in 2007 and based on her PhD thesis completed at the Institute of Cornish Studies, Catherine Lorigan is an accomplished local historian. In this book she demonstrates once more her great ability to hunt down key but often obscure documentary sources in all manner of archives and libraries, skilfully weaving her material together in a grand narrative that tells the story of Boconnoc in gripping detail. Her first five chapters present that story as a chronology, and in the final five she adopts a thematic approach, alighting on especially significant aspects of Boconnoc's past. We learn of the earliest traces of human activity in the locality, in the Bronze Age, and of the emergence of Boconnoc as a landed estate by the medieval period (it is mentioned in Domesday), entwined as it was in the fortunes of well-known Cornish and West Country families such as the Carminows, Courtenays and Mohuns. Less familiar among those medieval owners of Boconnoc is the wonderfully named Halnath Mauleverer, who acquired the estate in 1484 as a reward for his services to Richard III.

The Civil War, including the nearby Battle of Braddock Down, is covered here in vivid and illuminating detail, one of those moments when Boconnoc played a pivotal role in the history of Cornwall. Later, the estate was owned variously by Pitts, Grenvilles and Fortescues. As Catherine Lorigan explains, the house we see today was largely rebuilt by the influential Pitt family in the eighteenth century. By the mid-twentieth century, alas, it had fallen badly into decay, leading to the demolition of the unstable south-west wing in 1972. Yet there were brighter days ahead, and in 1996 the estate was taken over by Anthony and Elizabeth Fortescue, who together undertook the house's restoration – indeed, transformation – from 2001. All this Catherine Lorigan tells with insight and sympathy, her narrative encompassing not only house and church and gardens but also the estate's interests in the agricultural and mineral industries – including copper, tin, china clay and slate – and broader subjects such as emigration. Here again are themes that typify Cornish history. They lead Catherine to ponder whether Boconnoc should be considered an exemplar of Cornwall's story. Wisely, perhaps, she answers 'yes' and 'no'. But maybe it is best left to the reader to judge, as he or she becomes engrossed in this fascinating and extremely well crafted book.

Professor Philip Payton,
Flinders University, Australia

INTRODUCTION

'Boconnoc – it is the paradise of Cornwall.'

(BL: Add MS 69314, Hamoze, 19 September 1799, James Wallis to Lady Camelford, ff. 103–104)

This book has taken a long time to write, largely due to the enormous amount of information that came to light during the course of my research. The documents were held in a large number of archival repositories. The Fortescue archives held in the Cornwall and Devon Record Offices, the Phillimore papers in the Hampshire Record Office, the Dropmore papers in the British Library and the Pitt papers in The National Archives, necessitated many hours of reading and transcribing.

Two consequences became apparent when I realised the sheer volume of documentation that was involved and that the written records spanned the period from Domesday in the eleventh century to the present: first, that I would swiftly have to become an expert in every period of Cornish and English history to be in a position to put Boconnoc into its historical context. This initially seemed to be a daunting and challenging task, revising a number of topics that I had not studied for many years. In the end, it was a delight, for one week I was in the midst of the English Civil War, the next reading about the penalties imposed on tenants of the estate by the manorial courts in the fifteenth century and then with the Fortescue children growing up at Boconnoc in the nineteenth century. Where possible, I have allowed the people who have been part of the history of Boconnoc to speak for themselves, using their own words.

Second, it became clear that I could not write everything about everything. Some readers may therefore find that a subject in which they are particularly interested is only dealt with in a short paragraph or a sentence in passing or not at all. The history of Boconnoc had so many interesting aspects that there was no alternative but to synthesise and précis.

I also wanted to consider how far Boconnoc could be described as an exemplar of Cornish history. Is it a prism through which Cornwall can be viewed? Does it epitomise Cornwall over the centuries? The answer is, of course, yes and no. Yes, because the Carminows and Courtenays contributed to the unrest that epitomised the Cornish gentry in the fourteenth and fifteenth centuries, Lord Mohun supported the Royalist cause during the English Civil War, as did the rest of Cornwall, and many of the owners played leading roles in local government in the nineteenth century. In other ways, no, it did not – there was little engagement with Methodism or other forms of religious dissent, minimal interest in maritime activities (except for boating on the River Fowey) and in contrast with the enormous levels of emigration that took place from the west of the county in the nineteenth century, there was minimal movement of people from the Boconnoc estate.

All these topics and more will be discussed in the course of this book, which is divided into two parts, the first five chapters being chronological and the second five, thematic.

Catherine Lorigan
July 2017

CHAPTER 1

THE EARLY HISTORY OF BOCONNOC:
DOMESDAY BOOK, DE CANCIAS, CARMINOWS AND COURTENAYS

'Cornwall: Not only the ends of the earth, but the very ends of the ends thereof ...'
(Bishop Grandisson to his friends in Avignon, 1327, Grandisson Register, I, 97–98)

THE BRONZE AGE

The period known as the Neolithic, dating from six to four thousand years ago, was an era when the population started to clear woodland and to domesticate animals. However, in Cornwall, the prehistoric features that survive are primarily monuments and tombs, rather than farms and field systems. Bronze Age cultures first appeared in this area around 2,000 BC and five hundred years later, farming settlements were becoming established. The first farms, with round houses constructed of stone and thatch, were mainly on the upland areas of Bodmin Moor, West Penwith and the Lizard.[1]

Boconnoc is situated in south-east Cornwall, between Lostwithiel and Liskeard (see map on page 12). To date, no evidence has been found of any prehistoric settlement on the estate, although archaeological remains may have been lost through ploughing or excavations carried out by antiquaries in the nineteenth century. A Bronze Age barrow – a place for burial and ritual – and flint flakes have been found on Obelisk Hill in the Pineaster Plantation. In another barrow, opened in 1862, a pit was discovered containing a small piece of very coarse pottery and some iron or bone. Further barrows have been found to the east and in Clowne Plantation and the names Buckabarrow Plantation and Downs may suggest the presence of barrows as yet undiscovered. Although none of the known sites have been subjected to any modern archaeological techniques, they demonstrate that there was human activity at Boconnoc many millennia ago.[2]

BOCONNOC IN DOMESDAY BOOK — 1086

Following the victory of William the Conqueror in 1066, a new feudal system was imposed whereby a vassal or peasant was granted land by an overlord in return for the performance of various services, sometimes military. Society after the Conquest was structured around these relationships. In 1085, as recorded in the Anglo-Saxon Chronicle, 'the King had deep speech with his counsellors … and sent his men all over England to each shire commissioning them to find out how many hundreds of hides were in the shire … what or how much each landholder held … in land and livestock, and what it was worth'. Domesday Book is thus a survey describing the landholdings and resources of late eleventh-century England, listing the value before the Conquest, at the time of the Conquest and in 1086, providing the basis for a nationwide tax assessment.

The majority of the landowners listed in Domesday had fought with William at the Battle of Hastings, after which there had been a mass redistribution of resources, his followers being rewarded with land that had previously been owned by the English nobility. Some who had held property prior to the Conquest were allowed to retain their estates.

Boconnoc is listed as *Bochenod*, the dwelling of Conec or Konec. Prior to the Conquest, it was held by Osferth, a Saxon. Unlike many other estates in Cornwall, where the land was granted to William's Norman followers, Osferth was allowed to retain control of Boconnoc and of six other estates that he already held, under the tenant-in-chief, the Count of Mortain, William the Conqueror's half-brother. Osferth was also granted three additional estates after the Conquest and was a substantial landowner in the area.

The Domesday entry for Boconnoc shows that 'Osferth holds Boconnoc'. He also held it before 1066, and paid tax for 1 virgate of land; ½ hide there, however. Land for eight ploughs; one plough there; two villagers, six smallholders and one slave; Woodland, 100 acres; pasture, 40 acres. Formerly 40*s*; value now (in 1086) 10*s*; livestock, two unbroken mares; two cattle, twenty sheep; seven goats.[3] The value of the property had thus decreased following the Conquest.

THE EARLY MEDIEVAL PERIOD

Documentary evidence for Boconnoc in the early medieval period is sparse. Only two references have been found, both dating from the early thirteenth century. The first is in the Pleas before the King or his Justices held in 1201 at Launceston, relating to a case of novel disseisin. This was a type of medieval court action, providing a swift method for the recovery of land where the occupier (who was not necessarily the rightful owner) had been ejected. In this case, it was alleged that Robert Moderet had unjustly disseised Meliora, daughter of Thomas, of her free tenement in Boconnoc. The jury found for Meliora and ordered that Robert should pay damages of half a mark — that is, 6*s* 8*d*.[4]

The second reference is in the returns of an inquisition of 1212, which gives a list of knight's fees across the country in the Red Book of the Exchequer, where 'Ricardus de Bokenet' held 'j militem in Bokenet' – 1 knight's fee in Boconnoc of the Honour of Ongar in Essex, the principal holding of Richard de Lucy, appointed Chief Justiciar of England by Henry II, whose Cornish lands were held of the Honour of Ongar.[5]

THE DE CANCIA FAMILY

Thomas de Cancia

Although it is not known how he obtained the property, by 1266 Thomas de Cancia had become the owner of the Boconnoc estate. The patronage of the church was also in his hands so that he was responsible for appointing the clergyman for the parish. However, in 1269, Thomas de Cancia was excommunicated by Walter Bronescombe, Bishop of Exeter, after de Cancia 'ruined the Bishop's park'. Ultimately, he had to make his peace with the bishop as is detailed more fully in Chapter 8.

De Cancia was involved in several cases that were brought before the assize – the court – in which it was alleged that he had disseised various people from their free tenements. In 1289, an assize was granted to enquire if Thomas de Cancia and others had disseized Odo de Treures and Roesia, his wife, of their free tenement in Bosvoilgomneyl juxta Derwydel, when the verdict was given for Thomas.[6] In the following year, a further case involving Thomas de Cancia was heard at the assize on 5 October. This enquired whether de Kent (de Cancia) and others had unjustly disseised Robert de Trefret of his free tenement 'in the Ford next to Bockunet'. Thomas de Kent appeared before the court and argued that Robert had never been seised of the tenement and therefore could not be disseised. The jury found for Thomas and placed Robert 'in mercy', giving him a financial penalty, an amercement, at the 'mercy' of the king or his justices for making a false claim.[7]

De Cancia died in 1299 and was buried at Bodmin. William of Worcester gives the names of illustrious personages whose obits were kept in the church, including '1299 obit dominus Thomas de Cancia die 12 Januarij.'

THE DE CARMINOW FAMILY

Sir John de Carminow (d. 1331)

It is not known who inherited the Boconnoc estate after the death of Thomas de Cancia in 1299, but by 1317, John de Carminow was in possession, at which date he was given 'free warren in Buccucnok, Glyn, Penpont, Resker, Disart and Tregostentyn, county Cornwall'. Free warren was granted to the owner of an estate and conveyed the sole right to hunt game, including hares and rabbits, on his own land.[8]

The de Carminow Family

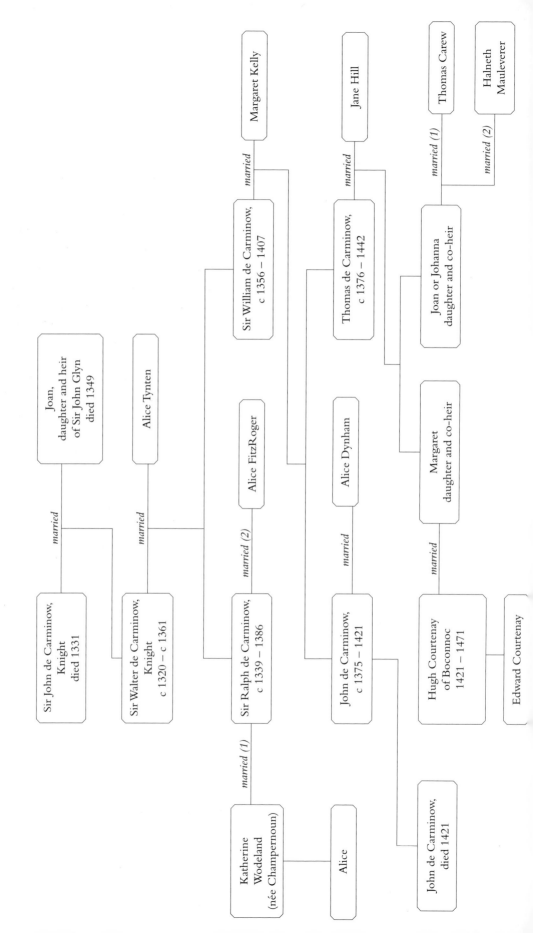

John de Carminow married Johanna or Joan, daughter and heiress of Sir John Glyn. They had four sons and one daughter and John's eldest son, Walter, was his heir.[9]

Sir John de Carminow and local administration

John de Carminow was enrolled in the military in 1323, made a knight in 1324 and as he held lands to the value of £40 per annum, he was summoned by general proclamation to attend the Great Councils at Westminster.

From the fourteenth century, commissions, composed of members of the local gentry, were appointed by the monarch and were given authority to control defence and criminal affairs and to enforce regulations that emanated from central government.[10] John de Carminow was one of those who was appointed by the Crown.

In 1330, he and William de Bello Campo were directed to enquire into a complaint made by Danesius de Acculeo and his associates of Leura, merchants of France. A vessel called *The Ship of St Peter in Poitou*, laden with a cargo of wine and other goods, had been driven ashore in Cornwall when local men had arrested the merchants and carried away the cargo. The king of France demanded redress and de Carminow and de Bello Campo were ordered to find out where the goods were, to recover what they could and to award damages to the merchants for those goods which were untraceable.

In contrast, members of the gentry who had allegedly committed a crime could also be placed under investigation. On 8 February 1318, a commission of *oyer and terminer* (a commission to 'hear and determine') was given to three men to investigate the complaint of John and Peter Domynges, merchants of Portugal, against John de Carminow and others. On a voyage to Flanders, a ship with a cargo of wine and other goods, on account of contrary winds, had had to anchor at Padstow. While there, the cables parted and the ship was cast ashore. The cargo was carried from the vessel onto the land by the Domynges. They argued that their goods, which had been recovered by their own efforts and not thrown onto the shore by the waves, should not be adjudged as 'wreck of the sea' which would, under common law, mean that the cargo would become the property of the Crown. A number of men, including John de Carminow, were convicted of removing the goods and fined for taking salvage of the ship.[11]

Keeper of the king's forests and parks

On 27 April 1331, John de Carminow was appointed Keeper of Trematon and Restormel castles and was made 'keeper of the king's forests, parks, woods and warrens as well as of vert [that is, everything that grows and bears a green leaf within the forest and the right or privilege of cutting growing wood] and of venison and of the King's game in the county of Cornwall'. The appointment was renewed on 12 October in the same year. As part of his commission, Carminow had to answer, on an annual basis, for the profits of pannage (the right to graze domestic pigs in a wood or forest) and herbage (pasturing cattle) within the forests, parks and woods owned by the king and had to appoint sub-keepers to assist him.[12]

The death of John de Carminow

John de Carminow only lived a short time after his appointment as Keeper of the King's forests. He died in October or November 1331. The escheator, the local official who had the responsibility for upholding the Crown's rights as feudal overlord, held an Inquisition Post Mortem (IPM) and thereafter an order was sent that he should take into his hands 'lands late of John de Carmynou, deceased, tenant-in-chief'. John's son and heir, Walter, being a minor at the date of his father's death, was made a ward of John of Eltham, 1st Earl of Cornwall (1316–36), the second son of Edward II of England and younger brother of Edward III.[13]

Walter de Carminow (*c.*?1320 – c.1361)

In 1333, Earl John transferred to Joan 'late the wife of John Carmynou' custody of her son and in addition, the Manor of Tamerton. Walter de Carminow's date of birth and his exact age at his father's death are unknown, but he witnessed a document on 4 May 1341, which suggests he had reached his majority by that date.[14] Sometime around the year 1340, he married Alice, daughter and heiress of Stephen de Tynten and through his marriage was granted the manor of Tynten. Walter and Alice had two sons, Ralph and William.

The Hundred Years' War – Walter de Carminow at the Battle of Crécy, 26 August 1346

The Hundred Years' War, a series of conflicts between 1337 and 1453, was fought mainly between England and France. After the death of the French monarch, Charles IV 'the Fair', in 1328, leaving no surviving male heir, the English King Edward III claimed the throne of France. Salic Law forbade inheritance by a woman, although not inheritance through the female line and Edward could thus claim the throne of France through his mother, Isabella, daughter of Philip IV and sister of Charles IV. A French court rejected Edward's claim and ruled that Charles's closest male relative was his first cousin, Philip, Count of Valois, who was crowned as Philip VI. In 1340, Edward declared himself king of France and deciding to pursue what he considered to be his entitlement by military means, he began to raise an army.

As part of the retinue of William de Bohun, Earl of Northampton, Walter de Carminow made the Channel crossing on 11 July 1346. On the battlefield at Crécy, the English king drew up his army into three divisions. The vanguard on the right was commanded by Edward, Prince of Wales, the 'Black Prince'; that on the left was commanded by William de Bohun, supported by the Earl of Arundel. The third was commanded by the king himself. William de Bohun's force consisted of one earl, two baronets, forty-six knights, 112 esquires and 141 mounted archers, a total of 302 men.[15] During the battle, the forces, under the command of Philip VI, flew the sacred banner of the French, the Oriflamme, which indicated that no quarter would be given and no surrender accepted. Any English soldier who was captured would be executed. To the enduring shame of the French, the Oriflamme was captured by the English who prevailed in the battle. Philip abandoned the field and fled.

Walter de Carminow's service in France was lengthy, for he was still there on 3 August 1347. At that date 'Walter de Carmynou, knight' was granted letters of protection as a member of de Bohun's retinue. These letters, granted to an individual who was overseas in the service of the Crown, prevented him from being prosecuted in the king's courts at home during his absence. The holder of the letters also had the right to appoint legal representatives in England by a Power of Attorney.[16]

Walter died in 1361 and since his son, Ralph, was still a minor, Sir John de Montacute, knight, held the wardship of the heir until he came of age.

Ralph de Carminow (*c.* 1339–86)

Ralph was born *c.* 1339. He married twice: first, to Katherine Wodeland (widow of Sir Walter Wodeland of Cockington, Devon) and daughter of Sir William Champernoun and second, by 1383, to Alice, widow of John FitzRoger. Ralph must have been of age by February 1360 for, at that date, he was able to grant away a manor in Bedfordshire. Two years later, Ralph had become the patron of the church at Boconnoc. He was also patron of the parish church at Menheniot and owned property there, at Carminow in Mawgan-in-Meneage and in St Tudy parish.[17]

The challenge to the validity of Ralph de Carminow's first marriage

In 1371, during a visit to Cornwall, Thomas de Brantyngham, Bishop of Exeter, adjudged that the marriage of Ralph and his wife Katherine was invalid, because they were descended from a common ancestor and were related by consanguinity, that is, by blood, within the prohibited degrees of kinship imposed by the Church and contrary to the tenets of Canon Law. Ralph and Katherine, when summoned to attend the bishop's court, produced letters that they had received from the Papal Nuncio, the Pope's diplomatic representative to England and France, Cardinal Simon Langham of St Sixtus. In the petition that they had presented to Langham at an earlier date, they had declared that they had married 'to preserve the friendship and agreement of both their parents, relatives and mutual friends, without gaining a dispensation'. As soon as they had realised that a dispensation was necessary, they had sent a request to the Nuncio asking him to regularise their position. Because the Carminows had shown themselves to be living honest lives and 'had many virtues', the Cardinal had granted the dispensation, allowing them to remain lawfully married and any children of their union to be deemed legitimate. Accordingly, the Carminows were granted 'an absolute dismissal from the case in our Court' by Bishop Brantyngham.[18]

Judicial and military offices and commissions

Being a member of an influential and important gentry family, Ralph de Carminow was appointed to judicial and military offices and commissions within Cornwall.[19] In 1377 and 1380, he was placed on commissions to equip all the men of the county to resist foreign invasion and to cause beacons to be set up that would give notice of the arrival of any enemy.[20] In 1381, the year of the Peasants' Revolt, and in 1382, he was appointed to commissions to put down rebellions.

As well as being instructed to deal with matters that were of national importance, he was appointed to enquire into local affairs. On 14 January 1379, de Carminow, in his capacity as Sheriff of Cornwall (with other Commissioners), was ordered to look into a complaint made by Lewis Gentil and three other Genoese merchants, that their ship had been wrecked, the cargo cast ashore and seized and the owner, merchants and mariners imprisoned. The Commissioners were ordered to ensure that the owner, merchants and mariners were released and the goods restored to their rightful owners, provided that the customs' dues and the cost of labour to those who had saved their goods were paid. As part of the same commission, de Carminow was instructed to release the owners of two carracks of Genoa, lately moored in front of 'Falemouth harbor', who had been unjustly arrested and to send them up to the king and Council at Westminster.[21]

In the same year, a commission ordered de Carminow to enquire into an allegation made by the Prior of Bodmin that eighteen men had felled his trees and carried away his fish. The following year, de Carminow investigated a similar complaint made by the Bishop of Exeter that men had broken into his park at Porton, had taken fish, deer and game birds and had assaulted the bishop's servants.[22]

Cornwall in the reign of Richard II (1377–99): conflict between members of the Cornish gentry

The reign of Richard II was a turbulent period in every part of the country, encompassing the Peasants' Revolt in 1381, which culminated in the murder of Simon of Sudbury, Archbishop of Canterbury and Lord Chancellor of England, by the London mob on Tower Hill on 14 June; the death of Wat Tyler, the leader of the rebels, at the hands of officers loyal to Richard II on 15 June; the conflict between the king and the Lords Appellant in 1387 and the deposition of Richard by his cousin, Henry Bolingbroke, who seized the throne as Henry IV in 1399. The 'turbulence at the centre of the realm visibly affected the Cornish locality'[23] and far from Cornwall and Boconnoc being isolated from what was taking place 'up-country', the county also suffered. The unrest contributed to an increasing number of disputes between members of the Cornish gentry, which included the Carminow family. Here Boconnoc exemplified the events that were being replicated across Cornwall.

In the absence of any ruling magnate in Cornwall and its geographical distance from the centre of power in London, the local elite ran the county and its government. The MPs, sheriffs, escheators and other senior office holders were drawn from the leading families such as the Bodrugans, Sergeaux (or Cergeaux) and Carminows. The gentry competed for the offices of local government, which increased their influence and power in the county.[24]

The holder of any of the offices had ample opportunity to settle old scores with other families with whom they had been or were in conflict, depending on who was holding which position and when. In the 1370s, the offices of Sheriff and Knight of the Shire were held on a number of occasions throughout this period by members of the Sergeaux and Carminow families.

Conflict with the Sergeaux family

Ralph de Carminow was particularly involved in a long-running and violent dispute with the Sergeaux family.[25] John Sergeaux and Ralph de Carminow were married respectively to two sisters, Elizabeth and Katherine, daughters of William Champernoun of Tywardreath. A disagreement arose over who had the right of inheritance to William's lands and property.

John Sergeaux and his brother, Richard (who was Sheriff from 1 October 1375 to 26 October 1376), each made use of the period when they held the office of Sheriff to harass the Carminows.[26] Ralph de Carminow and his brother, William, petitioned the king in Council in 1377–78, stating that Ralph and John Sergeaux had inherited the manors of William Champernoun 'by virtue of marrying his daughters and co-heiresses'. Ralph and William alleged that Sergeaux, with his allies, had come to Ralph's manor of Boconnoc 'and beat him and his daughter Alice, carrying away their goods to the value of £200, leaving the said Ralph for dead'. It was further alleged that Sergeaux had entered the manors of William and had removed goods and chattels to the value of £1,000. Ralph and William requested a remedy from the king against the members of the Sergeaux family who had carried out these violent attacks. An order was sent to the justices that they should enquire into the truth as between William de Carminow and John Sergeaux.[27]

The situation was reversed from November 1378 to November 1379, during Ralph de Carminow's term as Sheriff, when he took the opportunity to bring indictments alleging treason, rape and other felonies against his rivals.

In February 1381, four lawyers were appointed to a commission of peace to which (unusually) no members of the local gentry were appointed. This may have been an attempt by the central government to bring to an end the lengthy dispute between the two families and thereby to reduce both violence in the county and the increasingly lawless behaviour of the Cornish gentry. Although this action suggests that the king's ministers in London were aware of what was occurring in Cornwall, attempts to settle the conflict proved unsuccessful. In 1400, John Sergeaux was accused of employing three indicted felons to attack, among others, William de Carminow, Ralph's brother and heir.[28]

Conflict with William de Botreaux

In 1380, Ralph de Carminow was in dispute with William de Botreaux (1337–91), an important West Country baron during the reigns of both Edward III (1327–77) and Richard II (1377–99). Botreaux took part in an expedition to Saxony in 1359 and in 1380 was part of the army that was transported to the Iberian Peninsula to support Portugal in a conflict against its Spanish neighbour.

Carminow alleged that on the Wednesday after the feast of St John the Baptist (Wednesday, 27 July 1381), de Botreaux had gathered together eighty traitors who had come 'with force and arms against the peace to [Ralph] de Carminow's manor'. They broke and destroyed a door, a stone wall and de Carminow's park and released twenty of his animals, which they killed and took away to Botelet, near Herodsfoot, one of Botreaux's manors. In addition, they killed some of Carminow's servants at his manor of Boconnoc.[29]

William de Botreaux's wife, Elizabeth (née Daubnay), proved to the satisfaction of the local justices that, on the relevant dates, her husband had been abroad in the king's service in Portugal with Edmund, Earl of Cambridge, the king's uncle. In his absence, he had been wrongly indicted for treason in Cornwall. The indictment was suspended until further orders could be received from the king.

Although de Carminow and de Botreaux had ostensibly been at odds in 1381, three years later, William de Botreaux, William Sergeaux, Ralph de Carminow and others, were instructed to bring thirteen men (including the Ilcombe brothers) before the king and Council who 'when retained [in 1381] to go beyond the seas in an expedition with the King's uncle, Edmund, Earl of Cambridge behaved so rebelliously that he could not accomplish the object of his expedition'. Incentives had been offered in 1381 to persuade recruits to join the forces taking part in the overseas campaign and the two Cornish knights, Sir Henry and Sir William Ilcombe, both wanted for rape, had enlisted as a way (they believed) of evading justice. They were both initially pardoned for their crime on 23 October 1382 because of their 'good service in Portugal', but the pardons were withdrawn when it was shown that the Ilcombes had taken part in an insurrection against the Earl of Cambridge while he was abroad.[30]

The death of Ralph de Carminow

Sir Ralph, as MP for the county of Cornwall, was summoned to the Parliaments at Westminster on 26 October 1383, 12 November 1384 and 1 October 1386. Based on family tradition and the Heralds' Visitation of Cornwall, he delayed his departure for the Parliament due to be opened on 1 October 1386. On 9 October, he went hunting and 'Raphe was by a brase of greyhounds pulled over a cliff and died.'[31]

At the date of his death, Ralph de Carminow held not only ten manors and houses at Boconnoc, Mawgan-in-Meneage and St Tudy, but also the advowsons of the churches of Ladock, Boconnoc and Menheniot. He was receiving rents annually amounting to £11 from other properties in Cornwall and he owned three-quarters of the Manor of Ashwater, other land in Devon and the manor of Colway in Dorset.[32]

William de Carminow (c. 1356–1407)

Having died childless, Ralph's heir was his brother, William de Carminow, who was married to Margaret (née Kelly). In 1386, the escheator in Devon and Cornwall was ordered to take William's fealty, to give him full control of the manor of Polroda and to deliver to

William any rents taken since Ralph's death. William was named Lord of Boconnoc and Glynn (spelt in documents variously as Glyn, Glynn and Glynne).

The coat of arms dispute – Scrope v. de Carminow[33]

A knight fighting in battle or taking part in a tournament, with a closed helm, could not be identified except by his coat of arms. Richard Scrope, Chancellor of the Exchequer and William de Carminow, Sheriff of Cornwall, both accompanied Edward III to Paris, where it was discovered that they were using the same coat of arms, Azure, a Bend or: G = *gules*, red; Az = *azure*, silver; Or = gold. In order to arbitrate on disputes relating to heraldic devices, the king had established a forum called the Court of the Constable and the Marshal.

Both Scrope and de Carminow called witnesses and produced documents to support the claim that their respective forefathers had been entitled to use the disputed coat of arms. Richard Scrope maintained that it had been used by his family since the Norman Conquest, which was unlikely since the Normans had nothing that could be construed as heraldry. De Carminow put forward an equally improbable claim, that his family had been given the coat of arms by King Arthur, although the original grant had now been lost.

There are two versions of the court's decision. The first was that Scrope was awarded the right to the coat of arms and de Carminow was ordered to add a further device – a red label gules, that he should add to his coat of arms as a mark of difference. A second version gives joint title to Scrope and Carminow. The former verdict seems more likely, since by ordering de Carminow to use the label gules regularly, this would constitute a sufficient distinction from Scrope's coat of arms. The case had been settled by 1385.[34]

The last Carminows at Boconnoc, 1407–42

William de Carminow died on 8 February 1407. His son and heir was John (b. c. 1375–1421), who was married to Alice Dynham. John and Alice's son, also called John, died in the same year as his father, leaving no children, so his property reverted to his uncle, Thomas (b. c. 1376–1442), brother of his father, John. Thomas, married to Jane (née Hill), died on the Wednesday before Christmas Day in 1442. Having no sons, their daughters, Margaret and Joan or Johanna, were his co-heiresses. Margaret, the elder, aged 20, was married to Hugh Courtenay; Joan or Johanna, aged 15, was married, first to Thomas Carew and then to Halnath Mauleverer. Thomas was thus the last member of the Carminow family to own the Boconnoc estate.[35]

The Courtenay Family

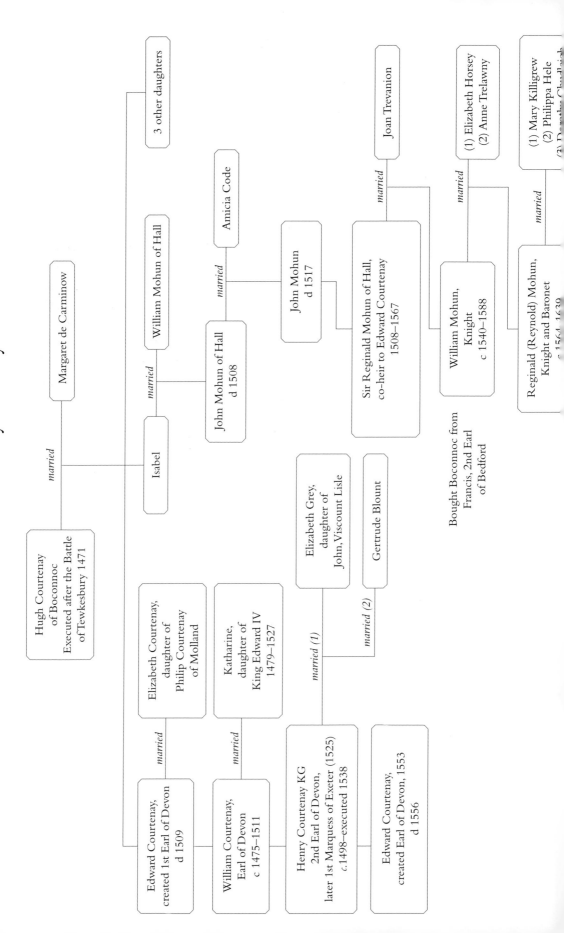

THE COURTENAY FAMILY

Hugh Courtenay (1421–71)

Sir Hugh Courtenay was the son of Sir Hugh Courtenay of Haccombe and a nephew of the third Earl of Devon. He married Margaret (née de Carminow) and in consequence of the marriage, became the owner of Boconnoc and was known thereafter as Sir Hugh 'of Boconnoc'.

The illegal activities of Hugh Courtenay

Hugh Courtenay was frequently engaged in illegal activities, particularly relating to acts of piracy around the coast of Cornwall. In November 1449, two ships from Fowey, part owned by Courtenay, sailed into Plymouth Sound and seized a Spanish vessel, despite the fact that the Spaniards were holding a pass which should have guaranteed them safe conduct. The ship was brought into Fowey where its cargo was put up for sale. Many of those who were appointed to commissions to enquire into acts of piracy were themselves receiving part of the stolen cargo or were operating pirate ships in their own right. In consequence, the Crown made minimal efforts to prevent the illegal behaviour, believing it to be a lost cause. Accordingly, Courtenay was able to continue sending vessels to sea unimpeded and 'manned with men of war well harnessed and arrayed'.

The pirates did not limit their attacks to foreign vessels. In February 1460, a commission was given to John Arundell, John Salter and the Sheriff of Cornwall to enquire into a complaint by fifteen merchants of Bristol. The merchants claimed that a ship called le Marie of Dansk alias Durdright (Dordrecht), master Herman Taillour, had been laden at Bordeaux with wine, wood, iron, saffron and other goods. The merchandise was due to be delivered to Bristol, but the ship was captured at 'Sylly' by pirates in two ships, one of them being le Petre Courtenay, owner Hugh Courtenay. The le Marie was taken to Fowey where the cargo sold for £2,713.13s.4d. Commissioners were ordered to discover into whose hands the ship and cargo had fallen and 'to arrest and restore the same or the value thereof, committing to prison such as refuse to make restitution'.[36]

A similar complaint was received in 1461 from le Margarete of Brittany. On 10 September, an inquisition held at Fowey learned that le Margarete had been captured at sea on 27 March by le Petre Courtenay, the carvel owned by Hugh Courtenay, master William Webbe. She, like other ships captured by Courtenay's crews, was brought into Fowey, the cargo sold and the sailors thrown into prison. On 9 March 1465, an order was given to arrest Sir Hugh, but the warrant seems never to have been executed, since it was renewed in June of the same year.[37] Courtenay was involved in piracy yet again in 1462 when the Edward of Polruan and the Macrell of Fowey captured and plundered the St Anthony & St Thomas, a Spanish galley, and removed merchandise to the value of £12,000.[38]

The Wars of the Roses – Lancaster v. York

The Wars of the Roses were a series of battles and conflicts in the fifteenth century, fought between the two rival royal houses of Lancaster and York, who were both attempting to seize and retain control of the English throne. The crown was held alternately by the Lancastrian, Henry VI, who reigned from 1422 to 1461 and then from 1470 to 1471 and his Yorkist protagonist, Edward IV, who reigned from 1461 to 1470 and from 1471 to 1483.

No battles were fought on Cornish soil that can be directly attributed to the Lancaster/York civil war, but the hatred between the Lancastrian Courtenay Earls of Devon and the Yorkist Sir William Bonville, 1st Baron Bonville, both major land owners in the West Country, led to bitter internecine warfare and slaughter during the same period, in which Sir Hugh Courtenay of Boconnoc was deeply involved. Bonville and the sheriffs of Devon and Cornwall were engaged to meet in Exeter in April 1455. Thomas Courtenay, 5th Earl of Devon, and Sir Hugh led their armed retainers into the city where they disrupted the meeting and attempted to ambush Bonville. In October of the same year, Courtenay and Sir Hugh attacked Nicholas Radford, the Recorder of Exeter at his manor of Upcott, when Radford was murdered by six of the earl's troops.

When the Courtenays subsequently laid siege to Powderham Castle, residence of their distant cousin, Philip Courtenay, the Bonvilles came to Philip's assistance and the two private armies engaged each other in a pitched battle at Clyst Heath. A sortie was then led by Thomas Carrewe to attack Bonville's manor at Shute which they pillaged, stealing animals and ransacking the house. This breakdown of law and order has been attributed to the lack of strong government during the reign of the frequently mentally incapacitated Henry VI.

In April 1457, a pardon was granted to Thomas Courtenay, Earl of Devon, Hugh Courtenay, knight and Thomas Carrewe esquire, for any felony or murder relating to the death of Nicholas Radford.

Although the Courtenays were always strongly Lancastrian in sympathy, during the first ten years of the reign of the Yorkist Edward IV, Hugh Courtenay was sufficiently trusted to be appointed to serve in local administration. In May 1462, he was a member of a commission to array and victual ships in the port of Fowey for the king's fleet to fight against his enemies and the following year, he was commissioned to carry out an Inquisition Post Mortem. Ironically, given his past history, in 1469, Courtenay was named as a Commissioner to investigate a complaint of piracy on Breton merchants by a ship based at Fowey.[39]

The Battle of Tewkesbury – 4 May 1471

When Margaret of Anjou, wife of Henry VI, landed in England in March 1471, Hugh Courtenay returned to his Lancastrian allegiance and joined her forces at Exeter. Denounced as a traitor by the Yorkists, Courtenay fought for Henry VI at the Battle of Tewkesbury, where he was captured and later executed. Not only did Sir Hugh perish at

Tewkesbury, but the last earl of the senior Courtenay line was also killed and Sir Hugh's son, Edward, became the male heir to the Earldom of Devon. No Inquisition Post Mortem was taken since Courtenay's lands were sequestrated by the Crown.[40] Edward IV reigned, in relative peace, for the next twelve years.

Edward Courtenay (d. 1509)

The dispute with Halnath Mauleverer

After the execution of Hugh Courtenay in 1471, his son Edward and Halnath Mauleverer became locked in a dispute about the inheritance to the Carminow lands. Mauleverer's wife, Johanna or Joan (née de Carminow) was the sister of Edward Courtenay's mother, Margaret. In 1476, an arbitration was made between Courtenay and Mauleverer which adjudged that Hugh and Margaret Courtenay were to have nine manors in Cornwall, including Boconnoc, together with the advowsons of the churches of Boconnoc and Broadoak (spelt variously as Broadoak, Bradoc or Braddock).[41]

Halnath and Johanna Mauleverer were to hold the manors of Ashwater, Loffyngcot and Beauworthy in Devon, the advowsons of the churches of Ashwater and Loffyngcot, other land in Devon and a number of tenements in Cornwall. Since their property was primarily situated east of the Tamar, the Mauleverers moved and settled in Devon.[42]

Edward Courtenay, Edward IV and Richard III

Hugh Courtenay, executed in 1471, left two sons and four daughters. Edward IV did not seek vengeance against the heirs of those who had fought for the Lancastrian cause and on 27 August 1472, Sir Hugh's goods and lands were granted to the executors of his will so that his wishes could be honoured. On 6 September, Edward, his son and heir, 'late of Bokenok, co. Cornwall', was granted a pardon by Edward IV.[43] Thereafter, men who (ostensibly) accepted Yorkist rule were given responsibility within local government, even in matters that could affect the security of the country, and between 1472 and 1477, Edward Courtenay was appointed to serve on several local commissions.[44]

In 1483, acting as regent for his nephew, now Edward V, Richard, Duke of Gloucester, summoned Courtenay to attend Edward's coronation, but the child king was never crowned because Gloucester seized the throne to reign as Richard III. Outwardly at least, Edward Courtenay appeared content to continue to live under the rule of another Yorkist king, but in October 1483, he joined the rebellion against Richard III led by Henry Stafford, 2nd Duke of Buckingham. Buckingham was married to Catherine Woodville, sister of Elizabeth Woodville, Edward IV's queen. He had helped Richard succeed to the throne, but thereafter had become disaffected and changed allegiance to support Henry Tudor, the surviving Lancastrian heir. Buckingham's rebellion failed and on 2 November 1483, he was executed for treason.

Sir John Scrope of Bolton, Edward Redmayne, Halvatheus Mallyvery (Halnath Mauleverer) and Peter Seyntaubyn were assigned by Richard III to enquire into various treasons and wrongdoings in the West Country. The presentment from the king alleged that Peter, Bishop of Exeter, (Edward) Courtenay of Boconnoc, John Trefry of Fowey with other unknown persons, on 3 November 1483 'with other traitors lately mustered for rebellion and war', had gathered at Bodmin with the intention of overthrowing Richard III and placing another (unspecified) king on the throne.[45] Before he could be detained, Courtenay escaped to the Continent where he joined Henry Tudor.

Halnath Mauleverer is granted Boconnoc

In the 1470s, Mauleverer had been appointed to a number of commissions. Together with George, Duke of Clarence, the king's brother, Richard, Earl of Warwick and Salisbury and others, he was ordered in 1470 to enquire into 'all felonies, murders, homicides and other offences, in the county of Cornwall and to arrest and imprison the offenders'. Unlike Courtenay, Mauleverer maintained his allegiance to Richard III. On 1 December 1484, as a reward for his good service against the Lancastrian rebels, he was granted the manors of 'Beconnek, of the yearly value of 38*l*.6*s*, Glyn, of the yearly value of 15*l*.8*s*.8*d*, and Brodak, of the yearly value of *13l.3s.*, late of Edward Courtenay, rebel'. In the same month, Mauleverer was appointed to commissions of array for Devon and Cornwall and on 17 December a grant for life was given to 'the king's servant Halnath Malyverer, one of the esquires of the body of the office of constable of the castle of Launceseton *alias* Dunheved, Co. Cornwall, with the accustomed fees from the issues of the castle'.[46]

On 22 August 1485, Mauleverer and his brothers, Thomas and Robert, fought with Richard III at Bosworth when Richard's forces were defeated by the army of Henry Tudor. 'Mauleverer *alias* late of Aysshewater, co. Devon, *alias* late of Boconnok, co. Cornwall' was granted a pardon by Henry VII on 24 November 1485.[47] He died in 1502 and in his will, Mauleverer, among other bequests, left forty shillings to the reparation of the body of the parish church of Ashwater that the parishioners there 'may pray for my soul'. The residue of his property he left to his wife, Johanna Mauleverer, who was his chief executrix.[48]

THE COURTENAYS DURING THE REIGNS OF HENRY VII (REIGNED 1485—1509) AND HENRY VIII (REIGNED 1509—47)

Edward Courtenay, 1st Earl of Devon (third creation, 1485) (d. 1509)

Edward Courtenay was knighted fifteen days prior to the Battle of Bosworth by Henry Tudor. By letters patent dated 16 October 1485, he was created Earl of Devon by the new king and carried the second sword at Henry's coronation.[49] Although he played little part in national events, he took an active part in the government of the South West, acting as a Justice of the Peace (JP) and being appointed the Constable of Restormel Castle in 1487. After the Pretender, Perkin Warbeck, purporting to be Richard, Duke of York, younger son of Edward IV, landed at Whitesand Bay in Cornwall on 7 September

1487 seeking to challenge Henry VII for the throne, Courtenay and the gentry of East Cornwall marched against Warbeck and his supporters.

In recognition of his support, the king granted to Edward Courtenay the lands traditionally associated with the Earldom of Devon, including sixty manors, eight boroughs and nine Hundreds and the Boconnoc estate. Courtenay was unable to reclaim the Boconnoc lands until 1502, as they had been granted by Richard III to Halnath Mauleverer as a reward for the latter's support in 1483.

Around 1475, Edward Courtenay, Earl of Devon, had married a distant cousin, Elizabeth, daughter of Sir Philip Courtenay of Molland. Courtenay made his will on 27 May 1509 and died the following day. He asked to be buried in the chapel at Tiverton next to his wife and left lands to the yearly value of £4 'for the performance of my chantrye in the said chapel which I intended there to have made …' He bequeathed 100 marks to be divided equally between Henry and Margaret Courtenay, his grandchildren, son and daughter of his heir, William.[50]

William Courtenay (*c.* 1475–1511) (created Earl of Devon, fourth creation, 1511)

Edward's heir, William Courtenay, was knighted in 1487 and in 1495 he married Katherine Plantagenet (1479–1527), ninth child and sixth daughter of Edward IV and Elizabeth Woodville. Katherine's sister, Elizabeth of York, was Henry VII's queen and William thus became closely related to King Henry VII. He was granted a number of prestigious honours, was made a Knight of the Bath at the coronation of the queen, Elizabeth of York, in 1487 and from March 1501, he was granted an annuity for his 'diligent attendance' on the king.[51]

While his close links to the royal family initially proved to be to his advantage, his fortunes changed in April 1502. He was accused of conspiring with Edmund de la Pole, Earl of Suffolk, the queen and his wife's cousin and the last surviving Yorkist heir, against Henry VII. In 1504, he was charged with treason, attainted and incarcerated in the Tower. William's father, Edward Courtenay, died in 1509, five years after his son had been imprisoned and since William was still under attainder, he was unable to inherit the Boconnoc estate and the other lands attached to the Earldom of Devon. Edward had, nonetheless, bequeathed the Boconnoc lands to William expressing the hope that ultimately, his son would be pardoned and could inherit: to 'my sonne Sir William Courtenay under condicion that he doe obteyne the king's grace and pardon' – that is, if the attainder was lifted and thereafter William maintained his allegiance to the king and his heirs.[52]

Courtenay had been transferred from the Tower to Calais Castle in October 1507 and it was rumoured that he was about to be executed. Instead, shortly after the accession of Henry VIII in 1509, he was released. On 10 May 1511, by letters patent, his father's lands and titles were restored to him and he was created Earl of Devon. Before he could be invested with the title or have his attainder formally reversed, he contracted pleurisy and died at Greenwich on 9 June.

Henry Courtenay, 2nd Earl of Devon and later 1st Marquess of Exeter (1498–1538)

Despite the fact that his father, William, had been attainted and imprisoned, Henry Courtenay received an education befitting his rank as a grandson of Edward IV and first cousin of Henry VIII. He was schooled by Giles Duwes, the tutor who taught French to the royal children and was described as 'the king's near kinsman, and hath been brought up of a childe with his grace in his chamber'.

A minor at the date of his father's death, Henry Courtenay obtained the reversal of his father's attainder, inherited the Earldom of Devon in 1512 and the Boconnoc lands sometime around 1515. Henry took part in the naval campaign in 1513 against France, was appointed a Privy Councillor and Gentleman of the Privy Chamber in 1520 and attended Henry VIII at the Field of the Cloth of Gold near Calais the same year. He was made Constable of Windsor Castle in April 1525. During the intrigue known as the 'King's Great Matter' when Henry VIII was attempting to obtain a divorce from his queen, Catherine of Aragon, Courtenay firmly supported the king and acted as one of the Commissioners for the deposition of Catherine in 1533. He was appointed High Steward of the Duchy of Cornwall and Lord Warden of the Stannaries and was created Marquess of Exeter in 1525. Much of his time was spent at court and the running of his estates was left in the hands of bailiffs, stewards and agents.

His close relationship with the royal family proved, as it had been to his father, initially advantageous, but ultimately led to his undoing. He was high in the line of succession to the throne and he became enmeshed in court politics, maintaining (probably unwisely) close connections with the Yorkist Pole and Neville families. He was accused of supporting them against the government of Thomas Cromwell, the king's principal secretary and chief minister. Cromwell was able to persuade the king that Courtenay constituted a serious threat to the continuing prosperity of the House of Tudor, particularly as Courtenay's second wife, Gertrude Blount, was a Catholic. She, unlike her husband, had supported Catherine of Aragon during the divorce proceedings. Information was laid against the Marquess that he had entered into a conspiracy with the Pole family. Perhaps anticipating future events, he made his will on 25 September 1538. Two months later, in November 1538, he was arrested and charged with treason. He, his wife and son Edward were sent to the Tower. Henry was taken before his peers in Westminster Hall on 3 December, found guilty and beheaded on Tower Hill on 9 December 1538. A week after his execution, he was proclaimed guilty of trying to encompass the death of the king and all his lands, property and estates, including Boconnoc, were forfeit to the Crown.[53]

NOTES AND REFERENCES

1. www.historical-cornwall.org.uk; www.cornwallheritagetrust.org/page-history-cornwall-bronze-age

2. Cornwall Historic Environment Service (HES), Cornwall Council, MCO 1068; Cornwall Record Office (CRO): X175/24, Diary of William Pease, 25 and 26 August 1862; HES, MCO 2263 and 2264.

3. Caroline and Frank Thorn, *Domesday Book, Cornwall*, Chichester, 1979, 5,13; www.britannia.com.

4. D.M. Stenton (ed.), *Pleas before the King or his Justices*, Selden Society, London, 1952, p. 172; Stephen Friar, *The Local History Companion*, Sutton, p. 296.

5. Email from Oliver Padel dated 9 November 2013; Hubert Hall (ed.), *The Red Book of the Exchequer*, Part II, HMSO, 1896, p. 612.

6. John Maclean, *The Parochial and Family History of the Deanery of Trigg Minor in the County of Cornwall*, Vol. 3, The Parish of St Minver, p. 67.

7. The National Archives (TNA): JUST1/1285, membrane 16r, 12 November 1289 to 19 November 1290.

8. Mini biographies: www.teachergenealogist; info.sjc.ox.ac.uk/forests/glossary, downloaded on 3 November 2015.

9. Several sources record that the Boconnoc estate at this date was owned by 'Sir Oliver Carminow who married a daughter of Joan Holland – the Fair Maid of Kent – a grand-daughter of Edward I. She married the Black Prince, son and heir of Edward III, as her second husband.' This information is totally inaccurate. It was not Sir Oliver who owned Boconnoc, but his brother, John. Sir Oliver married first, Elizabeth Pomeroy and second, Isould, daughter of Sir Reginald de Ferrers, but was never married to a daughter of Joan Holland.

10. James Whetter, *The Bodrugans. A Study of a Cornish Medieval Knightly Family*, St Austell, 1995, p. 94; John Carminow appears as a character in Daphne du Maurier's novel, *The House on the Strand*, 1969.

11. Calendar of Patent Rolls (CPR): Windsor, February 8 1318, 2 Edward II, London, p. 169; The Priory of Tywardreath: 'John de Carmynou' was a benefactor of the Priory of Tywardreath, near Fowey, a dependency of the abbey of Saints Sergius and Bacchus at Angers in Brittany. Before the outbreak of the Hundred Years War, the Priory had been in financial difficulties and Carminow had provided financial help. In 1328, the Priory was in debt to him: Oliver, Monasticon, pp. 34–36; CRO: AD1930/1/1.

12. Calendar of Fine Rolls (CFR): Eltham, 27 April and Westminster, 12 October 1331, 5 Edward III, pp. 249 and 277. A fine was a promise of money to the king in return for a concession or favour and the first purpose of the Fine Rolls was to record the money so offered.

13. CFR: Windsor, 14 November 1331, 5 Edward III, p. 288; CPR: Westminster, 26 January 1332, 6 Edward III, p. 242.

14. CPR: Westminster, 25 March 1332, 6 Edward III, p. 261; CPR: Westminster, 4 May 1341, 15 Edward III, p. 181.

15. Whetter, *op. cit.*, p. 105; Major-General the Hon. George Wrottesley, Crecy and Calais from the Original Records in the Public Record Office, London, 1898, p. 193.

16. Whetter, *op. cit.*, p. 105; Wrottesley, ibid., p. 133.

17. Nicholas Orme, *Cornish Wills, 1342–1540,* Devon and Cornwall Record Society, Exeter, 2007, pp. 219–220; F.C. Hingeston-Randolph (ed.), *Registers of Thomas de Brantyngham*, London and Exeter, 1901, (i), 373, 499; (ii) 586; Royal Institution of Cornwall (RIC): Henderson Calendars XVIII and XXIII, nd, p. 16.

18. Hingeston-Randolph (ed.), *ibid.*, London, 30 September 1371, pp. 270–271.

19. CPR: 1381–85, p. 652; Orme, *op. cit.*, p. 220.

20. CPR: Westminster, 1 July 1377, 1 Richard II, pp. 38–40; History of Parliament.

21. CPR: Westminster, 14 January 1379, 2 Richard II, pp. 311–312.

22. CPR: Westminster, 28 October 1379, 3 Richard II, p. 421 and Westminster, 12 February 1380, 3 Richard II, p. 466.
23. S.J. Drake, 'Policy and society in Richard II's Cornwall: a study in relations between centre and locality', *Journal of the Royal Institution of Cornwall*, 2013, p. 48.
24. Drake, *ibid.*, p. 28.
25. Whetter, *op. cit.*, pp. 121 and 129.
26. TNA: SC8/38/1868.
27. TNA: SC8/38/1867; Petitions to the King in Council, writ dated 10 December 1377, 1 Richard II.
28. C.J. Tyldesley, 'The Crown and the local communities in Devon and Cornwall from 1377–1422', unpublished PhD thesis, University of Exeter, 1978, *passim*; Drake, *op. cit.*, pp. 47–48.
29. TNA: SC8/277/13837.
30. Benjamin Trowbridge, 'English intervention in Iberia during the Hundred Years War: the English army and expedition to Portugal in 1381–2', unpublished MA(Res) degree in Medieval Studies, University of Reading, amended and updated 2009, pp. 38–39.
31. Lt Col J.L. Vivian and Henry H. Drake, *Heralds' Visitation of Cornwall in the year 1620*, Harleian Society, Vol. IX, 1874; Inquisition Post Mortem (IPM), 10 Richard II, No. 11.
32. Ralph de Carminow, History of Parliament.
33. Dom Pedro de Alcazar, *The Law of Arms in Medieval England*, © Craig Levin, heraldry.sca.org.
34. W.C. Wade, *Extinct Cornish Families*, 18 December 1890, pp. 10–11.
35. IPM, 8 Henry VI, No. 16; IPM, 21 Henry VI, No. 46; Calendar of Inquisitions Post Mortem, 21–25 Henry VI, 1442–47, Vol. XXVI, 2009, No. 97, p. 52.
36. J.A.F. Thomson, 'The Courtenay Family in the Yorkist Period', *Historical Research*, Vol. 45, Issue 112, November 1972, p. 233; CPR: Westminster, 27 February 1460, p. 612; Henry VI, 1452–61, pp. 649 and 650.
37. Whetter, *op. cit.*, p. 98; CPR: 1452–61, pp. 649–50; CPR: 1461–67, pp. 36, 452, 488, 489; Calendar of Close Rolls (CCR), 1461–68, p. 158.
38. Devon & Cornwall Notes & Queries, xii, January 1923, p. 230.
39. CPR: 1461–67, pp. 204 and 233; 1467–77, pp. 197–198, 612.
40. CPR: 1467–77, pp. 246–47, 249, 250, 251, 610, 612; CCR: 1468–76; CCR: 1468–76; *Paston Letters*, iii, p. 9.
41. Rosemary Horrox, *Richard III. A Study in Service*, Cambridge, 1989, p. 200.
42. Devon Record Office (DRO): 4088M/10/16.
43. CPR: 1467–77, Westminster, 6 September 1472, pp. 341, 374; Thomson, *op. cit.*, pp. 245 and 246.
44. CPR: 1467–77, pp. 403, 491, 573; CPR: 1476–85, p. 23.
45. Royal Institution of Cornwall (RIC): MS BV ¼, enquiry dated 3 December 1483.
46. CPR: Westminster, 27 October 1470, Edward IV to Henry VI, 1467–77, p. 246; CPR: Westminster, 17 December 1484, Edward IV, Edward V and Richard III, 1476–1485, p. 502.
47. www.girders.net; Anne P. Sutton and Rodney W. Hammond (eds), *The Coronation of Richard III: The Extant Documents*, 1984, p. 371; CPR: Westminster, 24 November 1485, 1 Henry VII, p. 39.
48. TNA: PROB/11/13, 1502.
49. Dictionary of National Biography (DNB): Edward Courtenay, 1st Earl of Devon.
50. TNA: PROB/11/16 – will proved on 11 July 1509.
51. DNB: William Courtenay.
52. TNA: PROB/11/16 – will proved on 11 July 1509.
53. Henry's son Edward Courtenay was held prisoner in the Tower of London for fifteen years and was not released until the beginning of the reign of Mary Tudor (1553–58). He was created Earl of Devon by the queen (fifth creation, 1553) and was considered as a potential consort for her, but no marriage took place. He was implicated in Wyatt's rebellion in 1554, an attempt to prevent Mary's marriage to Philip II of Spain and was again imprisoned in the Tower. In 1555, he was allowed to leave England for Italy and he died in Padua on 18 September 1556.

THE MOHUNS: 1563–1717

'His Majesty making his head Quarter at the Lord Mohun's House.'
(Edward Walker, *Historical Collections of Several Important Transactions relating to the late rebellion and Civil Wars of England*, London, 1707, p. 59)

JOHN RUSSELL, LATER EARL OF BEDFORD

In 1549, the government of Edward VI introduced measures in an attempt to further suppress the Roman Catholic religion. An order was issued that the Book of Common Prayer, in the English language, should be used in every church throughout the land on 9 June. Particularly in the Cornish-speaking west of Cornwall, discontent had already been rising due to a decline in living conditions and increasing levels of taxation. This edict from a government situated hundreds of miles away, was regarded as another affront to the Cornish and their traditions. Under the leadership of Sir Humphrey Arundell of Helland and John Winslade of Tregarrick, what became known as the Prayer Book Rebellion broke out in the western counties. Edward Seymour, 1st Earl of Somerset, Lord Protector for his nephew, Edward VI, ordered Lord John Russell to take an army into the west to quell the revolt. The rebellion was quickly extinguished and Arundell and Winslade were captured, transported to London and executed.

Yet, there was not universal support in Cornwall for Arundell and Winslade. A commission set up in 1550 was sent to take an inventory of 'all manner of plate and bells' belonging to every Cornish parish. The returns show that in some parishes, using the church property as collateral, the parishioners borrowed money to equip men who were riding west to fight 'the rebellers' – in the 'comocion' known as the Arundell rebellion.[1] The entry for Boconnoc reads:

The said pysheners have three belles hanging in their towre.

Itm, a chalys of sylver pcell gylte waying xiij unces & di.

Itm, a pixe of sylver weying one unce and half.

Upon the which chalys and pixes the said pysheners have borrowd of one John Deyngell and John Couche foure pounds for the charges of xviij men and as many horse for them meat drynk and wages when they rode westwards for to helpe resiste the last comocion by the assent and consent of the whole pysheners.

As his reward for crushing the rebellion, Russell was granted the Earldom of Bedford and land, valued in total at £399 per annum, spread over several counties, including the manor of Woburn and the estate at Boconnoc.

THE MOHUNS PURCHASE BOCONNOC

In 1563, John Russell's son, Francis, the 2nd Earl of Bedford sold the estate to Sir William Mohun for £1,740.[2] Three years later, in 1566, William sold Boconnoc to his father Reginald (sometimes known as Reynold or Reignolde) for £2,000. Reginald also owned a property called Hall House situated near Fowey.[3]

REGINALD MOHUN OF HALL
AND BOCONNOC (1508—67)

Reginald Mohun was an esquire to the body of King Edward VI and Sheriff of Cornwall in 1552–53 and 1559–60. He sat as an MP for five different constituencies in Devon and Cornwall between 1547 and 1563 and was a Justice of the Peace between 1547 and 1553. He became involved in disputes over land, his mother's inheritance and the dowry of his wife Joan Trevanion and was frequently involved in disputes with neighbours. In 1534, in the Star Chamber (a court of law that sat at Westminster), Reginald Mohun alleged that John Arundell's servants had damaged his property. Conversely, in 1565, Sir William Godolphin alleged that Mohun had unlawfully evicted tenants and stolen crops from his manor of Lelant.

The death of Reginald Mohun

Reginald Mohun died on 22 April 1567, owning considerable property in Devon and Cornwall. His Inquisition Post Mortem, taken at Bodmin on 17 January 1568, shows that he died 'seised of the Manor of Boconnock and Bodenych [Bodinnick]'.[4] The Mohuns and their successors at Boconnoc owned the rights to operate the ferries that ran between Fowey and either Polruan or Bodinnick for many centuries. This acquisition proved to be a mixed blessing for later owners – for more about the ferries, see Chapter 10.

The Mohun Family

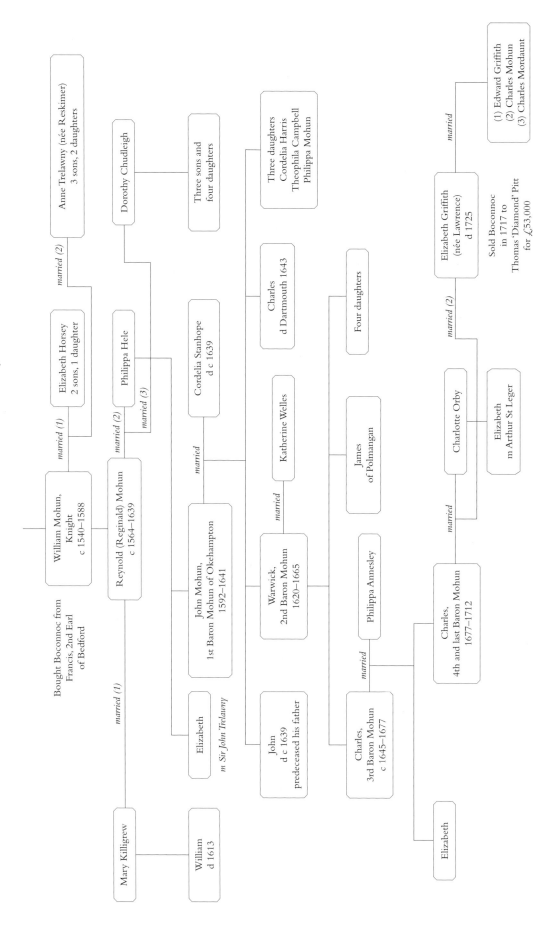

Bought Boconnoc from Francis, 2nd Earl of Bedford

William Mohun, Knight c 1540–1588

married (1) Elizabeth Horsey 2 sons, 1 daughter

married (2) Anne Trelawny (née Reskimer) 3 sons, 2 daughters

Reynold (Reginald) Mohun c 1564–1639

married (2) Philippa Hele

married (3) Dorothy Chudleigh

Three sons and four daughters

married (1) Mary Killigrew

William d 1613

Elizabeth m Sir John Trelawny

John Mohun, 1st Baron Mohun of Okehampton 1592–1641

married Cordelia Stanhope d c 1639

John d c 1639 predeceased his father

Warwick, 2nd Baron Mohun 1620–1665

married Katherine Welles

Charles d Dartmouth 1643

Three daughters
Cordelia Harris
Theophila Campbell
Philippa Mohun

James of Polmangan

Four daughters

Charles, 3rd Baron Mohun c 1645–1677

married Philippa Annesley

Elizabeth

Charles, 4th and last Baron Mohun 1677–1712

married Charlotte Orby

married (2) Elizabeth Griffith (née Lawrence) d 1725

Sold Boconnoc in 1717 to Thomas 'Diamond' Pitt for £53,000

Elizabeth m Arthur St Leger

Elizabeth Griffith (née Lawrence) d 1725

married
(1) Edward Griffith
(2) Charles Mohun
(3) Charles Mordaunt

WILLIAM MOHUN (C. 1540—88)

Reginald Mohun had four sons and four daughters, his eldest son William inheriting his father's property. William married twice: first to Elizabeth, daughter and heiress of Sir John Horsey, by whom he had two sons, his heir, Reginald and William and a daughter, Elizabeth; and second, to Anne, daughter and co-heiress of William Reskimer (and widow of Jonathan Trelawny of Menheniot) by whom he had three sons, William, Thomas and Arundel and two daughters, Jane (later Speccot) and Bridget (later Arundell).

In 1571, 1584 and 1586, he was elected as a Knight of the Shire, a gentleman who represented the interests of a shire or county in Parliament, was Sheriff of Cornwall in 1571–72 and 1577–78 and was knighted in 1583. He was also appointed to a number of committees and in 1577, he was a Commissioner for Piracy. He was appointed JP from around 1569 and when war with Spain broke out in 1585, he was made a Deputy Lieutenant for Cornwall.[5]

There is little evidence to show how often Mohun and his family were living at Boconnoc although, while attending Parliament, he must have been resident in London. A servant of William Mohun's, Richard Harvye, left a will which contained legacies to servants in Mohun's household.[6] Given the number mentioned in the will, this suggests that there was a substantial household and that the family was in residence for at least some part of the year. For more about life at Boconnoc, see Chapters 6 and 7.

When William Mohun died on 6 April 1588, he owned more than twenty manors in Cornwall. His will, made on the day of his death, appointed his eldest son, Reginald, aged about 23, as his executor.[7] To his elder son named William, by his first wife, Elizabeth (née Horsey) – confusingly, he had two sons named William, one by each of his wives – he bequeathed the manors of Bodmin, Tucoys and Mether; to his younger son called William, his first child and eldest son by his second wife, Anne (née Reskimer), the manors of St Mawes and Deviock; to Thomas (his second son by Anne), he gave an annuity of £40. His third son by Anne, Arundel, is not mentioned and had probably died by this date. To his two daughters, Jane and Bridget by Anne, he gave £500 each, when they reached the age of 14. Anne, William Mohun's widow, was left household goods, animals and farm equipment. Legacies were also left to several of his servants and 'for the stewardshippe of Boconnock, St Day, Amyll and Tregarick' William Grosse was left £5 yearly during his life.

As well as the property at Boconnoc, the family had retained the house at Hall at Bodinnick, near Fowey, which became the dower house for the Mohun widows. William Mohun's widow, Anne, lived at Hall for twenty years until her death in 1608. Her will (undated) and her inventory, dated 30 August 1608, demonstrate how wealthy the Mohun family had become. Over thirty rooms were listed in the house, including a hall, Ladies Chamber and a 'wyn seller'. She bequeathed a gold ring to each of her daughters and made a similar bequest to her grandson, Reginald (Reynold) Mohun; to her grandson, John Trelawny, she left her tin works; to her granddaughters, Anne and Bridget Arundell, dowries of £100 and £50 respectively, in addition to plate, bedding and furniture. Her sons, William and Thomas Mohun, received all her silver gilt vessels, silver bowls and spoons.[8]

Her wearing apparel was made of rich materials: 'a trayne of Taffaty', gowns made of velvet and a petticoat with a gold and silver fringe. She owned a satin bag, embroidered with silk and gold, jewels, silver gilt salts, Venetian glasses, china dishes and a pair of virginals. Her books were valued at forty shillings and in her purse was £221. In total, her inventory was valued at almost £400.

SIR REGINALD MOHUN (C. 1564–1639)

Reginald Mohun of Hall and Boconnoc, was the eldest surviving son of William Mohun and Elizabeth Horsey, his first wife.

Reginald was married three times, and the inheritance rights of his ten children by his several wives became the cause of protracted and increasingly acrimonious arguments within the family circle. Reginald married first, to Mary, daughter of Sir Henry Killigrew. By her, he had one son, William, who died in 1613, predeceasing his father. His second wife was Philippa, daughter of Sir John Hele. By her, he had two children: John, his heir and Elizabeth, who married Sir John Trelawny. His third wife was Dorothy, daughter of John Chudleigh of Aston, Devon. By her, he had three sons, Reynold, Ferdinand and George and four daughters, Dorothy (later Carew), Bridget (later Nicholls and then Smith), Penelope (later Drew) and Margaret (later Roscarrock).

A beautiful portrait of Reginald Mohun and Dorothy Chudleigh survives [*Plate 1*]. It is not known who the artist is, save that the painting is of the English School, *c.* 1604. Dorothy Chudleigh holds a pink rose in her right hand, a symbol of betrothal and sometimes of love. The couple's arms are intertwined and this portrait is believed to be the earliest known example of a full-length marriage portrait in English easel painting. The linked arms of the subjects give the painting 'an endearing characterisation and thus it is also perhaps the earliest instance of affection and tender feeling in English portraiture'.[9]

Sir Reginald became an important magnate in Cornwall. He was elected an MP for Fowey in 1584 and 1586, for East Looe in 1614 and for Lostwithiel in 1625. He was knighted by Edward VI in 1599 and in 1611 he was created one of the first baronets, 'a new dignitie between Barons and Knights' instituted by James I. However, Mohun had to pay £1,095 for this honour, which only succeeded in exacerbating his financial problems.

The security of the county

In 1600, Sir Reginald Mohun was appointed as a Deputy Lieutenant because 'he doth dwell in a convenient place … and is a gentleman of good sufficiency and credit …'[10] He and other members of the Cornish gentry were required to assist William, Earl of Pembroke, in protecting the Cornish coastline from invaders.[11]

From late in the reign of James I and between the accession of Charles I in 1625 and the commencement of the Civil War in 1642, there was continuing concern about the security of Cornwall. In the first quarter of the seventeenth century, England was at war with both Spain and France and later in the century with the Dutch. There was apprehension that a landing, by one, or all, of the Continental powers, was imminent. These concerns were intensified because the coastal defences of Cornwall were dilapidated and totally inadequate to prevent any invasion.[12] Naval protection was requested from the Crown on numerous occasions, but to little avail.

Not only was there anxiety about a possible invasion by the Continental powers, but also about increasing threats from 'Turkish' pirates, by which was meant men from Tripoli, Tunis and Algiers.

When the king requested financial assistance from the Cornish in order to support a naval presence, enthusiasm diminished rapidly. In 1626, the king had requested Ship Money, a tax that was assessed on subjects living on the coast. This had provoked opposition in Cornwall, as the king had already demanded a Forced Loan to finance the wars.[13] There was also dissension because no money was available from central government to accommodate the troops in taverns (as was the norm) and consequently, they had been billeted in the houses of civilians. Reginald Mohun, shortly after being appointed as a Deputy Lieutenant, wrote to the Privy Council, pointing out on behalf of the citizens of the western counties that 2,000 soldiers had been billeted in Devon and Cornwall and the civilian population was considerably out of pocket as a result.

The conflict between Sir Reginald and his son and heir, John

Sir Reginald had ten children, five sons (one of whom predeceased him) and five daughters. He became increasingly concerned about his debts and about how to provide for his seven children by his third wife, Dorothy Chudleigh. Reginald's heir was his son, John, born in 1592. His mother died when he was a young child and his relationship with his stepmother, Dorothy (née Chudleigh), was anything but amicable.

John Mohun married Lady Cordelia Aston (née Stanhope) on 2 July 1613.[14] She was the widow of Sir Roger Aston of Cranford, Middlesex and although she had a life interest in her late husband's estate, valued at around £7,500, she brought no dowry to her marriage. In return for Sir Reginald agreeing to let his son have the immediate use of the Mohun properties in Devon and Dorset, John agreed that he would take financial responsibility for his younger siblings should they be orphaned as minors. After the deal had been concluded, Sir Reginald had second thoughts and attempted to renege on the agreement. When John refused to agree to any changes, Sir Reginald took the unwise step (allegedly at the behest of his wife Dorothy) of forging deeds in an attempt to show that various properties had already been settled on his younger sons and therefore could not be included as part of John's inheritance. The allegation was made that Sir Reginald had 'gone mad' and although the forgeries were destroyed, the acrimony that had been created led to John commencing the first of a number of lawsuits that he launched against his father.

In 1616, a compromise was reached in the Court of Chancery, but when John Mohun returned to live in Cornwall the dispute was renewed. A Bill in the House of Commons in 1622 (confirmed in 1624) gave John significant additional rights over the Mohun properties and prevented Sir Reginald from granting leases and managing the estate at Boconnoc. Further, the clause that John should provide financially for his half-brothers and half-sisters was removed.[15] Even this was not the end, for in 1629 John, again sued his father, complaining that Sir Reginald had been wasting the Boconnoc estates.

The death of Sir Reginald Mohun

Reginald Mohun was still active in local government until the early part of 1639. Later that year, he became ill and although Dorothy Mohun's brother, George Chudleigh, wrote to her that he hoped for her husband's recovery, Mohun died on 26 December 1639.[16]

He had made his will on 30 January 1638, 'desiring to set his howse in order soe that peace and quietnes may Contynue therein' after his death. He requested that he be buried in the 'Chancell of the parish Church of Bocconnocke'. He left small bequests to his children and bequeathed twenty shillings each to the poor of the parishes of Boconnoc, St Nyott and Lanteglos-by-Fowey. All the residue of his goods and chattels he left to his wife Dorothy, who was named as his executrix rather than his son John which, given the strained relationship between father, stepmother and son, was unsurprising.[17]

Two days prior to making his will, on 28 January 1638, Reginald had had a note made of all his goods and chattels and had granted them to Sir George Chudleigh, his brother-in-law and Sir Henry Carew, his son-in-law, to be held in trust. These goods were to be used towards the satisfaction of his debts and legacies as he would give and devise in his will and testament.[18] The schedule gives interesting information about the contents and furnishings of Boconnoc House at this date, for which see Chapter 7.

JOHN MOHUN, LATER 1ST BARON MOHUN OF OKEHAMPTON (1592—1641)

John Mohun was born in 1592. His relationship with his stepmother was antagonistic and accordingly, he remained close to his mother's family, the Heles. He, together with his older half-brother William, went up to Exeter College, Oxford in 1605 where John graduated with a BA on 7 July 1608. In 1611, he proceeded to the Middle Temple. Two years later, William died and John became Sir Reginald's heir.[19]

John Mohun's political career and his alliance with Sir James Bagg

As a result of the lengthy conflict with his father and Sir Reginald's lack of political support for his son, the progress of John Mohun's career within Cornwall initially failed to achieve any momentum. This changed in 1622, when George Villiers, Duke of Buckingham (1592–1628) took control of the administration of the Duchy of Cornwall, hitherto held by three men, William Herbert, 3rd Earl of Pembroke, who was the Lord Warden of the Stannaries, William Coryton, the Vice-Warden and Sir John Eliot, the Vice-Admiral. Buckingham appointed Sir James Bagg as his agent in Cornwall and Coryton and Eliot were dismissed from their posts.

John Mohun formed a close alliance with Bagg, which enhanced the prospects of advancement in his career. He sat as an MP for Grampound and in May 1625 he was appointed a JP and had been appointed as a Deputy Lieutenant by the middle of 1626. In the latter year, he was also appointed by Buckingham to enquire into the activities of John Eliot during the time Eliot had held the position of Vice-Admiral. As a 'reward' for Mohun's diligence, Bagg recommended to Buckingham that Mohun should be appointed as Vice-Warden of the Stannaries in William Coryton's place, saying that 'he [Mohun] studies nothing more than to honour your Grace and to advantage his Majesty's commands'.[20]

The dispute between the different political factions in Cornwall reached new heights in 1628. Mohun and his allies attempted to prevent William Coryton being elected a Knight of the Shire and John Eliot as an MP, saying that their election 'would be contrary to the King's pleasure'. Despite Mohun's efforts to have Sir Richard Edgcumbe and himself elected, partly by issuing threats against his rivals, this had little effect on the electorate and Coryton and Eliot were convincingly returned. Mohun's defeat in the election of 1627–28 may have been an 'index of waning Court influence' which led, ultimately, to the conflict between king and Parliament in the Civil War.[21]

Mohun's conduct in threatening Coryton and Eliot was a step too far and on 16 April 1628, Eliot was appointed Chairman of a Committee set up to enquire into Mohun's possible abuse of his authority while he was Vice-Warden of the Stannaries. The House of Commons ordered all the protagonists to appear before them in London, but Mohun failed to attend. Despite Coryton and Eliot's attempts to bring Mohun to task to answer for his alleged abuses, no further action was taken.

Mohun had a long-held ambition of securing a peerage for himself. The only holder of such a title in Cornwall was Lord Robartes of Lanhydrock. On 15 April 1628, through Buckingham's influence, Mohun was created Baron Mohun of Okehampton and took his seat in the House of Lords on 12 May. Buckingham was assassinated in August 1628 and this brought Mohun's continuing political rise in Cornwall to a halt. His influence in the county declined and he was removed from the position of Vice-Warden in 1629.

John Mohun as Vice-Warden of the Stannaries

In 1628, Mohun and Bagg both intimated 'that the Crown should commit the direction of local business to select men in every county', meaning members of gentry families, which included both of them. The office of Vice-Warden of the Stannaries, to which Mohun has been appointed in 1626 (until 1629), was significant to the Cornish economy. Tinners were in a special position, so important in bringing in revenue to the Crown that they had their own Parliament. The holder of the office exercised jurisdiction over the tin-producing areas and the tinners. In theory, the Vice-Warden only had judicial power over lesser offences committed by tinners but, in practice, no one knew exactly who had jurisdiction over what, which gave Mohun considerable opportunity to extend his authority without any interference. He was accused of forcing local men to purchase the privileges that they should have had by right, by virtue of their being tin miners, distributing warrants stating 'to this submit or you will provoke me' and incarcerating any man whom he believed to be his enemy.[22]

In 1626, one of Mohun's supporters, Thomas Fitzwilliams, was arrested and imprisoned by William Mayowe, the Mayor of Looe. Mohun rode to Looe demanding that Fitzwilliams should be released from prison – the prison being 'a loathsome and filthy one bad ynough for the basest offender' – but Mayowe refused to release the prisoner into Mohun's custody. Accordingly, Mohun resurrected a claim against Mayowe for an unpaid debt and had the Mayor imprisoned.[23] After Mayowe reached agreement with his creditor and paid off the sum he owed, the Mayor was released by his gaoler, Hannibal Vyvyan of Trelowarren. Mohun had Mayowe rearrested and then had both Mayowe and Vyvyan thrown into prison. Vyvyan had significant influence in his own right, being MP for St Mawes and Comptroller of the Duchy. He brought a petition to the Commons on 10 April 1628, complaining that he had been falsely imprisoned for six months at Mohun's command, who was 'expressinge none spetiall cause in his warrant but contempt for not p[er]forming his order'.

From evidence collected by William Coryton and John Eliot, justice in the Stannaries under the rule of Mohun was both more expensive and more arbitrary, decisions being made according to his whims rather than according to the letter of the law. Mohun granted many Writs of Privilege which gave men tinners' rights, although they could not legitimately claim to be in that occupation. Further, Mohun levied the sum of £500 from the twenty-four Stannators, the men who controlled the Stannaries. He had himself nominated them, contrary to custom that decreed that the Stannators should be chosen by the Mayors of the four stannary towns (at various times, Penzance, St Austell, Lostwithiel, Bodmin, Liskeard, Helston and Truro). While Mohun declared that the money raised was for the maintenance of the Privilege of the Stannaries, Vyvyan believed that the money was really to be used by Mohun for his own purposes and that he 'doth use his power to the great greife of the whole countie of Cornwall'.[24]

The end of the Bagg faction – Mohun is sued by the Exchequer

The close relationship that Mohun had once enjoyed with James Bagg dissolved in the 1630s, to such an extent that Mohun accused Bagg of corruption and of embezzling £55,000. In turn, Bagg sued Mohun in the Star Chamber where Mohun was fined £500. Bagg died on 26 August 1638 and the faction that had been so important in Cornwall effectively disintegrated.

At the same time that Mohun was accusing Bagg of embezzlement, he was himself being sued by the Exchequer for (allegedly) attempting to export cloth illegally to the continent of Europe in a boat 'at near or aboute the port or Creake of ffowey in September now last past [1633] into the parts beyond the seas'. This was an attempt to avoid paying taxes and according to depositions given by numerous witnesses, Lord Mohun had brought cloth to the house of Degory George, a merchant at Fowey.[25] The cloth was due to be conveyed to a ship near Plymouth for onward transmission to Europe, but due to adverse winds the rendezvous did not take place and the cloth was deposited 'at a place called Cawsand'. It was alleged that Mohun had been intimidating witnesses to prevent them from giving testimony against him, but as nothing could be proved, no further action was taken.

John, 1st Lord Mohun died on 28 March 1641 and was succeeded by his son, Warwick, who inherited, aged 20.

WARWICK MOHUN, 2ND BARON MOHUN OF OKEHAMPTON (1620-65)

Warwick married Katherine Welles, of Brember in Hampshire. She was a Roman Catholic and the king in Council made an order that Lady Mohun 'shall give security to breed her children in the Protestant religion'.[26] By her, Warwick had five children, two sons, his heir, Charles, later 3rd Lord Mohun, James of Polmangan and three daughters, Cordelia, Catherine and Isabella.

Warwick, Lord Mohun and the English Civil War

The year 1642 marked the final breakdown of relations between king and Parliament which, ultimately, plunged the country into Civil War. For many months, the king and Parliament had been in conflict and in January the king tried to arrest those who were leading the opposition against him in the Commons. Failing to achieve this end, the king left London on 15 January. The country had no standing army, so the question of who commanded the Trained Bands or county militias, charged with the defence of the realm, was of significant interest to both factions. In January 1642 Parliament took control of the militias and in March of the same year the Militia Ordinance was passed in both Houses of Parliament. This gave Parliament the right to appoint their choice of Lieutenants to the militias which, until that date, had been the prerogative of the king.

On 12 August, Parliament voted to raise an army and placed it under the command of the Earl of Essex. When Charles raised the royal standard at Nottingham on 22 August, it signalled the commencement of the Civil War.[27]

Many years later, it was claimed that Lord Mohun had originally intended to join the Parliamentary cause and 'had forborne to join himself to the king's party' until the Royalists had triumphed at the Battle of Edgehill in October 1642.[28] Whether this was true or not, Lord Mohun declared that the increasingly bellicose situation made him concerned for his personal safety and he swiftly absented himself from Parliament and Westminster and fled London for Cornwall.

Preparations for war

In response to the passing of the Militia Ordinance by Parliament, the king sent out his own Commissions of Array in Cornwall to summon all men aged between 15 and 60 in the county to support his cause. With Warwick, Lord Mohun at their head, twenty-one gentlemen were appointed.[29] Mohun, Sir Nicholas Slanning, Sir Bevill (spelt variously) Grenville and John Arundell Junior of Trerice became the most active commissioners. Meetings were held at Boconnoc and at other venues around Cornwall. On 21 July 1642, Lord Mohun wrote to Francis Bassett of Tehidy:

> Bocconnocke - To my most respected friend Francis Bassett Esq there at Tehiddy present. My worthy friend, To lett you see what an Impudent beggar I am, I have sent this bearer to you, for the Barrell of Gunpowder, you promised mee, And likewise to give you notice that the commission of Array doe meet at Lostwithiell Wednesday next Pray doe mee the honor; to meet your friends Sir Nich: Slanning, Sir Bevill Grenville and Mr Arundle of Trerise heer on Tuesday, where we shal confere about some business concerning settling of this county.[30]

Parliament ordered that members of the Royalist faction, including Mohun, should be brought before the Lords in Parliament 'to Answer for high Comtempts Committed by them and so disturbing the peace of the kingdome, by receaving and endeavouring to execute a Commission of Array which is against the lawe of this realm. Take care to have their bodies well guarded that noe Rescues be made'.[31] The Royalists refused to attend, saying that the king had ordered them to remain in Cornwall and Mohun declared that 'it ill became his dignity as a peer to be summoned like a Common Rogue'.[32]

Raising an army

At the commencement of hostilities, Sir Ralph Hopton, an experienced soldier, was appointed by the king as Lieutenant-General for the Western Counties.[33] The Parliamentarians summoned the Trained Bands to meet at Bodmin on 28 September 1642 and they set off for Launceston under the command of Sir Richard Buller. In October, Hopton with his militia army moved towards Launceston, chasing the

Parliamentarians. Hopton had 3,000-4,000 men, but they were untrained and had only obsolete weapons.[34]

Believing that the Cornish militia could not be taken out of the county, Buller led his army back across the Tamar. Hopton was also uncertain whether he had a legal right to take his troops out of Cornwall into Devon, even if, as Coate put it, 'they were willing to go, which was unlikely'.[35] It was at this juncture that the Royalist leaders decided to raise a volunteer army, specifically recruited for the king's cause, that could cross out of Cornwall and into England.[36]

Warwick Mohun became one of the founding figures of the Cornish army.[37] The five Cornish regiments raised were initially led by their 'first Colonells: Sir William Godolphin of Godolphin, Warwick, Lord Mohun of Boconnoc, Colonel Nicholas Slanning of Maristow, Colonel John Trevanion of Caerhays and Sir Bevill Grenville of Stowe'.[38]

The Battle of Braddock Down, 19 January 1643

On 17 January 1643 three Parliamentary ships, loaded with weapons and money, were driven into Falmouth and captured by the Royalists, enabling Hopton to pay and supply his troops. On the following day, a Council of War was held in Boconnoc Park[39] and Hopton, Mohun and the other commanders agreed that, rather than waiting, they would actively seek out the Parliamentary army, led by Colonel Ruthin.[40]

However, on the morning of 19 January scouts reported that Ruthin had already deployed his troops on Braddock Down, 'on a pretty rising ground in the way towards Liskeard', south-west of Braddock Church. Here Hopton found the enemy's whole army 'upon a fair heath, between Boconnoc and Braddock Church'.[41] Hopton drew up his army to the north-east of Boconnoc. He placed the Cornish foot in the centre, flanked by the horse and the dragoons. Musketeers were in hiding behind hedges and Hopton arranged for 'two small iron minion drakes' – light field guns – to be brought from Boconnoc.[42] After two shots from the drakes, the Royalists advanced on Ruthin and his army. The Cornish 'being indeed excellent at hedge-work and that kind of fight' pushed Ruthin's army back and the retreat became a rout. All of Ruthin's ammunition was captured, together with eight colours, four pieces of ordnance and much baggage. Two hundred men were killed and 1,250 men were taken prisoner.[43]

Hopton and Mohun chased Ruthin and what remained of his army towards Saltash and then on to Plymouth. A conference was held between the two opposing sides in the city on Sunday 29 January in an attempt to arrange a cessation of hostilities, but no agreement could be reached. A temporary truce was agreed for March and part of April, giving the Royalists the opportunity to continue recruiting troops and raising money in Cornwall. The Cornish army was ordered to muster on Sunday 23 April, but when the truce expired the previous day, the Parliamentary troops, led by James Chudleigh, who had by then reached Launceston, commenced an attack.[44]

Beacon Hill and Sourton Down, 23 and 25 April 1643

Hopton drew up his army on Beacon Hill, known locally as Windmill Hill, to the east of Launceston.[45] Early on, the Parliamentarians outnumbered the Royalists, but during the course of the morning, Lord Mohun's regiment arrived to bolster Hopton's army. By 7 p.m., Chudleigh realised that he must abandon his attempt to take Launceston and withdrew his troops.[46]

Hopton followed the Parliamentarians across the Tamar towards Okehampton, but before they reached the town, Chudleigh set a trap for the Royalists on Sourton Down. At 11 p.m., as Hopton and Mohun were riding 'carelessly enterteyning themselves in the head of Dragoons', Chudleigh sprung his trap and the Royalists rode into an ambush. Hopton and Mohun's forces were fired upon and the Parliamentarian horse attacked, giving their foot soldiers sufficient time to retreat. Eventually, Chudleigh and the horse disappeared into the night.[47] Hopton and Mohun had very narrowly escaped capture.[48]

Hopton's troops were now scattered across Devon and Cornwall – 'the Lord *Mohune* his Regiment consisting of about 900; quartereth at *Liscard*, and the Parishes thereabouts, towards his mansion house near *Lostithell*'.[49]

The Battle of Stratton, 16 May 1643

A month later, the Cornish achieved a singular and somewhat unexpected victory. The Parliamentary army was drawn up by the Earl of Stamford at the top of what became known as Stamford Hill, near Stratton. At 5 a.m. Hopton gave the order to attack and the Royalists, in four sections, began to ascend the steep hill, Hopton and Mohun from the south. As the Cornish troops stormed up the hill and met their compatriots at the summit, the Parliamentary army broke and ran, which left the Royalists in complete control of the whole of Cornwall.[50]

Bristol, 26 July 1643

In July 1643, Prince Rupert, the king's nephew, had succeeded in capturing Bristol, although at the expense of enormous losses to the king's forces. Five hundred men died, including Nicholas Slanning and John Trevanion, two of the original Cornish Colonels. A third, Bevill Grenville, had already been killed on 5 July 1643 at Lansdown near Bath.

The loss of three of the Colonels had a serious effect on the morale of the Cornish army and left it 'terribly battered'. Although the Cornish regiments disappear from the record left by Hopton, this was not because they had been disbanded, but because after the fall of Bristol, Hopton's connections with them were severed. In fact, the Cornish regiments continued to form a vital part of the Royalist war-machine for many years to come.[51]

When Bristol was captured, Lord Mohun was still in command of his regiment, but in August, he was appointed Colonel-General of the Western Counties. He resigned his colonelcy to his 21-year-old brother, Sir Charles Mohun. Mohun's regiment took part in campaigns up to 1646, although when they finally surrendered is unknown. 'Thus, within two weeks of Bristol's fall, William Godolphin was the only one of the five original Cornish colonels to retain command of his regiment.'[52]

The Battle of Lostwithiel, August and September 1644

In May 1644, Mohun was replaced as Colonel-General, the appointment that he had been given the previous August. Two months later, the Earl of Essex, for Parliament, advanced into the west 'by the persuasion of Lord Roberts' (Lord Robartes of Lanhydrock), a 'sour Puritan' who assured Essex that he would receive great assistance in Cornwall, an assurance that proved to be totally inaccurate.[53] Closely pursued by the king and the Royalist army, Essex was due to rendezvous with a fleet at Fowey that was to bring him supplies, but due to the contrary winds along the Channel, the convoy of ships never left Portsmouth.

There are good eyewitness accounts of the Battle of Lostwithiel, including those of the diarist Richard Symonds (1618–80) and Edward Walker (1612–77).[54] Symonds joined the Royalist forces at Oxford in December 1643 as a trooper in the mounted lifeguards. Art historian Mary Beal argues convincingly that a painting of an identified man by Sir Peter Lely, now at Weston Park in Shropshire, is a portrait of Richard Symonds, while a seal showing Symonds in profile is held at the College of Arms[55] [Plate 2]. Symonds makes no mention of Mohun being present at Boconnoc when the king made his headquarters there in August 1644 (although that does not mean that he was not there), but Boconnoc, with or without Lord Mohun, still had a significant part to play.

Edward Walker was in constant attendance on Charles I and was in a unique position to give his account of the progress of the war:

> The day being the 4th of August a Party of Horse of Collonel *Richard Nevil's*, commanded by Sir *Bernard Gascoyn* an *Italian* and Volunteer in his Regiment, being sent out to secure the Country from Plunder, drew very near the Rebels Quarters at *Listithiel*, and being advertised by a Youth that divers of the Earl of *Essex's* officers were that Afternoon caressing [carousing] at *Boconnock* the Lord *Mohun's* House, he made haste thither presently, forced the Gates, and got Possession of the Dining Room. They still kept a Buttery at the end of it, until through the Door one of their Servants was slain; then they rendered themselves Prisoners, being Collonel Aldridge sometime Governour of *Alisbury*, Lieutenant Collonel *Butteler, Essex's* own Lieutenant Collonel, Lieutenant Collonel *Carleton,* Captain *Blyth*, and *Burdet, Essex's* Ensign; *Dalbier* Quarter Master General of the Rebels Army, was in their Power, but being without a Sword or Hat, he pretended himself a Servant of that House and so escaped, being unknown.[56]

The Royalists drew up their army and made 'the Rebels quit that part of the Heath which lyes between *Boconnock* and the Lord Mohun's warren they still keeping the Hill without *Boconnock Park*'.[57] On 8 August, the king 'lay in a field all night in his Coach on *Boconnock Downe*'. Still optimistic that a peaceful settlement might be negotiated, the Royalist officers sent a letter to Essex asking him to meet the king, but their approach was rebuffed, Essex replying that he had no authority to treat without the consent of Parliament. Thereafter, the king moved his headquarters and court to Boconnoc. He resided in the house (one bedroom still being called The King's Room), while his army camped in the surrounding fields and park.[58]

On Monday 12 August, Sir Richard Grenville rode from Bodmin and endeavored to possess 'Lanhetherock, [Lanhydrock] the Lord *Robert's* House two miles West of Boconnock'. Having captured Resprin Bridge close to Lanhydrock, Grenville marched on to Fowey, where he took control of the river banks to prevent Essex and his troops from reaching the foreshore.[59]

Simultaneously, Hall House (which still belonged to the Mohuns) and then Polruan Castle were recaptured by Sir Jacob Astley, preventing Essex's forces from receiving supplies from the seaward direction. On 16 August, as reported by Symonds: 'The King this day went on the other side of the river to the Lord Roberts his howse. Two of Essex's men who came in to us this day … told us that provisions were very scarce with Essex.'[60]

On Saturday 17 August, the king rode out from Boconnoc to make a reconnaissance of the Parliamentary Army's positions at Cliff and Hall Walk near Bodinnick.

> From thence his Majestie went to Lantegles to the manor howse belonging to the Lord Mohun just over against Foye, where his royall person ventured to goe into a walke there, which is within halfe musket shott from Foye, where a poore fisherman was killed in looking over, at the same time that his Majestie was in the walke, and in the place where the King a little afore passed by … [61]

Fighting continued sporadically during the next few days, until on the evening of 30 August, two deserters were brought to the king at Boconnoc.[62] 'At seven of the clock in the Evening upon Friday the 30th of *August*, two foot soldiers of the Rebels Army (whereof one was a *French* man) came over from them, and assured us, that they intended that Night to break through with their Horse …' Having been informed of the Parliamentarians' plan to escape, the king and queen's troops rode 'to Bocconoc, wither came newes that the enemyes horse were then upon the downe and coming up betweene the hills …' Shortly after dawn on 31 August, the king went in pursuit of Essex's force and after the fighting, 'this night the King lay under a hedge with his servants in one feild'.[63] The main body of the Royalist foot advanced and fighting continued around Lostwithiel and Castle Dore. The Royalists pushed the Parliamentarians back, step by step, hedge by hedge, field by field. The Parliamentary infantry retreated towards Fowey where they were trapped with their backs to the sea, surrounded by the Royalists and with no prospect of escape. In appalling weather and torrential rain, the Parliamentarians had no choice but to abandon their guns which, in any event, were impossible to move through the thick cloying mud. Despite the king's prompt action, the Parliamentary cavalry escaped and fled towards Plymouth.

On the night of 31 August, forced to accept that defeat was inevitable, Essex with Sir John Merrick and Lord Robartes sailed in a fishing boat for Plymouth, leaving Sir Philip Skippon in charge of what remained of the, by now, sodden, totally dispirited and broken Parliamentary army. Skippon was advised that the infantry would not be able to break out of the encirclement as the cavalry had done and the terms that the king offered being generous, he surrendered 6,000 infantry troops and all that remained of their guns, powder, bullets and arms.[64]

The king pardoned the infantry and allowed the chief officers to kiss his hand, except for Skippon, who was considered as too great an enemy to 'His Majesties Honour and safety'.[65]

Following this triumph, the king wrote to his nephew, Prince Rupert. Some of the letter was written in cypher, but is here transcribed:

> Boconoke, 3 Sep 1644
>
> Nepeue. Since my last, it hath pleased God to give me an unexpected victory, and you will fynde by the particulars (which I leave to others) that God's protection of a just cause was never more aparant then at this tyme, for had our success been ether deferd, or of an other kynde, nothing but a direct miracle could have saved us, and certainly nothing could be so unlooked for as that Essex in Cornwall should imitate (and outdoe) Meldrum at Newarke. Goring is now hemming in the Rebbelles' horse which broke from us, they lying neere Plimouth, and I have sent Sir Richard Grinefeeld with 1500 foot to assist him (who I hope is there by this tyme) following myself as fast as I may intending to bee the morrow at Liscard and Tavistock the next, and soon till we join. The Rebel Middleton is said to be about Barnstable; now I propose to you whether you will not think fit to march with speade unto Dorsetshire towards Sherborne, the case being altered with us both since my last, I not knowing then ye were at Bristol; yet by this I do not alter the main design, which [is] for you to join with me but as then, so now I refer it to you to do as you shall judge best for my service. So I rest
>
> Your loving Oncle and most faithfull frend, Charles R[66]

Having gained an epic victory, the king knighted the Sheriff of Cornwall, Francis Bassett of Tehidy and created Richard Vyvyan a baronet, rewarding them for their services to the royal cause. On 3 September, the king marched away from Boconnoc towards Liskeard and then across the Tamar and out of Cornwall.

The Prince of Wales – later Charles II

This was not the end of Boconnoc's association with royalty, for in January 1645, the king sent his son into the west of the country. Charles, Prince of Wales, was at Boconnoc on 10 November 1645, as appears from a warrant granted for fishing in the 'Larrin', signed by him as 'from our Court at Boconnoc'. Later in the year, the king ordered that the prince should be sent to France for his safety, but this order was disobeyed by Edward Hyde (later Earl of Clarendon) and Hopton, who believed that, should the prince leave the country, it would be a signal that the war was irretrievably lost to the Royalist cause.[67]

The end of the Civil War in the West

The Civil War in the country at large came to an end at the Battle of Worcester on 3 September 1651. The Royalist surrender in Cornwall had already taken effect on 15 March 1646 in Truro, when Sir Thomas Fairfax offered Ralph Hopton terms. By that date, Warwick, Lord Mohun had already submitted to Parliament.

In March 1655, Major-General John Desborough was placed in command of the six western counties. In order to suppress any further insurrections, a new militia force was to be formed in every county, paid for by taxing the Royalists.[68] Lord Mohun argued that, although he had fought for the king in 1642–43, he had not acted against Parliament since the autumn of the latter year and accordingly, he requested exemption from the tax, but Mohun finally had to compound for his estate at a fine of £2,090.17s.10d.

The death of Warwick, Lord Mohun

Lord Mohun died sometime between April and July 1665. His will was dated 30 April in that year and he asked that his body should be buried in Boconnoc church.[69] This request was granted for 'his corps in the parish church adjioyeinge to his said howse weare presently Interred'. The estate was to be held in trust by his wife Katherine and his three sisters, Dame Cordelia Harris, Theophila Campbell and Philippa Mohun until his son Charles, now 3rd Lord Mohun, came of age. When Charles reached his majority, he would inherit provided that he paid legacies to his younger brother James and to his three sisters. Warwick's widow and his sisters were made his executrixes and appointed as guardians of his children 'desireing that they may be piously brought up in the Protestant religion established according to law'.

Although the children had been left bequests of money when they respectively reached the age of 21, no provision had been made for their maintenance until they reached that age. Legal action was instituted by Cordelia Harris, who claimed that Lady Mohun had been left the estate in consideration of her accepting responsibility for the financial maintenance of the children until they reached their majority. Lady Mohun was now pretending that Lord Mohun's estate had only been worth £722.8s.4d, the sum being so low because of the debts incurred as a result of the Civil War. Rebutting Lady Mohun's claim, Cordelia alleged that a 'considerable part of the said Lord Mohuns Goods and personall estate were imbezilled and clearly omitted out of his Inventory … to conceale the same as well to the great prejudice of Charles now Lord Mohun sonne and heire'.[70] Whilst it is entirely possible that goods were omitted from the inventory, there is little doubt that the estate had been substantially impoverished by the fine that had been imposed by Parliament. This financially precarious state of affairs was to have repercussions for Lord Mohun's descendants and would be felt by the Boconnoc estate for many years to come.

CHARLES MOHUN, 3RD BARON MOHUN OF OKEHAMPTON (c. 1645-77)

Warwick, Lord Mohun was resident at Boconnoc for considerable periods of time, particularly after the Civil War, when he had retired from public life. His son Charles and his grandson, also named Charles, both eschewed the life of a country squire, spending the majority of their time in London.[71]

Charles Mohun, 3rd Baron of Okehampton, was still a minor at the date of his father's death.[72] While the estates in Devon and Cornwall were producing some income, it was largely expended in satisfying debts. In addition to the fines levied on Boconnoc by Parliament, Katherine, Lady Mohun, his mother, was entitled to £1,000 per annum as her jointure, a financial provision for a widow after the death of her husband, and she refused to agree to any reduction in her entitlement. In 1671, Mohun brought a case against his mother in the Court of Chancery, claiming that, although he had made 'dutiful applications' to her, she was refusing to return to him certain papers, 'deeds and writings' that he needed to protect his inheritance and that she was acting with 'undeserved unkindness to me'. Mohun's attempt to pressurize his mother came to nothing when the Court declined to take any action.[73]

One tried and tested way for Mohun to improve his financial situation was for him to marry an heiress. In November 1692, he appeared to have achieved that end when he asked for the hand of Lady Philippa Annesley, fifth daughter of Arthur, 1st Earl of Anglesey. However, Philippa came to the marriage with no dowry and the couple lived largely on credit and were frequently pursued by tradesmen for unpaid debts. The Mohuns moved to Drury Lane, but the marriage was a disaster from the outset, despite Lord Anglesey's attempts to arbitrate between the warring couple.[74]

On 23 November 1676, William, Lord Cavendish, son of the Earl of Devonshire, was involved in a duel with 'one Mr [John] Powre of Ireland' whose second was a Mr Bermingham, eldest son of Lord Bermingham. Mohun acted as Cavendish's second and in the course of the fracas, he became accidently entangled with the duelists, 'was run into the guts' and 'received a mortill wound, through the bottom of his belly into his thigh'.[75] He was taken to his home at Drury Lane, where his wife Philippa, who was pregnant, sent for physicians. Over the next months, Mohun was frequently reported to have had a relapse so that his life was despaired of and just as frequently to be on the road to recovery. He finally succumbed to his injuries on 29 September 1677 and was buried three days later at St Martin-in-the-Fields, under the floor at the east end of the chancel.[76]

CHARLES MOHUN, 4TH BARON MOHUN OF OKEHAMPTON (1677-1712) - 'THE GREATEST DEBAUCHEE AND BULLY OF THE AGE'[77]

Despite their marital difficulties, Charles, 3rd Lord Mohun and Philippa produced two children. The older child was a daughter, Elizabeth, born in 1675. The younger, Charles, later 4th Lord Mohun, was born on 11 April 1677, five months before his father's death. The children lived with their mother in London, but in severely straitened financial circumstances, their father having left debts of £16,000.

Philippa acted in a way that provided ample gossip for London's high society, becoming involved in a number of brawls, one of which came to the notice of the king:

> April 11th 1678. Lady Mohun and M[is] Browne, the deare friends … were att cards att one M[is] Roberts's lodgings, and one M[is] Love being landlady of the house …, Lady Mo[hun's] pages spit in that M[is] Love's daughter's face, and so the mother would have turned him out of the house, but he ran up to his lady, and so the woman followed him, and the quarell began between her and the lady with ill words and candlesticks … And it entertained the King [Charles II] mightily who was att the House, and desired that he might be judge whether the candlesticke had hurt my Lady Mo[hun's] knee.[78]

Being so young at the time of his father's death, trustees were appointed to oversee Charles's inheritance and property and one Sir Charles Orby became his guardian, although it is not known how the relationship between the Orby and Mohun families came about. Debts on the Boconnoc estate continued to mount and Mohun, as his father had attempted to do before him, married an heiress (or so he believed), in the hope of restoring his fortunes. In 1691, at the age of 14, he married Charlotte Orby, granddaughter of Charles Gerard, 1st Earl of Macclesfield and related to Mohun's guardian, Charles Orby. In many ways, the events leading to Mohun's marriage mirrored that of his parents. His prospective in-laws seem to have taken advantage of his youth and inexperience and Charlotte brought no dowry.[79] After the wedding, Charles and Charlotte may have visited Cornwall. According to Delarivière Manley, not only an English author, playwright and pamphleteer but a notorious and malicious gossip, the couple travelled to Boconnoc. Charles Mohun stayed only a short time before returning to London. Having left Charlotte with his uncle James at Polmangan, it was alleged that he seduced her and she became pregnant by him. Lady Mohun did give birth to a son in November 1692, who died shortly after his birth. A daughter called Elizabeth was born in 1693, but Charles Mohun repudiated her and always referred to her as his 'pretended daughter'.

After a short time, the marriage broke down and thereafter Mohun's behavior became increasingly erratic as he became involved in numerous brawls, duels and murders. A friend of Mohun's, Captain Richard Hill, was suffering from a youthful infatuation for a well-known actress called Anne Bracegirdle. According to the diarist, Narcissus Luttrell, Hill's feelings were not reciprocated by the lady, who was some years older than Hill. Hill and Mohun hatched a plan to kidnap her. Observing the disturbance in the street, William Mountfort, a colleague of Bracegirdle's, went to her assistance. 'That wretched creature my Lord Mohun, who is not sixteen years old till April next … Friday night, wth one Hill about his age, killed poore [William] Monfort the player, and as tis related, very barbarously.'[80]

On Thursday 31 January 1693, Mohun was brought to Westminster Hall to be tried by his peers with the king in attendance. The trial ended on 4 February when Mohun was acquitted, by sixty-nine votes to fourteen. The following year, Mohun returned to his wild life in the capital when on 7 October 1694 he tried to kill a coachman. In April 1697, he fought with a Captain Bingham in St James's Park and 'they were parted by the centinells'. Five months later (14 September 1697), he stabbed Captain Hill of the Footguards who later died. Despite a bill being brought against Mohun for murder, he obtained a pardon from King William III which rendered the verdict null.

The duel with the Duke of Hamilton

In November 1701, Mohun's patron, the 2nd Earl of Macclesfield, died childless. The wives of Mohun and James Douglas, 4th Duke of Hamilton were both nieces of the 2nd Earl and when Mohun was bequeathed much of Macclesfield's property, Hamilton, who considered that he had as good a claim to the inheritance as Mohun, instituted legal action. Over the next eleven years, the verdicts in court swung backwards and forwards, first favouring Mohun and then Hamilton. A few days before Hamilton was due to leave for Paris on 13 November 1712 to take up the position of a special envoy, Mohun (for reasons unknown), challenged Hamilton to a duel, which the latter accepted.

At 7 a.m. on 15 November, the men, with their seconds, met in Hyde Park where the protagonists fought 'like enraged lions'.[81] The Duke of Hamilton struck the first blow, thrusting his sword into Mohun's side so that it emerged from his back. Hamilton succeeded in cutting an artery in Mohun's groin and the 4th Baron fell backwards to lie bleeding to death in a ditch. Mohun wounded Hamilton in his right calf and right arm and plunged his sword eight inches into the duke's chest. Mohun was conveyed to Macclesfield House in Marlborough Street where he died, while the duke died in the park. Mohun was buried on 25 November in the same church as his father, St Martin-in-the-Fields. With his death, the line of the Cornish Mohuns came to an end.

Philippa, Lady Mohun, widow of the 3rd Baron, was in the unenviable position of having both her husband and her son killed in duels, but as Lyte remarked, 'it is doubtful whether she mourned much for either'.[82]

The aftermath of Charles Mohun's death

Charlotte Mohun (née Orby), the 4th Lord Mohun's wife, disappears from the written record and her fate is unknown. By 1709, Mohun was having an affair with Elizabeth Griffith, daughter of Thomas Lawrence, one of the king's physicians. When her husband died in 1711, she and Mohun married.

By his will, Lord Mohun left most of his property to his widow, Elizabeth, and £1,000 to his 'pretended daughter', also Elizabeth, by Charlotte Orby.[83] Despite the fact that Mohun never acknowledged her, she was born in wedlock and therefore had a strong claim on her father's estate, well beyond the legacy of £1,000. She challenged his will in Chancery and arguments continued through 1714. Mohun's daughter Elizabeth petitioned Queen Anne, asking the monarch to support her claim to her late father's estate.[84] The result is not known, but it was Elizabeth, Lady Mohun who, in 1717 after lengthy negotiations, sold the Boconnoc estate 'universally allowed to be the first seat in Cornwall' to Governor Thomas 'Diamond' Pitt for £53,000.

NOTES AND REFERENCES

1. H.M. Whitley, 'The church goods of Cornwall at the time of the Reformation', *Journal of the Royal Institution of Cornwall (RIC)*, Vol. VII, 1882, No. xxv, p. 87; A.L. Rowse, *Tudor Cornwall*, London, 1969, p. 258; Cornwall Record Office (CRO): P17/2/8, Record Book of Boconnoc and Braddock, 27 April 3 Edward VI, f. 25.
2. RIC, Henderson Calendar, 30 July 5 Elizabeth; CRO: F/4/71, 1563.
3. CRO: F/4/23, Calendar 9 Elizabeth, 1566–1567.
4. CRO: F/1/294, Inquisition Post Mortem, series II, Vol. 150, No. 186.
5. Rowse, *op. cit.*, p. 393.
6. The National Archives (TNA): PROB/11/70 – will proved on 26 May 1587.
7. TNA: PROB/11/72 – will proved on 21 June 1588.
8. N.A. Ackland and R.M. Druce, *Lanteglos-by-Fowey with Bodinnick*, Fowey, 1978, p. 9; CRO: AP/M141/1, 2 and 3, will and inventory dated 30 August 1608.
9. Weiss Gallery Catalogue, A Fashionable Likeness. Early Portraiture, 1550–1710, January 2006, p. 3.
10. Anne Duffin, 'The defence of Cornwall in the early seventeenth century', in Robert Higham (ed.), *Security & Defence in South-West England before 1800*, Exeter, 1987, p. 69.
11. CRO: CY 7260, 13 June 21 James I (1623).
12. Higham, *op. cit.*, p. 71.
13. Higham, *op. cit.*, pp. 75–76.
14. CRO: F/1/7.
15. CRO: F/1/7, Copies of a Private Act of Parliament (21 Jas I cap 30) for settling estates in Cornwall Devon and Dorset on Sir Reynold Mohun's son John, 1623.
16. British Library (BL): Add MS 11314, 11 November 1639, ff. 9–10.
17. TNA: PROB11/182, ff. 378v–379 – will proved on 30 April 1640.
18. BL: Add MS 11314, ff. 6–7.
19. John Mohun: History of Parliament; www.historyofparliamentonline.org.
20. TNA: SP16/37/91.
21. Richard Holmes, Civil War Battles in Cornwall, 1642 to 1646, Keele, 1989, p. 18.
22. CRO: EL/564.
23. CRO: EL/542/1-2, warrant for the arrest of imprisonment of William Mayowe, 1626.
24. CRO: EL 564; Anne Duffin, *Faction and Faith*, Exeter, 1996, p. 93.
25. TNA: E178/5199/8 Ch I.
26. HMC Twelfth Report Appendix, Part VII. *The Manuscripts of S H le Fleming of Rydal Hall*, 1020, 24 November 1668.
27. Holmes, *op. cit.*, p. 17.
28. Edward Hyde, Earl of Clarendon, *The History of the Great Rebellion*, Roger Lockyer (ed.), OUP for the Folio Society, London, MCMLXVIII (1968), p. 90.

29. Duffin, *op. cit.*, p. 193.
30. CRO: B35/37 and 58, Bocconocke, 21 July 1642.
31. CRO: FS/2/51 and BC/24/2, Antony documents, 31 August 1642.
32. Mary Coate, *Cornwall in the Great Civil War and Interregnum, 1642–1660*, Truro, 1993, pp. 34–35; Lords' Journal, vol. v, p. 363, letter from Lord Mohun, 7 September 1642.
33. Duffin, *op. cit.*, pp. 196–198.
34. Holmes, *op. cit.*, p. 21.
35. Coate, *op. cit.*, p. 37.
36. Coate, *op. cit.*, p. 37.
37. John Barratt, *The Civil War in the South-West*, Barnsley, 2005, p. 18.
38. Mark Stoyle, 'Afterlife of an army: the old Cornish regiments, 1643–44', in P. Payton (ed.), *Cornish Studies: Sixteen*, Exeter, 2008, pp. 24–47.
39. Coate, *op. cit.*, p. 41.
40. Coate, *op. cit.*, p. 42; Holmes, *op. cit.*, p. 25.
41. Letter from Bevill Grenville to Lady Grace Grenville at Stowe, Liskeard, 19 June 1642/3, cited in John Wallis, *The Cornwall Register*, Bodmin, 1847, p. 379.
42. Hyde, *op. cit.*, p. 92.
43. R. Hopton, *Bellum Civile*, C.E.H. Chadwyck-Healey (ed.), Somerset Record Society, 1902, p. 30.
44. Holmes, *op. cit.*, p. 29.
45. Coate, *op. cit.*, p. 60.
46. Hopton, *op. cit.*, p. 37; Coate, *op. cit.*, pp. 61 & 62; E102(17); Stuart Peachey, The Battles of Launceston and Sourton Down, Bristol, 1993, p. 30.
47. Coate, *op. cit.*, pp. 62–63.
48. Coate, *op. cit.*, p. 63; Sergeant Major Chudley, A full relation of the great defeat given to the Cornish Cavaliers, 3 May 1643, Thomason Tract, E100.20, London.
49. A True relation of the Proceedings of the Cornish Forces under the command of Lord Mohune and Sir Ralph Hopton, 1643, EEBO, British Library, Thomason Tract, E.102.17.
50. Hyde, *op. cit.*, pp. 125–127; Coate, *op. cit.*, p. 69; Holmes, *op. cit.*, p. 32.
51. Stoyle, *op. cit.*, p. 30.
52. Stoyle, *op. cit.*, p. 32.
53. Sir Edward Walker, Historical Discourses upon Severall Occasions, viz. The Happy Progress and Success of the Arms of K. Charles I, London, 1705, p. 48.
54. Richard Symonds, *Diary of the Marches of the Royal Army*, C.E. Long (ed.), Cambridge, 1997, p. xiii; Walker, *ibid.*, passim.
55. Mary Beal, 'The royalist Richard Symonds and an unclaimed portrait by Sir Peter Lely', *The British Art Journal*, Spring 2016, pp. 16-21.
56. Walker, *op. cit.*, pp. 51–52.
57. Walker, *op. cit.*, p. 58.
58. Symonds, *op. cit.*, p. 53; Stephen Ede-Borrett, Lostwithiel 1644, The Campaign and the Battles, Farnham, 2004, p. 23.
59. Walker, *op. cit.*, p. 62.
60. Symonds, *op. cit.*, p. 55.
61. Symonds, *op. cit.*, p. 55; it is tempting to speculate what would have happened if the king had been shot and killed at Hall Walk.
62. Walker, *op. cit.*, p. 70; Ede-Borrett, *op. cit.*, p. 37.
63. Symonds, *op. cit.*, p. 65.
64. Symonds, *op. cit.*, pp. 65–67.
65. Symonds, *op. cit.*, pp. 66–67.
66. The letter of Charles I is believed to have been purchased by Lord Grenville, who was interested in it as being dated from Boconnoc. S.R. Gardener (ed.), *The Fortescue Papers*, Camden Society, 1871, pp. 218–219, No. CLXI.

67. Wallis, *op. cit.*, p. 381.

68. Coate, *op. cit.*, pp. 292–293.

69. TNA: PROB11/317/262.

70. CRO: F/4/166-167; Katherine, Lady Mohun *v.* Cordelia Harris.

71. Victor Stater, *High Life, Low Morals*, London, 1999, passim.

72. H.C. Maxwell Lyte, *History of Dunster and of the Families of Mohun and Luttrell*, London, 1909, Appendix 1 of Volume II, The Mohuns of Hall and Boconnoc in Cornwall, pp. 9–11.

73. In a number of letters that Mohun wrote to Edmund Prideaux of Prideaux Place, near Padstow, he asked for Prideaux's support. CRO: PB8/9/96-97, 6 January 1671, Lord Mohun to Edmund Prideaux and CRO: PB8/9/101-103.

74. Lyte, *op. cit.*, p. 10; Stater, *op. cit.*, pp. 16–18.

75. HMC, Twelfth Report, Appendix Part V, *Manuscripts of the Duke of Rutland*, Lady Chaworth to her brother, Lord Roos, at Belvoir Castle, p. 32.

76. British Library (BL): Add MS 38141, Dugdale Papers.

77. Lyte, *op. cit.*, pp. 11–14; the Jacobite Thomas Hearn (1678–1735) called Charles, 4th Baron Mohun, 'the greatest debauchee and bully of the age'.

78. HMC, Twelfth Report, Appendix, Part V, *Manuscripts of the Duke of Rutland*, Lady Chaworth to her brother, Lord Roos, at Belvoir Castle, p. 49.

79. Stater, *op. cit.*, p. 94.

80. *Hatton correspondence*, Edward Maunde Thompson (ed.), Camden Society. A letter from the Countess of Nottingham, 13 December 1692.

81. Lyte, *op. cit.*, p. 13.

82. Lyte, *op. cit.*, p. 14.

83. TNA: PROB11/536, dated 23 March 1710 – will proved on 6 March 1713; TNA: C9/382/1, 18 November 1713.

84. BL: Add MS 69374, Indenture dated 27 March 1717; HMC, *Manuscripts of the Duke of Portland*, Vol. X, 1931, pp. 486–488.

CHAPTER 3

THE PITTS:
1717–1804

'The "Regent" was considered to be the finest diamond in the world.'
(www.louvre.fr – the 'Regent' diamond)

THE PITTS IN INDIA

Thomas 'Diamond' Pitt (I) (1653–1726)

Thomas Pitt, later known as 'Diamond' Pitt, was born on 5 July 1653 at Blandford Forum, the son of the rector of Blandford St Mary in Dorset (for the purpose of clarity, the four Thomas Pitts will be designated I to IV). Pitt departed for India in 1674 and initially he acted as an interloper, a merchant operating outside the control of the East India Company. The company ultimately recognised his talents and offered him employment and he was appointed Governor of Fort St George in Madras in 1697. Together with his older son Robert, he arrived to take up his position in July 1699.[1]

The officers of the East India Company were permitted to trade on their own account and Pitt acquired a considerable fortune which, since England was at war with France and Holland, he had to send home in the easily portable form of diamonds and other precious stones. During his time as Governor, Pitt wrote to a diamond merchant, Salvador Rodrigues:

> You being resolv'd to returne againe to ye Diamond Mines, I doe desire you to remember what you & I have discours'd fully here if you meet with any very large stones in every respect perfect as to their water and Modell, and that they can be purchas'd reasonable, I desire you to advise me thereof.[2]

The Pitt and Grenville Families

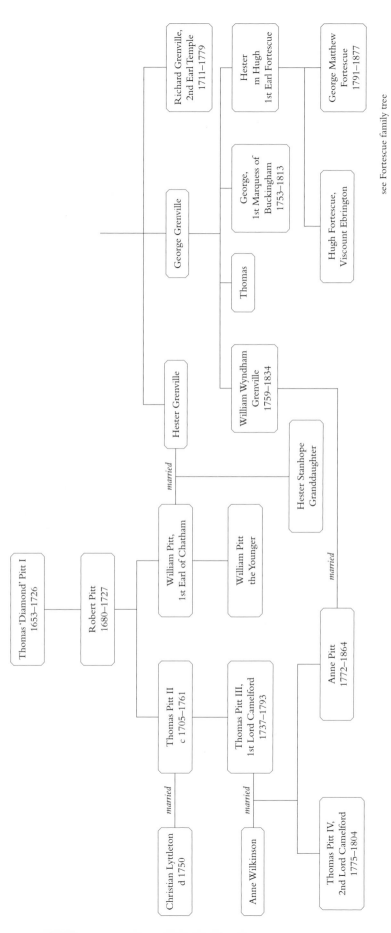

Thomas 'Diamond' Pitt I
1653–1726

Robert Pitt
1680–1727

William Pitt,
1st Earl of Chatham

William Pitt
the Younger

Hester Grenville

married

George Grenville

Hester Stanhope
Granddaughter

William Wyndham
Grenville
1759–1834

Thomas

George,
1st Marquess of
Buckingham
1753–1813

Richard Grenville,
2nd Earl Temple
1711–1779

Hester
m Hugh
1st Earl Fortescue

George Matthew
Fortescue
1791–1877

Hugh Fortescue,
Viscount Ebrington

Thomas Pitt II
c 1705–1761

married

Christian Lyttleton
d 1750

Thomas Pitt III,
1st Lord Camelford
1737–1793

married

Anne Wilkinson

Anne Pitt
1772–1864

married

Thomas Pitt IV,
2nd Lord Camelford
1775–1804

see Fortescue family tree

In December 1701, Pitt heard about a diamond which was brought to him by a merchant named Ramchund. The stone weighed 410 carats. There are several versions about the origin of the diamond, some of them highly improbable. One of the more believable was that a slave in the diamond mines in the Golkonda [Golconda] region of southern India, discovered the stone, cut his leg open and concealed the diamond in the wound. He bound up his leg and limped out past the guards. He was murdered by a seaman who stole the gem and the seaman, in turn, sold it to Ramchund.

Some years later, it was insinuated that Pitt 'had unfairly got possession of a large diamond'. On his way home from India, in an attempt to remove any suspicion of wrongdoing, he wrote his version of how he had acquired the stone. At first, he 'did not thinke of meddling with it' not knowing whether it would cut 'fowle or cleane, or the water goode'. Ramchund returned on a number of occasions and as the bartering continued and the price reduced, Pitt changed his mind and bought it for 48,000 pagodas, that is, about £24,000.[3]

Return to England

After making the purchase, Robert, Thomas Pitt's son, sailed home to England, taking the diamond with him. Tradition suggests that the stone was transported in the hollow heel of a boot that had been made specially for Robert for this purpose, although no documentary evidence has been found to support this version of events.[4]

Robert left for England on 9 October 1702 on the ship *Loyal Cooke* and arrived home in May of the following year, carrying with him the 'Grand Concern'. Governor Pitt wrote to his son: 'You must be very careful of this concern, on board your ship at sea or in harbour.'[5] His father was recalled to England in 1709 and landed in the autumn of 1710.

The cutting of the diamond was undertaken in London and thereafter, the Pitts spent many months attempting to sell the stone to the kings of France and Spain.[6] In June 1717, Phillippe d'Orléans, regent of France from 1715 to 1723, persuaded the Regency Council to purchase the diamond for £135,000. *The Regent*, as it became known, was considered to be the finest diamond in the world. It was set in the crown of the kings of France and was later placed by Napoleon Bonaparte in the hilt of his sword.[7]

After the sale of the diamond, Thomas Pitt (I) used the proceeds to buy property at Mawarden Court at Stratford, the Down House at Blandford, Kyneston Court in Dorset, Woodyates in Wiltshire, Abbot's Ann in Hampshire, Swallowfield Park in Berkshire and Boconnoc in Cornwall. In 1717, Elizabeth, Lady Mohun, the widow of the 4th Baron sold the Boconnoc estate for £53,000 and Pitt wrote to his son, 'when I can get matters settled about the Cornish estate, I think it would not be amiss if you went down'.[8]

Both 'Diamond' Pitt and Robert made a few fleeting visits to Cornwall.[9] Pitt appointed a steward, John Phillips, and gave Edward Rattew, the hind, that is, a farm servant, authority to act in some matters relating to the day-to-day management of the estate.

It soon became apparent that Boconnoc was by no means the bargain Pitt had believed it to be when he purchased it from Lady Mohun. In May 1720, he wrote to Robert from

Pall Mall in London, 'you know what a Condition Boconnock is in, & Ill assure you tis not better than we left it …'[10] He was at Boconnoc from August to October 1720 trying to get the estate into some sort of order.[11] The following year, Robert Pitt was resident at Boconnoc during August, when building works there were being overseen by John Moyle, for which see Chapter 7.[12]

Thomas Pitt's character

Pitt was an irascible character, ill-tempered and determined to retain strict control over family and servants alike. The hectoring letters written to his children continued until the time of his death on 28 April 1726, aged 73. He was buried at Blandford St Mary on 21 May 1726. Robert wrote to his son Thomas Pitt (II), 'I am under the dissatisfaction of being oblig'd to advise you of the Death of my father Thursday last at Swallowfield after two days illness, his Distemper was a mixture of apoplexy & Palsie'.[13]

Robert Pitt (1680–1727)

Robert had accompanied his father to India and made a number of voyages to China and other destinations in the East. Tiring of this peripatetic lifestyle, his desire to return home provided an ideal opportunity for him to carry the diamond.[14] Once back in England, Robert married Harriet, daughter of Edward Villiers, but failed to inform his father about his nuptials for seven months, concerned, no doubt, that Thomas Pitt would not approve of his choice of bride.[15] 'Diamond' Pitt continued to send letters to his son, reproving him for his lack of abilities, rebuking him for his extravagance and making it clear that Robert was a disappointment to his father. Despite the steps that had been taken to modernise the house at Boconnoc and make it into a more comfortable family home, Robert spent little time in Cornwall.

Robert Pitt only survived his father by just over a year, dying on 20 May 1727. He was described as 'a poor creature, mean, cantankerous, petty, unworthy of his notable father and the genius that was his son' and as 'a man of no importance'.[16] This is a harsh critique for a man who was completely overshadowed by a domineering and overbearing father, who treated his son more like a servant than as his heir.

Thomas Pitt (II) (c. 1705–61)

Boconnoc was not inherited by the 'genius' William Pitt, later Lord Chatham, but by William's older brother, also called Thomas (II). He married Christian Lyttelton, daughter of Sir Thomas Lyttelton, 4th Baronet of Hagley in Worcestershire. Their 'courtship', such as it was, lasted only twenty-four hours and the adage 'marry in haste, repent at leisure' might have been coined for them. It all began romantically enough, for Pitt, a friend of Christian's brother, 'saw a Daughter of Sʳ Thoˢ Lyttelton at the Opera; was struck with her extraordinary beauty, proposed the next day & was immediately accepted'.[17] Sir Thomas Lyttelton's consent was given without hesitation, but he was unaware that, although Pitt had substantial landholdings, his estates were heavily encumbered and his income was severely limited. Unfortunately for Christian, her husband turned out to be bad-tempered, foul-mouthed and unscrupulous. 'In truth Thomas Pitt was a terrible man, with more than a strain of the madness that ran though all his family.'[18] His son, Thomas Pitt (III) wrote that 'all his passions were violent by nature, particularly pride and ambition'. Much of his minimal income was dispensed to fund elections and fight lawsuits and in 1736, Pitt (II) wrote to General Stuart, 'It is a most melancholy thing to me to see the misfortunes, and distress which are fallen upon my family …'[19]

Much can be learnt about Thomas Pitt (II) from a lengthy document written by his son Thomas Pitt (III), later 1st Lord Camelford, for *his* son, Thomas Pitt (IV), later 2nd Lord Camelford. It is entitled *Family Characters and Anecdotes.*[20] Thomas Pitt (III) detailed what his mother Christian and other members of the family had had to endure at the hands of his father. Thomas Pitt (II) spent every winter in London, leaving his wife alone at Boconnoc, 'then the worst and the gloomiest habitation of any gentleman in England to which my mother cheerfully consented, though she had no amusements but books of piety and works of charity …'[21]

From the first moment of his marriage, Thomas Pitt's (II) ambition was to produce a son who, when he reached his majority, would be able to cut the entail on the Boconnoc estate and enable him to pay his debts and to provide for his other children.[22] After the birth of two daughters, Christian and Amelia, and then several miscarriages suffered by his wife, Pitt had almost given up hope, but in 1737, the much longed for son and heir was born at Boconnoc.[23] Thomas and Christian Pitt's marriage thereafter disintegrated and Pitt's feelings for his wife changed from indifference to dislike to positive aversion. She was forced to submit to what her son called 'every kind of insult … too painful to dwell upon'.[24] At the age of 7, Thomas Pitt (III) and his two older sisters were sent to school. Christian had endured her husband's behaviour for the sake of her children, but once they were all at school she decided that she would return, at least during the winter months when her husband was in London, to her father, Sir Thomas Lyttelton at Hagley. Ordered back to Boconnoc by her husband, a separation was agreed. Christian was granted an allowance of £100 per annum, to be doubled when her father died, but with the cruel proviso that she should never see her children again and nor did she.[25]

Thomas Pitt (II) was an adherent of Frederick, Prince of Wales (son of King George II) and under the prince's auspices, Pitt was appointed Paymaster of the Forces and Assay Master of Tin for the Duchy of Cornwall.[26] Despite these offices and the income they produced, he was still unable to live within his means and in 1749 he requested a loan of £4,000 from his brother-in-law and sometime rector of Boconnoc, Dr Francis Ayscough, who was holding in trust the monies that remained from the 1737 sale of 'Diamond' Pitt's Swallowfield estate.[27] Pitt sent Ayscough a wheedling letter arguing that, although the trustees might consider the loan to be a breach of trust, no fraud or embezzlement was intended and he hoped that Ayscough would be able to sufficiently sacrifice his scruples to lend him the money, the lack of which would lead to Pitt's inevitable ruin.

If Ayscough had not come to his rescue and had Pitt not received a further appointment from the Prince of Wales as Lord Warden of the Stannaries, it is likely that he would have been declared bankrupt. The prince granted him a salary of £1,500 per annum on condition that he should henceforth nominate the MPs for the borough of Old Sarum, hitherto under the control of the Pitt family. A year later, when even this salary proved insufficient, Pitt requested a further loan of £5,000 from Ayscough.

Frederick, Prince of Wales, died unexpectedly in 1751, extinguishing all hope that Pitt may have had of further advancement in his political career. Becoming increasingly extravagant, he sank deeper and deeper into debt.

By 1753, Thomas Pitt's (II) debts had become overwhelming. He wrote to his brother: 'my children I have taken from school and my son I shall get instructed in his Latin by Mr Leach, parson of Boconnoc till I can better afford to send him abroad to school again. My hounds I am oblig'd to part with and shall let this house [Boconnoc] as soon as a tenant offers for it'.[28]

Although the house had been made more comfortable by extensive rebuilding, Pitt had only returned to Cornwall out of economic necessity, for he had little interest in his children or their activities. His daughters were old enough to be introduced into society, but he chose that they should remain in isolation at Boconnoc.[29] Their brother, Thomas Pitt (III), was pleased to return to Cornwall, finding it 'highly advantageous, as I owe to it the little education I have to boast ...' His tutor, Mr Leach, was 'a studious man of good morals'.[30]

Thomas Pitt (II) attempted to prevent any communication between his children and their Lyttelton relatives, although unbeknown to Pitt, his daughters were receiving and sending letters to their uncle Charles Lyttelton, Dean of Exeter, about money bequeathed to them from their Lyttelton grandfather's estate. In a strange series of letters that passed between Christian, Amelia and Charles Lyttelton, the girls asked him to use their legacy to purchase lace for them, in preference to jewellery. The lace was sent to Pitt's house in London, but was returned 'the boxes unopened' to Lyttelton, Pitt writing an angry letter telling Lyttelton that he should not concern himself with Christian and Amelia's affairs.[31]

As Pitt became ever more mired in debt, he gave his children three options: first, to continue to live at Boconnoc in a confined and vastly reduced establishment; second, to live quietly in a country town in England; or third, to live abroad until his son Thomas Pitt (III) came of age, could break the entail and pay off his father's debts. The children favoured the third option. The Pitts left Boconnoc, to become neglected and at the mercy of Thomas's creditors, while his son thought he could hear the 'last cheer of the poor labourers', who assembled on the green before the house as the coach drove the family from the door.[32]

In March 1755, preparations were made for the family to leave the country. When they arrived in London, Thomas Pitt (III) was summoned by his uncles, William Pitt and Sir Richard Lyttelton, who suggested that he should not accompany his father and sisters on their European travels, concerned about the influence his father would have on him.

Knowing how his parent would react if he followed this advice, Thomas Pitt (III) escaped to Cambridge.[33] Thomas Pitt (II) ordered his son to rejoin the family in London, but supported by Francis Ayscough and his uncles, he refused to return and Thomas Pitt (II) was forced to leave England without his son. Thomas Pitt (III) wrote:

> My father almost broke my heart, but could not bend me from my purpose ... The violent emotions with which these scenes affected me left a sensible impression upon my health, and nervous disorders, which some time after increased upon me to a very alarming degree, owed their origin to anxiety of mind.[34]

The 'nervous disorders' were epileptic fits, from which he suffered for some years.

Thomas Pitt (II) left for the Continent with his daughters and was resident abroad for three years. In 1758, when Thomas Pitt (III) was nearing his majority, he received a letter saying that an old friend would be happy to meet him at a tavern in Bond Street. When he arrived, he was astonished to see his father emerge from behind a screen.[35] In bad health, Pitt (II) wanted to return to England permanently, but by appearing in London prior to agreeing any accommodation with his creditors, he was at risk of being arrested for debt. His son having agreed to pay his father's debts and to give £5,000 to each of his sisters, a document was prepared barring the entail from Thomas Pitt the elder to Thomas Pitt the younger, 'to facilitate the payment of the several debts ... and to make provision for Amelia Pitt and Christian Pitt his daughters'. Pitt's debts were indeed substantial, amounting in total to almost £17,000. The creditors included mercers, hatters, lacemen, a saddler, a peruke maker, apothecaries and merchants.[36]

In 1761, Pitt (II) re-married, his bride being the daughter of a General Murray. She did not find favour with Thomas Pitt (III), who described her as 'above 40 Years of Age without any advantages of mind or person or education'.[37] The newlywed couple travelled to Boconnoc for their honeymoon, but only a fortnight later, on 17 July 1761, Thomas Pitt died of a stroke. Thomas Pitt (III) learned of the death of his father from his uncle William Pitt. 'Dear Nephew, I am sorry to ... impart to you the loss of one so near to you. Your Father was seised with an apoplexy y[e] 16th and notwithstanding all proper assistance, expired y[e] next day.'[38] Thomas Pitt (III), who was in Florence with his uncle Sir Richard Lyttelton, returned to England to claim his inheritance.

Thomas Pitt (III), later 1st Lord Camelford (1737–93)

Thomas Pitt (III) was born on 3 March 1737. As we have seen, he was initially educated at school and then at Boconnoc. On 7 January 1754, he was admitted a fellow-commoner at Clare College, Cambridge and resided there until 1758. He obtained the degree of MA *per literas regias* in 1759.[39]

Visiting Boconnoc after his father's death, Thomas Pitt (III) wrote:

When I first visited Boconnoc after my return to England I could have shed tears at the Scene of desolation that presented itself to me. The Furniture had been sold by the Creditors by auction, and I had not a bed to lie upon. There remained nothing but the Books which were heirlooms & some boxes of old China that had been saved from the wreck. Without doors the Gardens were in weeds, the Woods had been cut down & the walks could no longer be traced. Fine Groves of old oaks had been destroy'd within sight of the Windows & the very lawns had been broken up & left in ridge & furrow by the carelessness of those who look'd only to draw from the Estate all the profit that could answer their purpose & leave it a wilderness to those who might come after them. The partiality I have ever had for the place of my nativity & of my earliest habits made me determine to stop the ruin if it were possible … I determined at least that it should not be totally abandon'd. I fitted up beds in the 4 attics I put some chairs & tables in the old eating room & in the Library; & in that manner provided for passing a month or two there every Summer. I pick'd up other things at auctions & by degrees made it a comfortable dwelling.[40]

Thomas Pitt (III) was active intermittently in politics. He sat as MP for Old Sarum from 1761 to 1768, the rotten borough in which the Pitt family had a controlling interest, for Okehampton from 1768 to 1774 and for Old Sarum again from 1774 to 1783. In December 1783, he was raised to the peerage. On accepting the honour, he chose the title of Lord Camelford in preference to 'dear Boconnoc', saying he preferred sound to sense, but 'tho' my stile be Camelford, I have requested my Barony may be attached to Boconnoc'.[41]

In 1771 Thomas Pitt (III) had married Anne Wilkinson, aged 33 and of 'a great fortune', she being the daughter of a wealthy London merchant, Pinckney Wilkinson. She brought a dowry of £40,000. They had two children – the elder, a daughter, born on 10 September 1772 in London: 'About half an hour after one this afternoon Mrs Pitt made me a present of a fine girl … Thank God both She and the child are well, and myself happier than I can describe.'[42] She was called Anne for her mother, but was known as Annette within the family circle. Three years later, a son and heir was born at Boconnoc. His birth was recorded in the family bible: 'Thomas born the 19:th of February 1775 ¼ after 5 o'clock in the morning.' The baby (Thomas IV, who would become the 2nd Lord Camelford) was baptised privately on 20 February 1775 and formally received into the congregation at Boconnoc church on 29 July.[43] Thomas Pitt (III) wrote to his aunt Hester, Lady Chatham to tell her of the 'Birth of our little Cornishman', Lord Chatham agreeing to be one of the child's sponsors.[44] After the christening in July, the Reverend Benjamin Forster, rector of Boconnoc, wrote of the festivities:

We have had all the bustle of a christening, with its appendages of concert and ball, and wrestlings, and a great supper of shew to 107 gentlemen and ladies; and the great house so dressed up and bedizened on the occasion that my hermitage became the retreat for two days of lordings and high dames of honours.[45]

Both the children, Thomas Pitt (IV) and his sister Anne, passed their early childhood at Boconnoc, Camelford House in London and at Petersham Lodge, near Richmond Park, but because of Lord Camelford's ill health, he, his wife and daughter spent many years abroad while their son was sent to school. Between 1786 and 1789 the family travelled to France, Germany, Italy and Monaco and between 1791 and 1792, they were in Belgium, Germany and Italy. Lord and Lady Camelford returned in 1792 for the nuptials of Anne and William Wyndham, Lord Grenville, but immediately after the wedding, her parents retreated to the Continent. From this journey, Thomas Pitt, 1st Lord Camelford did not return. He died in Florence on 19 January 1793, at the age of 55. His body was transported back to Cornwall and he was buried on 2 March on the north side of Boconnoc churchyard, but at his request, without tomb or gravestone.[46]

While the Pitts were abroad, their estates and property, including Boconnoc, were managed by stewards, on whom Benjamin Forster and the Cowper brothers, Spencer and Charles, lawyers who acted for the family, kept a watchful eye. They all kept in close touch by letter with the Camelfords, writing in exhaustive detail about any actions or decisions they were taking relating to the estate.

Thomas Pitt (IV), 2nd Lord Camelford (1775–1804)

Thomas Pitt (IV) (later 2nd Lord Camelford), in common with his Pitt ancestors, passed little of his childhood at Boconnoc and was there infrequently during his later life. At the age of 5, he was described as 'boisterous' and 'fond of his Papa'.[47] He wrote to his father (in French) asking to be forgiven for his little faults, which he attributed to his 'youth'. In a letter to his mother, probably written about 1784, he told her he was going to ask Mr Emly (his tutor), 'to teath [sic – teach] me the Moves at Chess to try when I see her [his sister] which can beat; I take your advise & will take pains to lern now', thanked her for the present of a watch and said he had been fishing with Mr Gilbert (a family friend who lived in Bodmin) for trout.[48]

Thomas Pitt's education at Boconnoc ended in 1785 when he was enrolled in Dr Kyte's school at Hammersmith, which only took twelve boys. 'Tom is the youngest and pet of the school. It is a Nursery for Westminster.' He was still there in February of the following year and was progressing well.[49]

Five months later, in July 1786, Thomas Pitt (IV) was taken abroad and placed by his parents in a French school at Liège with his tutor, now a Mr Wyatt.[50] He wrote to his friend W.F. Gilbert in Bodmin:

Dear Buddy, I am just arrived at Leage which in my opinion is a poor sort of place … I can hardly speak none in French except ask for some General things & them not quite esely. Mr Wyatt who is my second Mr Emly [his former tutor] seems to be a very good humour'd man.[51]

Camelford was disappointed that the young Thomas Pitt 'did not easily take to the polish of foreign manners' and his father removed him to an academy at Colmar in Alsace.[52] Camelford became dissatisfied with this school, but was unsure about where next to send his son.[53] Spencer Cowper believed that it would be more beneficial that Thomas should continue to be educated by his tutor Mr Wyatt because, although Thomas Pitt would mix at Colmar only with people of rank, given his disposition, he could seek out friends with whom he might get into mischief: 'particularly drinking and gaming'.[54] Cowper wrote again to Camelford: 'I grieve for what you say of your Son but I fear the Evil is without Remedy, it is in the Temper & Disposition, & from his earliest Age I have not been without Apprehensions on his Account. Nothing can make any Impression on him ...'[55]

From Colmar, Thomas Pitt (IV) was placed in a school at Neuchâtel in Switzerland, run by Henri de Meuron, who had an excellent reputation both as a philosopher and teacher.[56] This happy interlude was short-lived, for he was brought back to England and in July 1789, he was enrolled at Charterhouse. He was there for only nine days before running away.[57]

His parents were so angry that they forbade their son to write to them, but Thomas Pitt (IV) ignored this order and in a letter expressed sorrow for his disobedience.[58] Having failed to settle at Charterhouse, he revealed to his parents how much he disliked his studies and that he had an ambition to go to sea.[59] Lord Camelford, in order to reconcile his wife to the prospect of their son joining the navy, wrote to her that they could not eradicate what nature had implanted – their son had an untameable spirit, lived for the gratification of the moment and had a disregard for consequences.[60] Despite his parents' misgivings, on 9 September 1789 Thomas Pitt (IV) sailed on the *Guardian* as a midshipman under Captain Riou, the vessel carrying stores bound for the convict settlement at Botany Bay in Australia. Even at this early stage in his naval career, his conduct was already showing evidence of the waywardness that was to blight his career and ultimately, his life. 'I am sorry to say that for this one or two days past I am rather in the bad graces of the Captain the reason of it is that I have been idle ... I hope by working hard and behaving well I shall be able to regain the favour of M[r] Rioue upon which the comfort of my voyage depends so much.'[61]

The *Guardian* left Cape Town on 11 December. Ten days later, on 23 December, long before they reached their Australian destination, disaster struck the ship when an iceberg, twice as high as the mast according to the boatswain John Williams, hit the *Guardian* on its starboard beam, knocking away the rudder and breaking the tiller into three pieces. The cargo was jettisoned and the crew pumped out the ship continuously, but the water level kept rising. On Boxing Day, the majority of the officers and many of the seamen got into small boats and disembarked from the sinking vessel. The Commander, the carpenter, the boatswain and Midshipman Pitt remained, together with a number of others for whom there was no room in the boats. Assuming that the *Guardian* had sunk, the Camelfords were told that their son had drowned. Only four days later, to their relief and delight, a message was received that the *Guardian* had sailed into Table Bay in South

Africa. The Camelfords were, understandably, ecstatic and the Lostwithiel bells were set 'a ringing that the joyful Tidings might be spread as soon as possible'.[62]

Despite the fact that Pitt had not disembarked from the *Guardian* during the crisis, Captain Riou was not full of praise for his midshipman. He wrote from the Cape of Good Hope to Lord Camelford:

> If this were a place where your Son could learn anything worthy to be known, or had I any opportunity to watch sufficiently over a young person so much attached to Indolence as he is, I would keep him with me here, but this Country partakes in a great measure of the Luxury dissipation and debauchery of the Eastern World & I have no other means of insuring him <u>safe</u> than by following your Lordships method, of keeping him <u>money-less</u> – Your son tells me, he is still attached for a sea Life … but I must tell you the Truth that his Desires & Ambition are for low Company and low language.[63]

Pitt returned to England in 1790 and there were numerous discussions between Lord Camelford and Lord Grenville about what the destination should be on Midshipman Pitt's next voyage. Both lords were eager to limit the opportunities when Thomas Pitt would be able to go ashore, fearing that he would fall into bad company in sea ports.[64] It was agreed that he should join the crew of the *Discovery* which was to survey the Californian coast, under Captain George Vancouver. Pitt joined the ship on 12 March 1791, but his conduct on this voyage, as on the *Guardian*, did nothing to enhance his career prospects. On Vancouver's orders, Pitt (IV) was flogged for insubordination on several occasions and eventually he was discharged and put off the *Discovery* at Hawaii. Aged 16, he made his own way back to England, via Malacca and Madras.

In March 1795, Edward Packenham, Captain of HMS *Resistance*, met Thomas (IV), now Lord Camelford, at Malacca in the Malay Peninsula, on the latter's passage to the coast of India aboard a merchant ship from China. Packenham offered Camelford a situation as Acting Lieutenant and surprisingly, given Camelford's less than stellar naval career to this date, he acquitted himself to Packenham's total satisfaction, 'had shown great honour and personal courage' and was 'worthy of his ancestry and the name of Pitt'.[65]

Back in England, Camelford's (perceived) grievances against Vancouver still rankled. When Vancouver declined to meet him in a duel (a course of action wholly endorsed by Lord Grenville),[66] Camelford set upon him in Conduit Street, London and gave him a beating, an act of violence that filled many column inches in the newspapers. Camelford was bound over to keep the peace or failing that, to forfeit the sum of £10,000.

Going to sea again, sometimes as captain commanding his own ship, his career failed to prosper due to numerous incidents that brought his name further into disrepute. These included the shooting dead of Lieutenant Charles Peterson after an argument about who was the senior officer, the horsewhipping of George Kittoe, a storekeeper in Antigua, pressing men for his ship the *Favorite* in Barbados and firing on a British fort at Grenada.[67] In 1798, once more in England and despite it being a treasonable activity for anyone to attempt to sail for France, he set off incognito across the Channel, but was apprehended. The following year, he was again found in a boat which he had hired to go from Dover to France and was brought back to London in confinement. As his intentions were deemed to be 'tending to the service of his country' he was pardoned by the king.[68] The newspapers called him 'deranged' and once the Admiralty indicated that he would not be given command of any further vessels, he resigned his commission.[69]

As Camelford tried, somewhat unsuccessfully, to settle into civilian life, he became involved in a number of notorious and unpleasant incidents. On 2 April 1799, there was a scene in a Drury Lane theatre when a riot took place in the lobby caused by men who had had too much to drink. Lord Camelford, one of the ringleaders, was taken into custody and charged with knocking down a Mr Humphreys, nearly putting out one of his eyes and was fined £500.[70] In a further episode, Camelford and his companion, Captain Barrie, after a night out, attacked the nightwatchmen. Lady Camelford wrote to Charles Cowper: 'the Newspapers have as usual been the vehicle of sad information to me: my unfortunate ill judging Son has again been seeking broils and riots … I believe his poor Sister is not ignorant of the business … I know but too well that his strange conduct causes the misery of her life …'[71]

In February 1800, in a bizarre incident, he tried to force a duel on his friend Peter Abbott. On Tuesday 25 February, Abbott and Camelford had dined together. The conversation turned 'upon females of easy virtue – attachments and adventures with several persons of that character – and mutual jests were passed upon each others foibles'. Camelford alleged that Abbott had then suggested his suspicions of Camelford 'being addicted to the unnatural crime of S…..' Abbott denied this and said that the jests were on Camelford's 'extraordinary foibles for the fair sex even the most profligate of them'. Unaware of Camelford's intention that they should fight a duel, Abbott got into Camelford's coach. When Abbott noticed that there were pistols in the carriage, he finally realised the danger he was in and as soon as the conveyance came to a halt, Abbott jumped out and ran to a nearby cottage to seek refuge.[72] Abbott laid information against Camelford at Bow Street on 1 March 1800. Eventually, the criminal proceedings were dropped for reasons which will be recounted later in this chapter.

A strange event in Lord Camelford's life occurred in Hull shortly before his death, the background to which is totally obscure. Pursued by some Peace Officers who suspected him of being an Irish traitor, Camelford escaped and hid himself under a bridge, immersed up to the neck in water and suspended by a thorn bush. He was discovered by an old man called Edward Farrer who conducted Camelford to a friend of his called Wells. Wells provided Camelford with food and dry clothes. After Camelford's death, it was found that Wells had been left a monetary bequest in Camelford's will.[73] The belief was that the legacy had been intended for Farrer, but Camelford had mixed up the names. This created a further complicated and unfortunate situation that Lord Grenville and the lawyers had to resolve after the 2nd Lord's untimely death.[74]

Lord Camelford's private life

Camelford may possibly have had one or two illegitimate children. In April 1804, a letter was sent by Ann Panton to Lady Grenville, poorly written and badly spelt: 'I hope your Ladyship Will Excuse the Liberty I take of Writeing to you in Behalf of a Poor Distrest and Unfortunate Sister of Mine Who has lain in about five weeks of a Boy that she had By your Late Much Lamented Brother Lord Camelford.' The letter went on that the child had died and the mother, Mary Kirk, was dangerously ill 'Lying in Hospotle'. Ann Panton requested assistance for her sister.[75] It is not known what action, if any, was taken, nor indeed if Camelford was the father of the child.

In 1810, Lord Grenville received a letter signed 'C.T.' who it transpired was a man called Charles Trebeck, an agent for a number of important Irish and English families. He suggested, in oblique terms, that a girl he had adopted was the daughter of Lord Camelford and declared that he was not seeking monetary assistance, but contended that his intention was to let Grenville know that the child existed should Trebeck no longer be able to look after her. Frustratingly, as with the previous case, there is no information about how the matter was resolved.[76]

Camelford never married. Nikolai Tolstoy suggested that he was 'in love' with his cousin Hester Stanhope, the granddaughter of his great-uncle William Pitt, Earl of Chatham[77] (see family tree on page 62). Although he may have been fond of her, it is unlikely that he ever had any serious intentions towards her. Lady Grenville wrote from Dropmore on 8 January (the year is not stated, but possibly around 1801) to her mother Lady Camelford:

> A report perhaps without foundation has reached Lord Buckingham of Lady Hester Stanhope's being gone to Boconnoc. he fancies my Brother was to be there and if so fears she means something by her visit … even supposing her intentions to be what he supposes them I think we have good security in my Brother's extreme unwillingness to marry and that if she goes at all the visit will probably end without any cause of uneasiness. I at first determined not to trouble you with this report but recollecting that you asked me why I did not write to you when I before heard she was going into Cornwall I have thought it better that you should know what I have heard upon the subject … I cannot help adding that even if there should be anything to fear which I hope and believe there is not, the interference of friends might do mischief and I should be afraid ever of your writing.[78]

Peter Abbott, Lord Camelford and Lady Cox

The evidence that Peter Abbott had laid against Lord Camelford relating to the duel that he had tried to force on Abbott, was due to be heard in court in July 1800 and a barrister called Erskine was engaged to act as Camelford's defence counsel in the criminal case. The case was adjourned to November and Abbott wrote to a close 'friend', Sophia Turner, later Lady Cox, who lived in Slough: 'I find that they have taken steps to delay the Time for Lord Camelford's Tryall …'[79] In the interim, Abbott and Sophia Turner devised a scheme that they hoped would persuade Lord Camelford to pay Abbott to drop the case. Sophia was to approach Camelford, offer to intercede with Abbott and get him to withdraw the allegation. In return, an unspecified sum of money would be sought from Camelford by Sophia in recognition of her assistance, which she would share with Abbott.

This plot was developed in a number of letters that Abbott wrote to Sophia: 'if you see any Body about it my lovely Girl be very firm and very cautious what you say or do don't trust to fine Words and Promises. I will be with you on Sunday. God bless you my charming Sophia.' Other letters end: 'may you prosper my Angel' and 'bless you my lovely'.[80]

Unfortunately for Abbott, Sophia decided to take matters into her own hands. She contacted Camelford's solicitors and offered to give Abbott's letters to them for a pecuniary advantage of £500, thus cutting Abbott out of any potential deal. A representative of the solicitors travelled to Slough on Saturday 5 July to collect the first five (of seven) letters that Mrs Turner had received from Abbott outlining the scheme, and they were duly delivered to Camelford the following day.[81] She was paid an initial £150 for handing over the letters, but in 1806, she requested an interview with Lord Grenville saying she had papers 'which relates to Lord Camelford and wish Lord Grenville to peruse them'. It is not known what these papers contained, but a document dated 1815 confirms that Mrs Turner, afterwards Lady Cox, did receive the £150 in part payment of the £500 promised her for the letters, but whether she ever received the balance of the money is unclear.[82]

Lord Camelford at Boconnoc

Although Lord Camelford was rarely at Boconnoc, there are letters that refer to his infrequent visits. While his friends and neighbours were always pleased to see him, he was something of a trial to his steward Thomas Bennett. A letter from Mrs Gilbert of the Priory, Bodmin, to Lady Camelford extolled Camelford's virtues, imparting 'the satisfaction we felt in this visit of Lord Camelford: … he gave a great deal of comfort to the poor at Boconnoc, in a distribution of a large quantity of Flour & Meat: after that was done he went to look at the Clay at St Stephens; & return'd to the Priory at a four O'Clock dinner … he was so easy, so chearful, so sensible, & so kind to me …'[83]

Camelford was at Boconnoc in May 1799, when Bennett spent some hours with him. The following year, Bennett wrote to Charles Cowper about another visit that he had recently received:

My Lord Camelford came last Wednesday night late to Boconnoc, and sent for me early yesterday morning and desired to know what money I had, I said I might have about 100£ he said he wanted 500£. I told him I could not possibly get such Sum directly; he told me he must have it in Town by the 14th or 15th at farthest, & press'd me to say if I thought I might get such Sum … the coming of my Lord so suddenly & pressing me to raise such Sum was so unexpected that I did not know how to act & therefore did the best I thought I could do … His Lordship told me the money was wanted expressly in case he should lose at Newmarket on the 14th & then he should draw on the spot for it & therefore must not be disappointed.[84]

Was he mad?

The title of Nikolai Tolstoy's book about the 2nd Lord Camelford is *The Half-Mad Lord*. Was he mad or even half-mad? He was certainly strange. Tolstoy argues that, as a result of the isolation and 'neglect' the 2nd Lord Camelford, a sensitive boy, had endured during his childhood, left alone with his tutor at Boconnoc or sent to school, he felt his parents did not love him. He had a 'conviction of being actively rejected, shunned, hated'.[85] This is an unlikely scenario, for it was well known that 'no people dote more on their children than the Camelfords'.[86] Other children from aristocratic and gentry families received the same upbringing, but did not behave throughout their lives as Lord Camelford did. It will be remembered that his grandfather, Thomas Pitt (II), was a thoroughly unpleasant man with a violent temper and his great-great-grandfather, Thomas 'Diamond' Pitt (I), was similarly an irascible and domineering character. This may go some way to explain why the 2nd Lord Camelford turned out as he did.

The duel with Thomas Best

In March 1804, Camelford, with his usual indifference to any possible consequences, took offence at a remark made by his friend, Captain Thomas Best. Best, one of the most accurate shots in England, did his utmost to smooth things over, but Camelford insisted on challenging Best to a duel. They met in the early hours of the morning of 7 March, in the meadows surrounding Holland House, Kensington. Before Camelford had set out, he had added a declaration to his will in which he admitted that he had been the aggressor in the quarrel and if he was killed, he requested that no action should be taken against anyone who had taken part in the duel, duelling being illegal. He desired that this part of his will should be conveyed 'by a noble relative' to the king, so that royal clemency might be extended to the participants.

Camelford took the first shot but missed. Best's shot hit Camelford, who fell to the ground, mortally wounded. The sound of shots had been heard and the area was approached by Lord Holland's gardeners. The following is part of an eyewitness account (in the words and spelling of the witness):

> I, James Sheares On Wednesday Morning March 7th about Eight O Clock I was Digging in Lord Hollands Srubbery I herd the Report of two pistols I Said to My Fellow laberogh [labourer] I think that is A Dewel I ran Down to the pales and Saw the Smoke and one Gentleman Down and A Nother Supporting him … I Supported the gentleman by the Cape of his Cote and told his Frend that Surgeon Thomson Was the best Surgeon in Kensington … the gentleman [Camelford] then replide I Hown My Self to be the Ogreoser and I forgive him [Best] … my fellow laberoughs Came Up and One of them Went back for A Cheair and brought it Down by that time Surgeon Thomson Came Down … we then put the gentleman in the Chair and Carrid him to Mr Hottey's & put him upon the bed I then untied his Neck hancerchifs and Un buttend his Shirt Coller

and the Surgeon lookd at the Woond he then replied fetch Surgeon homes I then Ran as fast as I could to Sackaril Street and brought Surgeon homes Down with Me.[87]

Camelford was taken to Holland House and when the doctors arrived, the news about the duel and its result were conveyed to the Buckinghams at Stowe and the Grenvilles at their house at Dropmore. Hester Stanhope wrote in a letter to a friend: 'Lord Camelford has been shot in a duel and there is no chance of his recovering. You know my opinion of him, I believe, therefore can judge if I am not likely to lament his untimely end.' Lady Grenville was not allowed to see her brother, her husband fearing that it would be too upsetting for her. He lingered on for three days and died on 10 March 1804, aged 29. At the coroner's inquest, the verdict returned was of wilful murder or felonious homicide, by some person or persons to the jurors unknown.[88]

Lord Camelford's funeral

Lord Camelford's funeral was held on 17 March at St Anne's church, in Dean Street, Soho, London. The body was placed in the north vault and 2s.6d was paid for lights to illuminate that part of the church.[89] The funeral was elaborate, costing £176.13s.8d in total. This sum included inside and outside coffins, silk hatbands, men on horseback for the procession, a mourning coach and horses, mourning cloaks, a rich broad silk scarf and hatband and a pair of silk gloves for the Reverend Dr Eton of St Anne's, a silk scarf, hatband and silk gloves for the curate and an amount of £3.19s.2d to pay 'the dews of St Annes Vault'.[90]

In his will, Camelford stated that he did not wish to be buried at Boconnoc, but on the island of St Pierre in the Lake of Bienne in Switzerland, in a spot that he had picked out 'where the surrounding scenery will smile upon me'. Despite lengthy discussions taking place among the executors of his will about how Camelford's body could be transported to Switzerland, his wishes were never fulfilled and his coffin remained at St Anne's. The church was bombed during the Second World War and thereafter his (and other) coffins were removed from the church and there is now no record of his final resting place.

The 2nd Lord Camelford bequeathed the vast majority of his property to his sister Lady Grenville.

NOTES AND REFERENCES

1. Tresham Lever, *The House of Pitt. A Family Chronicle*, London. 1947, pp. 3–4.
2. Hampshire Record Office (HRO): 115M88/F3/3, Transcript of the story of the great Pitt diamond, taken from correspondence found by George Matthew Fortescue at Dropmore in 1868; British Library (BL): Add MS 22842, f. 55, Thomas Pitt to Salvadore Rodrigues, 12 March 1700, no 97.
3. HRO: 115M88/F3/3.

4. Dropmore Papers, Vol. 1, 1698–1790, pp. 48 & 49; Bergen, 10 July 1710, HRO 115M88/F3/3; Peter Douglas Brown, *William Pitt, Earl of Chatham, The Great Commoner*, Allen & Unwin, London, 1978, pp. 15–16. An undated newspaper article enclosed in a book in the Hampshire Record Office gives this version: <u>The Pitt Diamond</u>. History of gem recalled by will. Reference to the famous Pitt Diamond, now commonly known as the Regent Diamond, is made in the will of Mrs Caroline Mary Somes, of Bath. She bequeathed to Colonel Brownlow Villiers Layard 'the tortoise-shell snuff-box (with short account of same therein) in which Pitt brought over the Pitt Diamond from Golconda, and which he (Pitt) gave to my great-uncle the Duke of Ancaster'; HRO: 115M88/F3/3.

5. BL: Add MS 59479, 8 November 1702, f.11, Thomas Pitt to Robert Pitt; HRO: 115M88/F3/3.

6. BL: *ibid.*, 29 January 1702/3, f. 9.

7. www.louvre.fr/en/oeuvre-notices/diamond-known-regent (retrieved 26 November 2015).

8. Dropmore Papers, HMRC, Vol. 1, p. 62 Pall Mall 29 June 1717, Thomas Pitt to Robert Pitt; BL: Add MS 59469, Pall Mall, 29 June 1717, f. 173.

9. The National Archives (TNA): C108/422/21; 108/424/no 9 463, 18 October 1720.

10. BL: Add MS 59479, Pall Mall, 19 May 1720, f. 209, Thomas Pitt to Robert Pitt.

11. BL: Add MS 59479, Pall Mall, 18 August 1720, f. 211, Thomas Pitt to Robert Pitt at Boconnoc; TNA: C108/424/No 9 463, 18 October 1720.

12. BL: Add MS 59479, Pall Mall, 29 August 1721, f. 217, Thomas Pitt to Robert Pitt.

13. BL: Add MS 59482, f. 5, Pall Mall, Monday 2 May 1726, Robert Pitt to Thomas Pitt [II] Esqr at Utrecht.

14. BL: Add MS 59479, 9 October 1702, ff. 3 & 4.

15. Cornwall Record Office (CRO): X415/131, p. 6.

16. Lever, *op. cit.*, p. 59. The 'genius' was William Pitt the elder, later Lord Chatham; CRO: X415/131, p. 6.

17. Maud Wyndham, Chronicles of the Eighteenth Century, founded on the correspondence of Sir Thomas Lyttelton and his Family, Vol. II, London, 1924, p. 14; BL: Add MS 69333, f. 11.

18. Wyndham, ibid, p. 15.

19. BL: Add MS 69286, Boconnock, September 1736, f. 135.

20. BL: Add MS 69333, Family Characters and Anecdotes, passim.

21. Wyndham, *op. cit.*, p. 16; BL: Add MS 69288, Boconnock, 19 October 1731, Boconnoc was not a favourite residence of any members of the family. In 1731, William Pitt, later Lord Chatham, younger brother of Thomas Pitt (II) wrote of Boconnoc to his mother: 'Boconnock October ye 19, I am, after a long confinement at Quarters, at present confined here, by disagreeable dirty weather, which makes us all prisoner In this little house', William Pitt to Mrs Pitt at Bath, f. 32.

22. An entail was a device to restrict an owner of disposing of property by limiting the inheritance to the owner's lineal descendants, usually by primogeniture, the right of succession belonging to the firstborn son.

23. BL: Add MS 69333, *Family Characters and Anecdotes* by Lord Camelford, 1781 addressed to his son Thomas Pitt (IV), p. 43.

24. Lever, *op. cit.*, p. 66.

25. BL: Add MS 69333, *op. cit.*, p. 43.

26. CRO: F/1/353, 22 March 1737; Appointment of Thomas Pitt (II) to the Office of Assay Master of Tin for the Duchy of Cornwall.

27. BL: Add MS 59484, 5 May 1749, Thomas Pitt (II) to Dr Francis Ayscough, f. 64.

28. Lever, *op. cit.*, p. 88; BL: Add MS 69286, ff. 157 & 158, 1754.

29. CRO: F/1/223, Plymouth, 18 May 1753 to Thomas Pitt (II) from his sister Mary.

30. BL: Add MS 69333, *op. cit.*, p. 44.

31. Wyndham, *op. cit.*, pp. 20–22; Lever, *op. cit.*, p. 85.

32. Wyndham, *op. cit.*, pp. 23 & 24; BL Add MS 69333, *op. cit.*, p. 45.

33. BL: Add MS 69333, *ibid.*, pp. 47–48; Lever, *op. cit.*, p. 90.

34. Wyndham, *op. cit.*, p. 25, Lever, *op. cit.*, p. 90.

35. Wyndham, *op. cit.*, p. 27; BL: Add MS 69333, *op. cit.*, p. 51; Lever, *op. cit.*, p. 132.

36. CRO: F/1/13/3, 11 September 1759.

37. BL: Add MS 69333, *op. cit.*, pp. 57–58.

38. BL: Add MS 69288, St James's Square, 21 July 1761, ff. 60–61, William Pitt to Thomas Pitt (III).

39. Pitt, Thomas (PT754TA), *A Cambridge Alumni Database*, University of Cambridge.

40. BL: Add MS 69333, *op. cit.*, pp. 63–64.

41. BL: Add MS 59488, 26 December 1783, f. 77; BL: Add MS 69304, 30 December 1783, ff. 41–42.

42. As cited in Nikolai Tolstoy, *The Half-Mad Lord, Thomas Pitt, 2nd Baron Camelford (1775–1804)*, London, 1978, p. 6.

43. CRO: FP12/1/1, 1775. Baptisms: Boconnoc, 1709–1812.

44. BL: Add MS 59490, Hayes, 13 April 1775, f. 24 and 7 August 1775, f. 26.

45. As cited in Tolstoy, *op. cit.*, p. 7.

46. HRO: 115M88/F6/2.

47. BL: Add MS 59490, f. 5.

48. BL: Add MS 59491, ff. 2–3.

49. BL: Add MS 59488, 10 July 1785, f. 119; Add MS 69304, 25 February 1786, ff. 78–79; The school was one for the sons of noblemen. John Parker of Saltram, 1st Earl of Morley (1772–1840) and Granville Leveson Gower, 1st Earl Granville, both received their early education there. Regencyhistory.net.

50. BL: Add MS 69304, Spa, 20 July 1786, Lord Camelford to William Pennington, ff. 86–87.

51. BL: Add MS 69341, around 11 July 1786, Thomas Pitt (IV) to W.F. Gilbert, ff. 66–67.

52. BL: Add MS 69304, Montpellier, 10 November 1786, ff. 92–93 and Averze, 1 September 1788, Lord Camelford to William Pennington, ff. 104–105.

53. BL: Add MS 69304, Colmar, 22 June 1788, ff. 113–114.

54. BL: Add MS 69294, Kingston upon Thames, 17 May 1787, Spencer Cowper to Lord Camelford, ff. 116–117.

55. BL: Add MS 69295, 12 October 1788, Cowper to Lord Camelford at Lyons, ff. 51–52.

56. BL: Add MS 69312, 11 April 1789, Neuchâtel, Switzerland, Leministre Meuron to Lord Camelford, ff. 32–33.

57. Information from Catherine Smith, Archivist of Charterhouse, in an email dated 27 July 2015.

58. BL: Add MS 69341, before 30 July 1789, ff. 3–5.

59. BL: Add MS 69341, 3 August 1789, Thomas Pitt (IV) to his parents, ff. 8–9.

60. BL: Add MS 69290, before 17 February 1791, Lord Camelford to Lady Camelford, ff. 17–19.

61. BL: Add MS 69341, 29 September 1789, Thomas Pitt (IV) to Lord Camelford, ff. 14–15.

62. BL: Add MS 69341, Boconnoc, 8 September 1790, Lady Camelford to Thomas Pitt (IV), ff. 19–22; BL: Add MS 69303, Saturday evening 1 May 1790, Benjamin Forster to Lord Camelford, f. 114.

63. BL: Add MS 69342, Cape of Good Hope, 1 June 1790, E Riou to Lord Camelford, f. 165.

64. Lever, *op. cit.*, p. 270; BL Add MS 69042, November 1790, f. 37.

65. BL: Add MS 59492, 28 March 1795, Packenham to Grenville, f. 38; 30 March 1795, Packenham to Lady Camelford, f. 40; Packenham to Grenville, 26 November 1795, f. 49.

66. BL: Add MS 59492, Petersham, 27 October 1796, Lord Grenville to Captain Vancouver, f. 130.

67. BL: Add MS 59493, St John's Antigua, 15 March 1798, Wa: Colquhoun to Lord Grenville, ff. 17–22.

68. BL: Add MS 69360, Admiralty, January 1799, E. Nepean to H. Cowper, ff. 65–66.

69. BL: Add MS 69360, January 1799, H. Cowper to C. Cowper, ff. 74–77; January 1799, ff. 74–77 & 81–82.

70. CRO: X415/131.

71. BL: Add MS 69355, 6 May 1799, Lady Camelford to Charles Cowper, ff. 170–172.

72. BL: Add MS 69354, Examination of Peter Abbott at Bow Street, 1 March 1800, ff. 1–7; deposition of Lord Camelford, ff. 83–93.

73. BL: Add MS 69348 16 March 1799, Lord Camelford to Charles Cowper, ff. 3–4; BL: Add MS 69349, 2 August 1806, John Day to Charles Cowper, ff. 1–2; Add MS 69349, 26 August 1806, ff. 3–4.

74. BL: Add MS 69349, 26 August 1806, ff. 3–4.

75. BL: Add MS 69344, 17 April 1804, Ann Panton to Lady Grenville, f. 11.

76. Tolstoy, *op. cit.*, pp. 192–193.

77. Tolstoy, *op. cit.*, Chapter V, 'The lion tamed, Lord Camelford in love', pp. 84–98.

78. BL: Add MS 69043, 8 January, Lady Grenville to Lady Camelford, ff. 86–87.

79. BL: Add MS 69354, Peter Abbott to Mrs Turner, undated, ff. 63–95.

80. BL: Add MS 69354, Monday 4 o'clock, postmark 30 June 1800 Abbott to Mrs Turner; Abbott to Mrs Turner, letter not dated; Bolton Street, Monday 7 July 1800, Abbott to Mrs Turner, f. 101.

81. As cited in Stephen Banks, *A Polite Exchange of Bullets. The Duel and the English Gentleman 1750–1850*, Woodbridge, 2010, p. 164.

82. BL: Add MS 59494, Upper York Street, Cumberland Street, 24 October 1806, Lady Cox to Lord Grenville, f. 35; BL: Add MS 69374, Colonel Whaley's Statement 12 September 1815, ff. 12–17.

83. BL: Add MS 69359, Lostwithiel, 17 May 1799, ff. 58–59; BL: Add MS 69047, Priory, Bodmin 4 November 1800, Mrs Gilbert to Lady Grenville, ff. 20–21.

84. BL: Add MS 69359, Lostwithiel, 17 May 1799, ff. 58–59; BL: Add MS 69359, Lostwithiel, 11 April 1800, Bennett to Charles Cowper, ff. 37–38.

85. Tolstoy, *op. cit.*, p. 12; Lever, *op. cit.*, p. 222; BL: Add MS 59490.

86. BL: Add MS 59490, 24 March 1783, William Wyndham Grenville to his brother, Lord Temple; Lever, *op. cit.*, p. 222.

87. The *Sherborne Mercury*, 12 March 1804, p. 3; BL: Add MS 69344 f. 4; *The New Annual Register, or General Repository of History, Politics, Arts, Sciences and Literature for the Year 1804*, Vol. 47 by Andrew Kippis, pp. 25–29.

88. *The Sherborne Mercury*, 19 March 1804, p. 3.

89. Tolstoy, *op. cit.*, p. 228.

90. BL: Add MS 69344, A list of all the expenses of the funeral of Lord Camelford, ff. 60–61.

CHAPTER 4

THE GRENVILLES AND THE FORTESCUES: 1804—64

'We have just got to Boconnoc and have been looking about the dear old place.'
(George Matthew Fortescue to Anne, Lady Grenville, 1833)

THE GRENVILLES

Anne Pitt (1772–1864)

In 1804, after the death of her brother, Lady Grenville (née Pitt) inherited the majority of his property, including Camelford House in London and Boconnoc, the whole being in excess of 20,000 acres.

Unlike the distress that her brother's capricious behaviour caused to her parents, she was a well-behaved child. As William, Lord Chatham was Thomas Pitt's (IV) godfather, so Hester, Lady Chatham was Annette's godmother. She wrote frequently to Annette's parents asking after 'the pretty Cornish Damsel' and the 'little Fairy Mistress of Boconnoke'. In 1774, she wrote to Annette's mother, 'I shall expect to see my lovely little Goddaughter much grown, and at least with as many Graces as before; tho' she then had a larger share than was the right of her Age'.[1]

There is a vignette in a letter written by George Fortescue, describing a scene from her childhood at Boconnoc: 'The Xmas box you desired to be given to old Betty Richards … has been delivered in the shape of £1. Betty said it seemed but as yesterday that you liked to come in your little green bonnet & accompanied by Mrs Holroyd to see her.'[2]

The family was in London at the end of 1780 where the children, Thomas and Anne, were taking part in different activities. 'Tom is under the care of a Sergt of the guards and Annette under the famous Mme Simonet, both make a great proficiency.'[3] Madame Adelaide Simonet, 'an imposing figure', was a famous ballet dancer at the opera house.

In 1779, she placed an advertisement in the *London Courant*, announcing that she was opening a Dancing Academy 'for LADIES ONLY' at her house, No. 5, Dover-Street, London. From this, it can be surmised that Annette was having dancing lessons.[4]

In 1783, aged 11, she became very ill with a fever and nearly died, making but a slow recovery – ironically, having been considered delicate as a child, she outlived her husband by thirty years.[5]

Her father was proud of her and she was a much cherished daughter: 'the young lady is pomaturing and curling her Dolls to receive the Children of Lady Jersey who are to visit her tomorrow and dine with her for the first time – she improves every hour'. In 1786, from Montpellier: 'my girl also grows and is much admired' and later the same year: 'My girl is flatter'd wherever she goes and her modest timidity is a great grace to her in a country where that is so little their fault.'[6]

Despite the fact that she appeared to be a paragon of virtue, particularly when compared with her brother, her father wrote her a series of lengthy letters, which called attention to her faults and defects, pointing out that they needed correction and advising her how to behave. These are undated, but were probably given to her *c.* 1788 when she was about to make her debut in society.[7]

> The great essentials of character were <u>Religion</u> and <u>Virtue</u> but the constitutional vice of your character is <u>indolence</u>, which grieves me the more as I fear it is in some degree derived from me. Your indolence then takes shelter under an assumed indifference … it was thus that you have disappointed yourself of the great advantage which I proposed from carrying you abroad viz the giving you the familiar use of the Italian as well as the French language – the opportunity is now over.[8]

Anne is painted by Marie-Louise-Élisabeth Vigée le Brun (1755–1842)

In 1792, when in Rome, Anne was painted by the celebrated female artist Madame le Brun. She was one of the finest French eighteenth-century painters and among the most important of all women artists. In her biography, Madame le Brun recalled:

> I painted Miss Pitt, who was sixteen [she was actually 20] and extremely pretty. I represented her as Hebe, on some clouds, holding in her hand a goblet from which an eagle was about to drink. I did the eagle from life, and I thought he would eat me. He belonged to Cardinal de Bernis. The wretched beast, accustomed to being in the open air – for he was kept on a chain in the courtyard – was so enraged at finding himself in my room that he tried to fly at me. I admit I was dreadfully frightened.[9]

Anne was also painted by John Hoppner (1758–1810), an English portrait painter who was noted for being a brilliant colourist. His portrait of Anne Pitt is half-length and she is shown wearing a white dress with a blue sash. It is not known when it was painted, but it is first recorded at Dropmore in the year of her marriage, 1792, to Lord Grenville [*Plate 3*].

William Wyndham Grenville (1759–1834)

William Wyndham Grenville came from a family that rose from obscurity in the seventeenth century to become one of the most powerful in Britain. His father George Grenville was a successful politician, becoming Prime Minister in 1763. His aunt Hester Grenville, married William Pitt, Earl of Chatham, so that he was first cousin to William Pitt the younger. His uncle Richard Grenville-Temple, 2nd Earl Temple and his brother George Nugent-Temple-Grenville, 1st Marquess of Buckingham were successively the owners of Stowe House, a beautiful, now Grade I-listed, stately home in Buckinghamshire.

Grenville received his education at Eton College (1770–76), Christ Church, Oxford (1776–80) and Lincoln's Inn (1780–82), although he was never called to the Bar. He sat as MP for Buckingham from 1782, he was Speaker of the House of Commons for six months in 1789 and held many of the high offices of state: Home Secretary from June 1789 to June 1791, Foreign Secretary from June 1791 to February 1801, Auditor of the Exchequer from 1794 to 1834 and First Lord of the Treasury (in effect, the Prime Minister) from February 1806 to March 1807.

Grenville was known for his ungainly appearance, having a prominent head and dressing in dull and drab clothing.[10] He had a number of close personal friends, but his main interest was in the business of government, to which he devoted much of his career and in which he proved to be extremely competent [Plate 4].

Grenville had known Anne Pitt since she was born in 1772. In the spring of 1790, through the mediation of his brother the Marquess of Buckingham and Anne's father Lord Camelford, Grenville, whom she barely knew, proposed marriage to her. He was 30 and she was 18. Both Buckingham and Camelford were strong proponents of the match: Buckingham was keen to promote it because it would link the two families and Anne would bring a substantial dowry to his brother. Her father was equally enthusiastic, having known Grenville from an early age and admiring his character. In the end, Camelford advised her that she should make her own decision. Faced with this completely unexpected proposal, she refused Grenville, saying, 'he has had no opportunity of knowing me or I him'.[11]

Grenville was nothing if not persistent. Over the next two years, he bombarded her with a continuous stream of letters, repeating over and over again that he hoped for nothing more than 'a sincere and respectful friendship' between them. Reading between the lines (and there are many of them), he had obviously not given up hope that she would change her mind.

By the end of 1791, while the Pitts were travelling abroad, Grenville's persistence finally paid off and Anne agreed to become his wife. They were married on 18 July 1792: 'This morning was married by special licence, at Lord Camelford's house in Oxford Street, the Right Hon. Lord Grenville, to the Hon. Miss Anne Pitt, only daughter to Lord Camelford.'[12]

The next day, Lord Camelford wrote to his son 'yesterday my dear Boy, I disposed of your Sister's hand to Lord Grenville'.[13] He had given his consent as they had both had enough time for reflection and Grenville's perfect probity, his good sense, excellent judgement and amiable temper would ensure Anne's domestic happiness.

In anticipation of the marriage, Grenville had bought a small estate in Buckinghamshire that was to become their home at Dropmore. 'I am in treaty for a small house near Taplow, but it is so mere a cottage that if I make the purchase I must add something to the house immediately.'[14]

The marriage proved to be a great success. Correspondence that passed between them from 1802 to 1814 demonstrates the affectionate regard they had for each other. He started his letters with 'My dearest Angel' or 'My dearest love' and ended 'God bless you my dearest wife' or 'my dear little woman'.[15]

They had a love of dogs in common and she wrote amusing letters to him when they were apart, describing the canines she met on her travels.

> I am just returned from dining with the Hartwickes where I had unexpectedly the opportunity of making the acquaintance of Gen. Ramsay's <u>Poodle</u>. Tho' locked up in a Room he made his escape traced his master and came scratching at the door while we were at dinner. He sneezed at the word of command & is altogether a most admirable person.[16]

In turn, he wrote to her about their dog called Zephyr: 'Zephyr is so dear he will I really believe come to be a favourite. When we saw Bennett [at Boconnoc] on Sunday he perfectly understood before I said a word to him that we were going to church and he never offered to come with us.' On 1 October 1813, he wrote: 'Zeph is helping me to write this and desires to be particularly remembered to dear Mistress.'[17]

The late 2nd Lord Camelford

When the 2nd Lord Camelford died in 1804, leaving the bulk of his property to his sister, the aftermath of his 'misadventures' was to haunt Lord and Lady Grenville for many years to come. Camelford had paid £40,000 to purchase three ships and the sum of £16,000 was outstanding for articles that had been supplied to outfit them. Lord Grenville could raise some of the money from his own resources, but had to request a loan from the banker Thomas Coutts to satisfy the remainder of Camelford's debt.

Coutts replied: 'Your Lordship may depend that I will not allow Lady Grenville or yourself to appear in *The London Gazette*,' the publication where official notices of those being made bankrupt were listed, and offered Grenville a loan of the full amount if he could not raise the money by any other means.[18]

Eleven years later, another of Lord Camelford's 'imprudencies' came to light. Camelford had been in a partnership in a horse-racing concern with a Mr Whaley, a 'Gentleman of the Turf'. Although the partnership had been dissolved, the accounts had never been formally settled and as Whaley was detained as a prisoner of war in France for many years, Grenville believed that the money owed from Lord Camelford's estate would never have to be paid. To Grenville's mortification, when Whaley returned to England, he produced bonds and other legal instruments establishing a debt of almost £7,500, a large part of which was due for interest unpaid for the last ten years. Grenville, on the advice of his solicitors, was left in no doubt that he could not contest Whaley's claim. £3,000 was paid to him immediately, with the remainder in two further instalments in June 1817 and June 1818.[19]

The Grenvilles and Boconnoc

Grenville was very fond of Boconnoc and spent more time there than Lady Grenville, although as with many previous custodians of the estate, they were mainly absentee landlords. In September and October 1813, Lord Grenville was in residence at Boconnoc and there were frequent exchanges of letters between him and Lady Grenville, who was at Malvern taking the waters.

Apart from writing letters to his wife, Lord Grenville was having an enormously trying time. He had gone down to remonstrate with John Bowen, the steward, who had undertaken various works on the estate without authorisation from his employers. Grenville was also trying to get Bowen to produce the estate accounts. Chapter 6 will detail more about how the estate was run.

The Grenvilles were a contented couple for many years, but Lord Grenville suffered a stroke in 1823 and his health started to fail. By 1825, he was also suffering from gout and his eyesight was becoming progressively worse.[20] By the beginning of January 1834, he had become very frail and he died at Dropmore on 12 January.

Lord Grenville's funeral took place at Burnham on 20 January and was private, no one attending but those who had been present in the house when he died, including George Matthew Fortescue, Grenville's nephew.

> Lady Grenville was firm and composed as she followed the bier through the churchyard and during the first part of the beautiful service – but when we were standing round the vault and the second part of the service commenced, she was very much agitated, and I feared she would hardly be able to stand it – she made an effort however … and so continued till its close – as we went away she turned to take a last look at what for them & forty years had been the delight and comfort of her heart – the very soul of her existence.[21]

Having no children, Lord and Lady Grenville had to decide to whom the estates of Dropmore and Boconnoc and their other property should be bequeathed. Their choice fell on George Matthew Fortescue, the second son of Lord Grenville's sister Hester who had married Hugh, 1st Earl Fortescue. Everything was left to Lady Grenville for the duration of her lifetime and would thereafter pass to George Fortescue.

Shortly before Lord Grenville died, in 1833, George Matthew Fortescue had visited Boconnoc and in 1834, with Lady Grenville's permission, he and his wife, Lady Louisa (née Ryder), made their home there. This was the first time since Warwick, 2nd Lord Mohun had been resident in the seventeenth century that stewards were no longer left in day-to-day charge, but the reins of running the estate were taken over by a full time 'tenant'.

THE FORTESCUES

George Matthew Fortescue (1791–1877) and Lady Louisa Elizabeth Fortescue (née Ryder) (1813–99)

George Matthew Fortescue was born on 21 May 1791. He was educated at Eton, but did not shine academically. He hoped to follow a career in the army and his uncle Lord Grenville obtained a commission for him in Lord Bridgwater's regiment. While on his travels, he wrote letters to Lady Grenville, his aunt by marriage, in October 1811 from the Cape of Good Hope, where he said he was 'seeing the lions' and was sending to Lady Grenville samples of the bulbs that covered the mountains.[22]

By February of the following year he was in Calcutta, whence he sent Lady Grenville a shawl worked in gold, which he had purchased from the Persian interpreter to Lord Minto, who had received it as a present from a Rajah.

On his return from India, he travelled around Europe, visiting Rome and Verona and embarking on a series of 'ill-fated affairs of the heart'. In his young days, he was described by the 4th Lord Holland as 'very handsome and then an exquisite dandy of that time … he was universally popular and justly so …'[23]

On 19 February 1833, he married Lady Louisa Ryder, daughter of the Earl of Harrowby and youngest sister of Susan Ryder, who had married George Matthew Fortescue's older brother Hugh Fortescue, Viscount Ebrington: two brothers had married two sisters. Susan had died in 1827 and Louisa always felt that she was compared (unfavourably) with her sister. Despite the differences in their ages, George Matthew Fortescue was 42 and Lady Louisa 19, their marriage was very happy.

They settled very quickly in Cornwall. George Matthew wrote to Lady Grenville in June 1833: 'we have just got to Boconnoc and have been looking about the dear old place. My first ride was to the Obelisk which was on a bare bleak down [when he had last visited twenty-five years ago] and is now in a flourishing wood.'[24]

Figure 1 George Matthew and Lady Louisa Fortescue. (© Hampshire Record Office)

The Fortescue Family

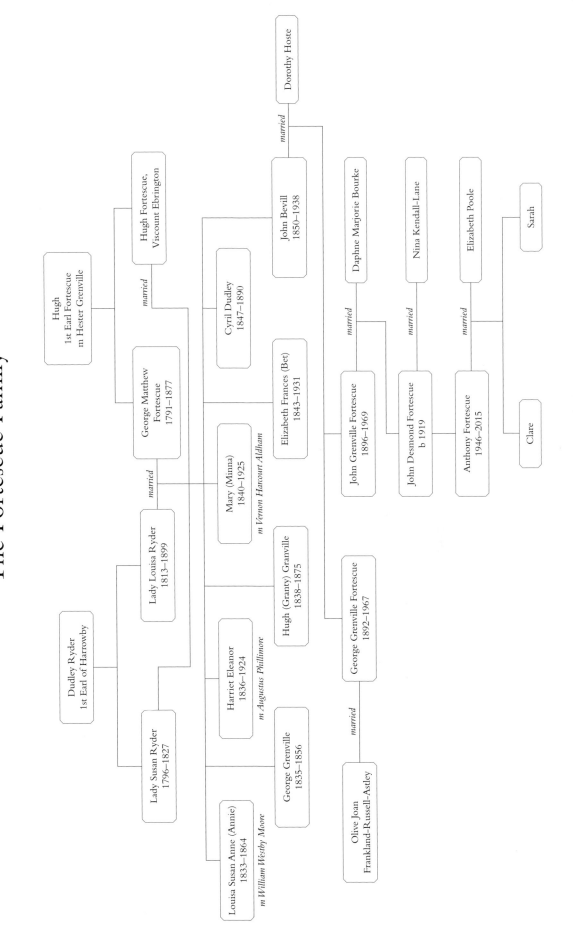

Hugh
1st Earl Fortescue
m Hester Grenville

Dudley Ryder
1st Earl of Harrowby

Hugh Fortescue,
Viscount Ebrington

married

George Matthew
Fortescue
1791–1877

Lady Louisa Ryder
1813–1899

married

Lady Susan Ryder
1796–1827

Cyril Dudley
1847–1890

Mary (Minna)
1840–1925
m Vernon Harcourt Aldham

Elizabeth Frances (Bet)
1843–1931

John Bevill
1850–1938

married

Dorothy Hoste

Harriet Eleanor
1836–1924
m Augustus Phillimore

Louisa Susan Anne (Annie)
1833–1864
m William Westhy Moore

Hugh (Granty) Granville
1838–1875

George Grenville
1835–1856

Daphne Marjorie Bourke

Nina Kendall-Lane

Elizabeth Poole

married

John Grenville Fortescue
1896–1969

married

John Desmond Fortescue
b 1919

married

Anthony Fortescue
1946–2015

George Grenville Fortescue
1892–1967

married

Olive Joan
Frankland-Russell-Astley

Sarah

Clare

Figure 2 Miss Fortescue, Miss E Fortescue, Cyril Fortescue, Dudley Ryder, Granty Fortescue.
(© Hampshire Record Office)

George and Lady Louisa brought up their eight children at Boconnoc, four sons and four daughters: Louisa Susan Anne (1833–64), named for her mother, her mother's late sister Susan, Viscountess Ebrington and Lady Grenville, known as Annie; George Grenville (1835–56); Harriet Eleanor (1836–1924), sometimes known as Pippy or Helen; Hugh Granville (1838–75), known as Granty; Mary (1840–1925), known as Minna; Elizabeth Frances (1843–1931), known as Bet or Bessie; Cyril Dudley (1847–90) and John Bevill (1850–1938), known as Bevill or Bev.

Country life suited them. On 3 November 1835, Ralph Sneyd, a long-time friend, wrote to Lady Harrowby that:

G is in better condition physically and morally than I have seen him for long years. His settled prospects and the occupation and amusement present and future which the possession of this place opens to him, added to the influences of a happy home, seems effectually to have dispelled those wayward clouds that used to gather over his mind and weigh down his spirits.[25]

In 1853, George Fortescue became very unwell, having gone out in snow and sleet to Liskeard on business. The doctor was called and diagnosed inflammation of the lung and the pleura from taking a chill. An abscess in his left lung burst and, fearing the worst, his sons George and Granty were recalled from their schools. By the end of March, he had 'turned the corner' and he eventually recovered.[26]

Despite his delight at living at Boconnoc, George Fortescue suffered badly from asthma throughout his life, which sometimes prevented him from taking an active part in local affairs. In May 1854, the slightest exertion or movement brought it on and he suffered from 'the most violent attack I have ever had …'[27]

On occasion, Lady Grenville made the long journey from London or Dropmore to Boconnoc.[28] Despite frequent requests from George Fortescue that Lady Grenville should visit, as the years passed and she grew increasingly infirm and unable to travel long distances, her visits became less and less frequent.

From 1833 until 1864, when Lady Grenville died, she and George maintained an almost daily exchange of letters, both being assiduous correspondents. When George was unable to write due to illness or absence, Lady Louisa took over the letter writing duties. Many hundreds of the letters survive, containing information about every aspect of the way the Fortescues spent their time in Cornwall, both on and off the estate. 'I can't tell you how much we both enjoy ourselves here and what a satisfaction it gives us to manage things for you …'[29]

Figure 3 George Matthew and Lady Louisa Fortescue. (© Hampshire Record Office)

Every day they went riding and walking, drove into Lostwithiel or visited friends and neighbours at Lanhydrock, Port Eliot, Carclew, Ethy, Menabilly, Tregothnan and Pencarrow, often for balls or parties. Annie and Harriet were particularly proficient at drawing and painting and they were frequently out capturing views of the estate as their sketchbooks show. The Fortescues were fond parents and when the 'children' were older, they went out riding or walking together as a family group. 'We rode yesterday in honour of Annie's birthday [her 21st] with all four girls to Berrydown.'[30]

The 'young ones' also undertook longer excursions. In October 1856, they rode to the Cheesewring, a distance of twenty-five or so miles. They ate lunch under the granite tor and visited the workshop where the porphyry sarcophagus was being prepared for the tomb of the Duke of Wellington.[31]

In 1861, Annie and Harriet had an adventure. They had gone off, with Lord Harrowby, to visit their cousin Captain Ryder on HMS *Hero* at Plymouth. The morning post brought a letter to Boconnoc saying that, having got on to the ship, the weather had become so bad that they could not safely leave and they were sleeping on board. The only inconvenience was passing a night in their day attire. Harriet wrote in her diary: '21 Thursday February. Dined in wardroom with Commanding officers – great fun, slept in Prince's cabin with A[nnie] in his cot', the cabin recently occupied by the Prince of Wales. Lord Harrowby's bed was a sofa covered with hair cloth, too short to enable him to stretch out his legs. Lady Grenville, now an elderly lady of 88, replied waspishly that 'she did not understand their coming back pleased with their excursion. The notion of visiting a ship in Plymouth as a morning amusement from Boconnoc is to me so new an idea that I can hardly take it in'.[32]

When home from school, the boys also made social visits. 'The two school Boys are come home in fair case (Cyril looks remarkably well) – and both with *excellent* characters. They passed the day yesterday at Lanhydrock – enlightening Charles Robartes as to the Eton rules of Football.'[33]

Life at Boconnoc, Dropmore and in London

For many years, the pattern that the Fortescues followed was that they were resident at Boconnoc from September until April. They then moved to Dropmore, as guests of Lady Grenville until her death in 1864, when George Matthew Fortescue inherited the estate. They hired a house in London for the season and resided there until it was time to return to Cornwall.

When they initially moved to Boconnoc, the house was in a poor state of repair, was not well furnished and was difficult to heat:

The cold has been severe and we have felt it keenly in the house you will not doubt when I tell you that in the library we with difficulty get the Thermometer up to 44 and that in the Gallery it is rarely as high as 50. We have abandoned the former altogether dining in the Gallery and sitting in the dining room; which latter we find very comfortable as well as our own apartment … in the billiard room – a Turkey carpet conceals the stone floor, with some old maroon curtains that we found here.

Over the years that they lived there, they transformed the house into a comfortable family home.[34]

George Fortescue was a very competent administrator. The steward, John Bowen, who had proved less than satisfactory was dismissed (finally) in 1850 and his place taken by William Pease, a very energetic (sometimes too energetic) and highly organised man (for which see Chapter 6). Between them Fortescue and Pease ensured that the estate was put into much better order and the income from it increased enormously.

George Grenville Fortescue (1835–56)

George and Lady Louisa's eldest son and heir, called George Grenville, was born at Weare Gifford on 3 January 1835. He spent his early childhood at Boconnoc and a fragment of a childhood journal survives from 1839 when he made the following entries:

> March 5 Froggot Butler came; March 6 Treffry viaduct founded; March 23 Saw Mohun coffins in church vault; May 15 Heavy snow. Thermometer 28; Aug 17 Annie and Dickie had Scarlet fever; Sept 12 The Herveys came; Oct 3 The Herveys went away; Nov 20 Left home with Clarkie [their nursery nurse] Harriet and Granty for Castle Hill; Papa Mama and Annie went to Port Eliot and Powderham. Joined us at C. Hill; Dec 13 1st Great coat of light Blue cloth.[35]

Lady Louisa kept a memorandum book, in which she wrote details about her children's progress. In 1840 she wrote: 'GG 5 years 3 weeks old. Always coming to morning prayers, knows many texts and some Hymns and Watts first catechism. Writes happier in pencil, knows some multiplication tables.'[36]

In another book, she wrote comments, letters and religious texts addressed to her eldest son. On 10 April 1844, when George was aged 10 and was going away to school for the first time, Lady Louisa wrote: 'My own dear Boy! this first time of your leaving me and your dear Father, your Brothers and Sisters, to take up your abode among strangers, must be an anxious and trying event for you and for us.' She told him to 'refuse the evil he might encounter away from the shield of Home and choose the good'.[37]

In 1847, he went to Harrow, but he was inattentive and was given unsatisfactory reports by his schoolmasters. The following year, he began to suffer from headaches and he returned to Boconnoc to recover. He had advanced to the fifth form at Harrow by January 1850, where Lady Louisa was glad to know he was 'not lying, drinking, smoking and betting', but he did not flourish and in March 1850, George and Lady Louisa decided to take him away from Harrow. They contacted the Reverend John Punnett, MA, formerly Fellow of Clare Hall, Cambridge and Vicar of St Erth, a 'good and clever man in the habit of taking pupils'.

The situation of the school near the coast was desirable for George's health and St Erth was only forty miles from Boconnoc.[38] The decision was made to send him there to continue his education.[39] He settled well and wrote to Lady Grenville: 'The situation of St Erth is very pretty and I have a very good view from my window of the sea; I like both the place and the inhabitants very much. Mr & Mrs Punnett are such very nice people, as is also his son who is a few months younger than I am.'[40]

During the time he was at St Erth, he wrote to his sisters Annie and Harriet, telling them about his activities: 'We went on a picnic to the Lands End … I was very much struck with the scenery, all along the coast it is very fine. We went also to the Logan Rock on which I got.' Perhaps there was still some need for him to work on English grammar![41]

In May 1853, George matriculated at Oxford.[42] He was pleased to feel that, being admitted as a member of the university, he had 'advanced a step in the scale of manhood'. His parents were particularly pleased that he had been admitted into a set of young men who had the reputation of being among the steadiest and most respectable at Christ Church, his Oxford college. He read law and history and was a model student, kept clear of extravagance and debt and passed his *little-go* (as Lady Louisa explained the first examination at Oxford was called) at the first attempt and at an earlier period of his university career than he need have done.[43]

On 3 January 1856, George reached the age of 21 and his mother wrote:

> It is a solemn thought that this anniversary of your Birth is that which for all business purposes launches you into the world as an independent member of society. My hope for you is a life sweetened at home by a *helpmeet* fulfilling her quieter share of patient and enduring domestic occupation, one who shall not *hinder* but *forward* you on your heavenward road![44]

Lady Grenville asked if some notice should be taken, in a quiet way, of George's 21st birthday, with no ostentatious display, but showing kindness to poor neighbours. George Matthew replied that the 3 January had not been 'unthought of' but as Lady Grenville had never authorised them to divulge her intentions as to her property, they had not encouraged George to assume the character of the future owner and the neighbours to look on him as such. As Lady Grenville had suggested a modest celebration, they would hold a servants' ball, a dinner in the barn for the labourers and their wives and organise a bonfire and fireworks.[45]

George Grenville recorded: 'Jan Thurs 3 Showers. Walked about. Planted trees. Came of age. Labourers dinner. Bonfire fireworks.' Harriet wrote in her diary: '3 January 1856 G's 21st birthday. Put up evergreens and arranged lots of flowers. Dinner to poor people and children in Carpenter's shop. Gave G malachite buttons – sang.'[46]

George Matthew reported to Lady Grenville:

The festivities did very tolerably. We began by planting ten trees in the lawn, first by Lou and the girls, second by the Boys and myself. We had a dinner for the labourers, their wives and children. 170 sat down. Our own dinner of 20 neighbours and lastly a bonfire – not up to Vauxhall but enjoyed by the children. Tonight is the Servants' ball and the end of the celebration.

And he reminded her of a link with the past: 'some old people present Martha Wilcocks and Belringer remembered the bonfire when Lord Camelford, your brother, came of age' in 1796.[47]

Lady Louisa wrote to her son:

Boconnoc January 13th 1856. I will add a few lines to those I wrote for your Birthday, expressing first my thankfulness that all our celebration of that day passed off so well and happily. May it please God that we should be spared all *10*, one united family group, like the trees we planted together … I am sure it must be a pleasant thought to you that this 3rd of January was a day of so much enjoyment to those who have so few holidays, who so seldom eat other food than that which their own hard labour has earned & to whom henceforth your name will be one of happy association! how strong are the claims of those who thus must live from hand to mouth, (whom every illness or misfortune, rise of prices, or even lack of thrift or continuance of bad weather deprives of all but daily bread, and sometimes not even that) on those who like you have an assured competence: you may not be able to afford yourself all the luxuries & enjoy-ments which many of your acquaintances partake of, but compare your lack of them with the lack of necessaries of others! remember how we are told that it is more blessed to give than to receive …

In 1856, George embarked on a cruise around the Mediterranean with Henry and Mary Moore (née Stuart-Wortley), the 3rd Marquess and Marchioness of Drogheda, the latter his mother's cousin, on the schooner *Fancy*. On Monday 18 August, they were off the island of Gozo. In October, the sailing party spent three days at Sebastopol. They were shown around by an aide-de-camp to places with very familiar names as a result of the Crimean War. The desolation, the solitude and the silence, with the marks of violence so universal and so recent, together with the sickening smell that prevailed, were described by George as most saddening. The *Fancy* continued on to Odessa.[48]

On 2 November, George climbed the 'main rigging for his amusement and which was no more than he had done before but either a sudden panic or giddiness must have seized him and he fell on the deck and died of the injuries he received in about four hours, never having come to …'[49]

Lady Drogheda wrote to Lady Louisa:

I do not wish to say more of ourselves but this I must tell you, that we had thro' the whole voyage looked on him as a brother and watched over him as such – I can hardly expect you to believe we were not careless in allowing him to climb the rigging, but I can truly assert that he was attempting nothing dangerous or that any man might not do – nothing can account for it but a sudden giddiness … words cannot describe how we miss the kindness and good humour, the incessant attention to every want of others, singular unselfishness that we experienced every hour in our friend and companion.[50]

George Grenville Fortescue was buried in the St Eugène Cemetery in Algiers. The service was performed by Her Majesty's Consul General in Algeria, John Bell, because there was no English clergyman in the town. He was covered with a white ensign, the red cross lying on him, and 'he looked perfectly calm and peaceful and there was no appearance of pain'.[51] The Droghedas ordered a white marble cross that was to be placed on the grave [*Plate 5*]. Lord Drogheda wrote to Earl Fortescue asking the latter to go to Boconnoc to give the news of their son's death to his parents. 'His death was caused by some internal injuries … the end was very sudden. I was holding his hand and feeling his pulse which at one minute was at 72 and the next had ceased for ever.'[52] In her diary, Harriet wrote: 'Uncle John and Glanville came to tell us of our darling George's death – Poor Papa and Mama much overcome.'[53]

His parents were particularly upset about the way in which he had died, where 'the act and exertion seemed so unnecessary'. Although they were sorely afflicted, they were thankful for the seven children that were spared to them. 'Poor dears it was a sad scene yesterday when we were all together on our knees praying …'[54] Many letters were received sending condolences, including one from Mr Punnett, under whose tutelage George had passed three-and-a-half years at St Erth and 'from whose kind and practical tutelage our dear Boy derived much'.[55]

To the Fortescues' second son, Hugh Granville Fortescue, known in the family as Granty, was given the unenviable task of travelling to Plymouth to collect his late brother's belongings. As the *Fancy* had been circumnavigating the Mediterranean, George had been buying keepsakes to give as gifts to members of the family on his return home. On 7 January 1857, the family met and 'allocated dear G's things'. The presents included silver hair pins and sleeve buttons bought at Constantinople for his younger sisters, a white Turkish tablecloth for his mother, one box of Smyrna figs for Bevill, his youngest brother, and even a keepsake for his old nurse – Clarkie. 'It was a painful task to look over these things and very saddening to see the clothes he had on and the straw hat he wore when he had the fatal fall!'[56]

Those on the Boconnoc estate were shocked at the tragedy and, organised by the rector Arthur Tatham and the steward William Pease, a subscription was taken up and the proceeds used to install a memorial window in the church, above the communion table, 'dedicated to the beloved memory of George Grenville Fortescue, who had made himself endeared to them by his gentle, considerate and amiable character, and whose sudden and premature loss they most deeply deplored'.[57] The list was headed by the Tatham and Pease families and the amounts ranged from Lady Grenville's contribution of £22.16s to that of Mary Belringer who gave 1d and C Yeo who gave ½d. The total sum raised was £95.10s.5d.[58] For the Fortescues, this was touching proof of the estimation in which their son had been held. A memorial was also erected to him in Christ Church Cathedral, Oxford.[59] [Plate 6].

In December 1856, the tragedy was brought home to them again when William Pond, the estate gardener, was buried at Boconnoc.

> Poor Pond was buried yesterday Lou G[lle] [Granty] and I attended and as we stood by his quiet Grave surrounded by familiar faces, close to the spot where we hope to lie and where we hoped our Children would lie, our thoughts naturally turned to that far off Grave in which just one month before, our own dear Boy was laid by strangers with no crowd of friendly mourners following … and the contrast added to our sadness.[60]

The family commissioned an inscribed slab of Cornish granite that would be sent out to Algiers to cover George's grave. George Matthew Fortescue lamented on this mournful occupation which contrasted sadly with their employment on the same day twelve months ago, when full of gratitude, hopefulness and joy they were making preparations for the festivities on the next day to mark George's 21st birthday.[61] On Tuesday 21 April, George Matthew, Lady Louisa and the four younger children went to St Blazey to see the granite slab. It was a fine piece of stone and the inscription was very well executed. It read: 'Georgius Grenville Fortescue Anglus de Boconnoc in Cornwall Armiger Immatura Morte Abruptus 11 [2nd] Die Novembris a MDCCCLVI Aetatatis Suae XXI Filio Primogenito Amamtissimo [sic] desideratissimo parentes eheu superstites' [George Grenville Fortescue, Englishman, of Boconnoc in Cornwall, knight, snatched away by an untimely death on the 2nd day of November 1856 at the age of 21. His parents, who alas survive him, (have erected this) for their ever-affectionate first-born son, most dearly beloved].[62] It gave them some satisfaction to have a link with a spot that they could never visit. The British Consul in Algeria, John Bell, wrote to tell George and Lady Louisa that the slab had arrived on 9 July 1857 and had been conveyed to St Eugène.[63]

From time to time over the years, various members of the family who were in Algiers went to find George's grave, Captain Alfred Ryder in March 1857 and the Courtenays in 1867. 'Recently when at Algiers, I made a point of visiting the cemetery there. I know it will be a comfort to you to know that it is nicely kept … I picked the enclosed wildflowers which grew against the stone and send them to you in case you may like to keep them.'[64]

In 1892, the British Consul, now R. Lambert Playfair, visited the grave and noted that it was in perfect condition.[65] Lady Louisa asked two of her sailor grandsons to look for the grave if they were ever in Algiers:

I must mention that having seen in the papers the fleet was likely to go to Algiers, I wish you w^d tell your sailors how desirous I am (sh^d they go there) for them to seek their Uncle George's grave. I wish to know the condition of our grave and that Dickie [Richard, her eldest grandson] w^d give orders for and defray expenses of any small needed repair as others have done for me, at intervals. It is longer than usual since I have had any report of it – They might also look out the marble tablet which the Harrowbys got Consul Playfair to erect in the English Church to dear G.[66]

In 1911, Richard Phillimore – Dickie, Harriet and Augustus Phillimore's eldest son – and a friend visited:

We had some difficulty in finding Uncle George's grave at first … but luckily Ruth remembered her Mother saying it was somewhere near the gate – and eventually we found it. It is really in good order, with the upright Algerian stone, the Boconnoc granite with the Cornish Cross on it – However the lettering on the granite is somewhat hard to make out and I have arranged with a stone mason to renew it, and paint the iron railings.[67]

The heir to the Boconnoc estate was George and Lady Louisa's second son, Hugh Granville Fortescue.

NOTES AND REFERENCES

1. British Library (BL): Add MS 59490, Burton Pynsent, Monday 13 September 1773, f. 10; Burton Pynsent, July 1733, f. 8; Hayes, Sunday 13 September 1774, Hester Chatham to Anne Pitt, f. 20.
2. BL: Add MS 69057, George Fortescue to Lady Grenville, 16 December 1855, ff. 196–198.
3. BL: Add MS 69304, Oxford Street, 23 December 1780, Thomas Pitt (III) to William Pennington, ff. 19–20.
4. The *London Courant*, 1779. I am grateful to Caitlyn Lehmann for this information.
5. BL: Add MS 59488, 6 February 1783, Thomas Pitt (III) to Benjamin Forster, f. 63.
6. BL: Add MS 69304, 31 January 1784, ff. 45–46, Thomas Pitt to William Pennington, ff. 45–46; Montpellier, 10 November 1786, Thomas Pitt, to William Pennington, ff. 92–93; Montpellier, 30 December 1786, Thomas Pitt to William Pennington, ff. 94–95.
7. BL: Add MS 59487, ff. 158–198; ff. 165–166. All undated.
8. BL: Add MS 59487, Thomas Pitt to Anne Pitt, undated, ff. 158–198.
9. www.batguano.com/vlbmemoirs1903; christies.com; Siân Evans (ed.), *The Memoirs of Elisabeth Vigée le Brun*, Camden Press, 1989.
10. The portrait of him at Christ Church, Oxford in which he is wearing the robes of Chancellor of the University, depicts him as a tall and distinguished figure.
11. BL: Add MS 59487, 1 September 1790, Camelford to Buckingham.
12. *The Astrologer's Magazine & Philosophical Miscellany*, Vol. 1, p. 493, *Domestic News*, July 1792. This publication gives the date of the wedding, erroneously, as 16 July.
13. BL: Add MS 59487, London, 19 July 1792, Lord Camelford to Thomas Pitt (IV), ff. 218–219.
14. BL: Add MS 69030, 2 December 1791, Lord Grenville to Anne Pitt, ff. 145–146.

15. Peter Jupp, *Lord Grenville. 1759–1834*, Oxford, 1985, p. 294; BL: Add MS 58873.

16. BL: Add MS 58873, Malvern, 16 September 1813, Lady Grenville to Lord Grenville, f. 115.

17. BL: Add MS 58873, Boconnoc, 17 September 1813, Lord Grenville to Lady Grenville, f. 114; Boconnoc, 1 October 1813, Lord Grenville to Lady Grenville, f. 180.

18. Cornwall Record Office (CRO): F/1/204, bundle of letters and accounts from Messrs Thomas Coutts' and Co., Bankers, London to Lord Grenville, 1786–1814.

19. BL: Add MS 59448, December 1815 to January 1816, ff. 124–149.

20. Jupp, *op. cit.*, pp. 460–461.

21. Hampshire Record Office (HRO): 115M88/1/2/2, Dropmore, GM Fortescue to his mother, 20 January 1834.

22. CRO: F/4/117/9, Cape of Good Hope, 20 October 1811, GM Fortescue to Lady Grenville.

23. CRO: F/4/117/9, 15 May 1820; History of Parliament.

24. BL: Add MS 69050, Boconnoc, 20 July 1833, GM Fortescue to Lady Grenville, ff. 169–174.

25. History of Parliament; Fortescue MSS FC39/78.

26. BL: Add MS 69054, Boconnoc, Tuesday 8 March 1853, Lady Louisa to Lady Grenville, ff. 143–144; Boconnoc, daily letters from Lady Louisa to Lady Grenville, March to April 1853, ff. 150–151 and ff. 163–206.

27. BL: Add MS 69056, Boconnoc, 15 May 1854, Boconnoc, GM Fortescue to Lady Grenville, ff. 69–71; 20 May 1854, GM Fortescue to Lady Grenville, ff. 80–81.

28. BL: Add MS 69052, Boconnoc, 29 October 1838, GM Fortescue to Lady Grenville, f. 1.

29. BL: Add MSS 69050-69064; CRO: F/4/117/9, Boconnoc, 20 August 1834, GM Fortescue to Lady Grenville.

30. BL: Add MS 69056, Boconnoc, 15 November 1854, GM Fortescue to Lady Grenville, ff. 194–195.

31. BL: Add MS 69058, Boconnoc, 21 October 1856, GM Fortescue to Lady Grenville, ff. 115–118; The duke's body lies inside a massive sarcophagus carved by F[rancis] C[ranmer] from ruddy brown Cornish porphyry, which it took two years to excavate by hand. It is inscribed with gilt letters.

32. BL: Add MS 69061, Boconnoc, 22 February 1861, GM Fortescue to Lady Grenville, ff. 188–189; Boconnoc, 24 February 1861, ff. 194–196, GM Fortescue to Lady Grenville; HRO: 115M88/F21/12, Harriet's diary, 1861; BL: Add MS 69061, Dropmore, 23 February 1861, Lady Grenville to GM Fortescue, ff. 192–193.

33. BL: Add MS 69062, Boconnoc, 24 December 1861, GM Fortescue to Lady Grenville, ff. 146–148.

34. CRO: F/4/117/9/46, Boconnoc, 14 June 1836, GM Fortescue to Lady Grenville; CRO: F/4/117/9, Boconnoc, 21 August 1839, GM Fortescue to Lady Grenville at Dropmore.

35. HRO: 115M88/F5/1, George Grenville's diary.

36. HRO: 115M88/F4/3, 23 January 1840, Memorandum book of Louisa Fortescue. Notes on children's education, growth rates, etc., f. 4.

37. HRO: 115M88/F5/2, Notebook of letters and religious texts by Louisa E Fortescue to her son, George Grenville Fortescue, up to his death in 1856 (from age 10) – 1844–1856. No page numbers. 'To my eldest son George Grenville Fortescue I commend the following pages written for him at divers times with much of anxious thought and earnest prayers (and first beginning on his leaving Home, and his Parents' wing) by his ever devotedly affectionate Mother.'

38. BL: Add MS 69054, Boconnoc, 16 March 1850, Lady Louisa to Lady Grenville, ff. 158–159.

39. BL: Add MS 69053, Boconnoc, 30 March 1850, Lady Louisa to Lady Grenville, ff. 78–81.

40. BL: Add MS 69053, St Erth, 1 July 1850, George Fortescue to Lady Grenville, ff. 128–129.

41. HRO: 115M88/C35/2/2/4, St Erth Vicarage, 15 August 1853, George Fortescue to his sisters, Annie and Harriet.

42. BL: Add MS 69055, Boconnoc, 5 May 1853, GM Fortescue to Lady Grenville, ff. 39–40.

43. BL: Add MS 69055, Boconnoc, Wednesday 15 February 1854, Lady Louisa to Lady Grenville, ff. 196–198.

44. HRO: 115M88/F5/2.
45. BL: Add MS 69057, 17 December 1885, Lady Grenville to GM Fortescue, f. 199; Boconnoc, 19 December 1855, GM Fortescue to Lady Grenville.
46. HRO: 115M88/F5; 115M88/F21/7, Harriet's diary 1856.
47. BL: Add MS 69058, Boconnoc, 7 January 1856, GM Fortescue to Lady Grenville, ff. 5–6.
48. BL: Add MS 69058, Boconnoc, 21 October 1856, GM Fortescue to Lady Grenville, ff. 115–118.
49. HRO: 115M88/C13/2/1, 4 November 1856, Lord Drogheda to Lord Fortescue.
50. HRO: 115M88/C12/1/2/1, Algiers, 5 November 1856.
51. HRO: 115M88/C12/1/2/1, Algiers, 5 November 1856.
52. HRO: 115M88/C13/2/1, RYS Sch^r Fancy, 4 November 1856, Lord Drogheda to Earl Fortescue.
53. HRO: 115M88/F21/7, Harriet's diary, 1856.
54. BL: Add MS 69058, Boconnoc, 14 November 1856, GM Fortescue to Lady Grenville, ff. 132–134.
55. BL: Add MS 69058, Boconnoc, 17 November 1856, GM Fortescue to Lady Grenville, ff. 135–136.
56. BL: Add MS 69058, Boconnoc, 21 January 1857, GM Fortescue to Lady Grenville, ff. 166–167; HRO: 115M88/F21/8, Harriet's diary, Wednesday 7 January 1857; BL: Add MS 69058, Boconnoc, 8 January 1857, GM Fortescue to Lady Grenville, ff. 168–170; HRO: 115M88/ C13/1/1, 5 November 1856, Memorandum; BL: Add MS 69058, Boconnoc, 8 January 1857, GM Fortescue to Lady Grenville, ff. 168–170.
57. BL: Add MS 69058, Boconnoc, 18 November 1856, GM Fortescue to Lady Grenville, ff. 137–138.
58. CRO: F/1/274.
59. BL: Add MS 69058, Boconnoc, 17 November 1856, GM Fortescue to Lady Grenville, ff. 135–136. There is also a memorial plaque and window in Christ Church Cathedral in Oxford. The window shows the Crucifixion and two scenes from the life of Christ by William Wailes, 1858. The inscription on the plaque in Latin is here transcribed: 'In Pious Memory of George Grenville Fortescue of Boconnoc in the county of Cornwall and at one time a Student of this House, whose body, when he had been snatched away by a sudden death, lies in Algeria among the Africans. His surviving friends saw to the decoration of this window with the stained glass. In the year of Our Saviour 1858.'
60. BL: Add MS 69058, Boconnoc, 5 December 1856, GM Fortescue to Lady Grenville, ff. 151–153.
61. BL: Add MS 69058, Boconnoc, 2 January 1857, GM Fortescue to Lady Grenville, ff. 166–167.
62. BL: Add MS 69372. The word 'amamtissimo' appears to be incorrect and should probably read 'amantissimo'. An implied grammatical completion of the meaning has been included (in brackets). My thanks to Alison Richards and Anne Graf for the translation.
63. BL: Add MS 69079, Boconnoc, Tuesday 21 April 1857, Lady Louisa to Lady Grenville, ff. 3–4; BL: Add MS 69372, f. 8.
64. BL: Add MS 69372, Algiers, 7 March 1857, Captain Ryder to the Fortescues, f. 5; Add MS 69372, 4 Berkeley Square, 30 March 1857, Courtenay to his aunt Lady Louisa, f. 10.
65. BL: Add MS 69372, 27 April 1892, R. Lambert Playfair to Lady Louisa, f. 19.
66. BL: Add MS 69372, a list of those who visited the grave up to 1911; HRO: 115M88/ C10/3/195/5, Polsden Lacy, 19 September 1890, Lady Louisa to Harriet Phillimore (née Fortescue).
67. BL: Add MS 69372, Chilworth Tower, Romsey, Hampshire, 11 February 1911, Richard Phillimore to Elizabeth Fortescue, f. 33. The author has made attempts to discover if the grave is still there, but was unable to obtain any information.

CHAPTER 5

THE FORTESCUES: 1864–1996

'Lady Grenville: The last link that binds to a past generation.'
(Lord Delamere to G.M. Fortescue, 15 June 1864)

A MOMENTOUS YEAR — 1864

The year 1864 was a momentous one for the Fortescue family, with the death of Annie after the birth of her child, the marriage of Harriet to Augustus Phillimore and the death of Lady Grenville, the last of the Pitts, on 13 June at the great age of 91.

Louisa Susan Anne Moore (née Fortescue) (1833–64)

Annie, the eldest child of George and Lady Louisa, with her siblings, spent an idyllic childhood at Boconnoc and was very close to her sisters Harriet, Mary and Elizabeth. In 1840, Lady Louisa wrote in her nursery memorandum book:

Annie is now 6 years 6 weeks old and has gone to Church every Sunday since her last birthday. She knows the 10 commandments, Watts first catechism, several hymns and texts. She reads fluently easy books, but with frequent mistakes from carelessness. Alternate days English and French which last she does not understand but pronounces tolerably. Geography and history, multiplication tables but incorrectly. Writes tolerably with a pen and ink, but spells indifferently. March 8th – Educating Annie. Threatening to put her on the floor often stops her crying. I slapped her hand for touching or squalling disobediently. I wish I could make her less troublesome when people are here![1]

On 18 July 1862, Annie left for a yachting trip to Scotland and Ireland with her relatives, Henry and Mary Moore, the Marquess and Marchioness of Drogheda and joined them at their home, Moore Abbey, where she enjoyed herself immensely, taking part in theatricals

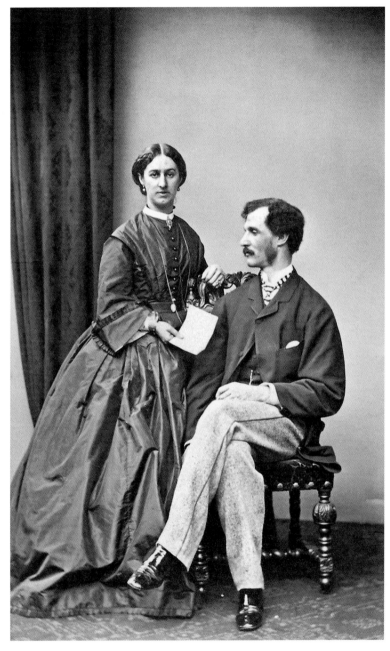

Figure 4 Louisa Susan Anne Moore [Annie] and William Westby Moore.
(© Hampshire Record Office)

and being invited to balls and parties.[2] While in Ireland, Annie was introduced to Captain William Westby Moore who was distantly related to the Droghedas and an aide-de-camp to the Earls of Eglinton and Carlisle, who were consecutively the Lord Lieutenant of Ireland between 1858 and 1864. His courtship of Annie progressed swiftly and they were married in London on 25 June 1863, at St George's, Hanover Square.

Annie had eight bridesmaids, including her three sisters. Her wedding dress was of white satin, while the bridesmaids were dressed in white muslin and tulle bonnets, the first four with trimmings of pink and the rest of Alexandra blue. Lady Grenville, aged 90, was present at the ceremony and after the service, a luncheon was provided for the guests. The newlywed couple went first to Dropmore and subsequently to Italy and Switzerland for their honeymoon.[3]

In August 1863, Annie and Willie Moore made their first visit to Cornwall as a married couple, when Annie confided to her mother that she was pregnant.[4] Later that month they travelled to Ireland, where they settled in Dublin in a pleasant Georgian property at 29 Fitzwilliam Street Upper, adjacent to Fitzwilliam Square Gardens.[5] The baby was due in March and Mary (Minna) Fortescue went to Ireland to attend her sister, during and after the birth. A daughter was born on 20 March and at first, Willie was sending encouraging telegrams about Annie and the baby's health to Boconnoc, while his sister-in-law Emma Moore wrote lengthy letters describing the new mother's progress.[6] However, Annie became ill with septicaemia and despite the best efforts of the doctors, she died on 31 March aged 31, two days after the marriage of her sister Harriet to Augustus Phillimore. Harriet wrote in her diary: '31 Thurs Heard by telegram that our darling Annie died at 1.30 am this morning.'[7]

On learning how ill Annie had become, her parents set out for Ireland, getting as far as Chester, but on hearing of her death, they turned round and returned to London. George Matthew Fortescue was almost overwhelmed with sorrow at the loss he had sustained.[8]

Mary wrote movingly to the family about her sister's last hours. Her husband had told her of her danger and although surprised, she was not agitated, nor dismayed. Conscious of her approaching end, Annie joined with Minna in repeating the 23rd Psalm. Her husband, her child, her parents and the old loved home at Boconnoc were among her final thoughts.[9] She had no pain and sank without a struggle. She was buried at Harold's Cross cemetery, Dublin (now Mount Jerome) on 2 April.[10] [Plate 7].

Emma Moore wrote to the Fortescues on 4 April 'my poor Willie is broken hearted …'[11] and a week later 'the dear Baby was christened this morning, it was a most melancholy ceremony. We have named her Anne Constance Louisa'.[12] The child, known by the name of Constance, was taken to Cornwall and brought up by her maternal grandparents.[13]

A service for Annie was held at Boconnoc church in April 1864, when the rector Arthur Tatham suggested that the hymn 'Nearer my God to thee', which had many associations with her, should be sung.[14]

Harriet Eleanor Phillimore (née Fortescue) (1836–1924)

Harriet, sometimes known as Pippy or Helen, was the third child and second daughter of George and Lady Louisa. Lady Louisa wrote in her nursery memorandum book in 1840: 'Helen [Harriet] nearly 3½ years old. Goes to morning prayers on Sunday, knows some hymns and texts, writes strokes with a pencil.'[15]

Diaries kept by Harriet from 1849, when she was 13 years of age, until 1864, when she married and left her parents' home, are an important source of information while the Fortescue children were growing up at Boconnoc.[16] The diaries do not reveal her innermost thoughts, but are a record of her activities and those of her parents and siblings: riding around the estate, lessons, visiting friends and neighbours, reading, attending dances and parties, recording news of the extended family and events in the wider world.

Here are two representative examples:

May 1849
1 Tuesday Fine. Played about the house. Walked to Beechwalk, Alder walk etc, Moved to the library.
2 Wednesday Expedition riding & driving to Lanteglos church. Dined at Bodinnick. Boated to Polruan & Readymoney cover. Swallows seen & cuckoo heard. Gloomy morning bright afternoon.
3 Thursday Walked to Millcombe and Brookses – picked pink anemones. Rode to Lostwithiel & heard & saw cuckoo. Patience exemplified in Throne towards Robin Hood. Wrote to Cissy [her cousin].
4 Friday Fine, warm, sunny. Walked to Kitchen garden. Walked to the School began reading "Letters from Palmyra" – began house.
5 Saturday Very hot & thundery. Walked to Rookery. Wrote Eva. Trees very green. Kitchen garden – Couch's mill – rode about lawn. Papa rode Brown Willy – Papa dined at Pelyn. Wrote "the Pearl of the Forest."
6 Sunday Fine. Boconnoc church. Sacrament Sunday. Flower garden, school, cows, bullock etc.
7 Monday Rain in m^g fine afternoon. Stayed in, wrote Eva. Rode with A[nnie] and Min [Mary] to Sladdsfoot sang songs G[eorge] went to school. Papa to Plymouth. Allowance 7^s.6^d.[17]

January 1862
4 Sat. Wet. American news more peaceful.
5 Sun. Stormy. Ch. "Sandon" for the 1st time – School – 64 children –
8 Wed. Fine. Walked C's mill. Visited A Cossentine – Began Granville's waistcoat –
11 Sat. Wet. Stayed in – finished Gr's waistcoat –
15 Wed. Fine. Walked K[itchen] G[arden] & Pinetum. Rode Lanhydrock – H^d of Mrs Sawle having been dangerously ill with diphtheria.
18 Sat. Cold. Wore our new black skirts.

21 Tu. Walked Park – put orange peel for deer –Visited the two Kittys.

22 Wed. Stormy. Tried to walk. Dear Cyril went – Rode Restormel – M^{rs} S much better.

26 Sun. Fair. Both Churches – A[nnie] distributed prizes to our class.

31 Fri. Stayed in all day – Bevill's bay Exmoor having come – [18]

Although not related, Lady Grenville had close connections with a family called Phillimore. They lived at Shiplake, Henley-on-Thames, about ten miles from Dropmore. Two of the Phillimore daughters, Elizabeth (known as Betha) and after Betha's death, her sister Mary, were Lady Grenville's companions for many years. Lady Grenville was very fond of all the members of the Phillimore family and as a result of her introduction, Augustus Phillimore, brother of Betha and Mary and a naval officer, was invited to Boconnoc.[19] In 1863, Augustus began to appear more and more frequently in Cornwall, where he made himself very agreeable and the family made him very welcome.[20] The attraction turned out not to be Boconnoc per se, but Harriet Fortescue. Augustus's repeated visits finally resulted in him proposing marriage to her. Harriet wrote in her diary: 'December 16 1863 Capt Phillimore wrote to ask me to be his wife – Rode ab^t Park Druid's Hill etc. Very happy.'[21]

Augustus's preference for Harriet had been noticed by her parents, but they had not been prepared for him to make so rapid a declaration, accelerated because Augustus was shortly to leave England with the navy and would be away for some months.[22] Harriet wanted to accept, but George Fortescue was concerned about his potential son-in-law's ability to support a wife and later a family. He wanted the couple to have a joint annual income of between £800 and £1,000 at the commencement of their married life, which he thought would generate a reasonable financial provision for Harriet's future comfort.[23]

Figure 5 Harriet and Augustus Phillimore. (© Hampshire Record Office)

Lady Grenville, delighted with the news of the impending marriage, had not been wholly unprepared having, as she put it, 'been aware of the strong western tendency, and finding that the west was only Boconnoc'.[24] She praised Augustus's character and commented, 'I have always thought his wife would be a most happy woman'. In the end, Lady Grenville came to the aid of the lovers and gave them a sum of money that would enable them to have an income of £1,200 a year, exclusive of Augustus's pay.[25]

The engagement was publicly announced on Thursday, 14 January 1864[26] and the wedding took place on 29 March at St George's, Hanover Square, with Lady Grenville in attendance. In addition to the money, she gave the bride a necklace with a large pearl as the centre ornament surrounded by diamonds, together with earrings of the same design.[27] At Lady Grenville's insistence, the newlywed couple honeymooned at Dropmore.

Despite George Fortescue's initial reservations about Augustus's prospects as a naval officer, his career proved to be an outstanding success. In 1868, he was appointed Commodore in Jamaica and from 1870 to 1873, he served as Senior Naval Commander in Gibraltar. He eventually achieved the rank of Admiral and was knighted.[28]

Harriet and Augustus's marriage proved to be very happy. They bought the Shedfield estate in Hampshire, where they brought up their seven children – six sons and one daughter, the latter called Violet, always known in the family as 'the one and only'.

The death of Lady Grenville

On 14 June, at 4 a.m. William Pease, the steward at Boconnoc, received a telegram from George Fortescue in London saying that 'all is over, come at once'. Lady Grenville had died at 10.10 p.m. the night before. Pease saw her just before she was put in her coffin and said she looked quite herself 'the same happy expression – but there was the pale marble like appearance' showing that the body was what he called 'tenantless'.[29]

In Lady Grenville's will, she left an annuity of £500 to Mary Phillimore, an annuity of £200 to be shared by her cousins, the three Misses Smith, and an annuity of £50 to her housekeeper Mary Gregory. With those exceptions, all was bequeathed, as she had promised, to George Matthew Fortescue.[30] Harriet recorded: '14th Tuesday. Will read. All left to Papa.'[31] John Fortescue wrote to his brother after hearing of the legacy:

> I had little doubt that our dear Aunt would not by her will disappoint all our expectations, but would do what was most liberal and considerate by you, but still with a person at her extremely advanced age and with such a very large property at her absolute disposal one never could feel quite sure what she would do.[32]

On Sunday the 19 at 7.30 p.m., George and Lady Louisa Fortescue, Mary and Elizabeth Fortescue, Captain Fortescue and Captain and Mrs Phillimore gathered at South Street and went into the room where the body of Lady Grenville lay. William Pease said that it was a touching sight to see the painting of Lady Grenville taken at Hebe when she was 20 years old looking down, as it were, on her own coffin. They all knelt and offered a prayer for her.[33]

Lord Delamere wrote to George Fortescue, saying, 'I rejoice to hear of so peaceful and calm a close to such a life as Lady Grenville's – with her death breaks almost if not quite the last link that binds to a past generation with whom we lived so much and whom we honoured and respected'.[34] Lady Grenville's funeral took place on Monday 20 June at Burnham in Buckinghamshire. It was attended by the family, Lady Grenville's servants and many members of the aristocracy. The procession of carriages was joined by the tenants in hatbands, together with sixteen bearers, all dressed in black, and was followed by other workmen. The church was crowded. The funeral service was over by 3.40 p.m., but it was past 5 p.m. before the church was cleared and the vault was closed.[35]

George Matthew Fortescue inherits Boconnoc

Although the correspondence between Lady Grenville and George Matthew Fortescue ceased after her death in 1864, fortuitously, after Harriet married Augustus Phillimore earlier in the same year, Lady Louisa took up her pen and wrote to her daughter several times a week, giving all the news from Boconnoc. These 3,000 letters are held in the Hampshire Record Office. Lady Louisa always started the letters 'My dearest Child', even when Harriet herself was a grandmother.[36]

Lady Louisa reported to Harriet on every topic that affected the Boconnoc estate: the weather, the servants, the health of George Fortescue (who was often incapacitated by his asthma), the dogs and horses (riding, buying and selling), the visitors they received and who they visited – their neighbours at Ethy, Lanhydrock, Trelawne, Glynn and Heligan – the churches they attended on Sunday, harvest festivals, the crops in the field and flowers in the park, dismay at the large number of dissenters that had come into Cornwall, the schools, the church choirs, shooting and fishing parties, Constance, and news of Harriet's children when they were left with their grandparents at Boconnoc while Harriet accompanied Augustus abroad.

Hugh Granville Fortescue (Granty) (1838–75)

Hugh Granville Fortescue, the fourth child and second son of George and Lady Louisa Fortescue, was born on 2 May 1838. After his older brother, George Grenville Fortescue, died in November 1856, Granty became the heir to his father and to the Boconnoc and Dropmore estates.

His school life was very unsettled. In 1850, he was at Winchester, but his parents decided not to send him back there.[37] In 1852, he was at Harrow, but he left there in 1853 and thereafter was sent to a private tutor.[38] Unlike his brothers, he did not go to university, but he was offered and accepted a commission in the Coldstream Guards. He joined as an ensign in the 1st Battalion on 1 April 1856, aged 17 years and 11 months.[39]

The Fortescues were – understandably – concerned about the safety of their second son after the loss of their first. George Fortescue wrote in January 1857:

Granty left us on Tuesday – we parted with him not without a pang, for besides that we shall miss his attention and cheerfulness which have been comforting to us in this season of sorrow – we can not after our late experience help casting a thought onwards, to what may happen before we meet again.[40]

He saw service in Ireland in 1857 and 1858.[41] He was garrisoned at Windsor for some months, where he was, on occasion, part of the Guard of Honour during the investiture ceremony for the Knights of the Bath.[42] He was well suited to an army career and George Matthew wrote: 'Granville … tho' young for his years, is far from wanting in intelligence … He has too during the 2½ years he has been in the Guards kept out of all scrapes avoiding getting into debt and has never given a moments uneasiness.'[43] This was not entirely accurate for, unbeknown to his parents, he was forced to borrow money from the steward William Pease to cover his debts. 'Mr G F informed me that he owes money for Bills and did not know how best to get money to pay them. He thought £100 would be sufficient to pay all.'[44] Granty would not allow Pease to tell his father of his impecunious circumstances, so Pease agreed to give him the money to repay the debts, provided that, in return, he received a promise from Granty that he would not borrow from the Jewish moneylenders. His two eldest sisters, Annie and Harriet, knew of his 'difficulty' and he had given Harriet a bundle of bills, which in the event of anything happening to him, he had asked be passed to Pease as he did not want them to be examined by his parents.[45]

He was gazetted Captain by purchase on 31 December 1861, the money being provided by Lady Grenville.[46] He enjoyed country pursuits: hunting, shooting and fishing. He was frequently at Heligan, Carclew and the other local estates taking part in shooting parties and he was not interested in shouldering the responsibilities that should have fallen to him as the heir to Boconnoc. His visits to Heligan seemed to be a particular favourite and were the subject of some irritation to Lady Louisa: 'Granty has disappointed us which I am very cross at. He stays at Heligan till Monday he says! He will have been there 12 days on this 2nd visit so … they will have had more of his society than we have!'[47]

In 1870, he started to suffer from a stiff neck and his health became increasingly uncertain.[48] By 1874, it was clear that something was seriously wrong. He became delusional and started to see 'creatures'.

Yesterday Gr. went in a chair with Constance and Bevill and they were glad to bring him home to Dr Clay [the doctor attending him] – Dr Clay sat with him in his room for an hour at a time and said but for what we told him, he should have said he [Granty] had improved – not looking about un-hearing and no mention of 'the creatures' … he must have a companion, a medical one.[49]

He continued to decline in health, walking becoming more and more difficult and there were suggestions that he should go to London to see Mr Maudsley, a rising doctor 'in line of Brain'.[50] Minna wrote to Harriet:

When he came in from his afternoon chairing with Mama, he told Cyril that the carriage had been full of those beasts – At dinner in the Study, he could hardly get on with his food, he was so tormented all the time – sometimes thinking they were taking his food from him, then that they were about my head, then shouting at them and insisting on going to demolish them with the forkes. About 11 he had a row with Smith … and got him by the throat. The boys both came and got him off Smith and back into bed and when they had calmed him down they fetched Mama who gave him a regular talking to.[51]

By early 1875, he was unable to get up stairs, had to be helped to his room and his right hand was affected.[52] He was daily losing power, had frequent falls which jarred and bruised him and he was no longer able to perform simple tasks, such as doing up his tie.[53] He became very violent and in November 1875, unable to manage Granty any longer at Boconnoc, it was decided that he should be moved. A cottage was rented at Wembury in south Devon and he was escorted there by Cyril, who reported that all was as comfortable as could be expected.[54] Lady Louisa received permission from the doctors to visit her son and, accompanied by Cyril and Bevill, she travelled to Wembury. She was encouraged that Granty recognised her, seemed pleased to see her and tried to join in when she said the Lord's Prayer.[55]

On Friday 19 November, Captain Hugh Granville Fortescue died at 5.30 a.m., aged 37. Pease wrote: 'Poor dear fellow he was always well with me – kind and considerate.'[56] His body was brought in a hearse from Wembury back to Cornwall and he was buried in the Boconnoc churchyard at 11.30 a.m. on Thursday 25 November. Granty never married and seemed to have no interest in women, although several young ladies had 'set their cap at him'. Having no children, the heir to the estate was now George and Lady Louisa's third son, Cyril Dudley Fortescue.

The death of George Matthew Fortescue

Through the years from 1850 until George Matthew died in 1877, he, together with his steward William Pease, ran the estate and gradually brought it into increasing financial prosperity and economic stability.

On Saturday, 20 January 1877, George Matthew Fortescue, aged 86, suffered a seizure while at dinner and was paralysed on his right side.[57] The next day, William Pease went with Lady Louisa into his bedroom and saw 'his dear kind friend lying on his back – eyes closed'. By 24 January, a great change had come over George Fortescue and he died at 11.15 a.m. with his family kneeling around his bed and Lady Louisa reading some prayers. Pease wrote: 'I have seen the last of my very dear kind friend.'[58]

On Monday 29 January, George Fortescue's will was read by Lord Devon. After bequests were made to family members and £300 left to William Pease, the bulk of the estate was bequeathed to Cyril Dudley Fortescue.

Following George Fortescue's funeral on Tuesday 30 January, Lady Louisa continued to live at Boconnoc and on 19 February that year, together with her daughters, she planted an Irish yew in the garden just before noon, at the hour she and George Fortescue had been married forty-four years before.[59]

Lady Louisa Elizabeth Fortescue (née Ryder)

After George Fortescue's death and with the next owner, Lady Louisa's son Cyril being a serving officer in the Coldstream Guards and away from home for many months at a time, she together with the steward became responsible for running both Boconnoc and Dropmore. During her time at Boconnoc, she established a Sunday school, at which she herself taught regularly until her seventieth year; she (and her husband) provided a parish nurse, who visited and attended the sick and infirm in nine parishes; she established Clothing and Provident Clubs, a lending library and a Cottage Garden Society; and gave donations towards the restoration of the churches of Boconnoc and Braddock.[60]

When her youngest son Bevill married Dorothy Hoste in 1891, she moved from Boconnoc to Dropmore. The residents on the Boconnoc estate wanted to mark the event and her son-in-law Vernon Harcourt Aldham, the rector of Boconnoc, prepared an address that would be made to her and another to Elizabeth (Bet), who was to accompany her mother. Anyone who wished could append their signature. Once the wording of the address had been agreed, the document was illuminated and bound up in book form, with the names of all those who had signed and with a photograph of Boconnoc as a frontispiece.[61]

Lady Louisa left Boconnoc, where she had lived for almost sixty years, continuing to write to Harriet several times a week and maintaining a strong interest in all the activities of her descendants; children, grandchildren and, eventually, great-grandchildren. She retained a sense of fun, greatly enjoying being pushed in a chair by her grandsons on the ice of a pool that had frozen over at Dropmore. She was a redoubtable woman, a matriarch, who held her family together through good times and bad. An obituary in the *Royal Cornwall Gazette* said that she and her husband had devoted themselves to the welfare of those dependent on them and though her life was visited with heavy sorrow, Lady Louisa's faith and cheerfulness never forsook her.[62]

In 1899, she was resident at Torquay, but was becoming increasingly frail. On 8 January 1899, she was sinking fast and died the following day. In 1900, a window was placed in Boconnoc church, dedicated to her memory.

The Fortescue children spent idyllic childhoods at Boconnoc. However, 'the heavy sorrow' that was referred to in Lady Louisa's obituary related to the deaths of her three sons, George, Granty and Cyril and her eldest daughter, Annie, who died at the ages of 21, 37, 43 and 31, respectively.

Cyril Dudley Fortescue (1847–90)

Cyril, the seventh child and third son of George and Lady Louisa Fortescue, was born on 19 September 1847. After his father's death, he inherited Boconnoc and other land in Cornwall, including the mines in the west, Dropmore and property in London. He was educated initially at a school in Malvern, then proceeded to Eton, whence he wrote letters to his parents and siblings, describing his lessons, sports, friends and the school activities in which he participated.[63]

A lengthy letter from Cyril described the events surrounding the wedding of the Prince of Wales (later Edward VII) and Princess Alexandra of Denmark. The royal couple were married on 10 March 1863 at St George's Chapel, Windsor. Part of the letter reads:

> The Prince himself was dressed in the robes of the Garter, he looked much better looking than usual. The Princess came in a carriage with her mother, she was dressed in white. I had a very good sight of her ... The Prince and Princess of Wales came out first together [from the Chapel] they appeared very happy and bowed vigorously, of course we shouted. I had leave with the Courtenays yesterday and I went over the Reception rooms built for the purpose [of the wedding] close to the Chapel they were wonderfully well done the Princes room had paper with feathers on them very handsome furniture the Princess's was hung with pink silk and satin covered with a garland round every looking glass and stand of flowers, the Carpet's pattern was feathers of A E ... Lady Caroline [Courtenay] gave me some of the Royal wedding cake to eat and I hid some of it in my pocket when no one was looking. I am afraid it is a very small piece but it was as much as I could spare & only cut a crumb myself please divide it if you can.[64]

After Eton, Cyril went up to Christ Church, Oxford, matriculating on 23 May 1866, aged 18, and graduating BA in 1869. His father had indicated to Lady Grenville many years before that 'we had always destined Cyril for the Church', but this was not his choice of career.[65] In 1870, he joined the Coldstream Guards, rising to the rank of Lieutenant-Colonel and serving for fifteen years until 1885.

Service in Ireland

During 1881 and 1882, the Coldstream Guards were ordered to Ireland. Evictions of Irish tenants had been ordered by courts in Co. Limerick and the battalion was sent there to protect the sheriff who was charged with enforcing the judgements. The battalion was also ordered to provide personal protection for certain landlords who, it was believed, were in serious danger from what were called 'outragemongers' in the country. Soldiers from both the Coldstream and Scots Guards were scattered in small groups of four or five on protection duty at gentlemen's houses all over Co. Clare. Cyril's duty was to visit them once a week. The police lent him a car and he drove about with a loaded revolver in his pocket. An order dated 17 March 1882, issued in London, recognised 'the valuable services rendered by Captain Fortescue, Coldstream Guards'.[66]

His time in Ireland was not all spent working, for he also went to stay with a brother officer, Lord Harlech's oldest son, visited the Droghedas at Moore Abbey, and attended polo pony races.[67]

Service in Egypt and the Sudan

The 'Urabi' or 'Arabi' revolt, led by Colonel Ahmed Urabi, was a national uprising in Egypt from 1879 to 1882, which attempted to end the influence of the British and French in the country. Cyril Fortescue was in Egypt in 1882 and was awarded the Egyptian medal.[68]

Three years later, in January 1885, General Charles George Gordon had been detailed to organise the evacuation of foreigners, officials and Egyptian soldiers from the Sudan. On 26 January, during the siege of Khartoum, the Anglo-Egyptian garrison was massacred and Gordon was murdered on the steps of the palace, hacked to pieces and beheaded by the forces of the Mahdi Muhammad Ahmad, the self-proclaimed redeemer of the Islamic faith.

Following the fall of Khartoum, the Coldstream Guards were sent out as part of the expeditionary force to Suakin in the Sudan with the aim of defeating the Mahdist forces. Before he embarked, Cyril returned to Boconnoc, where the whole family received Holy Communion together. Cyril had a long discussion with William Pease Junior, the steward 'speaking lightly and hopefully' and making appropriate arrangements for the running of the estate while he was abroad.[69]

'Two battalions of the Guards arrived on 9th March and marched to their camping ground ...'[70] They took part in two successful actions on 20 and 22 March, although no significant territorial gains were made. Cyril Fortescue was awarded the Suakin medal with clasp and the Bronze Star.[71] Two months later, the Gladstone government took the decision to abandon the campaign in the Sudan and the Suakin Field forces were evacuated on 17 May 1885.

Cyril Fortescue returns to civilian life

Lady Louisa commented that if only he could meet the right woman, now would be a good time for Cyril to leave the Guards. For what reason is unknown, except that it seemingly had nothing to do with a woman, Cyril fell out with the authorities and resigned his commission on 8 September 1885.[72] Almost immediately on his return to England, he had started to display symptoms of an illness. In September, his doctor, Frederick C. Wallis, who had been employed to accompany Cyril everywhere, suggested that he should be persuaded to make a will soon that would bequeath his unentailed property because medically, he would soon be unfit to do so.[73]

It is not clear if his health broke down as a result of his campaigning in Egypt and the Sudan as some newspapers suggested or whether this was the beginning of the same illness which had claimed the life of his brother, Hugh Granville, in 1875.[74] In 1885, Cyril was sleeping a lot, he was a good deal 'up and down' and the family was anxious and perplexed.[75] He spent the majority of his time at Boconnoc and despite being a Justice of the Peace and Deputy Lieutenant of Cornwall, he took little part in county affairs. Lady Louisa lamented the fact that Cyril was unwilling or unable to take up the responsibilities that came with running the estates at Boconnoc and Dropmore. When she wanted him to take the chair at a meeting of the Primrose League (an organisation founded to spread Conservative principles), he told her he would not go 'even if expected to do so'.[76]

In September 1885, Cyril was in London with his medical minder Dr Wallis and started to buy strange articles: a most absurd kind of 'trycycle' at a cost of £23, meant for a tradesman to carry his parcels, some paintings of questionable content, a watercolour which cost £37 and the heads of six deer for 80 guineas.[77] Dr Wallis wrote from London that the colonel was keeping well, but he was finding it a 'devil of a grind' to look after him alone.[78]

Cyril began to deteriorate, walking more feebly, frequently stumbling, sleeping for lengthy periods and taking hours to eat his meals. He became increasingly restless, fiddling incessantly with string, balls of twine and his rings and perpetually rearranging the wraps on his legs when he was out in the carriage.[79] He talked wildly and his moods became more and more erratic and difficult to manage.[80]

Cyril Dudley Fortescue died on 26 October 1890 at Boconnoc, aged only 43.[81] After his death, the newspapers reported that 'in business matters, he was very liberal, and death has deprived the tenantry (by whom he was held in high esteem) of a good landlord and a kind friend. In politics the Colonel was a Conservative, but ill-health prevented him from taking an active part in political matters, although he was much interested in the welfare of his party'.[82]

In the quiet and secluded churchyard of Boconnoc, Cyril Fortescue was buried on Wednesday, 29 October 1890. His body was taken into the church in an oak coffin that had been made by the carpenters on the estate with the bearers being some of the workmen. Though the funeral was private, a large number of his friends and many of the tenants were present. The coffin was covered with wreaths, including one sent by officers of the 1st Battalion, the Coldstream Guards.

In 1891, a memorial to Cyril was placed in the church at Boconnoc.[83] He was unmarried and his heir was his younger brother, John Bevill Fortescue, the only surviving son of George and Lady Louisa.

Mary (Minna) Aldham (née Fortescue) (1840–1925) and Elizabeth (Bet or Bessie) Frances Fortescue (1843–1931)

Mention must be made of the two remaining Fortescue daughters, Mary (known as Minna) – the fifth child and third daughter of George and Lady Louisa - and Elizabeth – the sixth child and fourth daughter. Both seemed to be rather unhealthy as children, suffering from numerous minor illnesses, headaches, colds, coughs and the like and Lady Louisa bemoaned the fact that one or the other (or both) frequently lost their speaking voices so that they could not sing.[84]

Vernon Harcourt Aldham was the rector of Boconnoc from 1874 to 1916 and an Honorary Canon of Truro Cathedral from 1889 to 1916. Aldham was a widower with four children. Cyril wrote to William Pease Junior on 16 June 1884 that 'I suppose you have heard that my sister Minna is going to marry Mr Aldham. I was very much surprised

Figure 6 Mary Aldham. (© National Trust/Anne Chapman and David Presswell)

Figure 7 Elizabeth Fortescue. (© Hampshire Record Office)

when I heard of it …,'[85] The couple were married on 22 July 1884 at St Mark's, North Audley-street, and after lunch they went to spend a few days at Dropmore and then travelled on to Switzerland. Mary moved from Boconnoc to Braddock Rectory to start life with her husband.

Elizabeth, Bet or Bessie, never married. After the marriage of her brother Bevill to Dorothy Hoste, she accompanied her mother Lady Louisa to Dropmore where she lived until Lady Louisa's death in 1899. She then moved to Chilworth Towers in Hampshire, close to the Shedfield estate owned by her sister and brother-in-law Harriet and Augustus Phillimore, and lived there until her death in 1931, aged 88.

John Bevill Fortescue (1850–1938)

John Bevill Fortescue, known as Bevill or Bev, was the eighth child and fourth son of George and Lady Louisa Fortescue. He was born on 1 November 1850 in Cornwall. He was first educated at a school in Brighton and went on to Eton where he became 1st Oppidan.[86]

After Eton, he matriculated at Balliol College, Oxford, where he read law and graduated in 1873. While still at university, on 17 April 1871 aged 20, he was admitted to the Inner Temple with a view to following a career as a barrister. He was called to the Bar on 26 January 1875 and joined chambers at 5 Pump Court.

In 1891, a year after he inherited Boconnoc, Bevill became engaged to Dorothy Augusta Hoste, only daughter of the late Admiral Sir William Hoste and the Dowager Lady Hoste.[87] His mother wrote to Harriet:

> As you are out of town – Bev does not object to my telling <u>you</u> – what is hitherto only announced to <u>me</u> and to Bet – that tomorrow morning I am going to receive Dorothy Hoste as my future daughter-in-law! From one or two indications previously, I was not altogether surprised when on Saturday he told me only, that he was intending (hopefully) to propose in a day or two, and yesterday afternoon, added with much satisfaction, that he was accepted ... You know perfectly well our past thoughts on the subject, but now the matter is settled, I desire to consider it as God's answer to my constant prayer for a 'help-meet for him', & it is my most earnest desire that neither to him or her or anyone else, should the impression be conveyed of her not being fully welcomed into the family! so that our new relations may be of the happiest.[88]

Lady Louisa, while sad at the thought of having to leave Boconnoc, her 'dear idolized home' of more than half a century, was delighted that her son was to be married.

The engagement was announced in *The Morning Post* on Wednesday, 8 July 1891 and the wedding took place on Wednesday 26 August at 2.30 p.m. at St Paul's, Knightsbridge. The bride was given away by her mother, the Dowager Lady Hoste, and was accompanied to the altar by her uncle, Lady Hoste's brother Charles Prideaux-Brune of Prideaux Place, Padstow. Dorothy wore a white satin gown, with a draping of fine old Venetian lace given by Lady Louisa and a tulle veil, looped up with a diamond stay, the gift of her mother. The officiating clergymen were the Reverend Canon Hoste (brother-in-law of the bride) and the Reverend Canon Aldham (brother-in-law of the bridegroom). The bridesmaids were Miss Ethel Greene (step-sister of the bride), Lady Frances Fortescue (cousin of the bridegroom), Miss Violet Phillimore (Harriet and

Figure 8 John Bevill Fortescue.
(© Hampshire Record Office)

Augustus's daughter) and Miss Constance Moore (Annie and Willie's daughter), (nieces of the bridegroom), Miss Mary Prideaux-Brune, Miss Seymour and Miss Hilda Barnard (cousins of the bride) and the Hon. Catherine Beresford. The bridesmaids wore white muslin gowns, trimmed with Valenciennes lace, gathered in with a rose pink band and carried bouquets of 'Malmaison' carnations. Each wore a trefoil brooch, made of diamonds with a pearl centre, the gift of the bridegroom. The Hon. Lionel Fortescue (cousin of the bridegroom), acted as best man. As the bride's family was in mourning, only close relatives and friends were present at the church. After the ceremony, the wedding guests were received by Lady Hoste at a reception and in the afternoon, Bevill and Dorothy left for Dropmore, where they spent the early part of their honeymoon.[89]

The wedding presents were listed in the *Royal Cornwall Gazette* dated Thursday, 3 September 1891. They included four silver salt cellars from the Boconnoc keepers and a large clock from the Boconnoc and Braddock workmen. The tenants at Boconnoc bought a two handled Cup in Silver Gilt, dated 1755, for £120 and had it engraved 'Presented to John Bevill Fortescue Esq[re] on the occasion of his marriage August 26th 1891 by his tenantry with their heartiest good wishes for the future happiness of himself and his bride'.[90]

After their honeymoon, Bevill and Dorothy returned home to Boconnoc and were greeted by a large gathering, including seventy of the home court tenantry mounted on horseback, and servants from the estate and the household. Four decorated arches were erected at various points through the park and a procession was formed, headed by the horse riders. At Thorney Bridge, Bevill Fortescue thanked them for their welcome. The horses were taken out of the carriage and it was drawn by a host of hands to the mansion where refreshments were provided in the grounds adjoining the front entrance.[91] By this date, Lady Louisa had got to know Dorothy and had concluded that 'in all essentials she is very satisfactory'[92] and was pleased to find that her daughter-in-law was taking a great interest in everything at Boconnoc.[93]

Lady Louisa visited Boconnoc in 1892 and 1893, but her visits to Cornwall became fewer and fewer as she advanced in age. While she saw with pleasure that Bevill and Dorothy were happy, the latter had superseded Lady Louisa as 'First Lady of the Estate' and Lady Louisa now took second place, a difficult transition for her to make, she having effectively run Boconnoc for so many decades.

In 1892, to celebrate their marriage, Bevill and Dorothy entertained the tenantry. A sumptuous dinner for two hundred people was held in a marquee. Following the meal, Bevill proposed the health of the tenantry, said what a pleasure it was to introduce his wife to them and thanked them for their wedding present.[94] There were speeches and fireworks and the whole thing was 'a gigantic success'.

On 24 December 1892, in London, Dorothy gave birth to a son who was called George Grenville.[95] A second son was born on 3 May 1896 and was called John Grenville.

Bevill Fortescue as High Sheriff of Cornwall

The right to choose the High Sheriff of Cornwall is vested in the Duchy of Cornwall and HRH the Prince of Wales, rather than in the Privy Council and the monarch. Following in the steps of members of other gentry families like the Bassetts, Boscawens, Treffrys and Rashleighs, Bevill Fortescue was appointed High Sheriff of Cornwall from February 1894, following the Shrievalty of William Bolitho.[96] He was already a Justice of the Peace and a Deputy Lieutenant of Cornwall. The Letters Patent and the forms of Declaration appointing Bevill Fortescue had been sent from the Duchy Office on 31 January 1894, together with similar forms appointing William Pease Junior (son of the former steward of Boconnoc and a solicitor) as Under-Sheriff, who dealt with the administration.

The office was (and is) for one year only and is largely ceremonial, but being independent and non-political, the Sheriff had the ability to bring together a wide range of people from all sections of the community.[97] His principal duties were to accompany royal visitors to the county, support High Court Justices when they were on circuit and offer them hospitality, and to attend the Lord Lieutenant. During his year as Sheriff, Bevill Fortescue hosted (at least) two dinners for the county gentry at the Royal Hotel in Bodmin in June and November 1894. The bill for the latter came to £50.12s.6d and included the costs of dinner, dessert, champagne, sherry, claret, port, coffee and cigars. Since the office of High Sheriff was (and is) purely voluntary, with no part of the expenses of the office coming from the public purse, the cost would have come from Bevill Fortescue's personal fortune.

At the end of his year of office, Bevill was asked to nominate five men who could be recommended to HRH when the Duchy Council met as Sheriff for the following year. His preferred candidate was Sir William Trelawny, who was appointed for the year 1895.

Bevill Fortescue as owner of Boconnoc

After Bevill inherited Boconnoc and Dropmore, he and Dorothy divided their time between the two estates. He, together with William Pease Junior and after the latter's retirement with other stewards, ran both properties. Bevill Fortescue died on 27 May 1938.

George Grenville Fortescue (1892–1967)

George Grenville, the older son of Bevill and Dorothy, inherited his father's estates in 1938. On 15 December 1927, he married Olive Joan Frankland-Russell-Astley. He was also educated at Eton and was appointed Sheriff of Cornwall in 1943. George Fortescue saw active service in the First World War, was wounded and suffered severely from the effects of shellshock.

The Second World War

During the Second World War, Cornwall provided accommodation for both troops and storage facilities prior to the invasion of mainland Europe. Commanded by Major-General Charles H. Gerhardt, the 29th US Division was stationed in camps between Falmouth and Plymouth, before their embarkation to Omaha Beach during the D-Day landings. The camps, providing tents for the troops and areas where equipment could be stored, were situated in wooded areas near small roads in the county. The Boconnoc estate, having many paved roads and extensive woodland, was a prime site for munitions to be deposited and was requisitioned by the Americans. Ammunition dumps and tanks were scattered across the estate. The house was occupied by several American units, while the troops were camped in the park.[98]

David Chapman, an estate worker, recalled that the Americans were popular with the children and that the troops sometimes went swimming in the Bath House pool. Chapman also remembered the airplane that crashed at Boconnoc:

> A German airplane landed in the wood near the school. My father (who worked for many years on the estate with the horses) took me to see it – we didn't get too close in case the Germans were still alive and had a gun. We could see the plane burning. Most of the crew were dead. One was injured and was taken to hospital but he died. The plane was shot down over Plymouth and came in among the chestnut trees. The plane was hit badly and only just made it to Boconnoc. We could see the fire on the tail as it was flying. It was not high enough for the crew to eject.[99]

Compensation was paid to the Fortescues after the war for the use that had been made of the estate and from 1945 until 1964, George Fortescue and his wife resided in the house, which became progressively more and more dilapidated. Brad Perkins, an American academic, with his wife Nancy, spent the year between 1950 and 1951 in Britain undertaking research for his PhD on the subject of Anglo-American relations between 1795 and 1805. Some of Lord Grenville's papers were still held by the Fortescue family at Boconnoc and the couple travelled to Cornwall to examine them. Of the forty rooms in the house, only about six were heated and the Fortescues lived mostly in their kitchen. The gardens were overgrown, except for the deer park where the grass was grazed by cows belonging to the local farmers. As far as Brad Perkins could tell, Mr Fortescue had no employment and no source of income so that, on a daily basis, he and his wife appeared to be living on the poverty line in severely straitened circumstances.

For about two weeks, Brad Perkins and his wife worked in an unheated room on the third floor of the house. There was no electricity, so that their working days were sometimes curtailed, governed by how long the sun shone and the light lasted.

On the last day that the Perkins were at Boconnoc, George Fortescue asked if they would like to see some family treasures. In a cupboard in the room where they had been working, they were shown forty place settings of Meissen or Sèvres china. In the long gallery, with

French windows on one side and fireplaces on the other, there were a large number of family portraits, including Gainsboroughs, Romneys and a Hoppner. Perkins commented on the dichotomy between the poverty and extravagance in which the Fortescues existed.[100]

John Grenville Fortescue (1896–1969)

In 1967, John Grenville Fortescue, the younger son of Bevill and Dorothy, inherited the estate on the death of his brother George, who had died childless. In June 1917, John Grenville married Daphne Marjorie Bourke (1895–1962) at the Guards' Chapel, Wellington Barracks; he was then a lieutenant in the Coldstream Guards and subsequently lieutenant-colonel. They had a society wedding when she was given away by her father and there were a large number of guests. The reception was held in London and their honeymoon, as had been the case with other members of the family, was spent at Dropmore.

Daphne's father, the Hon. Algernon Henry 'Algy' Bourke (1854–1922) was a colourful character and one of the fashionable men in London in late Victorian society and political circles. Falling heavily into debt, he was made bankrupt and passed the last twenty-two years of his life in Italy and Fulham, making a living by buying and selling Italian antique statuary.[101]

John and Daphne had three children: John Desmond Grenville – known as Desmond (b. 1919), who married Nina Kendall-Lane; Rose (1920–2010) and June Diana (b. 1924). In 1959, Desmond Grenville was invited to live on the estate and take over its management during the lifetime of his uncle George.

In 1996, Anthony Fortescue, Desmond's son, and his wife Elizabeth (née Poole) took over responsibility for the estate. The house had been abandoned and unoccupied for thirty years, but despite many declaring that restoration was impossible, Anthony and Elizabeth Fortescue were determined to prove the naysayers wrong and to restore this great house and estate to its former glory. More details about how the renovation was achieved are to be found in Chapter 7.

NOTES AND REFERENCES

1. Hampshire Record Office (HRO): 115M88/F4/3/f.1 and f. 7.
2. British Library (BL): Add MS 69063, Boconnoc, Xmas Day 1862, GM Fortescue to Lady Grenville, ff. 111–113; William Westby Moore's father was the Rt Hon Richard Moore, PC, one of the Judges of the Court of Queen's Bench in Ireland.
3. *Royal Cornwall Gazette*, Friday 3 July 1863.
4. BL: Add MS 69063, Boconnoc, 1 August 1863, Lady Louisa to Lady Grenville, ff. 172–173.
5. BL: Add MS 69063, Boconnoc, 21 September 1863, Lady Louisa to Lady Grenville, ff. 198–200.
6. HRO: 115M88/C41.
7. HRO: 115M88/F21/15/1864, Harriet's diary.
8. Cornwall Record Office (CRO): X715/26, William Pease's diary, 1864.
9. BL: Add MS 69064, 3 Park Place, Friday 1 April 1864, GM Fortescue to Lady Grenville, ff. 134–135.

10. BL: Add MS 69064, Park Lane, 2 April 1864, Lady Louisa to Lady Grenville, ff. 136–137; CRO: F/3/10/510, 17 June 1878, CD Fortescue to William Pease; the reference of her grave vault at Harold's Cross cemetery, now Mount Jerome, is vault number C87-2354. In 1868, William Moore remarried Isabella Sophia Anne, daughter of the Hon. Granville Ryder, second son of Dudley Ryder, 1st Earl of Harrowby. She died on 31 January 1884. The Hon. Granville Ryder was Lady Louisa Fortescue's brother. Isabella was thus Lady Louisa's niece and Annie's first cousin.

11. HRO: 115M88/C41/1/1/5, ff. 1–2.

12. HRO: 115M88/C41/1/1/6, 11 April 1864.

13. HRO: 115M88/C10/3/25/12, pp. 3–4.

14. CRO: F/3/10/100, Broadoak, 2 April 1864.

15. HRO: 115M88/F4/3.

16. HRO: 115M88/F21/1-57. The diaries run until 1909, but contain much less information relating to Boconnoc after 1864.

17. HRO: 115M88/F21/1, Harriet's diary, 1849. The diaries are tiny – around 2 inches by 1½ inches and are difficult to read in places.

18. HRO: 115M88/F21/13, Harriet's diary, 1862.

19. BL: Add MS 69058, Dropmore, 10 September 1856, Lady Grenville to GM Fortescue, ff. 111–112.

20. BL: Add MS 69064, Boconnoc, 26 October 1863, GM Fortescue to Lady Grenville, ff. 8–9; 1 December 1863, GM Fortescue to Lady Grenville, ff. 37–38.

21. HRO: 115M88/F21/14, Harriet's diary, 1863.

22. BL: Add MS 69064, Boconnoc, 16 December 1863, GM Fortescue to Lady Grenville, ff. 55–56.

23. BL: Add MS 69064, 17 December 1863, Lady Grenville to GM Fortescue, ff. 57–59.

24. BL: Add MS 69064, Boconnoc, 17 December 1863, GM Fortescue to Lady Grenville, ff. 57–59; Torquay, 17 December 1863, Lady Grenville to GM Fortescue, ff. 60–61.

25. BL: Add MS 69064, Boconnoc, 21 January 1864, GM Fortescue to Lady Grenville, ff. 114–115.

26. CRO: X715/26, William Pease's diary, 1864.

27. BL: Add MS 69064, Stratton Street, 17 March 1864, GM Fortescue to Lady Grenville, ff. 120–122.

28. HRO: 115M88/C10/3/37/8, 22 February 1868.

29. CRO: X715/26, William Pease's diary, 1864.

30. CRO: F/1/14.

31. HRO: 115M88/F21/15, Harriet's diary, 1864.

32. BL: Add MS 69371, Poltimore Rectory, 17 June 1864, John Fortescue to GM Fortescue, ff. 139–140.

33. CRO: X715/26, William Pease's diary, 1864.

34. BL: Add MS 69371, Hertford Street, 15 June 1864, Lord Delamere to GM Fortescue, f. 124.

35. CRO: X715/26, William Pease's diary, 1864.

36. HRO: 115M88/C10/3/1-293, 1842 to 1898.

37. BL: Add MS 69053, Boconnoc, 30 March 1850, Lady Louisa to Lady Grenville, ff. 78–81.

38. BL: Add MS 69055, Boconnoc, 6 December 1853, Lady Louisa to Lady Grenville, ff. 136–137; email from Tace Fox, Archivist of Harrow School, dated 21 January 2016.

39. BL: Add MS 69058, Boconnoc, 7 January 1856, GM Fortescue to Lady Grenville, ff. 5–6; letter and information from Major Robert de L. Cazenove, Regimental Archivist of the Coldstream Guards in a letter dated 17 September 2015.

40. BL: Add MS 69058, Boconnoc, 8 January 1857, GM Fortescue to Lady Grenville, ff. 168–170.

41. BL: Add MS 69058, Boconnoc, 12 September 1857, GM Fortescue to Lady Grenville, ff. 40–41; BL: Add MS 69059, Boconnoc, 3 April 1858, ff. 125–126.

42. BL: Add MS 69058, Boconnoc, 3 February 1857, GM Fortescue to Lady Grenville, ff. 185–186.
43. BL: Add MS 69060, Boconnoc, 17 October 1858, GM Fortescue to Lady Grenville, ff. 6–8.
44. CRO: X715/21, William Pease's diary, Friday 8 April 1859.
45. CRO: X715/21, William Pease's diary, 9 and 15 April, 1859.
46. BL: Add MS 69062, Boconnoc, 1 January 1862, GM Fortescue to Lady Grenville, ff. 151–153.
47. HRO: 115M88/C10/3/37/11, Boconnoc, 29 February 1868, Lady Louisa to Lady Grenville.
48. HRO: 115M88/C10/3/50/15-16, Boconnoc, 16 December 1870.
49. HRO: 115M88/C10/3/56/3, Boconnoc, 2 April 1874.
50. HRO: 115M88/C10/3/56/4, Boconnoc, 4 April 1874, Minna to Harriet.
51. HRO: 115M88/C10/3/56/5, Boconnoc, 6 April 1874, Minna to Harriet.
52. HRO: 115M88/C10/2/62/5, Boconnoc, 13 April 1875.
53. HRO: 115M88/C10/3/63/9, Boconnoc, 7 May 1875.
54. HRO: 115M88/C10/3/67/1, Powderham, 4 November 1875; HRO: 115M88/C10/33/67/2, Boconnoc, 7 November 1875.
55. HRO: 115M88/C10/3/67/5, 17 November 1875.
56. CRO: X/715/37, William Pease's diary, 1875.
57. HRO: 115M88/F21/29, Harriet's diary, 1977; CRO: X715/39, William Pease's diary, 1877.
58. CRO: X715/39, William Pease's diary, 24 January 1877.
59. HRO: 115M88/C10/3/74/9, Boconnoc, 19 February 1877.
60. *Royal Cornwall Gazette*, Thursday 5 July 1900, p. 3.
61. CRO: F/3/10/220, Braddock Rectory, 19 August 1891, VH Aldham to William Pease Junior; CRO: F/3/10/220, Braddock Rectory, 5 September 1891, VH Aldham to William Pease Junior.
62. CRO: F/3/10/518, Dropmore, 6 January 1893, Elizabeth Fortescue to William Pease; *Royal Cornwall Gazette*, Thursday 5 July 1900, p. 3.
63. HRO: 115M88/C37, 1860–1863.
64. HRO: 115M88/C37/2/4/9, 11 March 1863, Cyril to Lady Louisa.
65. BL: Add MS 69054, Boconnoc, 27 December 1851, GM Fortescue to Lady Grenville, ff. 67–68.
66. CRO: F/3/10/511, 13 January 1882; Sir John Ross of Bladenburg, *A History of the Coldstream Guards, 1815–1896*, p. 346.
67. CRO: F/3/10/511, 10 January 1881, 14 February 1881 and 6 July 1881.
68. Information from Major Robert de L. Cazenove, Regimental Archivist of the Coldstream Guards in a letter dated 17 September 2015.
69. HRO: 115M88/C10/3/129/3, Boconnoc, 12 February 1885, Lady Louisa to Harriet Phillimore.
70. E. Gambier-Parry, *Suakin 1885 being a sketch of the campaign of this year, by An Officer who was there*, London, 1885, p. 48.
71. Information from Major Robert de L. Cazenove, Regimental Archivist of the Coldstream Guards in a letter dated 17 September 2015; *The Daily News*, Monday 27 October 1890.
72. HRO: 115M88/C10/3/134/1, 6 July 1885, Lady Louisa to Harriet Phillimore.
73. CRO: F/3/10/196, 4 September 1885.
74. *The Daily News*, Monday 27 October 1890; *Royal Cornwall Gazette*, 30 October 1890.
75. HRO: 115M88/C10/3/135/2, Boconnoc, 18 August 1885, Lady Louisa to Harriet Phillimore.
76. HRO: 115M88/C10/3/142/4, Boconnoc, 5 April 1886.
77. CRO: F/3/10/196, September 1885 from FJH Somerset.
78. CRO: F/3/10/204, 7 June 1887.
79. HRO: 115M88/C10/3/151/3, 7 January 1887; C10/3/151/5, 12 January 1887; C10/3/151/8, 19 January 1887.
80. HRO: 115M88/C10/3/151/11, Boconnoc, 25 January 1887.

81. CRO: F/3/10/217, Saturday 25 October 1890.

82. *The Daily News*, 27 October 1890; *Royal Cornwall Gazette*, 30 October 1890.

83. HRO: 115M88/C10/3/204/9, Boconnoc, 30 May 1891, Lady Louisa to Harriet Phillimore.

84. HRO: 115M88/C10/3/50/21-22.

85. CRO: F/3/10/513; *Royal Cornwall Gazette*, Friday 25 July 1884.

86. Etoncollege.com. At Eton, King's Scholars were awarded Foundation Scholarships and were known as Collagers, one of whom was always Captain of the whole school. The Oppidans entered Eton via Common Entrance and had the letters 'OS' after their name in the school lists.

87. CRO: F/3/10/220, 8 July 1891.

88. HRO: 115M88/C10/3/206/2, 51 Upper Berkeley Street, London, 6 July 1891, Lady Louisa to Harriet Phillimore.

89. *The Morning Post*, Thursday 27 August 1891; *Royal Cornwall Gazette*, Thursday 3 September 1891.

90. CRO: F/3/10/7, pp. 874 & 890.

91. *Royal Cornwall Gazette*, Thursday 8 October 1891.

92..HRO: 115M88/C10/3/210/9, Dropmore, 28 November 1891.

93. CRO: F/3/10/221, Braddock Rectory, 28 November 1891, Mary Aldham to William Pease.

94. *Royal Cornwall Gazette*, Festivities at Boconnoc, Thursday 25 August 1892.

95. *Royal Cornwall Gazette*, Thursday 29 December 1892.

96. CRO: F/1/491; *Bristol Mercury & Daily Post*, Thursday 1 February 1894.

97. www.highsheriffs.com.

98. Information from Min Wood in an email dated 5 August 2014.

99. Oral history interview with David Chapman, 24 March 2013.

100. Information from Min Wood in an email dated 16 October 2003.

101. Kildare Hubert Bourke-Borrowes, 'Hon Algernon Henry 'Algy' Bourke, A Short Biography', 2012, unpublished.

CHAPTER 6

RUNNING THE ESTATE

'12d was received from the heir of Thomas Penerell for the
confirmation of the use of the fishtrap at Daunettismyll.'
(Cornwall Record Office: F/4/3, bailiff's accounts, 29 September 1431 to 30 September 1432)

THE MIDDLE AGES TO THE
EARLY SEVENTEENTH CENTURY

The manor

During the Middle Ages, the manor was an estate held by what was known as feudal tenure. The king held all the land in the country and devolved estates to tenants-in-chief, who in turn could grant land to their adherents. Part of an estate consisted of the demesne, which the lord held for his own use. The rest was cultivated by tenants or retained as common land or waste. The tenants were of two types – villeins, who rendered labour services to the lord, cultivating his demesne in return for an allocation of land, and those who paid a rent in money. The bailiff was the officer appointed to oversee the estate, collect the rents, prepare the accounts and execute the decisions of the manorial court.[1]

From the early thirteenth century, many lords employed local officials to manage their affairs and to draw up manorial accounts known as *compoti*. These provide much information about how the manor functioned as an economic unit. The accounting year generally ran from Michaelmas (29 September) to Michaelmas, following the natural rhythm of the harvest year.[2]

The first documents found that relate to the workings of the Boconnoc estate are bailiff's accounts dating from the early fifteenth century.[3] The bailiff is named as Richard Menebryll and the account is for the period from Michaelmas 1431 to Michaelmas 1432. King Henry VI was on the throne and the lord of the manor was Thomas Carminow.

The accounts follow the usual pattern of first listing the receipts received by the bailiff from the rents of land, the sale of labour services (where the lord had remitted labour services for a monetary payment), profits from the manor, the rents from the demesne land

and the profits of the manorial court: 12*d* was received from the heir of Thomas Penerell for the confirmation of the use of the fishtrap at 'Daunettismyll' (probably Dawnahat on the River Lerryn), 12*d* was received from the sale of four works of reaping and 4*s*.4*d* from the sale of thirteen works of carrying for the lord.

The amount of demesne land that was rented out varied from year to year. In this particular year, much of it was being held in hand – 'concerning a close called Redpark that was accustomed to be answerable for 6 shillings a year, nothing because it is in the lord's hand this year'. The total of all the receipts received by Richard Menebryll was £65.2*s*.8½*d*.

The second half of the accounts lists the expenditure paid out by the bailiff including any rents lost by the lord because of grants of land made rent-free to tenants and pensions given to servants for good service: the bailiff, Richard Menebryll, was granted a pension of 13*s*.4*d* per annum for life.

The costs associated with the manor house were then listed, for which see details in Chapter 7. These were followed by the costs of 'necessities': 40 shillings and 33*s*.4*d* paid to Thomas Kendale and Thomas Flemmyng for 'Ereschclothe' (a course woolen cloth), a payment of 8*s*.4*d* to the rector of Boconnoc for the tithe and three gowns given to John Pride, Walter Rule and John Hunt for their children at a cost of 43*s*.5*d*. The lord had bought from 'Aysshwater in Devon' five yards of cloth for his marriage, costing 4*s*.2*d* and three pairs of shoes at a cost of 18*d*. The total of all payments and expenses was £38.10*s*.6*d*.

The bailiff then accounted for amounts he had received from other sources: 15*s*.1*d* from the sale of 1 quarter and 7 bushels of corn, 23*s*.11*d* received from John Burgeys, reeve of Westdraynes, 17*s*.0*d* from Vincent Burgeys, reeve of Eastdraynes, and 66*s*.8*d* from John Body, reeve of Glynne.

Finally, there are listed the harvest works, the works that the tenants had to perform for the lord on the demesne land. These included ploughing, reaping, fencing and carrying the corn with their own horses to the lord's grange.[4] At the end of the account, the bailiff declared how much money he owed to the lord.

The manorial court

The lord of the manor had the responsibility for holding two different types of manorial court which preserved the lord's rights and his financial interests, and regulated the relationships of the tenants with each other.

The first, called the court baron, was held every three weeks. This dealt with land use and tenure, payment of dues, how the works due to the lord were to be performed and had other functions, including dealing with disputes among tenants and appointing the reeve, who acted as an overseer.

The second type of court, the court leet, was held every six months, in the spring and autumn. This court dealt with the view of frankpledge, a system consisting of a grouping of ten adult males. Each person in the group, called a *tything*, was responsible for the actions of the other members. The head was called a tithing-man, who could be fined for failing to produce any male alleged to have committed a crime. In addition, the court dealt with minor offences and was empowered to fine or imprison offenders and to deal with the regulation of agricultural practices on the manor such as crop rotation.

The court rolls

The tenants, who were obliged to attend the manor court, were known collectively as 'the homage'.[5] When a fine or amercement was imposed by the court, the amount was decided by the assessors and in the court roll, the amount of the fine is often inserted over the name of the offender. Some of the entries for Boconnoc (Bodconneck) are:[6]

> The homage presents the absence of James [3d] Durneforth, John [3d] Anstoll, the heirs of [3d] Delawydell and William [3d] Lona who owe suit to this day and are not come. Therefore they are amerced – 12[d]. The homage elects Nicholas Notell to the office of reeve of Bedowe who is sworn. Also they elect Laurence Hey to the office of tithing-man who is pledged to the hundred.[7]
>
> The homage presents that Robert Tonker who held one holding in Connenc from the lord has died. Whereupon there falls due a cow, value 6s.8d. as a heriot to the lord.[8]
>
> The jury presents that Richard Lyon allows a bakehouse to be ruinous and he is given notice to repair it before the next feast of St Michael the Archangel under a penalty of 20d.[9]
>
> John Tonker puts himself in the grace of the lord because he took, unjustly, several loppings of oak without the permission of the lord or his officer. Penalty 2d.[10]
>
> Item that William Levan and Richard Illary obstruct 1 footpath at attehill and attewyll to the hurt of all tenants of the lord.
>
> A certain unknown ploughed 100 acres of Boconnok downe to the hurt of all the tenants. Thomas Davy occupies the pasture of the lord at Boconnok and Whiteburgh downe with his beasts.[11]

Court rolls from the late sixteenth and early seventeenth centuries

Court rolls also survive from the reigns of Edward VI, Philip and Mary and Elizabeth I, when William Mohun was lord of the manor, and draft court rolls dating from c. 1594–1600, when Reginald Mohun was lord of the manor. Two of the entries are as follows:

> The jury presented John [8d] Robyns because he assailed and treated badly the wife of Edward Peron against the peace of the lady Queen [Elizabeth I]. John amerced 8d.
>
> Richard Corche complains against William Peron the elder in a plea of trespass whereupon the said plaintiff … saythe that the said defendant here at Nether Town on the 10th August in the 36th year of the reign of the present Queen the corne of the plaintiff lying cut for tithing there before the delivery thereof to the parson of Bocconnock the defendant's two pygges did eat consume and devour and other enormytes to the value of 5s. and therefore presents his suite. And the defendant appears and says: that true it is that trespass was done but through the defaulte of the plaintiff …[12]

Ministers' accounts

The next documents chronologically are a series of ministers' accounts dating from 1511 to 1544.[13] It is unclear why these accounts were prepared, save that William Courtenay, son of the owner of Boconnoc, had been attainted and could not inherit. Some control may have been retained by central government for one account (*compotus*), was prepared by William Loure Esq., the Receiver Particular, for the Crown.

The Mohuns

The Mohuns bought the estate in 1563. The will of Richard Harvye, a servant of the Mohuns at Boconnoc, provides information about the various servants that were employed. Harvye gave bequests in money to four chambermaids, to the maidservants, to every one of the 'howshould handes' and to two brewers, John Harrye and a man called Trethewe, for whom no Christian name was given. He gave to John Hutchin the 'boye of the buttery all my cards and dice with the games already given', his canvas doublet to Clementes, the hind, his best hat to John Ale, his master's cook and to Edward Pointye, another servant, 'my newe lawne bande'. He owed his master's bailiff, Peter, ten shillings.[14]

From the time of the 2nd Lord Mohun until George Matthew Fortescue and his wife Lady Louisa moved to Boconnoc and made it their family home in 1834, running the estate was left largely in the hands of stewards.

The Pitts

When Thomas 'Diamond' Pitt (I) bought the estate in 1717, he appointed John Phillips as his land agent and steward in Cornwall, but this was far from an ideal situation, since Phillips lived in Camelford, about twenty miles from Boconnoc. Accordingly, Edward Rattew, the hind, was instructed to look after some of the day-to-day management.[15]

Pitt convinced himself that Phillips, Rattew and the other servants were cheating him of income: 'And that dog of a Hind with his cursed ffamily is the destruction of yᵉ barton of Boconnock where yᵉ villain has filled his Pocketts and empty'd mine … you amongst you made me repent that ever I meddled with my Lady Mohun's Estate.' He complained incessantly that too much money was being spent and he was even considering disposing of Boconnoc. 'I have for above a twelve month not received one penny for my estate in Cornwall, from which I should have received three or four thousand pounds which so perplexes my thoughts that I am thinking of selling my estates there.'[16]

Becoming more and more enraged that the servants were living the 'high life' at his expense, he wanted to know how many people were eating in the house, called Rattew a 'dumb beast' and wrote that Phillips was 'the vilest unfaithfulest wretch yᵗ ever was employed by man'.[17]

Phillips and Rattew protested that they were doing their best and when 'Diamond' Pitt (I) died in 1726, Phillips was still in his employ. Robert, Pitt's eldest son, did not long outlive his father and Robert's older son Thomas Pitt (II) (1705–61) inherited in 1727. In

1747, John Bennett was appointed steward.[18] Like his predecessors, he wrote letters to the absent owner, outlining what was happening in Cornwall.[19]

Bennett continued as steward after Thomas Pitt (III) (later 1st Lord Camelford) inherited in 1761 and he was prompt in dealing with estate matters. These included making an advantageous bargain in selling 120 acres of timber in Largin Wood for £10 per acre,[20] arranging for an orchard to be planted[21] and dealing with poachers after the gamekeeper had caught some 'fellows shooting pluvers' and hunting hares with hounds.[22] He forwarded accounts prepared by the gamekeeper and the gardener to his employer, but in 1765 pointed out that 'money goes away fast'.[23] John Bennett died in March 1782 and his son Thomas inherited his father's duties.[24]

Thomas Bennett was (apparently) an efficient administrator and when his responsibilities were increased after 1786, when the Pitts were travelling abroad, he employed a deputy called William Beard to assist him.[25] The lack of personal supervision from their employers meant that the stewards were left to their own devices, often for many months at a time. Three of them, Thomas Bennett, Watson Sharman and John Bowen initially 'gave satisfaction', but all three of them ended up in financial difficulties, having to repay the debts that had been incurred in running the estate.

The Grenvilles

After Lady Grenville inherited in 1804, her husband on her behalf wrote letter after letter to Thomas Bennett requesting the estate accounts. Grenville's patience finally ran out in November 1804 when he reminded Bennett that more than seven months had elapsed since he had first requested the financial statements, which were now more than three years in arrears. Once Grenville had finally received them, it became clear why Bennett had been so reluctant to produce them. There was a deficit of £2,000, for which Bennett could provide no explanation. There was no suggestion that the money had been embezzled, but the arrears had accumulated primarily due to the lax and inefficient running of the estate. Bennett requested a period of grace within which he would liquidate the debt,[26] but when it was still unpaid in 1806, Grenville threatened that if the money did not arrive promptly he would commence a prosecution.[27] Long, rambling letters with further excuses emanated from Bennett, but after many further exchanges, an agreement was reached: if Bennett was unable to pay off the debt by 22 August 1806, he would transfer property which he owned to Lady Grenville.[28]

Having reached an accommodation with Bennett, the Grenvilles must have hoped that the situation would improve, but this was not the case. Latterly, Bennett had been assisted by a man called Watson Sharman, who became steward in his turn. At Christmas 1806, Sharman started to exhibit the symptoms of a serious medical condition, probably epilepsy. When riding to Bodmin, he was seized with a fit before he reached the town and fell from his horse.[29] Realising he needed assistance to enable him to continue to undertake his duties, Sharman called on the services of a man called John Bowen. In 1810, when Sharman was confined to bed,[30] Bowen reported to Grenville that there was no money to cover any unsettled bills, nor to pay the arrears of wages due to the labourers of nearly £200.[31] Almost six months passed before Grenville heard from Sharman, who eventually produced a list of the substantial expenses associated with the estate, a total of £1,150 per annum.[32] In addition, there were costs associated with the maintenance and upkeep of the mansion, park, farm houses and other buildings.[33] The high level of expenses and lack of income were the reasons why Sharman was unable to pay bills and wages. When Sharman suffered a fresh attack of his malady in January 1811, it was agreed that he and Bowen should be jointly appointed to run the estate, with Bowen to succeed to sole management in due course.

John Bowen

Sharman died in August 1812 and Bowen became steward. John Bowen was born on 13 August 1782 and died on 18 October 1873. He worked as an engineer at Trinity House, then for the Bridgwater Turnpike Trust and finally as steward and land agent for Lord and Lady Grenville.[34] Records in the Cornwall Record Office and British Library include hundreds (if not thousands) of letters he wrote, maps he prepared, account books and ledgers he maintained, lists of wages he paid to workmen and servants, and records of money he received and expended on behalf of the estate, all meticulously kept.[35] Many of the letters and papers include beautifully crafted sketches of buildings or tiny maps of the areas about which he was writing. He undertook numerous tasks, not only acting as steward, but as assistant commissioner and surveyor during the process of enclosure in the early nineteenth century and as tithe commissioner in the 1830s.

Enclosure

In the eighteenth and early nineteenth centuries, enclosure, creating one large farming area from a number of small landholdings, together with the fencing in of common land, was in progress. The land enclosed was mainly arable and pasture, but could include areas of waste. Thereafter, it became the private property of one owner and ceased to be available for communal use. The advantage was that, by bringing land into more efficient agricultural use, productivity was improved.

From 1750, enclosure by Act of Parliament had become the norm. The process commenced when the lord of the manor introduced a bill into Parliament that requested enclosure. Notice was given to all parties concerned by attaching a notice to the door of the parish church and by placing advertisements in local newspapers. A meeting was called of the land owners and the holders of the common rights, usually the right to graze animals in common pasture, who, if their interests were to be extinguished, could claim compensation in the form of a monetary payment or an allotment of land elsewhere. Once consent had been obtained from all parties, a statement was drawn up giving a description of the land to be enclosed. After the Act had been passed by Parliament, a commissioner was appointed to oversee the enclosure and to take control of the fields while the terms of the Act were implemented.

Commissioners and surveyors were appointed to deal with matters at a local level. Sometimes, as with Boconnoc, the two designations were rolled into one and John Bowen was appointed the sole commissioner for enclosing 2,300 acres of land in the three parishes of Boconnoc, Braddock and St Winnow. Bowen gave notice that he would hold his first sitting, or attendance, at the house of John Vandersluys, called the Western Taphouse, in Braddock, on Tuesday, 13 June 1809. Any person who had or claimed to be entitled to any rights of pasturage or turbary (the right to cut turf and furze for fuel) or any other right was instructed to deliver a schedule in writing to Bowen, setting out their claim and stating the number of cattle (if any) which had a right of pasturage. From 2 June, the right of turbary was suspended until Bowen had made his final award.[36]

Bowen also announced that he intended to perambulate the parishes on Monday 19 June to fix their boundaries. All interested parties were invited to meet at Trecan Gate at 10 a.m. At the perambulation, representatives of a number of the local landowners were present.[37] There were disputes about where the borders ran between the respective parishes and old maps and plans were produced as evidence: 'Mr Job, acting for Sir Harry Trelawny, described a boundary and said that he would bring documents 500 years old to prove his opinion ...'.[38] Bowen had to record who owned what in the pre-enclosure landscape, so that he could devise a formula for re-allocating the land.

A further meeting was held on Monday 17 July and thereafter, Bowen was able to plot the new boundaries, produce the award, set out obligations relating to the new roads, hedges and walls, and describe how any exchange of land would be managed.[39] On 28 August 1809, he gave notice of the lands that were to be enclosed and produced the schedule showing the amount of land to which each proprietor was entitled. If any of the owners to the rights of pasturage preferred to receive compensation in money, rather than incurring the expense of enclosure – the new proprietors being responsible for creating the fencing or hedges – the value of their rights in money would be assessed.[40]

The leaseholders who held tenements with commonable rights came to give their decisions as to whether they wanted compensation in money or an allotment of land. Thomas Bryant Junior of Kilgeare, Thomas A'Lee of Upper Trebarrett, Penesta and Lower Kilgeare, James Roskilly of Hill, Thomas Hawken of Upper Kilgeare and William Phillips of Grimshall, all requested compensation in money.[41] John Penrose requested an allotment of land.

For a nominated period after the new boundaries had been set, gaps were left in the hedges and walls so that livestock, farm machinery and implements could be moved around.[42] All rights of common or commonable rights over the downs and lands to be enclosed were extinguished immediately and Bowen delivered to each claimant of rights of pasturage and turbary a description of their allotment.[43] As from 5 August 1814, any stock found on the downs of the manors of Boconnoc, Braddock and St Winnow, would be impounded.[44] Prosecutions would be brought against any person who allowed stock belonging to them to commit trespass.[45] Thus was the process of enclosure concluded on the Boconnoc estate and Grenville was thereafter able to meld the landscape of the plantations with the newly enclosed 2,000 acres of open downland between Boconnoc and Braddock into one harmonious whole.

Working the estate

John Bowen's tenure as steward

Bowen was extraordinarily busy with minimal assistance and like Thomas Bennett and Watson Sharman before him, his stewardship ended with the estate accounts being in less than pristine order. The financial situation at the outset of Bowen's employment had been far from satisfactory with the expenses for 1808 and 1809 being in total £7,183. These were predicted to increase as much of the property, the buildings, fences and gates, had been neglected for many years and were seriously dilapidated.[46]

In 1813, Grenville spent some months at Boconnoc.[47] He had travelled to Cornwall to remonstrate with John Bowen – who was already beginning to sink under the weight of his administrative duties – about work that Bowen had instructed should be done on the estate, but which had not been authorised by the Grenvilles, cutting down trees of which they were particularly fond and building hedges, walls and buildings that Grenville considered to be eyesores. Grenville spent his time walking about, becoming more and more irritated and frustrated and writing increasingly frantic letters to Lady Grenville about the steward's activities. Grenville berated and scolded Bowen, 'until I put myself in a passion and till he almost cried'.[48] He wrote to Lady Grenville: 'I am sorry to say my walk has increased my vexation, the group we were so fond of under Beech walk is reduced to one naked tree … It grieves me when I think of the pleasure you had in the place to see it is so much injured by the folly and vanities of this blockhead and by my own over confidence in thinking he had judgement and discretion.'[49] Grenville asked for his wife's advice about whether they should consider replacing Bowen as their agent.

Lady Grenville responded to her husband's letters, attempting from a distance to sooth his ruffled feathers.[50] Not only did Grenville criticise Bowen for what had been done on the estate, but he was attempting (mostly unsuccessfully) to get his steward to produce the accounts, months, if not years, in arrears, while Bowen prevaricated and kept promising to produce them 'tomorrow'.[51] Bowen, nervously anticipating that his services were shortly to be dispensed with, wrote a penitent letter to Lady Grenville, begging not to be dismissed, which would 'prove to be his family's utter ruin'. The final decision on his future prospects was suspended until the accounts had been produced. Some eventually appeared at the end of September and seemed to be accurate and correct.[52] By the middle of October, Grenville was still waiting for the detail which would show the exact nature of the enormous amounts that had been expended. Grenville had believed that Bowen's substantial financial outlays would be repaid by increasing the value of the estate overall, but this did not prove to be a correct assessment and Grenville was in no doubt that, in future years, the ordinary expenses would be difficult to reduce.[53]

The Grenvilles eventually decided that Bowen's services and tenure as steward should not be terminated, but the amount of discretion he would be allowed was henceforth strictly defined and he could not take any steps without first obtaining Lord and Lady Grenville's positive approbation.[54]

William Pond

Other employees were not as dilatory as Bowen. From November 1817 to 1829, William Pond, foreman and wood bailiff at Boconnoc, sent a weekly report to Lord Grenville detailing how the workmen were being employed and the costs associated with the work. In June 1819, he reported that the men had been cleaning the road at the front door of Boconnoc House and at the Bath House and Shrubbery. When those tasks had been completed, he had put them to fagoting the wood in the plantations. In other months, they were gathering hawthorn berries, planting laurel cuttings, weeding in the nursery, tying up apple trees, digging and turning the soil, cutting furze and thinning and pruning in the plantations.[55]

John Bowen and the tithe maps

For many centuries, tithes, one tenth of annual produce, payable on the fruits of the earth such as corn, hay or fruit, on animals and animal products such as calves or wool, and on earnings made by fishermen and millers, had been levied as a tax for the support of the established church and clergy. Tithes were a heavy tax, particularly on farming, and by the 1830s there was increasing opposition to their payment, particularly from dissenters and nonconformists. Farmers who had the foresight to improve their land ended up paying more in tithes, contributing to increasing dissatisfaction with the whole system.

In the nineteenth century, the government decided that the question of tithes should be addressed, concerned that a continuation of the system would result in unrest. Accordingly, the Tithe Commutation Act of 1836 was passed, 'an important measure for reform, that commuted arbitrary and uncertain levies of tithes in kind into annual monetary payments regulated on a uniform national basis'.[56] In order to assess what the monetary payments should be, maps were produced for every parish, together with an apportionment. The latter listed every map item by number and each entry included the name of the landowner, occupier and tenant (if any), the area and the name or description of the land or field, its state of cultivation, the rent charge and the tithe owner.

Between 1838 and 1845, Bowen, as the cartographer, prepared tithe maps for six parishes: St Winnow, St Sampsons Golant, St Keyne, Tywardreath, Fowey and Lanteglos-by-Fowey, all of which were signed by him. In addition, although unsigned, Bowen's distinctive style means that further maps can be credited to him: Boconnoc, Bradock, St Veep, St Stephens in Brannel and Lanhydrock. In all the latter parishes, except Lanhydrock, the Grenvilles owned property so that he would have known the terrain well.[57] [Plate 8].

John Bowen and George Matthew Fortescue

Bowen escaped, by the narrowest of margins, from being dismissed by Lord and Lady Grenville. When George and Lady Louisa Fortescue arrived to set up their home at Boconnoc in the early nineteenth century, he was still employed there. George Fortescue thought that Bowen was prepared for *some* change in his circumstances, although having weathered the arrival of the Fortescues, he felt that he was, for a season at least, safe.[58] Bowen was slow and always glad of an excuse to put off any daily task. George Fortescue reported to Lady Grenville: 'He finds, I fear, the minute inspection which I make of every *issue*, not a little tiresome, the more so as I see frequent occasion to find fault, not with his want of honesty, but with his indolence and good nature, both of which have frequently interfered with your interests …'[59]

When the accounts were finally presented to George Fortescue, a close examination showed that there were arrears of around £1,200. Farms and buildings were in a deplorable state. The outlay required for repairs in 1835 was £1,600 and would probably be the same in 1836, labour was not used to its best advantage and wages were too high. Fortescue suggested that Bowen should be asked to repay £700 of the arrears and the remaining £500 should be forgiven him, a solution to which Lady Grenville agreed.[60]

Despite George Fortescue's best efforts to rein in expenditure, the debts continued to rise, partly due to Bowen's persistence in 'robbing Peter to pay Paul'.[61] He collected the rents from the tenants, paid off the most pressing creditors and bills and then, finding himself short of money, borrowed again, so that the downward spiral was continuously perpetuated. Lady Grenville and George Fortescue agreed that the time was now long overdue when Bowen had to be replaced.[62] Lady Grenville believed that the further debts incurred by Bowen were irrecoverable and the only thing to be done was to get rid of him gently, it being 'disagreeable', as she put it, to dismiss him after a service of forty years.[63] She generously decided to entirely write off his further debt to her of £1,206 (although that still left him with a similar amount to find that he owed to others) and to allow him £100 per annum as a pension. Despite Lady Grenville's exhortation to Bowen that he should reveal everything that related to the estate's financial position – whether good or bad – George Fortescue was later to find, to his considerable annoyance, that Bowen had been less than forthcoming and truthful and had concealed large debts. These additional liabilities, together with the sums that had been given to the former steward or that he had not been required to repay, had crippled the estate financially. He was even more annoyed to find that the house at Lostwithiel where Bowen was living was 'well furnished, comfortable and very clean, very different from the state in which he had left the Stewardry'.[64]

William Pease

After Bowen's departure, the thoughts of Lady Grenville and George Fortescue turned to finding his successor. William Pease had been an employee of Joseph Thomas Austen, who, in 1808, when he inherited the 'Big House' at Place above Fowey, changed his name

Figure 9 William Pease. (© Hampshire Record Office)

by deed poll to Treffry.[65] Treffry was an industrialist, engineer, mining adventurer and land-owner. In 1831, he sent Pease as an apprentice to learn a trade with Harvey & Co. at Hayle, an engineer-ing company which had a world-class reputation. Pease was later appointed to oversee the trade at Par, where Treffry had built a harbour which enabled his tin ore to be transported out of Cornwall.[66]

After Treffry died on 29 January 1850, Pease was seeking a new situation and after some dis-cussion with George Fortescue, he was offered the position as steward and land agent at Boconnoc. The advent of William Pease marked a significant turning point in the fortunes of the estate, which was now run with great efficiency by an energetic stew-ard. This was in contrast to George Fortescue's endeavours being continually defeated by 'poor Mr Bowen's kind of passive resistance and the sort of cloud he continued to throw around the accounts'.[67]

William Pease's diaries, covering the years from 1832 (when he was working for Treffry) to within a month of his death on 14 September 1881, are a treasure trove of informa-tion about the running of Boconnoc, containing details of tenants' disputes, holding courts, collecting rents, examining property, authorising repairs, drafting leases and much more. He was continually travelling around Cornwall, to the north coast, 'down west' and nearer to home at St Stephens and West Taphouse, either on horseback or in a carriage or dog-cart, in fact, anywhere where Lady Grenville and George Fortescue held land or property. Fortuitously, the early diaries of Harriet Phillimore (née Fortescue) cover the same period and so it is possible to cross-reference details of the professional and social aspects of life at Boconnoc.[68] To the Fortescues, Pease became more than an employee. He never overstepped the mark, nor took advantage of his position as confidante to George Fortescue, Lady Louisa and their eight children. He was almost (but not quite) accepted as an equal.

William Pease established a network of what might be called sub-agents who were employed across the county to oversee the interests of Boconnoc. Each man was appointed to be responsible for a particular area and reported to Pease, who in turn reported to George Fortescue or whichever of his sons was the current owner of Boconnoc. For example, Simeon Truscott who lived at Brannel Grampound Road, reported on 19 March 1877 about the Yellands who owed money to the estate:

> I regret to state that H Yelland or his wife (who is no better than she ought to be & rules the old man as she likes) allowed Wm Brokenshire to take one of the Cows on Friday afternoon for rent of the house they occupy and goods had from his shop … The only thing they have on the premises (besides their furniture which is very little) is a Cart worth about £2 …[69]

Pease attended divine service every Sunday wherever he happened to be. Despite being a strong adherent of the Church of England, he nevertheless took part in some strange activities, notably table turning at Boconnoc and séances in London. The movement of modern spiritualism was initiated in America and reached Europe in 1852–53. It was a popular method of consulting spirits where participants sat around a table on which they rested their hands and waited for the table to move and it became a fashionable diversion all over the country, including at Boconnoc.

In 1853, 'Caroline [Mrs Pease] and I took tea and spent the evening at Mr Fortescue's – Lady Louisa Miss F[ortescue] Miss Wallis Miss Bessy and I tried some table moving and succeeded very nicely – the Table Moved after sitting about 20 Minutes.'[70] Harriet's diary for the same date reads: 'Mama Miss W[allis] A[nnie] B[essy] & Mr Pease tried table moving with great success Table moving round ab^t the room so fast as to make them run – no pain felt only Miss W a little giddy. They sat for 10 minutes before it began swaying.'[71]

Pease was married to Caroline (née Cossentine). They had two children, William Junior and Ann. Pease became so busy that his son was employed to assist his father and after the latter died in 1881, he took over as steward in his turn. Thereafter, William Pease Junior ran the estate with assistance from various under-stewards, William Dunbar, Thomas Oates, A.E.S. Scantelbery and Fitzroy Somerset, among others. There are thousands of documents in the Cornwall Record Office which are invaluable in detailing how the estate was run from 1882 to 1930: letter books containing outgoing correspondence, mining sett and china-clay leases, papers relating to quarrying concerns, agreements relating to railway lines, leases of land, letting agreements and information about land management, property and plans of new buildings. Incoming correspondence includes advertisements for farm machinery, requests for donations and subscriptions, applications for jobs, requests for tenancies of houses and land, and letters about disputes between tenants on the estate.[72]

Profit and loss

There are numerous account books, ledgers and wages books in the Cornwall Record Office relating to the financial position of the estate. It would need the expertise of a forensic accountant to unravel all the information, to say nothing of the many months that it would take to examine so many documents. It is therefore difficult to assess how much financial profit (if any) the owners of Boconnoc enjoyed from the estate as the evidence is largely anecdotal. It was heavily mortgaged during the era of the Mohuns. Thomas 'Diamond' Pitt (I) was constantly complaining that Boconnoc was not producing any income for him and would prove to be his ruin. Grenville was concerned about the amount of money that was being spent, to the extent of telling the gardener to only do what planting was absolutely necessary and was considering selling off the deer in the park. The gross product of the Cornish estates between 1770 and 1785 was in total £33,655, in 1803, £3,150, in 1804, £2,925 and in 1805, £2,965. In 1815, Grenville asked Bowen what cash he could raise as he was short of money.[73] The following year he said that in view of the disappointing receipts, he had had to take out a mortgage of £15,000.[74] Although income from the estate was low, between 1811 and 1820 at about £1,500 per annum, in the years to 1834 it increased and fluctuated between £4,000 and £6,000 per annum and Boconnoc began to account for an increasing proportion of Grenville's income.[75]

When George Fortescue was resident at Boconnoc forty years later, he wrote to Lady Grenville, saying that he had been living at a rate of £600 a year beyond his income. Due to Pease's exertions, there had been a considerable improvement in the affairs at Boconnoc and he asked Lady Grenville to allow him an increase in income from the estate.[76] Two years later, he was writing to Lady Grenville again saying that at the beginning of the year, his funds were very low and he was renewing his application for her assistance. On both occasions, Lady Grenville agreed to come to his aid.[77]

George Fortescue and his son Bevill received substantial amounts from their interests in tin mining and china clay extraction. Despite this, they were frequently 'land rich but cash poor'. In addition, the house at Dropmore, which needed substantial and essential renovation, was a continuing and heavy drain on financial resources. After George Fortescue died in 1877, there were lengthy discussions within the family circle about whether Dropmore should be sold. Although it was eventually decided that the house should be kept, land in outlying areas of the estate was offered for sale.

There are some figures for the year to the end of June 1885, when Cyril Fortescue was the owner of the estate and which had proved to be a satisfactory year. The total receipts were £27,296.19s.3d, about the same as in the previous year. Rents had amounted to £14,383.2s.4d, an increase on the previous year of £612.13s.7d, notwithstanding the allowances that had been made to those tenants who had been struggling to pay their rents in north Cornwall and in St Stephens. Income from mineral dues had gone down from £9,931.1s.10d to £8,621.9s.7d, a decrease of £1,309.12s.3d. The £8,621.9s.7d included a payment of £6,832.5s.10d from the West of England Clay Company. Expenditure for the year was £28,456.14s.0d, a decrease of £411.6s.5d. Remittances and annuities for the year had amounted to £15,634.1s.3d, which included £9,000 remitted to Cyril. The balance in hand at the beginning of the year was £2,471.1s.0d and at the end of the year, £315.6s.3d.[78]

By the time Bevill Fortescue was owner of Boconnoc in the late nineteenth and early twentieth centuries, he was offering farms and land for sale, particularly after the First World War. In 1919, Helland Farm, near Delabole in north Cornwall was sold to the tenant. Later in the same year, farms were being offered for sale by auction and in the 1920s Bevill Fortescue indicated that he must sell as much of his landed property as possible.[79] After the Second World War, the house and estate became progressively less prosperous financially, until responsibility for Boconnoc was taken over by Anthony and Elizabeth Fortescue in the 1990s and its fortunes began to slowly improve.

THE SERVANTS AND THE ESTATE WORKERS IN THE NINETEENTH CENTURY

Much of the information about the servants and estate workers, particularly in the nineteenth century, comes from the letters of the stewards, from Lady Louisa's letters and from the diaries of William Pease and Harriet Phillimore (née Fortescue). Keeping servants proved difficult, either because they disliked the remoteness of Boconnoc and the lack of social interaction and activities in which they could take part or because they proved unable to carry out their duties to the satisfaction of the Fortescues. Lady Louisa spent a considerable amount of time seeking replacements for the staff who left. The following are some examples.

The butler and cook
In March 1836, it was found that the butler was a habitual drunkard. One evening, being tipsy, his behaviour was such that George Fortescue sent him out of the room during dinner and he was discharged the next morning.[80]

A cook called Gover was employed in 1841. She looked clean and healthy and had a quiet, sensible and respectable manner. Once she took up her duties, it was found that she was 'a failure with puddings and bread' and being aged only 21 and not 25 as they had believed, she was unable to exercise any authority over the staff in the kitchen. When it was discovered that the bill of fare for the day was being prepared by the kitchen maid and not by the cook, Gover and the Fortescues soon parted company.[81]

The governess
The Fortescue daughters were educated at home by a governess. She also taught the boys until they went away to school. One, a Miss Newton, was with them for three years, but

as Annie, the eldest daughter, became a teenager, the governess believed that 'Annie's influence militated against hers with the younger ones' and that, combined with the 'lack of society' made her decide to seek employment elsewhere.[82]

Jane Clarke, known as 'Clarkie'

One servant who was particularly close to and valued by the family was Jane Clarke, known as 'Clarkie', who was nursery maid to all the Fortescue children.[83] She attended Lady Louisa when her youngest son Bevill was born on 1 November 1850 and Harriet Phillimore (née Fortescue) when her eldest son Richard was born in 1864. She frequently accompanied Lady Louisa and some or all of her charges on outings: on one occasion in 1846 with the four girls to see the queen who was on a visit to Fowey, and on another to Lanhydrock with the four youngest children.[84]

She lived initially at Buckshead on the Boconnoc estate, but after retiring she moved to Lostwithiel, where members of the Fortescue family frequently visited her, often taking small gifts, such as a shawl or a pair of slippers. Once Harriet had her own children, Clarkie gave her small sums of money and toys for them. She died on Thursday, 16 May 1889, aged 81, and was buried at Lostwithiel on 22 May.[85]

Figure 10 Jane Clarke. (© Hampshire Record Office)

CHARITY

The stewards, John and Thomas Bennett, were regularly ordered by Lord and Lady Camelford to distribute assistance to their tenants and workers on the estate, although, in 1763, John Bennett wrote to Lord Camelford that 'there are few very poor in Boconnoc and the Winter has been remarkably mild and ffine'.[86]

In contrast, in the 1780s and 1790s, the poor were suffering from the severe weather and Camelford told Benjamin Forster, the rector, to apply to the steward for assistance for whatever was necessary for their relief.[87] On another occasion, Lady Camelford provided blankets, warm clothing, corn and barrels of salt pork to the labourers on the estate during a time when there was a scarcity of food, while the 'Garden Stuff' was also liberally distributed among them.[88] When there was a lack of corn in 1796, it was only distributed to labourers on the estate[89] and additional wheat and barley was bought and divided into portions appropriate to the number of people contained in each family.[90]

Weaving was undertaken by workers at a manufactory at Brookes's on the estate and was subsequently made into cloth for 'comfortable inner garments for the poor'.[91] Bennett wrote to Lady Camelford that:

> The poor are, as they ought to be, very grateful for the favors conferred upon them and God knows! it never could come in a better time as the distress of the lower classes of the people never, in this County I believe, were so great as at this time; and was it not for the very liberal subscriptions of the Nobility & Gentry they must inevitably have starved.[92]

On special occasions, for example at Christmas, gifts of meat were distributed to the workers: at Christmas 1807, two bullocks were divided up between tenants on the estate.[93]

The Fortescues and Lady Grenville were generous to both their current and former servants. At Christmas 1855, £1 was given to Betty Richards, who was 'well and cheerful, sitting by the fire in the warm woollen gown you [Lady Grenville] gave her last Christmas. She is within 3 months of 90'.[94]

Three years later, at Christmas 1858, Lady Louisa distributed presents and gowns to five under-maids and three other servants, gave 'a shawl to little Jane, a piece of lace to Clarkie (who was enraptured with it) and a flannel petticoat to Cath Mattie'.[95]

Another pensioner, Martha Willcocks, one of the few remaining who remembered Lady Grenville from her childhood at Boconnoc, was visited every day by a member of the Fortescue family and they always took her 'some little comfort from our own table' and on one occasion, a gift of five shillings from Lady Grenville.[96]

St Faith's House of Mercy, Lostwithiel, Cornwall

One charity with which Lady Louisa was involved was the home called St Faith's House of Mercy, established in 1861 for 'fallen girls', some of whom were rescued from Bodmin Gaol. Construction of the house started in 1862 and a chapel, added in 1876, was dedicated to the memory of the Reverend Arthur Tatham, one of the founders of the house and long-time rector of Boconnoc. It was run by a Church of England order of nuns from St Mary's, Wantage and the girls worked in the laundry and received instruction in needlework.

The 1881 census shows that the head of the house was Sister Anna Jones from Witney, in Oxfordshire. She was assisted by five other Sisters of Mercy and there were twenty-five inmates. Sister Anna was often at Boconnoc and Lady Louisa gave financial assistance towards the running of the house and visited it on a number of occasions.[97]

Charities

The owners of Boconnoc supported a large number of charities. Between 1811 and 1866, these included the Cornwall Sailors' Home, the Bodmin Lunatic Asylum, the Clergymen's Fund, the Bodmin Dispensary, the Cornwall Female Refuge, the Truro Mining School, the Boconnoc Horticultural Show, the Fowey Lifeboat and thirteen local schools.[98] The amounts donated were modest, the lowest being £1 and the highest £12.

Pensioners

A number of elderly former workers were granted pensions and on occasion, allowances of money were made to the very poor. In 1811, John Bowen sent a list to Lady Grenville showing the amount of money that was being expended on a weekly basis for three women. Catherine Prior received 4s.6d, Elizabeth Ratty 3s.9d and Jane Wilcock 3s.4d – a total of £29.5s.0d per annum.

Two men, both unemployed, were recommended by Bowen to receive Lady Grenville's bounty because of their age or infirmities: one was William Broad, who had worked in the gardens for many years and lived in one of the cottages on the lawn. His wife was very ill and was never again likely to be able to earn her own living. The other was William Hitchin, who had been employed in thatching and in general business about Boconnoc. He was more than 70 years of age and was the sexton of the parish, for which he earned 10s.6d per year. Given his age, he was unlikely to be able to continue to fill that position for much longer. In addition, Mary Rowe, who had been carrying letters and parcels to Boconnoc for many years, had received from Mrs Rhind (the housekeeper), five shillings in this year and would be very grateful to receive any permanent addition to that amount. She was of such an age that she was incapable of labour.

An order was given by Lord Grenville that payments to those already in receipt of pensions should be continued and Bowen was asked to suggest what amounts should be allowed to Broad, Hitchin and Mary Rowe.[99]

Scandal and tragedy

During the 1850s, the steward William Pease employed a young man called John Chegwidden as a general clerk. Chegwidden lived at Polpiece, was unmarried and was aged 23 in 1851.[100]

At the same time, the Pond family was living at Couch's Mill Lodge: William Pond, wood bailiff, his wife, Mary, their daughter Leonora, aged 14, and three further children. Their son, Francis, was not living at home.[101] In January 1855, George Fortescue told Pease that he had received a report that Leonora Pond was 'with child' by 'Mr J W C' – John Chegwidden. He was 27 and she was 18. Once this had been confirmed, Pease informed Chegwidden that he would have to leave George Fortescue's employment. Leonora's father, William, and Chegwidden met before the latter quitted Boconnoc and came to an agreement that Chegwidden would make one payment of £25 and thereafter be clear of all future liability for Leonora and the child.

When Leonora Pond's father died in December 1856, no will was found, nor was there any sign of the £400 or £500 that he been bequeathed to him by a colleague. The £25 received from John Chegwidden had similarly disappeared.[102] Despite these serious financial discrepancies, it was anticipated that when all Pond's property had been sold and his estate wound up, the children would inherit about £20 each. Two years later, it was discovered that the Pond girls would not have a farthing since the 'rascal' Francis, their brother, had run into debt beyond any means he had of paying, had got hold of the whole of their father's money and had spent it.[103] The Fortescues rallied round and Lady Louisa found places for the three girls, including Leonora.[104]

Insanity

There are several instances of servants or workmen being adjudged insane. The wife of John Talling, a labourer who had been employed on the estate since 1807, had been placed in the lunatic asylum in Exeter. Returning to Boconnoc, Mary Talling was in no better state of mind. As the couple lived in the Dairy House, which was very close to the mansion, Bowen requested instructions from Lord Grenville about whether, when the Grenvilles visited, the Tallings should be moved out.[105] The situation was resolved without any intervention from Grenville for in 1815 'the poor woman Mary Talling who lives in the Dairy House and has been deranged about two years past … died this morning'.[106]

A workman on the estate called Robert Libby who was 'out of his mind' remained at home with two men to control him. At times, he was rational, but at others, he wanted to murder his children. It was anticipated that he would be removed to the asylum at Bodmin.[107]

The workmen

There is not space within the confines of this book to write in detail about the workmen on the estate, save to say that there were a large number of employees, encompassing carpenters, gardeners, coachmen, grooms, woodmen, millers, blacksmiths and gamekeepers.

Figure 11 Near the sawmill, Boconnoc estate, *c.* 1870s. (© Hampshire Record Office)

From time to time, the working men requested an increase in wages or, alternatively, a decrease in the number of hours they worked.[108] Whether these requests were granted or not was dependent on the health of the estate's finances at the date the requests were made.[109]

The mills

There are references, some dating from the sixteenth century, that make mention of mills on the estate. In September 1561, at a survey-court to allocate land, John Robyns the elder took from Francis, Earl of Bedford, one tenement of two mills and one fulling mill in Grymshall (Grims Hall). Fulling was a process in woollen cloth-making which involved cleansing the cloth of impurities, particularly oil and dirt.[110]

At a court held at Boconnoc in November in the forty-second year of Elizabeth I (17 November 1599–16 November 1600), the homage and the bailiff presented that Thomas Peren, the tenant of a mill called 'a soken Myll' had died and the lord was entitled to a heriot of a cow valued at 46*s*.8*d*. Thomas's widow, Alice, was the next tenant for the duration of her widowhood. In the medieval period, milling was controlled by the customary law of Mill Soke. The mill was built at the cost of the lord of the manor in return for which his tenants were obliged to bring their own corn to be ground by the lord's miller, who received a percentage of the flour ground in payment, his 'toll', usually about a sixteenth.[111]

Grist mills at Trewynnard, which ground grain into flour, were let by Warwick, Lord Mohun to Sampson Heyne for four years from 30 September 1644 at a rent of £16 per annum.

In 1765, the Boconnoc Mills were destroyed and the manor mill was moved to Couch's Mill, a small hamlet on the estate. The Couch family were the millers there from at least the eighteenth century and for many generations. In 2013, the BBC genealogical programme *Who Do You Think You Are?* featured the actor Nigel Havers. The son of Sir Michael Havers, distinguished QC, MP and sometime Lord Chancellor, Nigel Havers is well known for playing upper-class characters such as Lord Andrew Lindsay in the film *Chariots of Fire*. His ancestral roots, however, turned out to be somewhat humbler than might have been expected. Research revealed that, on his mother's side, he was descended from the Cornish millers, the Couchs, and his great-great-grandfather, David Couch, had fathered an illegitimate child. 'Not too far back in my family,' said Nigel, 'there were totally normal working-class people … there is a drop of blood in my veins that belongs to those people back then.'[112]

An application was received in 1828 from a Mr Giles Freethy for the grant of a part of Colvethick Wood for a sawing mill, while in 1851, a saw mill, established by George Fortescue, promised to 'answer well'.[113]

Much more recently, Anthony Fortescue restored the old nineteenth-century water-powered saw mill, which cut much of the timber used in the restoration of Boconnoc House in the early twenty-first century.

Events on the estate
In the nineteenth century, many events were held on the estate, including the annual Boconnoc Cottage Garden Society meeting, when monetary prizes were given for the best displays of vegetables. Other events included Teetotal Festivals, Primrose League fêtes, garden parties, teas for the tenants, workmen and their families, and concerts.[114]

Cricket
The Boconnoc Cricket Club was established in 1846. The members played (and still play) in the deer park, which lays claim to being the longest continuous use of any cricket ground in Cornwall. A match in August 1855, when 'the young ones' were fully involved with the preparations, was followed by a dinner for 200 and afterwards dancing from 6 p.m. to 10 p.m.[115]

Festivities on royal occasions
The anniversary of George III's birthday, 4 June, was celebrated in 1789 'with great Festivity at Boconnoc House, the seat of Lord Camelford'. A dinner was held for his tenants and after the meal there were rural games, foot-races, wrestling and dancing. At 10 p.m., the house was illuminated and neighbouring gentry were invited to partake of a cold collation, followed by fireworks on the lawn in front of the house. The food that

remained was distributed to the labourers, together with a small donation in money to every poor family in the parishes of Boconnoc and Bradoc.[116]

To celebrate the marriage of the Prince of Wales (later Edward VII) and Princess Alexandra of Denmark on 10 March 1863, bonfires were lit in the county and from near each, three skyrockets were sent up as the clock struck 10 p.m., including from close to the bonfire on the Boconnoc estate at Druid's Hill.[117]

In June 1887, the Queen's Jubilee was marked by Colonel Fortescue and Lady Louisa entertaining the workmen and their families to a luncheon and a tea on the cricket ground, followed by sports.[118]

On Thursday, 19 March 1981, the wedding day of Charles, Prince of Wales and Lady Diana Spencer, Captain Desmond Fortescue arranged for a short service of thanksgiving to be held at 3 p.m. in the church, followed by a parish tea and sports.[119]

NOTES AND REFERENCES

1. Dennis Stuart, *Manorial Records*, Chichester, 2010; www.lancaster.ac.uk/fass/projects/manorialrecords/manors
2. Stuart, *ibid.*, p. 59; paleo.anglo-norman.org/account2.html
3. Cornwall Record Office (CRO): F/3/3, 29 September 1431 to 30 September 1432.
4. It may be that part of these accounts are missing as they include no information, as would be expected, about the animals to be found on the manor.
5. Stuart, *op. cit.*, p. 2.
6. CRO: F/4/1.
7. CRO: F/4/1: Law-Day court held there [Bodconneck] on Friday next before the feast of St Dennis in the 36th year of the reign of king Henry VIth, Friday, 7 October 1457.
8. CRO: F/4/1: Court held on Wednesday the feast of St Peter in the Cathedral, Wednesday, 22 February 1458; heriot – the lord had the right, on the death of a tenant, to seize the tenant's best beast – often a cow or horse or alternatively, chattels. Sometimes payment would be taken in money.
9. Court held on Monday, 10 April 1458.
10. Court held on Tuesday, 16 May 1458.
11. Court held on 17 April 18 Edward IV.
12. Devon Record Office (DRO), W1258M/E17; CRO: F/1/463; Law-Day Court (View of Frankpledge) held there 28 October in the 36th year [1594] of the reign of our lady Elizabeth now Queen of England, 17 November 1593 to 16 November 1594.
13. The National Archives (TNA): SC6/HENVIII/6159-6167.
14. TNA: PROB11/70, will made on 30 December 29 Elizabeth, 17 November 1586–16 November 1587, probate 26 May 1587.
15. While absentee landlords and owners are potentially bad for their estates, they are good for the historian. If the owner lived on the estate full time, there would be no need for letters or documents to go between him or her and the steward or agent. Any discussion of business matters would have taken place face-to-face and instructions given orally and not necessarily recorded fully in writing.
16. TNA: C108/424/no 9, letter 607, Pall Mall, 13 December 1722, Thomas Pitt to John Phillips; TNA: C108/424/ #15, 28 June 1722.
17. TNA: C108/424 #14, 13 February 1721; C108/424/No. 9. 531, 16 January 1721/22; C108/424, #15; C108/424, #17, 22 October 1723.

18. CRO: F/4/76, 16 November 1796.
19. CRO: F/1/223; St Nyott, 21 December 1747, John Bennett to Thomas Pitt II; F/1/223, Lostwithiel, 21 December 1754 and 30 December 1754.
20. British Library (BL); Add MS 69320, Lostwithiel, 30 July 1762, Bennett to Pitt, f. 31.
21. BL: Add MS 69321, Lostwithiel, 25 September 1764, Bennett to Pitt, f. 25.
22. BL: Add MS 69322, Lostwithiel, 27 November 1764, Bennett to Pitt, f. 34.
23. BL: Add MS 69322, Lostwithiel, 18 March 1765, Bennett to Pitt, ff. 11–12.
24. BL: Add MS 59489, Collon, 12 March 1782, Thomas Bennett to Pitt, f. 10.
25. BL: Add MS 59489, Collon, 10 May 1786, Bennett to Lord Camelford, f. 86.
26. BL: Add MS 69176, Lostwithiel, 4 October 1805, ff. 21–22 and 4 November 1805, Bennett to Lord Grenville, ff. 32–33.
27. BL: Add MS 69176, Downing Street, 2 June 1806, Grenville to Bennett, ff. 61–62.
28. BL: Add MS 69176, agreement between Grenville and Bennett, 22 August 1806, ff. 80–81.
29. BL: Add MS 69177, Boconnoc, 3 June 1809, Elizabeth Sharman to Lord Grenville, ff. 92–93.
30. BL: Add MS 71594, Boconnoc, 29 January 1810, John Bowen to Lord Grenville at Camelford House, f. 11.
31. BL: Add MS 71594, Boconnoc, 5 February 1810, f. 13; 21 February 1810, Bowen to Grenville, ff. 23–24.
32. BL: Add MS 71594, Dropmore, 21 August 1810, Lord Grenville to Sharman, f. 39.
33. BL: Add MS 71594, Boconnoc, 13 August 1810, Sharman to Lord Grenville, f. 40.
34. Dictionary of Land Surveyors and Local Mapmakers of Great Britain and Ireland, 1530–1850, British Library, 1997.
35. BL: Add MSS 59440-59443, 1810–1818; Add MS 69178, 1824–1829.
36. CRO: F/1/240, draft award, Boconnoc Enclosure, 1815; F/1/223.
37. CRO: F/1/233, f. 5.
38. CRO: F/1/233, f. 3.
39. Steven Hollowell, *Enclosure Records for Historians*, Chichester, 2000, p. 100.
40. CRO: F/1/233, Bodmin, 30 January 1810, f. 13.
41. CRO: F/1/233, 16 February 1810, ff. 13–15.
42. Hollowell, *op. cit.*, p. 70.
43. CRO: F/1/233, f. 29.
44. CRO: F/1/233, f. 33.
45. CRO: F/1/233, f. 34; Historians are divided about whether enclosure created a landless working class that contributed to the Industrial Revolution by providing the labour required in the new industries in the north of England.
46. BL: Add MS 59440, Boconnoc, 4 and 5 March 1810, Bowen to Grenville, ff. 1–4.
47. BL: Add MS 59440, 28 July 1813, f. 41; 23 August 1813, f. 59.
48. BL: Add MS 58873, 6 September 1813, Lord Grenville to Lady Grenville, f. 30.
49. BL: Add MS 58873, 7 September 1813, Lord Grenville to Lady Grenville, ff. 36–37.
50. BL: Add MS 58873, Malvern, 10 September 1813, Lady Grenville to Lord Grenville, f. 69.
51. BL: Add MS 58873, Boconnoc, 8 September 1813, Lord Grenville to Lady Grenville, ff. 50–55.
52. BL: Add MS 58873, Boconnoc, 27 September 1813, Lord Grenville to Lady Grenville, ff. 159–164.
53. BL: Add MS 58873, Boconnoc, 10 October 1813, Lord Grenville to Lady Grenville, ff. 212–215.
54. BL: Add MS 58873, Malvern, 10 September 1813, Lady Grenville to Lord Grenville, f. 69.
55. BL: Add MS 69179, Accompt of Mens labour, Boconnoc, *passim*.
56. Roger J.P. Kain and Hugh C. Prince, *Tithe Surveys for Historians*, Chichester, 2000, p. ix.
57. CRO: Tithe maps, TM/253/1; TM/204; TM/101; TM/242; TM/66; TM/116; TM/12; FTM/17 or FS/3/924; TM/243; TM/212; TM/109.
58. BL: Add MS 69052, 14 December 1838, GM Fortescue to Lady Grenville, f. 27.

59. CRO: F/4/117/9, Boconnoc, 20 August 1834, GM Fortescue to Lady Grenville.

60. CRO: F/4/117/9, Boconnoc 26 August 1834 and 24 September 1834; Boconnoc, 22 November 1836, GM Fortescue to Lady Grenville.

61. BL: Add MS 69053, Boconnoc, 12 June 1849, GM Fortescue to Lady Grenville, ff. 27–28.

62. BL: Add MS 69053, Dropmore, 25 February 1850, Lady Grenville to GM Fortescue.

63. BL: Add MS 69053, South Street, 2 March 1850, f. 63; 4 March 1850, f. 64–65; 7 March 1850, ff. 66–67, Lady Grenville to GM Fortescue.

64. BL: Add MS 69053, South Street, London, 4 March 1850, Lady Grenville to GM Fortescue; BL: Add MS 69053, Boconnoc, 7 July 1850, GM Fortescue to Lady Grenville, ff. 130–131; Boconnoc, 13 August 1850, GM Fortescue to Lady Grenville, ff. 138–139.

65. CRO: FS3/1120, biography of William Pease by CR Clinker.

66. John Keast, *The King of Mid-Cornwall. The Life of Joseph Thomas Treffry, 1782–1805*, Redruth, 1982, p. 70.

67. BL: Add MS 69054, 16 March 1850, Lady Louisa to Lady Grenville, ff. 158–159.

68. CRO: X715/1-43, Pease's diaries and HRO: 115M88/F21/1-57, Harriet's diaries.

69. CRO: F/3/10/147.

70. CRO: X715/15, Pease's diary, 23 May 1853.

71. Hampshire Record Office (HRO): 115M88/F21/4, Harriet's diary, 23 May 1853.

72. See CRO catalogue: F1–F4.

73. BL: Add MS 59422, Dropmore, 23 December 1815, Lord Grenville to Bowen, f. 123.

74. BL: Add MS 59443, 2 May 1817, Lord Grenville to John Bowen, f. 119.

75. Peter Jupp, *Lord Grenville, 1759–1834*, Oxford, 1985, p. 461.

76. BL: Add MS 69055, Boconnoc, 9 June 1853, GM Fortescue to Lady Grenville, ff. 55–58.

77. BL: Add MS 69057, South Street, 25 July 1855, Lady Grenville to GM Fortescue, ff. 129–134.

78. CRO: F/3/10/513, 15 July 1885, William Pease to Cyril Fortescue.

79. CRO: F/3/10/26, FJH Somerset to J Wilson, February 1919; F/3/10/27, FJH Somerset to J Wilson, 20 April 1920.

80. CRO: F/4/117/9, Boconnoc, 18 March 1836, G M Fortescue to Lady Grenville, f. 39.

81. BL: Add MS 69052, Boconnoc, 29 January ?1838–1841, GM Fortescue to Lady Grenville, f. 41.

82. BL: Add MS 69363, Boconnoc, 22 May 1847, Lady Louisa to GM Fortescue, ff. 129–132.

83. In the 1841 census, she is enumerated as Jane Clarke, 33, Female Servant, Census, 1841, HO107/153.

84. BL: Add MS 69363, Boconnoc, 9 September 1846, ff. 36–39; Thursday, 10 September 1846, Lady Louisa to GM Fortescue, ff. 40–43.

85. HRO: 115M88/F21/39, 1889, Harriet's diary.

86. BL: Add MS 69320, 26 February 1763, John Bennett to Lord Camelford, f. 44.

87. BL: Add MS 59488, 11 February 1784, Thomas Pitt to Benjamin Forster, f. 85.

88. BL: Add MS 69303, 4 January 1795; CRO: F/4/76, 3 August 1795, Boconnoc House, William Beard to Lady Camelford.

89. CRO: F/4/76, 7 September 1795, Thomas Bennett to Lady Camelford.

90. CRO: F/4/76, Lostwithiel, 19 February 1796, Thomas Bennett to Lady Camelford.

91. CRO: F/4/76, Lostwithiel, 8 February 1800, A Collier Bennett to Lady Camelford, f. 41.

92. CRO: F/4/76, Lostwithiel, 18 May 1800, A Collier Bennett to Lady Camelford, f. 42.

93. BL: Add MS 69177, Boconnoc House, 19 December 1807, Walter Sharman to Lord Grenville, ff. 36–37.

94. BL: Add MS 69057, 17 December 1855, GM Fortescue to Lady Grenville, f. 199.

95. BL: Add MS 69363, Boconnoc, Tuesday 5 December 1858, Lady Louisa to GM Fortescue, ff. 178–181.

96. BL: Add MS 69061, Boconnoc, 18 January 1861, GM Fortescue to Lady Grenville, ff. 162–163; Boconnoc, 21 January 1861, GM Fortescue to Lady Grenville, ff. 166–167.

97. HRO: 115M88/F21/37 and 38, 1887 and 1888, Harriet's diaries: 'Monday 6th February 1888, Drove with Mama to St Faith's Mercy House.'

98. BL: Add MS 71594, Lostwithiel, 19 April 1811, John Bowen to Lady Grenville; CRO: F/1/242.

99. BL: Add MS 71594, Lostwithiel, 19 April 1811, John Bowen to Lady Grenville, f. 96; Dropmore, 17 June 1811, Lord Grenville to Bowen, f. 117.

100. 1851 census, HO/107/1903.

101. 1851 census, HO/107/1903.

102. BL: Add MS 69058, 5 December 1856, GM Fortescue to Lady Grenville.

103. BL: Add MS 69059, Boconnoc, 13 January 1858, GM Fortescue to Lady Grenville, ff. 114–116.

104. BL: Add MS 69059, Boconnoc, 9 January 1858, GM Fortescue to Lady Grenville, ff. 109–111.

105. BL: Add MS 59441, 11 June 1814, John Bowen to Lord Grenville, f. 43.

106. BL: Add MS 59442, 3 March 1815, John Bowen to Lord Grenville, f. 36.

107. BL: Add MS 69363, 23 May 1847, GM Fortescue to Lady Grenville, ff. 133–136; 26 May 1847, GM Fortescue to Lady Grenville, ff. 147–150.

108. CRO: F/3/12/8, 11 October 1891.

109. CRO: F/3/10/456, Lostwithiel, 24 April 1900, William Pease to Bevill Fortescue.

110. Devon Record Office (DRO): W1255M/E17 and E19; Images of England Number 60502.

111. CRO: F/1/463; information from Mildred Cookson, Trustee of the Mills Archive in Reading, Berkshire and traditional water miller of thirty years.

112. bbc.co.uk; *The Daily Mirror*, 30 July 2013, article by Nicola Methven. The author of this book took part in the programme which was transmitted in July 2013. It was a most interesting and entertaining experience, during which much was learned about how television programmes are made.

113. CRO: F/4/72/20; BL: Add MS 69178, Boconnoc, 28 January 1828. Application for a grant of Colvethick Wood, ff. 46–49; BL: Add MS 69054, Boconnoc, 9 November 1851, GM Fortescue to Lady Grenville, ff. 46–47.

114. BL: Add MS 69057, Boconnoc, 27 July 1855, GM Fortescue to Lady Grenville, ff. 135–136; *Royal Cornwall Gazette*, 14 August 1857; CRO: F/1/287; CRO: F/1/487–490; CRO: F/3/10/225, 28 July 1892; CRO: F/3/10/9, Lostwithiel, 14 July 1893, William Pease to Bevill Fortescue; CRO: F/3/10/26, 28 February 1917.

115. CRO: F/4/78/2, Rules of the Boconnoc Cricket Club; website of the Boconnoc Cricket Club; BL: Add MS 69057, Boconnoc, 25 August 1855, GM Fortescue to Lady Grenville, ff. 139–140.

116. BL: Add MS 69303, Boconnoc Parsonage, 7 June 1789, Benjamin Forster to Lord Camelford in France, ff. 101–102. King George III was born on Wednesday 4 June 1738.

117. CRO: F/3/10/95, Lostwithiel, 5 March 1863, George Richardson to William Pease.

118. *Royal Cornwall Gazette*, Friday, 3 June 1887.

119. CRO: P12/7/1.

⁀ᴀᴧᴧᴧᴧᴧᴧᴧ⁀

THE HOUSE, GROUNDS AND GARDENS IN THE LANDSCAPE:

THE FOURTEENTH TO THE TWENTY-FIRST CENTURY

'Boconnoc, Cornwall is a great scale of a place with fine bold varieties
of ground – deep vallies – sweeping woods and bright gushing streams.'
(Sneyd Manuscript, S[RS/HWV] 58, University of Keele, 18 November 1835,
Ralph Sneyd to H.W. Vincent)

THE HOUSE

The medieval and early modern house

The manor house was the centre of administration for an estate and manifested the status of
the owner, financially and as the lord of the manor. The first documentary evidence referring to the house at Boconnoc is in the Calendar of Patent Rolls, dated 21 May 1393:

> Licence, for 20s, paid by William Carmynowe to the king, for him to enclose a way
> in Boconek, 400 perches long and 27 feet wide, adjoining his house, leading from
> Lostwythyell to Leskerid, on condition that in lieu of it he causes another of the same
> length and breadth to be made on his own ground as sufficient for travellers thereby.[1]

It is unclear whether this house was on the same site as the present house, but although
scarcely conclusive evidence, a straight line drawn between Lostwithiel and Liskeard does
go past the front door of the current mansion.

The Boconnoc tithe map shows an area called 'Boconnoc Lawn', sometimes called, incorrectly, the Park. The lawn was an area that was historically farmed and predominantly grazed since the date of Domesday in the eleventh century. The landscape was not a 'designed setting for a house', but buildings were placed adjacent to what was already agricultural land.

The bailiff's accounts of September 1431–32 list some of the costs expended for the maintenance of the house and other buildings:

> In payment to the carpenter for making a dressing of the timber for the Lord's lodge 25s. In payment for the work of the lath layer in the same 10s.8d of laths bought 26s.10d. In 10,000 nails bought for lath rails 25s.8d at 20d per thousand. In nails bought for mending the joists 4s.2d. In 12,000 stones bought for mending the joists 4s.2d. In 12,000 stones bought, price per 1000 4s.8d. 56s in floor tiles for tiling the lodge. Also for carrying the timber from the Lord's park to the manor house 8s. total: £10.15s.7½d.[2]

In 1478, the medieval fortified tower house was described by William of Worcester as 'a turreted old mansion then lately the seat of Sir Hugh Courtenay'. The tower was incorporated into a courtyard house: in such houses, the rooms were arranged around a central courtyard, the accommodation looking inwards, with semi-fortified walls. These buildings occupied a place somewhere between a castle, built for defence, and a country house, built by gentry families in later centuries when there was no longer any necessity to consider whether the site was defensible.

The entrance to the house at Boconnoc was then facing west, that is, on the opposite side to the entrance as it is today.[3] The original timbers of the great hall roof survive above the current east-facing drawing room and dendrochronology has established the felling date of the timbers as between 1492 and 1517.[4] It is likely that as C.S. Gilbert puts it 'the ancient buildings were most probably erected by the Courtenays'.

There are two representations of the early house, both dating from the sixteenth century. The first is on the map of Henry VIII's coastal fortifications, c. 1540, which shows the house with a tower, surrounded by the deer park[5] [Plate 9]. The second representation is on a map listed as 'Draft of the East Commons' which shows 'Boconack howse'[6] [Plate 10]. It is undated, but refers to 'the Queenes high waye from Foye to Launceston'. It has been assumed that the queen was Elizabeth I who reigned from 1558 to 1603. The map shows a patchwork of fields with beehives, a gallows, Penventon House and Braddock church to the north. The fortified 'Boconack howse' is shown at the end of a driveway. It has two towers: the one on the left is circular with castellations, flies a flag and has arrow hoops on the ground floor, narrow openings incorporated into the walls that enabled those defending the building to fire arrows at attackers. The larger tower on the right has a dome, is also flying a flag and has arrow hoops in the walls. Between the two towers, there is a cupola, a small structure on the top of the building, sometimes used to provide a position for a lookout or to admit light and air. The doorway is slightly off-centre and the map appears to suggest that the entrance was leading into a cobbled central courtyard. The roof is covered with tiles, possibly made of slate.

Dating from around fifty years later, when the house was owned by Sir Reynold Mohun, an inventory from January 1638 gives information about the furniture, furnishings and hangings in the house:

> At Boconnock house one and Twentie feather bedds with theire furniture
> In Sʳ Reynolds Mohuns owne lodginge chamber 6 piece of leather guilded
> hangings and one suit of hanginge of greene sea
> Five piece of Arroes hangings in the Cellar chamber there
> Five piece of Arroes hangings in the Parloʳ chamber there
> One suite of yellowe sea hangings in the Tower Chamber there
> Fower piece of stuffe hangings in the Parloʳ there[7]

When Richard Symonds was at the house in 1644, he wrote in his diary that in the great parlour of the house were 'twenty-five quarterings of the Mohuns'. For centuries, the house remained an S-shaped building and was recorded in the Hearth Tax assessment of 1664 as having twenty-five hearths, the largest number of any house in the Hundred of West.[8]

The Pitts

In 1717, Thomas 'Diamond' Pitt (I) found that the house was in a dilapidated condition. Four years later, he employed John Moyle of Exeter, a master builder of some repute, who had already been working at Antony and Powderham Castle, to redesign the east side of Boconnoc House, which contained the entrance hall, dining room and billiard room, remodelling the earlier house. On 19 January 1721, Pitt asked John Phillips, the Boconnoc steward, to 'gett all materials in place for yt Moyle will be down to begin in 3 weeks' and to employ a man called Pardew to do all the carpentry work.[9] In turn, Moyle was to send to Rattew the 'Dementions' about what stone needed to be sourced from the quarries at Purbeck. Pyne, a mason, was to finish the building that was to support the tower.[10]

In August 1721, a ceiling had fallen down in one of the rooms. The following year, Robert Pitt wrote to his father that 'ye great parlour & all ye rooms over it are so crazy' that 'tis dangerous to inhabit them' and Moyle was instructed to rebuild that part of the house.[11]

After the marriage of Thomas Pitt (II) to Christian Lyttelton failed and he had to move abroad in order to escape his creditors, the estate was abandoned and Pitt (II) only returned shortly before his death in 1761. Thomas Pitt (III) (created 1st Lord Camelford in 1784), hearing of his father's death while abroad, returned to England, finding a scene of desolation at Boconnoc.[12]

Thomas Pitt (III) was a talented amateur architect, designing the Palladian bridge and the alcove supported by the bridge at Hagley 'built after young Mr Pitt's design', c. 1762 for his uncle, Sir Richard Lyttelton. Between 1772 and 1777, Pitt (to an altered version of a design made by Robert Adam), remodelled the south front at Stowe House in Buckinghamshire and his was the design of the corinthian arch which dominates the prospect of the house towards the town of Buckingham. After 1761, Pitt (III) started to put plans into effect to restore the house, grounds and gardens at Boconnoc and between 1765 and 1775, he transformed it from an Elizabethan house into a gentry residence, making drawings of possible additions to the property although the arch shown in Plate 11 was never built [*Plate 11*].

Charles Rawlinson (1729–86)

An estate map by I. Black, dated *c.* 1761–71, shows the east-facing S-shaped house, to which were attached two single-storey service buildings[13] [*Plate 12*]. In 1772, Thomas Pitt commissioned the carpenter, architect and builder Charles Rawlinson of Lostwithiel to build a new south-facing wing which would replace the two single-storey buildings and include a library and picture gallery. On 12 November 1771, Rawlinson submitted an estimate for 'Building and furnishing an Addition to Boconnock House for Thos Pitt Esqr'. The estimate came to £4,387 and the whole was due to be 'covered in', that is, the roof would be on by 29 September 1772.

One clause in the contract provided for Rawlinson to build a new staircase, which was to prove a significant and successful improvement to the house. The staircase was to start in the room on the left-hand side of the vestibule and lead upstairs to a corridor on the first floor, where a door to the left would lead into a gallery, the present library at one end and a dressing-room at the other. The new staircase would have 'oak steps and risors' and a mahogany hand rail.[14]

Letters from Rawlinson to Pitt document how the work was proceeding. On 3 April 1772: 'I have the pleasure to inform you the foundation of the Building was begun last Monday in sight of a great number of spectators. On the 1st Stone is Engraved T + A, a new halfpenny under. It now goes on briskly … I have drew out the working plans.' Despite the initial optimism, the building work did not proceed smoothly because Rawlinson seemed unable to instigate any action or make any major decisions without explicit instructions from his employer and by May 1772, delays had already occurred.[15]

In September 1772, Rawlinson was experiencing problems with workmen. They had left the site and a number of days had been lost during the Lostwithiel feast that had 'ingaged the men more than Boconnick work this week'. By 11 September, it was clear that the building would not be completed by the date specified in the contract. Rawlinson had to 'put the law in forse' to get all the men back to work. One man called Jefferies had been gaoled, where Rawlinson intended to keep him as long as he could, Jefferies being the man who was 'spiriting' (i.e. encouraging) the rest of the men to leave the work when they pleased.[16]

Rawlinson continued to make excuses about why the roof was not on, citing the 'badness of the wether' and alleging that he was being harassed by Pitt's 'domesticks', whom he claimed had been trying to send away some of his best masons. The roof was almost complete by April of the following year when a hurricane struck Boconnoc and slates were disturbed and blown off from the old part of the house. Rawlinson was regretting that he had ever taken on the job of building the new wing: 'I wish with all my Hart you had any person to have built your house but myself', and claiming that some of the problems had been due to Pitt not being present at Boconnoc to give the requisite orders.[17]

While Pitt was abroad, Thomas Toms of Exeter was commissioned to give his opinion on Rawlinson's roof and the covering of the new apartments of Boconnoc House. He pointed out that Rawlinson had placed the roof timbers too far apart and the beams were inadequate to support the span. Only by expending a substantial sum of money to replace timbers could the roof be made watertight. A year later, Rawlinson was still making excuses and explaining (yet again) how he would rectify the problems.[18]

Pitt can have had little idea that Rawlinson's work would be of such poor quality. During the course of the next two decades, repairs were frequently necessary, undertaken by Rawlinson himself, who, surprisingly, was not dismissed by Pitt. Even more surprisingly, Rawlinson was employed to make additional improvements and changes to the east side of the house where the main entrance was sited.[19]

The saga of the leaking roof continued for many years to come and was an insoluble problem until John Soane arrived at Boconnoc in 1786.

Vincenzo Valdrè (Waldre) (1740–1814)

The estimate submitted by Rawlinson for the rebuilding and refurbishment of the house specifically excluded decoration and painting. The Cornwall *Pevsner* gives the following description:

> The outstanding feature of the interior is the entrance hall and to its left, the stair hall … The latter contains a majestic imperial stair and, above a ground floor of painted ashlar, is richly decorated in Neoclassical style with caryatids and porticos to the side, a coffered niche with Nike on the landing, and a ceiling of panels with grotesques and illusionistic reliefs of classical sacrifices.[20]

The question arises as to who executed the paintings on the walls and ceiling in the stairwell. The leading candidate is Vincenzo Valdrè or Waldre, an Italian artist born in Faenza in 1740. Valdrè studied at the Academy of Fine Arts in Parma and then, with a financial grant from the Grand Duke of Parma, attended the French Academy in Rome in 1768 where he studied painting and architecture. By 1774, he was living in London and between 1777 and 1778, he was employed at the King's Theatre in the Haymarket, designing scenery for operas by composers that included J.C. Bach, Piccinni and Giordani.[21]

Valdrè was at Boconnoc in 1778 as is evidenced by a letter from Benjamin Forster, the rector, to Mrs Pitt: 'Lord Temple wrote to me two Posts ago desiring that I would copy and send to him a Receipt from a Book called Iconologie which Waldré had seen in Mr Pitt's library [at Boconnoc] … I ransacked the library and am pretty confident there is not such Book there … & I wrote to Waldré what sort of Book it was referred to, and where it was to be found.'[22] [Plate 13].

Given the different styles of the paintings on the walls and in the stairwell, it is possible that it is the work of two (or even three) different artists. If Valdrè did have an assistant, it may have been one Antonio Poggi. Poggi had married an English woman at Plymouth and Pitt (III) wrote a glowing reference to John Strange, the English resident in Venice about Poggi, referring to him as 'an ingenious Artist well known to Sir Joshua Reynolds ...'[23] Despite Poggi's connection with the West Country, there is no direct evidence that he was ever at Boconnoc.

The decoration and painting were undertaken contemporaneously with the rebuilding [Plates 14, 15 & 16] and only a few months later, water had already caused a problem. William Pennington, a friend of the Pitts, reported on damage in the corner of the gallery and feared that the image of the muse over the false door on the staircase was 'irrevocably lost'.[24]

After his sojourn at Boconnoc, Valdrè was employed by Richard Grenville-Temple, 2nd Earl Temple (1711–79), who owned Stowe House and subsequently, by Temple's nephew and heir, George Nugent-Temple-Grenville, 1st Marquess of Buckingham (1753–1813), both related to Thomas Pitt (III) through marriage. Valdrè was employed to decorate both interiors and exteriors [Plate 17] and was responsible for creating and decorating a number of new structures in the gardens, in particular the menagerie, built c. 1781 [Plate 18].

One of Valdrè's most spectacular creations at Stowe is *The Dance of the Hours* on the ceiling in the music room, probably finished in the early 1780s[25] [Plate 19]. Vincenzo Valdrè was 'a man for all seasons', 'a talented Italian artist who could turn his hand to pretty well anything'. According to John Gilmartin, 'he was a very versatile artist; not only did he paint large historical canvasses, easel paintings and stage scenery, but he designed decorations and illuminations for the Viceroy's Court in Ireland, painting the ceilings of St Patrick's Hall in Dublin Castle'.[26]

The Dance of the Hours at Stowe was recently the subject of a major restoration. One of the conservators writes:

> There is little doubt in my mind that the grisaille wall paintings on the staircase at Boconnoc are designed and painted by Valdrè. I fully agree that they are close to the ceiling paintings in the Menagerie at Stowe.[27]

John Soane (1753–1837)

The saga of the leaking roof continued for ten years. After Rawlinson died in 1786, Pitt brought the rising architect John Soane to Boconnoc.[28] Soane made several visits to Cornwall, but his work at Boconnoc between 1785 and 1788 largely consisted of repairs and attempts to rectify Rawlinson's shoddy work. From the notes and plans he made on his first visit, it is clear that there were serious structural problems. Apart from the leaking roof, the south wall was bowing and some parts of the building had subsidence.

Like Rawlinson, Soane suffered difficulties with the workmen. In August 1786, Soane told Pitt that the season was too late for any work to be done in Cornwall, citing the problems of exposing the roof to high winds during the winter season and 'the plague of workmen and the difficulty of procuring good ones …'[29] Work began again in May and continued into June 1787 when Soane was at Boconnoc. The roof was still leaking, which meant that the front roof of the new building had to be 'stript' and new rafters put in, and it was discovered that the gutters and dormer windows were rotten. In other places, the woodwork was entirely perished, fungus had been found in the south front of the eating room, which was in a ruinous state, and dry rot in the billiard room had destroyed all the woodwork next to the east front. The roofing to the whole of the old part of the house was in very bad repair and had to be replaced. All these defects were being remedied under Soane's direction.[30]

By 1789, the work was sufficiently advanced that Lord Camelford was able to discuss the colours of the paint that he wanted in the house:

> … the garrets should have the doors and skirting boards chocolate, but in all the rooms we inhabit they should be white like the rest of the painting. The vestibule, billiard room, eating room and in general all the doors upon that floor must be dark to prevent the appearance of dirty paws. The stucco of the Vestibule should be a light grey … I need not say that all the best rooms must be dead white.[31]

The work was completed in July 1790 and although the final cost was considerably more than Camelford had anticipated, he was relieved that it had been completed as he was 'tired of repairing'. The bill was settled on 30 May 1791 and Soane was paid a gratuity of £50.[32] Lord Camelford's death in January 1793 was a blow for Soane, but his work at Boconnoc and elsewhere in Cornwall launched his career and led to him being offered further commissions.

Thomas Pitt (IV), 2nd Lord Camelford left the running of the estate to his stewards William Bragge and William Beard. A description of the house, woods and garden was written in 1800 by a visitor, Thomas Staniforth (1735–1803).

> Saturday August 16th Hext & I set out on horseback for Boconnoc, the seat of Lord Camelford where Mrs Staniforth, Miss Hext and Mrs Hext met us, found Mr Beard the steward ready to receive us & went with us thro' the house, which appears to be a comfortable habitation & was a great indulgence to my good wife whose passion for old china was highly indulged the collection being a very fine one … having refreshed ourselves we mounted our horses & accompany'd by Mr Beard Hext & I rode thro' the woods for near 2 hours – we then returned to the house & adjourned to the garden, saw the orangery, hot and greenhouses & drank tea in the Green House Parlour, saw 2 snow drop trees in fine health 10 or 12 feet high. The house is well elevated and the lawn & plantations surrounding it very fine …'[33]

The Grenvilles

The plan of manors shows the extent of the property owned by the Grenvilles in Cornwall [*Plate 20*]. In 1804, after Lord Camelford's property had been inherited by Lady Grenville, John Mulholland wrote a report describing the condition of Boconnoc House and the numerous other buildings on the estate: stables and coach house, piggeries, cowsheds, greenhouses, blacksmith's shop, slaughter house, wash house, laundry, poultry sheds, carpenter's house, hot house, 'cyder' mill, dairy and gardener's house and suggesting what work should be undertaken.[34]

The new owners decided to add to the property. In 1808, James Chapple & Son wrote to Grenville sending the plans of the intended additions and alterations to the house, with a specification and estimate amounting to £567, but it is unclear to which part of the house the specification relates.[35] In November 1808, a carpenter, Thomas Rogers, similarly sent a specification and estimate for improvements to the house at a cost of £500 'of the additional part intended to be erected to Boconnoc House, 1808'. The specification included such items as flooring over an old staircase, building a new chimney, making doorways through old walls and sash frames of red deal wood for the windows. The outside was to be rough cast, to match with the old building.[36] An illustration of the house was made in 1820 by John C. Buckler.

In 1829, John Bowen wrote about the dilapidated condition of the northward walls of the mansion, to which temporary repairs could be made, but serious improvements would ultimately be required.[37]

Figure 12 Boconnoc House, 1821, by J.C. Buckler. (© British Library)

The Fortescues

Seven years later, in June 1836, Bowen was describing plans for the removal of an old wing and a proposed new building, extending from the billiard room, to create, in the north-west corner, a new hall, a side garden entrance and a bathroom with a water closet, the latter to be built on the ground floor over the basement or cellar storey. On the middle floor, a dressing room or needle room was to be built over the ground floor.[38] These plans were never implemented for there are further drawings dated 1862, which show a four-storey high tower on the same site. The completion of the tower was overseen by George Fortescue.

A conservatory had been constructed in 1835, but in 1872, George Fortescue's son Cyril commissioned T.G. Messenger of Loughborough to replace it with a custom-built edifice, 50 feet long, including a covered way which connected it to the tower at the north end of the house at a cost of £329.5s. The conservatory was to grow camellias and had a stove at one end to provide warmth for the plants.[39] A Francis Frith photograph of 1898 shows the eastern frontage of the house with the conservatory attached.

In 1882, architect Richard Coad visited Boconnoc and Lady Louisa wrote to Harriet, 'Mr Coad (architect) was here on Tuesday and with him, your brothers and Mr Pease'.[40] Coad was employed to prepare a specification for yet another addition and he forwarded plans of the ground, first and second floors of the portion of Boconnoc House to which the addition was to be made.[41] These were approved by Lady Louisa and Cyril Fortescue.[42] Three years later, Coad was employed to add a smoking room in the tower.

Figure 13 Boconnoc House, c. 1898. (© The Francis Frith Collection)

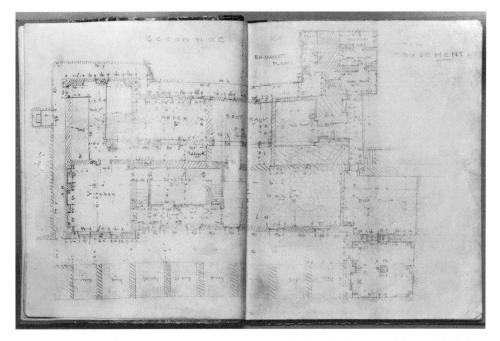

Figure 14 Plan of the basement of Boconnoc House by Richard Coad. (© Cornwall Record Office)

Figure 15 Boconnoc House, 1960s. (© Historic England. Commander R. Phillimore Collection)

Some of Coad's plans (undated) and a sketch book (also undated) in Coad's hand are held in the Cornwall Record Office. The latter shows the basement rooms with their service areas, the ground floor with the hall leading into the dining room and billiard room, the staircase, the mezzanine and the upper floors with gallery and bedrooms.[43] The photograph at Figure 15 shows one of the rooms in the 1960s.

This marked the end of any substantial repairs and additions in the nineteenth century. After the Second World War, during which the house had been occupied by American troops, George Grenville Fortescue and his wife returned to live in the house. In 1959, during the life of his uncle George, Desmond Fortescue was invited to live on the estate and take over its management. His family moved to the Stewardry and on inheriting in 1969, Desmond Fortescue had no option but to sell 2,000 acres of land to pay substantial death duties. When George Fortescue's widow Joan vacated the 'Big House', she took with her many of the contents, leaving much of the house empty. It was then discovered that the mansion was in a precarious state, suffering from major subsidence. There was a possibility that the roof might collapse, the walls were bulging and crumbling and the south wall of the gallery was unstable and leaning out. The roof was letting in water, causing severe damage to the interior and, particularly, to the important plasterwork and paintings on the staircase.[44] In 1972, the decision was taken to demolish part of the south wing that had been built by Charles Rawlinson. The house was abandoned and eventually fell into total disrepair.

When Anthony Fortescue (Desmond's son) and his wife Elizabeth took over responsibility for Boconnoc in 1996, they in their turn were faced with a seemingly irretrievable situation. Nevertheless, they were determined to bring the house back to its former glory. In an interview in *Country Life* in November 2008, Anthony Fortescue was quoted as saying that he recalled the long years in which the house stood empty. 'I'd wander the passages saying, how could we do it. I felt driven by an inner determination to make something happen.'[45] Making something happen was even more difficult because the Fortescues chose not to apply for any grants to raise the finance to enable the work to be done. Instead, there was some limited selling of redundant buildings and revenue raised from events on the estate was devoted to the repairs and restoration and, little by little, room by room, they rebuilt, renovated and refurbished. The house, now beautifully redecorated, is in regular use for events: weddings, parties, concerts, art courses, lunches and lectures.

In 2012, Anthony and Elizabeth instituted the Boconnoc Music Award, whereby an ensemble comprising students from the Royal College of Music is selected and they become musicians in residence. They give a concert in the house, followed several days later by one in the church. Over the past five years, the selected ensembles have been three string quartets, one wind quintet and one saxophone quartet.[46]

In addition to the restoration of the house, three cottages have also been renovated: Dairy Cottage, situated next to the main house and where the dining room table is made of oak from the estate; the Groom's House, overlooking the church and parkland; and the Head Groom's House, looking onto the stable yard.

Following the enormously successful restoration of the Grade II★ listed house, the achievement was recognised by two prestigious awards. Anthony Fortescue received the Historic Houses Association/Sotheby's Restoration Award in 2012. James Stourton, chairman of Sotheby's UK, said: 'This magical house sits in one of the most beautiful settings in Cornwall and was crying out to be restored and used. It is wonderful to see it come back to life.' In the same year, Boconnoc was joint-winner of the 'Restoration of a Georgian House' category at the Georgian Group Architectural Awards. Anthony Fortescue, on receiving the award, said: 'The house is now the heart of the estate again, something I have dreamt of since I first laid eyes on the house as a child.'[47]

THE GROUNDS AND GARDENS

The map showing 'the Queenes high waye' [Plate 10] portrays the house surrounded with fences, small fields and diagrammatic trees. The land around the house was divided into compartments and although there is little evidence about what it was used for, it was probably primarily grazing for animals and pasture.[48]

A three-quarter length portrait of Sir Reginald Mohun [Plate 21], dating from the 1620s, might represent part of the Boconnoc garden, although if it is Boconnoc it is not known which part of the garden is portrayed. Between two groups of trees can be seen a two-storeyed building with a gabled end with garden implements leaning against it, possibly a hut used for storing tools. Garden beds are shown divided by paths and in the background is an arched doorway in a wall.

The Pitts

In letters from the steward John Bennett, when the estate was owned by Thomas Pitt (II), Bennett mentioned (between 1749 and 1754) an orchard and garden, warren, barn, linhay, stables, pigeon house, hop garden, theatre, nursery and dog kennel. On the Black map dated *c.* 1761–71 some of these features can be identified, including compartment divisions, drives and garden buildings[49] [Plate 12].

As we have seen in Chapter 3, when Thomas Pitt (III) inherited in 1761 the gardens were unkempt, many of the trees had been felled and the lawns had been broken up into ridge and furrow. Pitt initiated major improvements, not only to the house, but also to the grounds and gardens so that any further ruin was halted and improvements were made gradually.

At Boconnoc, Pitt was able to indulge his own preference for working with nature rather than tidying it away through stiff design. The word *naturesque* is applicable, that is, something with striking natural beauty.[50]

Pitt appeared to have two aims: first, to unite the house and gardens into a single and pleasing entity and second, to improve the appearance of the grounds including the gardens. A document entitled 'Works to be done at Boconnoc' in Pitt's hand details the improvements made from 1764 to 1785. In order to address his first aim of unit-ing the aspects of the house and gardens, one of the instructions that Pitt gave Charles Rawlinson was to place pieces of a mirror into the lower panes of the window shutters in the drawing room at the end of the gallery so that the shutters in the house would reflect the prospect of the grounds.[51]

The second aim, to improve the appearance of the gardens and grounds, involved creating a 'rosary', a rose garden, and replanting a shrubbery to the south-east of the house, opposite the churchyard, which was laid out with serpentine paths, evergreens and 'Sweets', that is, ornamental plants. In 1769, hedge building, ornamental tree planting and a new 'Pidgeon Cote' were all recorded.[52] In addition, a further series of rides and walks through the park were created and unsightly buildings were removed.

Pitt planned that the existing ways, rides and walks should be extended and linked together to form continuous routes around the estate. In 1765, the circuit of the park was measured as three and a quarter miles. By 1790, it had been extended to six miles. All parts of the park could thus be accessed and every circuit offered ever-changing views of the scenery.[53] One of the routes is now known as the Stewardry Walk, formerly the Rookery. This runs behind the mansion, through the woods, to what was until 1808 the parsonage.[54] Another of the walks was described as follows: 'Measured from the Back of the house thro the flowergarden, the great Beeches by the Parsonage, over the boarden-bridge by the lead mine along the Park walk by the Bastion and thro the melancholy walk, home $2^M2^F32^P4^Y$'.[55]

Unsightly buildings were removed or demolished. The manor mill was moved to Couch's Mill while the old stew-pond under the house was cleared and made 'staunch for fish'. Pitt also 'Intended to remove the present fruit garden which stands in the Orchard under the House, into the old Nursery by the Church, concealing it by Shrubs and firr-trees from the Avenue. Intended to remove the Brew-house Laundry and Dairy now under the Study windows, into the Court near the Stables ...' The latter was completed in 1767.[56] George Grenville (father of William Wyndham Grenville who later married Pitt's daughter Anne) visited in that year and wrote in his diary: 'Boconnock 26 June 1767. Our landlord here has made this place which in itself has many great Beauties from the finest vallies filled with old timber and little Rivulets ... still more agreeable.'[57] Improvements took place every year due to Thomas Pitt's (III) efforts.

After Pitt married heiress Anne Wilkinson in 1771, his financial position was greatly improved and the garden accounts for 1773 and 1774 show a greater outlay for both labour and materials.[58] In 1775, the estate was visited by Josiah Wedgwood who wrote: 'June 3rd 1775 Buconic the seat of Mr Thos Pitt ... which is extremely rural and retired, we found him at home, and he took us a walk before dinner, down a sweet valley, with hanging woods on each side, and a clear purling stream in the bottom ...'[59]

When at Boconnoc, Pitt played a direct part in the adjustments made to the landscape on the estate while the employees continued to make improvements as instructed. A new gardener, Mr Rhind, was employed in 1785 and he undertook extensive work in the park and, in 1791, planted 3,000 fir trees in the plantation.[60]

Pitt (III) also improved the horticulture of the gardens. The shrubbery (now the Dorothy Garden) was replanted and a new shrubbery created on the former glebe.

The 2nd Lord Camelford had little to do with the landscape, but Bennett and his successor as steward, William Beard, recorded that Lord Camelford visited in 1797 and 1799 and had made certain (unspecified) suggestions about improvements that could be made to the estate.[61]

The Grenvilles

Both Lady Grenville and her husband shared her father's interest in planting and in creating landscapes in harmony with nature, not to any formal design, but revealing natural features to their best advantage. The 1st Lord Camelford established a pattern in the landscape which his daughter Anne and her husband Lord Grenville followed.

The Grenvilles wish to proceed with planting was partly curtailed by shortage of funds, even though there were home-grown trees enough on the estate in the nursery run by Mr Rhind and then by Mr Pond. In 1813, Grenville wrote to his wife 'the place looks beautiful, and one sees everywhere the want of more trees, and the success of those we have already planted …'[62]

The Fortescues

Ultimately, it was left to Anne Grenville and George Fortescue to complete the planting over the next half century. When George Fortescue became resident at Boconnoc in the early 1830s, formal terraces were planted near the house, together with a flower garden and two shrubberies. A new rose garden was created, beds were filled with bright coloured flowers and a pond and fountain were installed.[63] Plants and seedlings were exchanged between Dropmore and Boconnoc.[64] George Fortescue wrote to Lady Grenville: 'The rhododendrons in sight of my window are seven feet high and as many in diameter and in spite of the rain, they are covered with the brightest cherry and coloured blossoms.'[65] The photograph album of Louisa Fortescue from the 1870s to the 1890s shows that the Fortescues followed the practice of the Pitts and the Grenvilles in planting, and the southern area of the lawns became dotted with young trees.[66] Trees were planted by members of the family to celebrate special occasions such as birthdays and wedding anniversaries. The Fortescue daughters spent many hours painting and drawing various aspects of the landscape on the estate [Plate 22].

George Fortescue proved a very able administrator for the estate, with the steward John Bowen until 1850 and then with William Pease. When Fortescue died in 1877, the estate passed to his third son, Cyril Dudley Fortescue. The gardens were well maintained, the walks lined with trees and flower beds laid out in front of the orangery. Later, when Bevill Fortescue had inherited, the flower garden was renamed the Dorothy Garden in honour of his wife.

The two world wars ended several centuries of improvements on many estates in Cornwall and Boconnoc was no exception. During the time that Captain Desmond Fortescue owned the estate few changes were made to the gardens, for he believed it was important 'to keep the amenity value and character of this part of the Estate unchanged'.[67] Some of the historic landscapes have been conserved due to the introduction of the Higher Level Stewardship Scheme and the Boconnoc Lawns and Deer Park are part of an area of 340 hectares which are included in a Grade II★ landscape. The tenant of the Home Farm is returning some parts of the lawn that had been used for arable farming to pasture and has been re-planting trees from where they have been lost in former years.[68] The character is preserved, incorporating many of the ideas and designs that the Pitts, Grenvilles and Fortescues introduced when they were respectively the custodians of the estate.

The improvements made by Anthony and Elizabeth Fortescue included replacing the eighteenth- and nineteenth-century tree planting and efficiently managing the large acreage of woodland. The clearing of rhododendron ponticum from a considerable amount of the estate has enabled the original pattern of planting, commenced by Lord and Lady Grenville and George Fortescue, to be newly identified.

THE TREES

Lady Grenville was fond of Lucombe oak trees and she wrote to Lord Grenville from Malvern, saying, 'pray tell Pond to graft as many Lucombe Oaks as he can in the spring'.[69] The oaks (*Quercus χ hispanica* 'Lucombeana') provide a feature on the lawns. They retain their glossy green leaves throughout the winter, dropping them in the spring when other trees are beginning to come into leaf.

George Fortescue wrote on a number of occasions to Lady Grenville to report on trees that had been blown down during storms. In December 1856, one of the Scotch firs in the flower garden had lost two limbs and the fine beech in Sowdens opposite the mine, one of the largest on the estate, was split.[70] Some years later, during a heavy storm from the west and north-west, one of the fine beeches in the Rookery went down with a loud crash and injured its neighbour, a very large and beautiful beech.[71]

The Wellington clump

On the date that the Duke of Wellington was buried in St Paul's Cathedral, a clump of trees was planted on the lawns at Boconnoc. On a broken column is inscribed:

> These trees natives of various lands which were rendered famous by the birth defended by the victories or exalted by the patriotism of Arthur Duke of Wellington were planted on the day when his remains followed by a nations tears were consigned to the tomb. Nov. 18 1852.

The trees are Irish yew to celebrate his birth in Dublin; a Deodar cedar for the years he spent as a soldier in India during the period when his brother Lord Mornington was Governor-General; a holm oak for his service during the Peninsula campaign in

Portugal; a Spanish chestnut for his advance through Spain towards France; an elm, the tree under which he stood in the shade during the battle of Waterloo; and an oak to represent his time as Prime Minister.

THE BUILDINGS IN THE GROUNDS AND GARDENS

There are a number of buildings in the grounds and gardens, erected between 1763 and 1790, including a 'summer house'[72] and a Palladian bridge created by Thomas Pitt (III). On 14 October 1780, Pitt wrote to Benjamin Forster, 'I am delighted that you have improved your scene with an opening to my bridge'.[73] In addition, there were greenhouses where grapes were grown and a 'Pinery' for pineapples, which were 'prosperous and flourishing'. The fruit was sent to friends and neighbours.

The Obelisk

The Obelisk, which still stands in the grounds, was erected by Thomas Pitt (III) in 1771 in memory of his uncle Sir Richard Lyttelton, who had given Pitt assistance in his youth and had supported him while the latter was in dispute with his father Thomas Pitt (II). The inscription reads: 'In gratitude and affection to the memory of Sir Richard Lyttelton, and to perpetuate the remembrance of that peculiar character of benevolence, which rendered him the delight of his own age, and worthy the veneration of posterity. 1771.'

In July 1783, during one of his visits, John Soane was charged with repairing the 123-foot high structure, which had been struck by lightning. By 1838, a large amount of woodland with wide drives had been planted around the monument.[74]

Lady Grenville and G.M. Fortescue continued planting and the remarkable pattern they made in the landscape as seen from the Obelisk Drive has been once again revealed after the recent removal of the invasive rhododendron ponticum which had spread from the plantations onto the open areas.

The Bath House

In a wooded area, enclosed by high stone walls, the Bath House, which incorporates a rectangular sunken bathing pool, is situated 500 feet north-west of the mansion. The pool is lined with ashlar granite blocks and stone steps lead down on the north-east corner. On the west side, a fountain has carved stone lions' heads in moulded stone. In the south-east corner over the entrance is a fifteenth- or sixteenth-century two-centred moulded doorway [*Plates 23 & 24*].

John Mulholland, a pupil of James Wyatt the architect, designed the Bath House on the orders of the 2nd Lord Camelford. Building commenced in 1804 and was completed in 1806. In July 1805, John Mulholland wrote to the gardener Mr Rhind to ask what quantity of stone was on the spot at Boconnoc, asking Rhind to order moorstone, ashlar and paving and instruct Pyne the mason to begin work.[75]

1. Sir Reginald Mohun and Dorothy Chudleigh, *c*. 1604. (© The Weiss Gallery, London)

2. Richard Symonds in profile. (© Reproduced by permission of the Kings, Heralds and Pursuivants of Arms, The College of Arms)

3. Portrait of Anne, Lady Grenville by John Hoppner. (© Christie's Images Limited)

4. Portrait of William Wyndham, Lord Grenville by William Owen. (© The Governing Body of Christ Church, Oxford)

5. Painting of George Grenville Fortescue's grave. (© Hampshire Record Office)

6. Memorial in Christ Church Cathedral, Oxford to George Grenville Fortescue. (© the author)

7. Grave of Annie Moore in Dublin. (© the author)

8. Detail of the tithe map of Boconnoc parish, 1838. (© Cornwall Record Office)

9. Detail of Henry VIII's map of coastal fortifications. (© British Library)

10. Detail of the map of the East Commons. (© Cornwall Record Office)

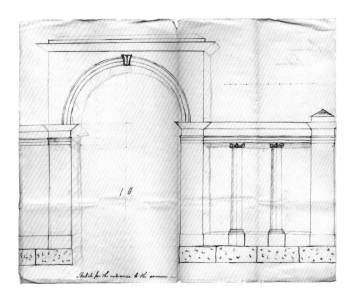

11. Drawing of an arch for Boconnoc by Thomas Pitt (III). (© Sir John Soane's Museum, London)

12. Detail of a map by I. Black. (© Cornwall Record Office)

13. Boconnoc House, 2016. (© the author)

14. The staircase at Boconnoc. (© Boconnoc estate)

15. Painting on the staircase at Boconnoc. (© Min Wood)

16. Detail of painting on the staircase at Boconnoc. (© Min Wood)

17. Stowe House, Buckinghamshire. (© the author)

18. The Menagerie, Stowe House. (© the author)

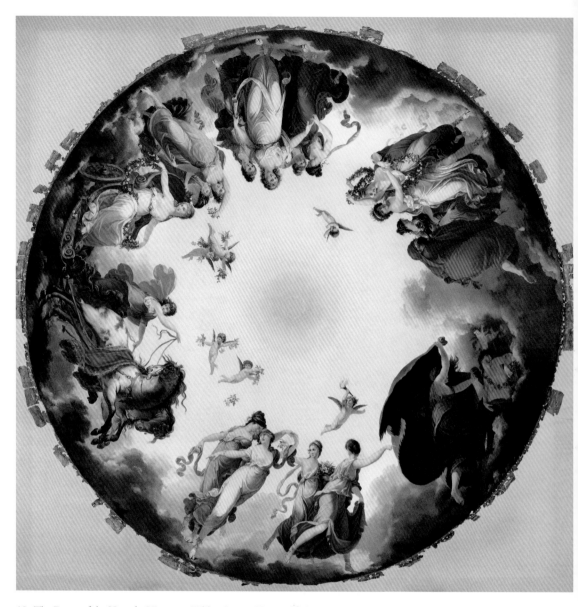

19. *The Dance of the Hours* by Vincenzo Valdre, Stowe House. (© Stowe House Preservation Trust)

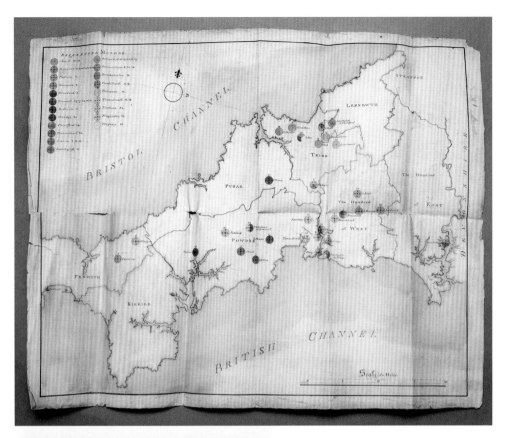

20. Plan of manors owned by Lord and Lady Grenville, nineteenth century. (© Cornwall Record Office)

21. Sir Reginald Mohun in later life, c. 1620s. (© Emma Trelawny-Vernon)

22. The stream in Valley Crucis, sketched by Annie Fortescue, 1856. (© Hampshire Record Office)

23. The entrance to the Bath House, Boconnoc. (© the author)

24. Interior of the Bath House. (© the author)

25. The Dovecote, Boconnoc. (© the author)

26. The wheel-headed wayside cross in Boconnoc churchyard. (© the author)

27. The font in Boconnoc church. (© Drawing book owned by Harriet Buller)

28. The Carminow brass plate in Menheniot church. (© the author)

29. Engraving of the harbour of Fowey by Willem Schellinks, 1662, the ferry, bottom right. (© Österreichische Nationalbibliothek, Vienna)

30. Boconnoc House and church, 2016. (© the author)

Today, the pool is no longer filled with water, but is used as a highly unusual venue for wedding ceremonies.

The Orangery

In 1835, George Fortescue had an orangery built in the gardens. Finished in November 1835, it was light and lofty and had two wings that made it look very imposing.[76]

The Dovecote

The early eighteenth-century circular dovecote is situated to the north of Boconnoc House. It has stone walls with a conical slate roof. Built of two storeys, the ground floor was probably used for a different purpose than the dovecote on the higher storey. The entrance to the latter is approached by six steps to the north side. There is a panelled timber door and above the door, to the south-east, a window[77] [*Plate 25*].

THE DEER PARK

The true deer park was an enclosure of some hundreds of acres, surrounded by a dike or palisade, lying a mile or more from the lord's residence within groves of trees and with a stream of water running through it.[78]

The first mention of the deer park at Boconnoc is in the bailiff's accounts for 1431–32 when the estate was owned by Thomas de Carminow.[79] Tenants of manors with deer parks were expected to render assistance to the lord, or someone else in his name, who wanted to hunt in the park. On this occasion, rather than being out in the field with the lord or his substitute, the *stabulagium*, that is, the hunting 'rent', had been commuted to a payment in money, sixteen tenants paying 4½d each, giving a total of six shillings.

The illustration of Boconnoc in Henry VIII's map of coastal fortifications (*c.* 1540), shows the house and deer park surrounded by a fence[80] [*Plate 9*].

In 1763, John Bennett suggested to Thomas Pitt (III) that owners of other deer parks, for example Humphry Morice of Werrington and Sir Christopher Treise of Lavethan, should be asked for any deer that they could conveniently spare to bolster the numbers and improve the breeding stock at Boconnoc. In addition, deer were also acquired from other parks, those coming from Mount Edgcumbe being carried in panniers on horseback and those from Lanhydrock being transported in a cart.[81]

The deer caused many problems because they kept breaking out from their enclosure. In April 1763, John Bennett wrote to Thomas Pitt (III):

We have had an abundance of trouble with the deer, they breake out every Day and every morning the men go after 'em to Bring 'em in again, last week we had an account of one in St Veep Parish, which John Roberts endeavour'd to Drive Home with the Spaniels, but could not succeed, and therefore went to my nephew for the Beagles, but the Deer never shew'd any Inclination to Returne to the Park, and was therefore quite run down. John Roberts carry'd him several fields afterwards on his Back, where the poor Creature Expired: this has vexed me greatly and the more because it Happens to be one of those brought from Mount Edgcumbe.[82]

Mr Leach, the rector, reported that one of the bucks was devouring his 'Beans and Pease' and if not controlled would, no doubt, eat his whole field of wheat, the animal being one of the 'Roving Brood'.[83] In 1808, because the fence around the park had been neglected, the deer escaped again and had been particularly mischievous, getting as far as Braddock and nearly to Lerryn and Restormel. Frost, the gamekeeper, had got them back, but they caused the steward Watson Sharman great vexation and he complained that they had been in his garden and he had not a shrub left.[84]

A year later, farmer Thomas Richards wrote to Lady Grenville, saying that deer had been breaking from her park for several years past onto his farm and destroying his corn and grass. Although he had applied to her servants to repair the fence, they had taken no notice of him. As it was coming on to harvest, he would have all his corn destroyed. He asked that she give an order that the fence should be made up.[85]

Figure 16 Gamekeepers at Boconnoc, John Frost, bottom right. (© Historic England. Commander R. Phillimore Collection)

Due to the 'prodigous expense in keeping the deer in', Lord Grenville seriously considered disposing of them. John Bowen produced a valuation and devised an advertisement that was to be placed in the local newspapers offering them for sale.[86] Grenville eventually decided that the animals should remain, despite the costs of maintaining them. In 1813, the cost of fencing the park was £400, much more than he had anticipated. At that date, there were 325 deer in the park, thirty bucks of the age of three upwards, does, teggs, pricketts and fawns. The ground was wet and boggy and cold to the foot, though sheltered from the wind, and Bowen suggested that twenty to thirty females should be shot which would be to the general benefit of the park.[87]

The situation was kept under review and the steward's accounts for 1818–19 contain a memorandum: 'to see whether the park can be managed so as to pay nearly its Expences and Gamekeeper's wages amounting to £200. Or if that cannot be done to write immediately to Lord Grenville to that effect and that it may be disparked.' Ultimately, no action was taken to close the park and the deer continued to provide venison for local dignitaries, Lord and Lady Grenville and the family at Boconnoc, but little financial profit was ever made from the animals.

The deer park still exists at Boconnoc and new blood was introduced into the breeding stock when a buck was brought from Gunton Park in Norfolk. The park is dominated by beech trees with abundant numbers of oaks and ash and willow around the lake. The old-growth sessile oak (*Quercus petraea*), growing in ravines and on woodland slopes, contains an internationally important assemblage of rare lichens. Some 188 species have been identified, including the only known British site for *Porcina hibernica*, making it one of the most important sites in Europe. The site is also considered to be the best 'old-growth, southern-oceanic oak woodland' in the South West and is a Site of Special Scientific Interest.[88]

STONE AND MEMORIAL CROSSES

In the nineteenth century, two crosses were removed to Boconnoc from Lanlivery. One of the crosses was set up in the old deer park in 1840 by George Matthew Fortescue as a memorial to his uncle William Wyndham, Lord Grenville. The inscription has two incised letter Cs facing each other in a square format: [ ] with a cross between them.

The second cross is on Druid's Hill, north-east of the house. The upper part of the cross was removed from Lanlivery in 1846 and was then erected on a modern shaft and pedestal.[89]

There is a memorial cross in front of the house which lists the names of those men who were killed in the two world wars. In the First World War: John Benallack, Frederick Hambly, William John Hambly, Sir William Hoste, Bart., Leslie F. Ellington Leslie, William Rogers and Thomas White. In the Second World War: Francis John Keast, Herbert Wilton and Harold Tucker.[90]

EVENTS IN THE GROUNDS

Today, as numerous events are held in the house, similarly many are held in the grounds. These include the Boconnoc Steam Fair, Carriage Driving, Sheep Dog Trials, a Motorsport Carnival and the Endurance GB horse ride. In April 2016, as part of the Cornwall Garden Society Spring Flower Show, two episodes of the BBC Radio 4 programme *Gardeners' Question Time* were recorded inside the house.[91]

NOTES AND REFERENCES

1. I am very grateful to Min Wood for much of the information about the grounds and gardens that is contained in this chapter; Calendar of Patent Rolls (CPR), Richard II 1391–96, Vol. V, London, 1905, p. 274.

2. Cornwall Record Office (CRO); F/4/3, Bailiff's Accounts, September 1431 to September 1432.

3. Marcus Binney, 'A restoration inspired by history', *Country Life*, 19 November 2008, pp. 46–50.

4. English Heritage, *Boconnoc House and Boconnoc Park report,* 77/2007, tree-ring analysis; personal communication from Dr Dan Miles, dendrochronologist.

5. British Library (BL): MS Cotton Augustus, I.i.38.

6. CRO: AD 644 & F/2/40; The Cornwall Record Office catalogue entry reads as follows: 'The map was purchased from the contents of Ethy House in June 1977. Bound stones are shown on the commons, and gates and fields are also shown. Names include Boconnack House, the way to Dulaw [Duloe], a gallows and the road from Boconnoc to Bradoc.'

7. BL: Add MS 11314, 28 January 1638; Sea or Say. 'A very ancient English fabric of twill weave, originally woven from worsted, but could also be made of silk. It was manufactured mostly in Norfolk, Suffolk and Essex, and is found in the majority of sixteenth-century inventories, used for bed and wall hangings, table carpets and later, window curtains.' Pamela Clabburn, *The National Trust Book of Furnishing Textiles*, London, 1988, p. 254; Arras (arroes) were wall hangings made of a rich tapestry fabric.

8. T.L. Stoate (ed.), Cornwall Hearth and Poll Taxes, 1660–1664, Direct Taxation in Cornwall in the Reign of Charles II, Bristol, 1981, p. xxi.

9. The National Archives (TNA): C108/424 #12 Notebook No. 3, October 1720–19 January 1721; 19 January 1721 and 1 December 1720; TNA: C108/424 # Notebook No. 6, April 1722 to November 1722, 26 April 1722.

10. TNA: C108/424 #13, Notebook No. 4: C108/424/no 9, Pall Mall, 4 November 1721, f. 517.

11. TNA: C108/424 #14, Notebook No. 5, 19 June 1721 to April 1722, 10 August 1721; C108/424/no 9, Pall Mall, 10 April 1722 to John Phillips, f. 563; C108/424 #14, Notebook No. 5, 19 June 1721 to April 1722.

12. BL: Add MS 69333, *Family Characters and Anecdotes*, Petersham, Lord Camelford to his son Thomas Pitt (IV), December 1781, f. 63.

13. CRO: F/3/14/11, map by I. Black.

14. BL: Add MS 69176, The Boconnoc Minute Book, ff. 171–174; BL: Add MS 59489, ff. 118–119; The intended addition to the House containing Gallery, drawing room and family apartment over the offices begun 1772 and finished 1774, the Estimate above 5000£.

15. BL: Add MS 69328, 3 April 1772, f. 1; Lostwithiel, 9 May 1772, f. 4.

16. BL: Add MS 69328, 6 September, f. 7; 11 September 1722, f. 8; 24 September 1772, f. 9; 11 October 1772, f. 10.

17. BL: Add MS 69328, 25 October 1772, f. 12; Lostwithiel, 22 November 1772, ff. 13–14; 13 December 1772, f. 14; 24 January 1773, f. 15; 12 March 1773, f. 17; 23 March 1773, f. 19; 30 April 1773, f. 5.

18. BL: Add MS 59489, Exeter, 21 April 1779, f. 129; Exeter, 11 December 1779, f. 130; 6 May 1781, f. 141 and Lostwithiel, 15 September 1782, f. 147.

19. L: Add MS 69328, 4 January 1774, f. 38; 15 March 1775, f. 23.

20. Peter Beacham and Nikolaus Pevsner, *The Buildings of England: Cornwall*, Yale University Press, New Haven, CT and London, 2014, p. 104.

21. Edward Croft Murray, Decorative Painting in England, 1537–1837, Vol. 2, The Eighteenth and Early Nineteenth Centuries, MCMLXX, published by Country Life, pp. 288–289.

22. BL: Add MS 60303, letter from Benjamin Forster at Boconnoc Parsonage to Mrs Pitt, December 29 1778, ff. 8–9; Thomas Pitt's (III) uncle, William Pitt, 1st Earl of Chatham married Hester Grenville, sister of the 2nd Earl Temple and aunt of the 1st Marquess of Buckingham.

23. BL: Egerton MS 1969, Oxford Street, 22 April 1776, Thomas Pitt to John Strange, f. 142.

24. BL: Add MS 69304, Bodmyn [*sic*], 1 January 1780, William Pennington to Mrs Pitt, ff. 5–6. The painting of the muse is still somewhat strange and looks as though she is wearing a mask.

25. Conservation and repair work began on the music room at Stowe in April 2012 and was completed in October 2012. The project involved the conservation of the Vincenzo Valdrè painted panels and ceiling – wmf.org.uk. *The Dance of the Hours* has now been reinstated on the ceiling of the music room.

26. M.L. Gibbon, 'Lord Buckingham and the completion of the interior', *The Stoic*, December 1875, p. 2221; Vincent Waldre's ceiling paintings in Dublin Castle, *Apollo*, January 1872, p. 43.

27. Grisaille: painting executed in neutral colours or in shades of grey, used in large decorative schemes, often in imitation of sculpture; email from Emma Boyce, Paintings Conservator, dated 22 April 2015.

28. Talk by Susan Palmer, Archivist at the John Soane Museum, 'The adventures of a Regency Architect in the West County', given at Boconnoc House to the Cornwall Branch of the Art Fund, on 15 November 2008.

29. BL: Add MS 69238, Soane to Camelford in Lausanne, Switzerland, 18 August 1786, f. 42.

30. BL: Add MS 69328, 8 May 1787, Soane to Lord Camelford at Montpellier; Boconnoc, 19 June 1787, Soane to Lord Camelford, ff. 54–56; Sir John Soane Museum Archives. Rome, 3 December 1787, Lord Camelford to John Soane; 4 August 1788, Soane to Lord Camelford at Colmar, Alsace, f. 62.

31. Sir John Soane Museum Archives, PRIV COR IV, p. 2 (32), 6 May 1789, Lord Camelford to Soane.

32. Sir John Soane Museum Archives, Florence, 1 May 1788, Lord Camelford to Soane.

33. Jean Hext (ed.), *The Staniforth Diary, A Visit to Cornwall in 1800*, Truro, 1965, p. 18.

34. BL: Add MS 69177, Correspondence to Lord Grenville from the Stewards, 4 and 5 September 1804, ff. 111–119.

35. BL: Add MS 69176, Bodmin, 15 December 1808, James Chapple & Son to Lord Grenville, ff. 149–152.

36. CRO: F/1/220, 62 Princes Street, Plymouth Dock, 15 November 1808, Thomas Rogers to Mr Shearman [*sic*], at Boconnoc.

37. BL: Add MS 69178, Boconnoc, 12 March 1829, Bowen to Lord Grenville, ff. 81–82.

38. CRO: F/4/78/4, Boconnoc, 27 June 1836, John Bowen to GM Fortescue.

39. CRO: F/1/304, Midlands Horticultural Works, Loughborough, 10 April and 17 June 1874.

40. Hampshire Record Office (HRO): 115M88/C10/3/120/1, Boconnoc 4 November 1882, Lady Louisa Fortescue to Harriet Phillimore (née Fortescue).

41. CRO: F/3/10/2, Lostwithiel, 7 December 1882, ff. 406–407.

42. CRO: F/3/10/2/676, 4 June 1883, William Pease Junior to Lady Louisa; F/3/10/2/739, 26 June 1883, William Pease Junior to Cyril Fortescue.

43. CRO: X939. Building plans for Boconnoc house, details of smoking room, windows and doors; X847/RL/2, proposed alterations, chimney piece on the first floor, casement window in the smoking room; F/1/306, Coad plans.

44. Binney, *op. cit.*, pp. 46–50; Cornwall Garden Trust Journal, 2004, report by Pam Dodds and Joy

Wilson. The author remembers visiting the house some fifteen years ago, when it was in a parlous state – everywhere was in ruin and it was possible to see the sky through the roof.

45. Binney, *op. cit.*, pp. 46–50.

46. The ensembles have been from 2012: the Danchin Quartet (string quartet), the Cataleya Quintet (wind), the Laefer Quartet (saxophones), the Arcos Quartet (string quartet) and the Alke Quartet (string quartet).

47. *Cornish Guardian*, Friday, 10 August 2012; *Cornish Guardian*, Friday, 9 November 2012; www.savinggeorgianbuildings.blogspot.co.uk/.

48. CRO: AD/644.

49. CRO: F/3/14/11, map by I. Black.

50. Information from Min Wood.

51. Joanna Vernon, 'Thomas Pitt, Lord Camelford, amateur architect, connoisseur and patron of the arts: a case study in the history of taste 1760–93', presented for the degree of Master of Philosophy, 1993, Royal Holloway and Bedford New College, University of London, p. 194, 15 January 1782.

52. Vernon, *ibid.*, p. 178; CRO: F/4/88.

53. Cynthia K. Troup, 'Lady Anne Grenville: an unsung heroine in garden history', dissertation submitted for the degree of MA in Garden History, 2004, History of Art Department, University of Bristol, p. 47.

54. Cornwall Gardens Trust report, 2007, pp. 4–5; CRO: F/4/120/13 and F/1/159.

55. BL: Add MS 69176, Boconnoc Minute Book, f. 171.

56. BL: Add MS 69176, Boconnoc Minute Book, f. 170 and ff. 171–172.

57. Huntingdon Library, San Marino, California, USA. George Grenville's diary, Boconnock, 26 June 1767, ST Vol. 7, 1764–1769.

58. Cornwall Gardens Trust report, 2007, p. 18.

59. CRO: AD621/11, Diary of Josiah Wedgwood, 1775.

60. CRO: F/4/120/13.

61. CRO: F/4/76.

62. BL: Add MS 58873, 1 October 1813, Lord Grenville to Lady Grenville, ff. 182–183.

63. CRO: F/4, letters of George Fortescue to Lady Grenville, 1810–1840.

64. CRO: F/1/163; F/4/117/9, Boconnoc, 25 April 1839, GM Fortescue and Lady Louisa to Lady Grenville.

65. BL: Add MS 69063, Boconnoc, 1 April 1862, GM Fortescue to Lady Grenville, ff. 1–4.

66. Min Wood, 'Parks and lawns. The making of the Boconnoc landscape', 21 January 2015, unpublished report, p. 4.

67. Cornwall Gardens Trust report, p. 23.

68. Wood, *op. cit.*, p. 6.

69. BL: Add MS 58873, Malvern, 9 September 1813, Lady Grenville to Lord Grenville, ff. 61–62.

70. BL: Add MS 69058, Boconnoc, 12 December 1856, GM Fortescue to Lady Grenville, ff. 154–155.

71. BL: Add MS 69060, Boconnoc, 1 November 1859, GM Fortescue to Lady Grenville, ff. 157–159.

72. BL: Add MS 9489, 20 July 1785, T. Bennett to Lord Camelford.

73. Vernon, *op. cit.*, p. 177.

74. Troup, *op. cit.*, p. 48.

75. Images of England, No. 60511; CRO: F/1/220, John Mulholland to Mr Rhind, 25 July 1805; measurement of the Bath.

76. CRO: F/4/117/9/47, Boconnoc, 4 November 1836, GM Fortescue to Lady Grenville; F/4/117/9, Boconnoc, 6 November 1835, GM Fortescue to Lady Grenville at Dropmore, f. 35; Boconnoc, 17 November 1835, GM Fortescue to Lady Grenville, f. 36.

77. Images of England, No. 60510.

78. Charles Henderson, A.L. Rowse and M.I. Henderson (eds), 'Cornish deer parks', *Essays in Cornish History*, Oxford, 1935, pp. 157–162.

THE HISTORY OF A CORNISH ESTATE

79. CRO: F/4/3, 29 September 1431 to 30 September 1432.

80. BL: MS Cotton, Augustus I.i.38; the owners of Boconnoc, such as Thomas 'Diamond' Pitt (I), ordered their stewards to send venison to various friends and acquaintances. Those who were on the list to receive venison were often also sent pineapples; CRO: F/4/76.

81. BL: Add MS 69320, Lostwithiel, 24 January 1763, John Bennett to Thomas Pitt (III), f. 39; Lostwithiel, 8 March 1763, John Bennett to Thomas Pitt (III), f. 46; Add MS 69321, 18 March 1763, Thomas Bennett to Thomas Pitt, f. 2.

82. BL: Add MS 69321, Lostwithiel, 26 April 1763, John Bennett to Thomas Pitt, f. 6.

83. BL: Add MS 69322, Lostwithiel, 4 April 1766, f. 51.

84. BL: Add MS 69177, 10 January 1808, Watson Sharman to Lord Grenville, ff. 60–65.

85. BL: Add MS 69176, Boconnoc, 16 July 1809, Thomas Richards to Lady Grenville, ff. 166–167.

86. BL: Add MS 71594, Boconnoc, 10 February 1811, Sharman to Lady Grenville, f. 73; Lostwithiel, 31 May 1811, Bowen to Lord Grenville, f. 113; Dropmore, 17 June 1811, Lord Grenville to Bowen, f. 117; Valuation of deer, 13 August 1811, f. 139.

87. BL: Add MS 58873, Boconnoc, 9 October 1813, Lord Grenville to Lady Grenville, ff. 204–211; Add MS 59440, Boconnoc, 31 December 1813, J Bowen to Lord Grenville, f. 110; 12 January 1814, Grenville to Bowen, f. 120; 9 December 1813, J Bowen to Grenville, f. 101.

88. Neil A. Sanderson, 'Wildlife reports – lichens', December 2014; Nick Wright, *British Wildlife*, 26(2), pp. 139–140. ISSN 0958-0956; SSSI site notified to the Secretary of State on 14 November 1986.

89. Arthur G. Langdon, *Old Cornish Crosses*, Cornwall Books, 1896, pp. 20, 51–52, 291; Andrew Langdon, *Stone Crosses in Mid Cornwall*, Federation of Old Cornwall Societies, 1994.

90. CRO: P12/2/4/1.

91. Boconnoc.com

CHAPTER 8

THE CHURCH

'The massive oak altar table is inscribed "made by me, Sir Raynold Mohun 1621".'
(Peter Beacham and Nikolaus Pevsner, *The Buildings of England: Cornwall*,
New Haven and London, 2014, p. 105)

THE CHURCH BUILDING

The church, which is the parish church and not a private chapel, is situated on a hillock to the north-east of Boconnoc House and is in a close relationship with the mansion, similar to the configuration at Lanhydrock. The saint or saints to whom it was dedicated are not known. Some parts of the church date from the fourteenth century, but substantial restoration took place in 1873. The building consists of a chancel, nave, a north chancel aisle, a south aisle and a porch to the south. The chancel, nave and porch retain their wagon roofs and that of the north aisle has been partly restored. At the west end of the south aisle there is a musicians' gallery.

Figure 17 Drawing of Boconnoc church tower. (© Hampshire Record Office)

On the south-west of the church, there is a turret or tower, added to the building by G.M. Fortescue in 1838.[1] On removing the old vestry wall of the church it was found to be in a ruinous state so that a buttress was necessary. The tower was the substitute and cost about £60. In the early nineteenth century, there were four bells, nearly on a level with the ground, under a shed in the yard, which were sounded by moving a wooden handle similar to that of a pump. Three of them were broken up and stolen and the fourth, having been recast, was in 1839 suspended in the new turret.[2]

In 1886, when a new organ-chamber was constructed in Boconnoc church, a wheel-headed wayside or churchyard cross was discovered. It is incised on both sides with a cross and has been dated to the eighth or ninth century. It was placed in the churchyard, near to the gate that leads to Boconnoc House [*Plate 26*].

The church windows

When Richards Symonds was at Boconnoc with Charles I's army in 1644, he described the windows and monuments in his diary. The east and west windows and the east window in the 'south yle' were 'old' and portrayed the coats of arms of the Carminow, Courtenay and Mohun families.[3]

A plan of the church dated *c*. 1835, shows where the Grenvilles and their servants would sit during the services.

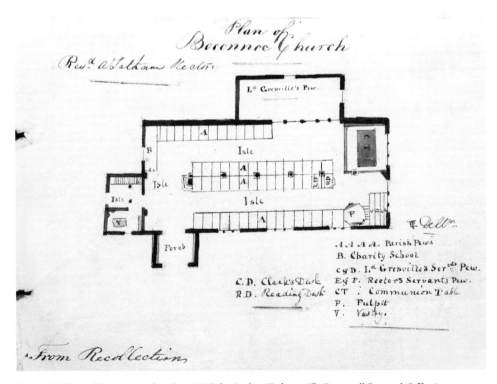

Figure 18 Plan of Boconnoc church, *c*. 1835, by Arthur Tatham. (© Cornwall Record Office)

In 1873, when the church was restored, the arcade of the south aisle was rebuilt and many of the windows were replaced, largely paid for by members of the Fortescue family. The main subjects include Christ stilling the waves on the window dedicated to George Grenville Fortescue, perhaps a reference to his death on the yacht in the Mediterranean, the Sermon on the Mount, the Adoration of the Shepherds and the Magi, the Feeding of the 5,000 and other stories from the Bible. The window dedicated to Mary Aldham (née Fortescue) shows Mary of Bethany sitting at the foot of Christ.[4]

Some of the windows were made by well-known companies. The windows in the south aisle, dedicated to Lady Louisa Fortescue, were by Burlison & Grylls, a company with an excellent reputation for its fine work.[5] The window dedicated to Mary Aldham was by Clayton & Bell, one of the most prolific English workshops producing stained glass during the latter half of the nineteenth century and the early part of the twentieth. Their products were highly sought after due to the excellence of their designs, their glass typified by brilliant luminosity and their use of colour.

The church furniture

The font in the church can be dated from its decoration to the fifteenth century [*Plate 27*]. The reredos of 1888 was created by Harry Hams of Exeter from wood taken from the house. The rood screen, which may have been moved to Boconnoc from Braddock church, has been utilised as a parclose screen to separate the north chapel from the rest of the church.

The oak altar table is inscribed 'made by me, Sir Raynold Mohun 1621'. The Mohuns' coat of arms is on the front. The octagonal pulpit, dated 1629, has carvings of cherubs who are holding musical instruments, including a lysaden constructed in an 'S' shape, also known as a tenor cornett, for which composers were writing mainly in the early seventeenth century.

On the wall are the royal arms of Charles I in painted plaster, dated 1639.

Memorials and monuments

High above the south arcade in the nave are two fine carved reliefs. On the east are the figures of death, time with an hourglass and a sleeping figure. On the west is a kneeling woman, Penelope Drew (née Mohun), wife of William Drew, who was buried on 30 March 1637. Above the figure are the words: 'To the memory of the trewly vertuous Penelope the daughter of Sr Raynold Mohun Knight and Barronett [*c.* 1564–1639] for a short tyme wife unto William Drew of Broad Henbury [Broadhembury] in the County of Devon esquire.' Below the figure is the following verse, including a pun upon her husband's name:

My name was Mohun, my fates like various were;
My short life's often changes make it cleare.
A virgin star on earth a wife I shind

With noted splendour cheifly of the mind,
Till my Will. Drew me to his nuptial bed,
Then soone by God's high call to heaven I fled,
Not without hope in Christ to live agen,
Set in the walls of his Jerusalem.[6]

Symonds also wrote about a 'faire monument' on the north wall of the chancel, the picture of a man and two women, six sons and three daughters with the inscription, 'Here lyeth the body of Sir William Mohun, who dyed 6 April, 1588.' Over the heads of the sons are shown the coats of arms of Mohun and his wife and over the daughters, the names and the coats of their husbands.[7]

Another monument at the east end has portraits of three children and the coats of arms of Mohun and of Chudleigh. 'Here lyeth interred three children of Sir Reynold Mohun, Knt. and Baronet, whome he had by his wife, the Lady Dorothy Mohun, Sir Reynold's third wife, née Chudleigh.'

After the death of the 1st Lord Camelford in 1793, there was discussion about creating a monument to him in the church. John Flaxman (1755–1826), a British sculptor and draughtsman, was a leading figure in British and European Neoclassicism. At the beginning of his career, he worked as a modeller for Josiah Wedgwood's pottery and subsequently he became a prolific maker of funery monuments. In 1797 he wrote to Lord Grenville, saying that he had received the plans of Boconnoc church in which a monument was to be erected to the late Lord Camelford. He had two or three questions to ask about the nature and situation of the work before he started preparing the designs. In the end, the project did not proceed.[8]

THE DE CANCIAS

In 1266, the de Cancia family had the right to appoint the priest. Walter Peverel was admitted to the church of 'Boskenech' on 15 April 1266, Patron, Sir Thomas de Cancia.[9] (For a full list of the rectors, see Appendix 1 on page 234)

In the year 1269, the Bishop of Exeter, Walter Bronescombe (known as 'the Good') had purchased Gargaul (or Cargoll) in the parish of St Newlyn East which was to become the site of a medieval palace for the Bishops of Exeter.[10] Thomas de Cancia 'ruined the park of Gargaul' and Bronescombe excommunicated him. This was a serious punishment, for the malefactor was deprived of the sacraments and expelled from the church community. If he died, still excommunicate, his soul would be consigned to hell for all eternity and his body could not be buried in consecrated ground. Given these potential consequences, de Cancia had no alternative but to make his peace with the bishop. On 15 June 1275, he wrote a letter admitting his offence and that he had been 'involved in violence and insults unjustly used against priests and clerks att Gargaul' and had been guilty of other offences against the church and the bishop. He expressed his repentance and promised to pay fifty marks to the bishop on fixed dates as reparation. He also promised not to commit any further such offences and accepted that if he reneged on his promise, the sentence of excommunication would be reimposed. A footnote in the Bishop's Register confirms that the bishop had received fifty marks from Thomas de Cancia.[11]

In 1282, the rector Thomas de Ken (or de Cancia) obtained licence to study theology or canon law as he might decide, in Paris or at Oxford, for three years.[12] The next rector, Walter de Kent, was probably a relative of Thomas.

Being a clergyman did not prevent Walter from being accused of criminal activity. In the Cornwall Eyre of 1302, Richard, son of William de Tregadener, presented himself against eight men, including Walter de Kent 'parson of the church of Boccunekes' and claimed that at 'Lostwythiel' they had made 'an assault and beat wounded and badly maltreated and inflicted other enormities upon him to the injury of Richard himself of one hundred marks and against the king's peace'. Walter and two other men were arrested and they were 'in mercy'.[13] The sheriff was ordered to distrain them, that is to seize their property, but unfortunately there is no information about how the case was resolved.

THE CARMINOWS

By 1321, the right to appoint the priest had passed, with the manor, to the Carminows.[14] On 18 October of that year, Bishop Stapledon dedicated the church, although the saint or saints to whom it was dedicated are unknown.[15] A letter written by the Reverend Martin Picken to the rector of Boconnoc, Percy Austin Openshaw, makes the following suggestions:

Boconnoc is a corruption of Bod-Conoc = Conoc's house. 'Bod' is usually found in placenames with only secular associations so Bod-conoc, prima facie, would not suggest that Conoc was a Cornish 'saint'. Nevertheless it is a very curious coincidence that the 9th century author of the "Life of S. Winnoc" (patron of St Winnow parish) names as one of S. Winnoc's 'companions'… a man whose name, Ingenoc, is quite possibly a version of Conoc. The Conoc of Boconnoc might also be identified with the St Cynog (the pronunciation would be the same), one of the children of Brychan of the Welsh traditions. It is possible that Conoc, though probably not the patron of the church, may actually have been another Celtic saint. He may have been that Welshman whose connections, the 'children' of Brychan, are patrons of so many parishes near Boconnoc – Fowey, Lanreath, Pelynt, Morval and St Keyne. He may also – not necessarily alternatively – have been that rather mysterious Igenoc, companion of S Winnoc because Boconnoc was one of the chapelries of S Winnow parish through the middle ages.[16]

The church visitations – 1281 and 1331

The basic unit of the church in Cornwall, as elsewhere, was the parish. There were some complications in the general situation, for there were what were called 'peculiar jurisdictions', which were not part of a rural deanery and therefore outside the normal system. The cathedral of Exeter had two peculiar churches. One of these was St Winnow, which included Boconnoc and Bradoc (Braddock or Broadoak), which was administered as a separate entity by the cathedral and had its own officers and courts.[17]

From the thirteenth century, the Church authorities made inspections of parish churches. These records provide information about church fabric, ornaments, vestments and books.[18] The visitation of 1281 did not include Boconnoc, but that in 1331 did, in addition to thirteen other churches and three chapels. By that date, John Grandisson, Bishop of Exeter, had been in office for four years. Being a reformer, he wanted to ensure that all the churches and clergy in his diocese were functioning properly.[19]

The visitation of 1331 was carried out after Easter (*post Festum Pasche*), which in that year was on 31 March, by a cathedral canon, Sir Richard de Brayleghe, a special representative of the Dean and Chapter of Exeter deputed to tour Cornwall. The regulations specified that each church should possess a silver chalice for use at mass, other decent vessels, suitable linen such as a frontal (a decorative cloth hanging down in front of the altar), appropriate service books, at least two sets of vestments, a stone font, a woman's veil for marriages, a pall to cover bodies at funerals, and a cross and banner for processions.[20] The reality often fell far short of the ideal, as can be seen from the entry for Boconnoc:

Boconnoc [Bodkonok] is in St Winnow within the peculiar jurisdiction of the Dean and Chapter of Exeter. It is wanting a communion cup for the sick. There are two corporal cloths without suitable storage places. It is wanting one set of vestments. It is wanting adornment [embroidery] for altar-cloths for the high altar. It is wanting one surplice. It is wanting one rochet. It is wanting the Lenten and marriage veil. It lacks a burial pall and altar frontal. The missal is in poor [inadequate] condition. There is a dilapidated [worn] troper. It lacks an order of service book [ordinal]. The pyx lacks locks and fastening. The chrismatory is dilapidated and lacks a lock. The lattice to the pax-board is inadequate. The cruets are dilapidated. It lacks a vessel for the incense and the Easter [paschal] candlestick. The portable cross is dilapidated. The font is without lock. It lacks a canopy over the high altar.[21]

At the time of the visitation, the rector was Peter Castle or de Castro, who had been instituted on 19 May in that year. Nicholas Orme suggests that he was a clergyman of the diocese who had building skills and may have been brought in by the Chapter or by Bishop Grandisson to help with the building of the cathedral at Exeter. He had died by 10 December 1334.[22]

Ralph de Carminow

During the time that Ralph de Carminow was the owner of Boconnoc, the rector, John Phelipp, issued a letter appointing Walter Braddon as his attorney in order that Walter could deliver to Ralph de Carminow and Alice his wife seisin (possession) of land and a tenement in the 'manor of Asfitzwater'. John placed his seal on the document, which was 'given at Bodconek on Friday next after the feast of Saint Barnabus the apostle in the fiftieth year of the reign of king Edward the third after the conquest' (Friday, 13 June 1376).[23]

In the medieval period a grant or gift of land was signified by *livery of seisin*, that was the ceremony of taking possession by physical transfer of a turf or a key. The deed or charter was prepared subsequently and was regarded as no more than evidence of an event which had already taken place. On occasions the grantor was precluded from delivering seisin, and in these circumstances would appoint another, or an attorney, to act in his stead.

In 1383, Ralph and his wife were given licence by the Bishop of Exeter to celebrate divine services *in capella sive oratio* (in a chapel or oratory) in their 'manor of Bodconoke'. The chapel or oratory may have been in a building separate from the house.[24]

Ralph de Carminow, who died on 9 October 1386, was also patron of the parish church of Menheniot, as well as of Ladock and Boconnoc. In his will, he asked to be buried in Menheniot church, where the Latin inscription of his tomb's brass plate, probably the oldest brass in Cornwall, survives on the floor of the nave, close to the chancel steps. It is undated, but the inscription reads: *Orate pro anima domini Radulphi Carmynow militis cuius anime propicietur deus Amen* (Pray for the soul of Sir Radulph Carmynow, knight, on whose soul may God have mercy. Amen) [*Plate 28*].

Ralph de Carminow bequeathed the sum of £40 for his burial. In total, his monetary bequests amounted to £109. To Agnes, 'maid of my wife', he left twenty shillings, to Alice his daughter and only child, the sum of ten marks, but she had predeceased him. He left to all the convents of mendicant friars of Devon and Cornwall £40 and forty shillings for masses to be said. The executors of his will were *Aliciam consortem meam* (Alice, my consort), Sir John Kentwood, steward of the Duchy of Cornwall and Sir John Phelipp, who by 1382 had moved from Boconnoc and had been presented to the living of Menheniot by de Carminow. Bishop Brantyngham of Exeter heard of de Carminow's death three days after it occurred *non absque gravi cordis dolore* (not without severe heart pain – with heavy sorrow and grief), although that did not prevent him from sequestrating de Carminow's property, allowing payments to be released only for funeral expenses. John Phelipp refused to accept the sequestration and was cited to appear before the bishop for disobedience. It was now that it was revealed that Carminow had been very closely associated with the bishop as his tenant and had worn the bishop's livery.[25] The Archbishop of Canterbury, William Courtenay, annulled the probate of Sir Ralph's testament, granted by the commissary of the Bishop of Exeter, claiming that because Ralph de Carminow had owned moveable and immoveable goods in different dioceses of the province of Canterbury, his will should be proved in the Prerogative Court of Canterbury. Since one of the executors named in the will, Sir John Phelipp, together now with Sir William Searle, rectors of the churches of Menheniot (Mahennyet) and Bradoc (Broadoak or Braddock), refused the burden of administration, power was committed to the Prior of Launceston. Ultimately, the undated will was proved in the Archbishop's Chapel at Lambeth on 30 January 1387.[26]

On 29 May 1397, a further grant of an oratory in the manor of Boconnoc (Bokoenek) was given to William de Carminow and his wife Margaret.[27]

THE FIFTEENTH TO SEVENTEENTH CENTURIES

On 1 March 1445, Nicholas Radeforde, Richard Arscote, clerk, rector of Ashwater in Devon and John Palmere presented Thomas Olertone, chaplain, to the bishop for the parish church of Boconnoc 'said to be vacant'. John Houper (or Hopere) had been instituted on 25 February 1418 and had drawn his last breath on 15 February 1445 and that was the day when the living had become vacant. A Commission of Enquiry was held in St Nectan's Chapel before six of the rectors of the local churches, Lanreath, Broadoak (Braddock), Warleggan, St Neot, St Winnow and Lanlivery, to decide who now had the right to present to the living. On a previous occasion, Thomas Montague, Earl of Salisbury, had presented to Boconnoc, as guardian of John de Carminow, true patron of the church, but who was at the time a minor. The right to present had then been passed to Nicholas Radeforde, Richard Arscote and John Palmere by reason of a feoffment (a grant of ownership) made to them by Thomas de Carminow. Under these circumstances, Thomas Olertone was accepted by the bishop, presented to the church and ordained, aged 35, on 3 March 1445.[28]

Olertone was born in 1410. He was a Vicar Choral of Wells Cathedral and then a Vicar Choral of Exeter from 1437 in the stall of John Hody, who was Chancellor of Wells Cathedral and possibly brought Olertone to Exeter. Following Olertone's resignation in 1454, Sir Walter Colle was instituted on 15 March, when the patrons were still Nicholas Radeforde, Richard Arscote and John Palmere. He was followed in 1462 by John Pawton, who may have taken his surname from Pawton in St Breock parish.[29] In the 1440s, he was described by the city authorities of Exeter as one of the 'rioters' among the clergy of the cathedral close, who impeded city officers and 'caused noise and affray in the city'. He was instituted as rector of Boconnoc on 20 December 1462.[30]

In 1646, after the Civil War, many clergymen were ejected from parishes in Cornwall because they were accused of 'Royalism'. This included John Hardinge at Boconnoc, but together with other Cornish clergy in 1660 he was restored to his living.[31]

THE EIGHTEENTH AND NINETEENTH CENTURIES

Charles Peters (1690–1774)

Hebraist and Church of England clergyman, Charles Peters was born at Tregony on 1 December 1690. He received the early part of his education at Mr Daddow's school in his home village. He matriculated at Exeter College, Oxford on 3 April 1707, aged 16, when he was described as 'the son of Richard Peters, pleb of Tregony'. He graduated BA on 27 October 1710 and MA on 6 June 1713. He was instituted to Boconnoc on 21 March 1714, by the patron Elizabeth, Lady Mohun. He was still there in 1723 and during his incumbency he built the south front of the old parsonage house (later the stewardry). He was appointed to Bratton Clovelly in 1723 and in November 1726 to the rectory of St Mabyn, and he held both with Boconnoc. While at St Mabyn, he was able to pursue his studies without interruption and he published a number of books, including *A Critical Dissertation on the Book of Job* in 1751. After his death, his nephew, Jonathan Peters, vicar of St Clements in Truro, published a volume of his sermons. He was known for an 'uninterrupted enjoyment of health', which was attributed to 'that happy relief which his bodily exercises afforded to his sedentary habits'. He died on 11 February 1774, aged 83.[32] His curate at Boconnoc was Thomas Whitford.

The churchwardens' accounts

Churchwardens' account books survive from 1773–1846.[33] Churchwardens were lay officials whose primary job was (and is) to procure and disburse funds for the maintenance of the parish church and other buildings owned by the parish and to offer aid to the poor. They were elected to their positions by members of the laity and usually served a single term of one year.

From Easter 1782 to Easter 1783, the churchwardens were Thomas Bryant and Thomas Alee. Some of the sums they disbursed were: 'for Bread and wine for two Sacraments, 10s.4d; Sixton wages and washing ye Cirplice, 13s.6d; Thomas Alee's Bill for killing Vermons, 4s.0d.'

In other years, sums were paid out to 'a poor man in distress not incerted in ye Poor book, 1s.0d; for a singing feast for the choir, £2.2s.0d; to Mr Soloman for Instructing Singers, £2.0s.0d; Clearing the Iveys from the wall, 1s.0d; to George Motton for work Cleaning the Seats, 9s.2½d'. Motton was also paid 9s.0d for 'Cleaning 6 Windows and Repairing Glass and the casements; and for putting in a new Window and glass work done on the Church, £4.1s.11d'. A note in the book records that the rector thought that George Motton's bill for 9s.0d for cleaning the windows was exorbitant and 'therefore should be enquired into and ratified before this acc^t can be passed'.

In 1823–24, amounts were also expended on 'A Base [*sic*] Viol £4.0s.0d, a Bagg for the viol, 3s.6d, strings for the viol, 5s.0d and for repairing the instrument, strings and candles, 11s.2d'.[34]

Benjamin Forster (1736–1805)

Benjamin Forster was born in London on 7 August 1736. He was educated at Hertford School and Corpus Christi College, Cambridge. He became rector of Boconnoc, Broadoak (Braddock) and Caerhayes in Cornwall in 1773. Forster was eccentric, surrounding himself with a menagerie of pet animals, but his letters show him to have been a man of taste and learning and a proficient antiquary.

In a return requested from him by Bishop Ross in 1779, Forster wrote:

> This parish was united to Bradoc by Act of Parliament in 1742 and are under the peculiar jurisdiction of the Dean and Chapter. I reside at the Parsonage at Boconnoc. I have a curate Mr Dixon who lives with me in the Parsonage and to whom I pay £50. There are 4 Celebrations in each Church. Communicants Boconnoc 20, Bradoc 23. Families Boconnoc 43 Bradoc 40. No Dissenters. I also hold the Vicarage and sinecure Rectory of Carhais, St Stephens and St Dennis.

The patron was Thomas Pitt of Boconnoc.[35]

Forster was a strange character. In December 1780, Thomas Pitt (III) wrote to William Pennington: 'Poor Forster is got into a squabble with his Lostwithiel friends about a hunting party who have been frighting the wood nymphs from their hallow'd haunts' and Pitt made reference to Forster's 'awkwardness and want of method in his domestic matters'.[36] While Pitt and Forster were close friends, on occasion Pitt worried about Forster's conduct. In 1786, Pitt wrote: 'I am always sorry when you tell me traits of Forster that are recountable from nothing but a tendency to insanity – I am sure I do not wish he should control either his sentiments or society in conformity to mine nor do I pretend to have any such right over him; but I cannot help thinking it odd that his opinions and personal preferences should happen almost invariably to run in direct opposition to me.'[37]

In the following year, Pitt wrote: 'I had a serious letter from Forster admirably well written as a sort of justification of his way of passing his time in answer to a word that had fallen in one of my letters – I have no other right to interest myself in except from the interest I take in his happiness and estimation in the World which cannot make me indifferent to what tends at the same time to distress his finances and to cheapen his fame.'[38]

It is evident that Forster was not universally popular. A man called James Wallis wrote that he was very pleased to hear the manner in which the 2nd Lord Camelford had addressed 'that creature Mr Foster [sic]'. 'It is a pity that so old a Clergyman is so bad a man …'[39]

Whatever might have been thought of him, Forster was cultured and a scholar. He wrote a stanza relating to the rectory in which he lived, sited behind Boconnoc House, in a beautifully secluded valley, among majestic trees:

A little lowly hermitage it was,
Down in a dale, hard by a forest's side,
Far from resort of people it did pass
In travail to and fro.

Thomas Gray (1716–71)

Thomas Gray, the poet who wrote *Elegy Written in a Country Churchyard*, was a friend and frequent guest of Forster. It has been suggested that some lines in his *Elegy* may have been inspired by a beech tree on the Boconnoc estate. This seems unlikely as Forster did not become rector of Boconnoc until 1773 and the *Elegy* was published in 1751. It is more likely that this rumour was inadvertently started by Thomas Pitt (III) during a visit by Josiah Wedgwood in 1775. Pitt gave Wedgwood a tour of the estate during which he repeated these lines from the *Elegy*:

There at the foot of yonder nodding beech
That wreathes its old fantastic roots so high,
His listless length at noontide would he stretch,
And pore upon the brook that babbles by.

In a book of sketches and verses created and compiled by Annie and Harriet Fortescue, dedicated to their father George Matthew Fortescue, they wrote a number of sonnets about various aspects of the estate, including one that makes reference to Gray's *Elegy* and the beech tree. This one was written by Harriet:

Notes on Sonnet III Gray's Beech, April 1, 1852.
If thou wouldst meditate a while alone
Go: seek sweet Valley Crucis' solitude,
When thou mayst wander freely thro' the wood
And hear no other footsteps than thine own.
But should the heat oppress thee, thou mayst lie
To rest beneath the old and "nodding beech".
Where Gray of yore 'his listless length would stretch'
And pore upon the brook that babbles by –
Here, food for meditation may be found
Here, thou mayst sit nor living thing be near
Save birds that warble round thee, & the deer
That lightly bound across the rushy ground,
Or pause to scan with timid curious eye
The bold intruder on their privacy
HEF Ap 1. 1852[40]

The last living limb of the tree fell in the winter of 1850 and the whole has now disappeared.

The death and funeral of Benjamin Forster

In October 1805, Forster became very ill of the yellow jaundice and he died on 2 December at Boconnoc Parsonage, unmarried and aged 70 years of age.[41] He wrote a lengthy preamble to his will, setting out how he wanted his funeral to be conducted. Having lived among his parishioners for 'three and thirty years' as a friend and protector, he hoped they would lament his loss. He had made arrangements for a frugal funeral and desired that his body should not be carried into the church, but met 'at the church yard stile' by the officiating minister and from there process immediately to the grave. He wished that his remains should be 'inclosed in a plain flat coffin' like those of the neighbouring farmers without any pall or mark of distinction. Four labouring men should be the bearers and each should be given five shillings. The funeral should be held at about 11 a.m. and his final resting place was to be under a sycamore tree on the north side of the church.[42]

He made detailed provisions in his will about which members of his family should receive which books from his library. The books included Edmund Spenser's *Fairie Queene*, the works of Chaucer, *Elymologieum Magnum* (a very rare and valuable book), an edition of *Erasmus's Greek Testament*, a book in his own hand containing music by Pergolasi, and Mason's *Memoirs of Gray*.

Thomas Bennett

Thomas Bennett was instituted to the United Rectories of Boconnoc and Braddock, vacant by the death of Benjamin Forster, on the presentation of Lord and Lady Grenville. Bennett was rector until May 1832.[43]

It did not take John Bowen long to try to exploit the situation of the living being vacant to his own advantage when he asked Lord and Lady Grenville to appoint one of his sons to the benefice, which 'would open up the prospect of a settlement for him and a home for his sisters in the event of their loss in me', despite the fact that none of Bowen's sons were in or considering taking holy orders.[44]

Arthur Tatham (1808–74)

Arthur Tatham was born on 22 September 1808 at York Place, Marylebone, London. He was educated at St Paul's School, Cheapside in London, which he entered on 1 June 1818, aged 9, and then proceeded to Magdalene College, Cambridge where he graduated BA in 1832 and MA in 1835. He was an affiliate of an association known as the Shoreham Ancients, an art group whose members were followers of William Blake.

In 1832, his father, Charles Heathcote Tatham, who followed Samuel Wyatt as architect of Dropmore and was warden of Greenwich Hospital, wrote to introduce Arthur to Lord Grenville's notice with a view to his son being presented to the vacant living of Boconnoc and Braddock.[45] Grenville set out the requirements that he believed a good rector should possess, namely that he should have an impression of the awful responsibility that he was taking on behalf of those committed to his charge, a faithful duty to them with earnest,

Figure 19 Reverend Arthur Tatham.
(© Hampshire Record Office)

zealous and unwearied diligence, pure morals, exemplary piety and a sincere attachment to the established principles of the Church, whose doctrines he would inculcate and enforce by persuasion and his conduct. If Lord Grenville could be persuaded by Tatham's father that his son possessed all these attributes, Lady Grenville would offer him the living. The usual income was about £450 per annum and there was a house provided in which he would be expected to reside.[46] The Grenvilles must have been convinced, for despite the fact that he was only 23 years old, Arthur Tatham was offered the living.

The Tathams, father and son, arrived at Boconnoc early in October and were received by John Bowen. They were disappointed to find, after a survey of the rectory house and outbuildings, that they were in a very forlorn and dilapidated state and could not be repaired and fitted for occupation until the spring of the following year. The gates, glebe and fences were in the same poor condition. In view of these circumstances, Arthur Tatham was given permission to live in the mansion until the rectory was put into repair, to the delight of Mrs Rhind, the housekeeper, who was very happy at the prospect of having 'Company' in the house during the winter months.[47]

Charles Heathcote Tatham had some observations to make about Boconnoc church:

> The Pews of Boconnoc are in good order, that of your Ladyship's I greatly admire, but I think the pulpit is very awkwardly placed for light and for the Clergyman being seen and heard by his Congregation – it might be transposed against the external wall, where I am told it formerly stood, at a very easy charge to the Parish.[48]

Arthur Tatham was ordained priest on 28 October 1832 at Exeter and the following day was instituted to the rectory of Boconnoc.[49] The tithe was £390 and there were eighty-two acres of glebe. At the time he became rector, the population of Boconnoc was 323 and of Broadoak, 274.

In 1833, candidates were put forward for confirmation at Boconnoc. They were aged between 14 and 40 years of age and there were ten males and seven females, including Thomas Wills, John Rickards and Elizabeth Carne, all of whom were residing at the stewardry.[50] Elizabeth Carne was (probably) the same Elizabeth who was bound a parish apprentice to Lord Grenville and resided with John Bowen until shortly after Lord Grenville's death in January 1835. For more about her settlement and her removal to Boconnoc parish in 1849 under the Poor Law regulations, see Chapter 10.

On 22 June 1835, Tatham married Harriet Edwards. She gave birth to a stillborn son in 1838 and they had no further children. Harriet died on 2 May 1843 and ten years later, on 19 May 1853, he married Jemima Amabel Glanville. They had four children: Harriet Amabel (b. 1854), Mary Agneta (b. 1855), Arthur Glanville (b. 1856) and George Julius (b. 1858).[51]

In 1859, Tatham was trying to raise money to buy a new harmonium for the church. George Fortescue donated £5 and the singers in the choir offered to give up their singing feast that year and contribute the £3 that it would have cost towards the new instrument. There was an 'old Base [sic] Viol', the property of the parish that could be sold for £1 or upwards, the proceeds of which could be applied to the same object.[52]

In addition to being rector of Boconnoc and Broadoak, Tatham was a prebendary of Exeter Cathedral from 1860 to 1874. He wrote several pamphlets and tracts: *Prayers for the Use of the Members of the Church of England during the present troubles* (1851), and *A Cornish Bishopric, the Necessity and Means for its Restoration* (1859).[53] Apart from the duties attached to his parishes, he sat as a magistrate for more than forty years.

Arthur Tatham died at Broadoak Rectory on 22 February 1874.[54] According to a letter from Arthur's brother, Frederick in north-west London, to another brother, Robert Bristow Tatham in South Africa, dated 31 March 1877, Arthur's death was 'very sad and his suffering great'.[55]

An advertisement in a local newspaper, dated 11 March 1874, gave notice of a sale by auction at Glebe Farm, Broadoak of the whole of the farm stock, implements of husbandry, corn and hay, the property of the late Reverend Prebendary Tatham.

William Pease wrote in his diary:

We heard this morning that the Reverend Arthur Tatham of Braddock died last night about 10 pm. Anne and I attended Mr Tatham's funeral which was fixed for 1.30. A large number attended. He was 65 years old and was Rector of the Parishes of Boconnoc and Braddock between 41 and 42 years. The grave was bricked round to little more than the height of the coffin and then filled up with Earth – no stones have been placed over the coffin.[56]

Vernon Harcourt Aldham (1844–1929)

The next rector was Vernon Harcourt Aldham, who preached for the first time on Sunday, 12 April 1874 and 'was generally liked'. Aldham was born in 1844 in Stoke Prior, Worcestershire. He married Jane Seymour (née Carr-Lloyd) and the couple had four children: George Seymour Harcourt, Constance Mary, Michael Seymour and Rachel Dorothy. In the 1881 census of Boconnoc, the children were aged 9, 7, 5 and 3. Jane Aldham died at Broadoak Rectory on 5 January 1878, aged only 35.[57]

Six years after his wife's death, to the surprise of the Fortescue family, Aldham and Mary Fortescue announced their engagement. Harriet wrote in her diary: 'I was much startled but not sorry to hear from dear M that she is engaged to Mr Aldham.'[58] They were married on 22 July 1884. Harriet's diary for that date reads: 'Busy preparing favours. Dear Minna married to Mr Aldham at St Mark's. Constance, Francie and Miss Pierson bridesmaids. M looked very nice – all went well – large muster of family. Couple off to Dropmore after lunch.'[59]

THE TWENTIETH CENTURY

Minutes of the Parochial Church Council dating from 1922 to 1989 report on matters relating to the maintenance, care and upgrading of the church.[60] In 1924, Mrs Fortescue had given the gift of electric light to the church. In January 1933, G. Fortescue (Bevill and Dorothy's son) was elected Chairman of the Council. On 19 February 1934, it was noted that the slate of the church roof was in very bad condition and a report commissioned by the Church Council showed a very serious state of affairs with the laths of the ceiling being entirely perished and other woodwork and the main beams wormeaten. The cost of repairs was estimated to be from £450 to £500 and an appeal for funds was made to the parishioners.

Public teas were always held on the occasion of the induction and institution of a new rector; the Reverend Charles Percival Triplett (1936–43), the Reverend Evan Thomas (1943–44), the Reverend Harold Dalton Streatfield (1945–52), the Reverend Percy Austin Openshaw (1952–57) and in the 1950s and 1960s, the Reverend George Robert Owen Jones, the Reverend Laurence William Day and the Reverend Canon Alfred Edwin Peaston.

When Canon Peaston retired in June 1972, a priest-in-charge was appointed, as distinct from a fully inducted rector. Minutes of a meeting held on 21 June 1972 reported that Canon Peaston's successor was to be Mark Bevan Kennaway. He would take up his duties on 1 September. Mr Kennaway moved on early in June 1974 and the next priest-in-charge was Geoffrey Gilbert Pinnock.

In March 1980, the Rural Dean reported on a proposal that the joint benefice of Boconnoc and Braddock which had existed since 1742, should be dissolved and Boconnoc attached to the Liskeard Team Ministry, while Braddock would be linked with

Duloe. At the PCC meeting on 21 June 1980, it was pointed out that the two parishes were a united community and always joined together for services and social occasions. Ultimately, it was confirmed that the two parishes would remain united, but new arrangements were put into place in 1988, listing Boconnoc with St Winnow, St Veep and Lostwithiel in an unofficial partnership. In about 1990, Boconnoc parish was subsumed into the benefice of Lostwithiel, St Winnow with St Nectan's Chapel, and St Veep.

THE TWENTY-FIRST CENTURY

As with other parishes in Cornwall, the shortage of clergymen and women now means that many parishes share a priest. Boconnoc remains part of a group of parishes around Lostwithiel: St Bartholomew, St Winnow and St Nectan's Chapel, St Saviour in Bridgend and St Veep (St Cyricius and St Julitta). Members of the congregation at Boconnoc take some of the services.

NOTES AND REFERENCES

1. British Library (BL): Add MS 69052, 1 November 1838, GM Fortescue to Lady Grenville, f. 3.
2. Cornwall Record Office (CRO): John Wallis, *The Cornwall Register*, Bodmin, 1847, p. 383.
3. Richard Symonds, C.E. Long (ed.), *Diary of the Marches of the Royal Army*, Cambridge, 1997, pp. 50–52.
4. The donors and dedicatees include: 1843, in the south aisle east, donor, Elizabeth Frances Fortescue, dedicatee, the children of the Honourable George Matthew Fortescue and Lady Louisa Fortescue; 1856, in the chancel east, donors, the Parishioners, dedicatee, George Grenville Fortescue; 1877, in the north aisle north, no donor, dedicatee, the Honourable George Matthew Fortescue; 1881, in the nave north, donors, the Fortescues in memory of William Pease (the Steward); 1890, in the north aisle west, no donor, dedicatee, Lieutenant-Colonel Cyril Dudley Fortescue; 1900, south aisle, donated by the family in memory of Lady Louisa Fortescue and 1927, south aisle, donor, Elizabeth Frances Fortescue in memory of Mary Aldham (née Fortescue); www.cornishstainedglass.org.uk.
5. flickr.com; Clayton & Bell were commissioned by John Loughborough Pearson to provide the windows for the newly constructed Truro Cathedral.
6. Symonds, *op. cit.*, p. 52; Peter Beacham and Nikolaus Pevsner, The Buildings of England: Cornwall, New Haven, CT and London, 2014, p. 105; Cornwall Historic Churches Trust, www.chct.info.histories.Boconnoc.
7. Symonds, *op. cit.*, p. 51.
8. BL: Add MS 59492, 27 July 1797, John Flaxman to Lord Grenville, f. 146.
9. Register of Bishop Bronescombe, 1257–1280, F.C. Hingeston-Randolph (ed.), London and Exeter, 1889, p. 40 and p. 115.
10. Images of England, No. 63970.
11. Bronescombe Register, 1257–80, *op. cit.*, p. 242.
12. Register of Bishop Quivil, 1280–1291, F.C. Hingeston-Randolph (ed.), London and Exeter, 1889, p. 315.
13. The National Archives (TNA): JUST1/117A, membrane 4.
14. CRO: AD409/22-26; a complete index of the rectors of Boconnoc is to be found in Appendix 1.

15. Register of Bishop Stapledon, 1307–1326, F.C. Hingeston-Randolph (ed.), London and Exeter, 1892, p. 55; Nicholas Orme, *English Church Dedications*, Exeter, 1996, pp. 69–70.

16. CRO: P17/2/8, 29 May 1953, Martin Picken to Percy Austin Openshaw, Rector of Boconnoc.

17. Nicholas Orme, *Cornwall and the Cross. Christianity 500–1560*, Chichester, 2007, pp. 30–31.

18. Nicholas Orme, 'Visitations of Cornish churches, 1281–1331', in Philip Payton (ed.), *Cornish Studies 21*, 2013, pp. 76–103.

19. Orme, *ibid.*, p. 78.

20. Orme, *Cornwall and the Cross, op. cit.*, pp. 55–57.

21. Register of Bishop Grandisson, Part II, 1331–1360, F.C. Hingeston-Randolph (ed.), London and Exeter, 1897, p. 605; Suitable storage places – burses, a pouch or case for some special purpose; surplice – a linen garment with wide sleeves for the priest; rocket – similar to a surplice but with close-fitting sleeves for the parish clerk; marriage veil – a nuptial veil made available for brides at a wedding; burial pall – a cloth that covered the coffin; troper – a medieval book containing tropes or sequences for farsing, a word or phrase interpolated as a embellishment in the sung parts of medieval liturgies or the sung parts of the mass; pyx – a receptacle to carry the consecrated host; chrismatory – an ampulla or jar, usually made of silver or pewter, used for containing chrism oil, consecrated oil for sacraments; pax board – most churches had a pax board, direct kissing giving the sign of peace among the celebrants and congregation was replaced by each in turn kissing the pax board, which usually included a flat surface to be kissed and was carried around among those present. Translation from the Latin by Jim Sutton.

22. Nicholas Orme, *The Minor Clergy of Exeter Cathedral, Biographies: 1250–1548*, Exeter, 2013, p. 73.

23. Devon Record Office (DRO): 4088M/10/8; information about livery of seisin from Jim Sutton.

24 Register of Thomas de Brantyngham, Part I, 1370–1394, F.C. Hingeston-Randolph (ed.), London and Exeter, 1901, p. 499; Canon J.H. Adams, 'The Medieval Chapels of Cornwall', *Journal of the Royal Institution of Cornwall* (JRIC), Vol. III, New Series, Part I, 1957, pp. 48–65.

25. History of Parliament – Ralph de Carminow.

26. Nicholas Orme, *Cornish Wills 1342–1540*, Exeter, 2007, pp. 39–40; Ralph de Carminow, History of Parliament; London, Lambeth Palace Library, The Register of William Courtenay, f. 221r; Orme, *Cornish Wills, op. cit.*, pp. 39–40.

27. Register of Edmund Stafford, 1395–1419, F.C. Hingeston-Randolph (ed.), London and Exeter, 1886, p. 272.

28. Bishop Lacy's Register, 1420–55, F.C. Hingeston-Randolph (ed.), London and Exeter, 1909, pp. 295–296, ff. 214–215; Register of Bishop Stafford, *op. cit.*; RIC: Henderson Calendar, XVIII, p. 15.

29. This information comes from Nicholas Orme, *Minor Clergy, op. cit.*, passim.

30. Orme, *ibid.*, pp. 212–213.

31. Mary Coate, *Cornwall in the Great Civil War and Interregnum, 1642–1660*, pp. 331–332 and p. 350.

32. Dictionary of National Biography; CRO: Index of Clergy, AD409/22.

33. CRO: P12/5/1; Easter 1797 to Easter 1798.

34. This is of particular interest to the author, who plays the viol.

35. CRO: AD409/22, Index of clergy.

36. L: Add MS 69304, Oxford Street, 23 December 1780, Thomas Pitt (III) to William Pennington, ff. 19–20; Oxford Street, Tuesday, 16 December 1782, Thomas Pitt (III) to William Pennington, ff. 31–32.

37. BL: Add MS 69304, Montpellier, 30 December 1786, Thomas Pitt (III) to William Pennington, ff. 94–95.

38. BL: Add MS 69304, Montpellier, 7 February 1787, Pitt to William Pennington, ff. 98–99.

39. BL: Add MS 69314, Decade, Hamoze, 19 September 1799, James Wallis to Lady Camelford, ff. 103–104; sermons given by Forster are in the CRO: EN/2003.

40. The *Elegy* was completed in 1750 and published in 1751; Hampshire Record Office (HRO): 115M88/F6/2, Book of sketches and verses relating to Boconnoc by Louisa S.A. Fortescue and Harriet E. Fortescue, 1852.
41. BL: Add MS 69176, Lostwithiel, 31 October 1805, Thomas Bennett to Lord Grenville, ff. 25–26; St Teath, 3 December 1805, Thomas Bennett to Lord Grenville, ff. 42–43.
42. TNA: Will of Benjamin Forster, PROB11/1436, probate granted 14 January 1806.
43. Thursday, 6 March 1806, *Trewman's Exeter Flying Post*; CRO: F/3/10/519, Boconnoc, John Bowen to Lady Grenville; *Liverpool Mercury*, Friday, 1 June 1832.
44. BL: Add MS 59468, 25 May 1832, John Lakes to William Rashleigh, f. 113; CRO: F/3/10/519, Boconnoc, John Bowen to Lord and Lady Grenville, 31 May and 9 June 1832.
45. BL: Add MS 58997, 34 Alpha Road, Regents Park, 9 August 1832, CH Tatham to Lord Grenville, f. 103.
46. BL: Add MS 58997, Dropmore, 4 September 1832, Lord Grenville to CH Tatham, ff. 103–105.
47. BL: Add MS 58997, Boconnoc, 27 October 1832, CH Tatham to Lady Grenville, ff. 122–123.
48. BL: Add MS 58997, Boconnoc, 27 October 1832, CH Tatham to Lady Grenville, ff. 122–123.
49. BL: Add MS 58997, 24 September 1832, CH Tatham to Lord Grenville, ff. 116–117.
50. CRO: P17/2/4.
51. *Trewman's Exeter Flying Post and Plymouth and Cornish Advertiser*, 24 May 1838; Harriet Tatham, 14 March 1803 to 2 May 1843; Jemima Amabel Glanville, 23 November 1823 to 16 February 1892.
52. CRO: F/3/10/80, 12 July 1859.
53. CRO: TCM/155.
54. *Royal Cornwall Gazette, Falmouth Packet* and *General Advertiser*, 28 February 1874.
55. saxonlodge.net
56. CRO: X715/36, Monday 23 February 1874, Pease's diary; X715/36, Saturday 28 February 1874.
57. CRO: X715/36, Sunday 12 April 1874, Pease's diary; *Royal Cornwall Gazette*, 11 January 1878, p. 8.
58. HRO: 115M88/F21/35B, Saturday 31 May 1884, Harriet's diary.
59. HRO: 115M88/F21/35B, Tuesday 22 July 1884, Harriet's diary.
60. CRO: P12/7/1.

CHAPTER 9

INDUSTRY AND AGRICULTURE

'I first discovered the petuntse in the parish of Germo, in a hill called Tregonnin Hill.'
(William Cookworthy, on discovering china-clay deposits in Cornwall)

MINING

Mining in Cornwall began around the year 2150 BC in the Early Bronze Age. It ceased 4,000 years later in 1998, when the mine at South Crofty closed. The metals that were extracted were primarily copper and tin, although over time the former was gradually superseded by the latter. There were references to a tin mine owned by the Boconnoc estate at Blaketorr, from which the profits were accounted for by John Weryng in 1511–12.[1] In the early seventeenth century, Anne Mohun bequeathed 'all my Tynn works within the County of Cornwaill' to her grandson John Trelawny.[2]

Land both 'down west' and in the parish of St Stephens-in-Brannel, which was owned by the Boconnoc estate, was mined extensively. Thomas Pitt (III), later Lord Camelford, was sent the lease of a sett in 1784 by his steward Thomas Bennett: 'under cover I have sent the sett for the new Adventure in St Stephens which I hope will be of some consequence in a few years, as there is certainly a good quantity of Tin in the Ground which is granted'.[3]

The Condurrow and Grenville mines
Mining reached its zenith in Cornwall in the nineteenth century. Important copper and tin mines were situated near Troon, including the Grenville mines. Wheal Grenville was close to the Great Flat Lode, an enormous vein composed primarily of tin. At an angle of dip of about forty-five degrees, it was shallower and flatter to the ground than other deposits, making it easier to extract the ore. Working commenced at Wheal Grenville in the 1820s, though it only became productive and profitable many decades later.[4]

In 1845, Lady Grenville, the 'lord' and owner of the mineral rights, granted a lease to The Wheal Grenville Company, run by Captains Thomas and Lyle, which incorporated earlier workings, such as those at Polgine and Newton Moor. Thomas and Lyle worked the mine for six years and it was then purchased by John Taylor & Sons. Mines to the east were producing significant amounts of copper, which ensured that the area remained of interest to potential new investors.

The company was sold in 1855 for £2,040 and work commenced to dewater the mine and deepen the shafts. In the 1860s, about 240 people were employed, about 160 miners working underground and eighty women and boys at the surface. About 250 tons of copper and 80 tons of tin were raised in 1860, but by the end of that decade, the copper had been worked out and production was switched to tin, which had to be mined at much lower levels.[5]

During the depression of the 1870s, the profitability of Wheal Grenville declined, but a new management team under the chairmanship of R.W. Goold and mine captain T. Hodge turned the mine's fortunes around. They were able to persuade investors to provide new capital and a shaft called Goold's broke into the Great Flat Lode in 1878. In 1881, dividends were paid for the first time and during the course of the next ten years the mine became very profitable.

After Captain Hodge's death in 1889, a new mine captain, Charles F. Bishop, was appointed who proved to be as efficient as Hodge. The management decided to expand the workings eastward and a new shaft called Fortescue's was begun and sunk to a depth of 2,370 feet. Between 1893 and 1894 production was the highest ever. While prices in general were once again depressed, Wheal Grenville was one of the few tin mines in Cornwall which not only survived, but recorded a profit.

The next decade proved difficult and the committee running the mine asked Bevill Fortescue on numerous occasions to either reduce, forego or only claim the dues when a profit was made. He became increasingly irritated with these constant requests. In April 1897, William Pease wrote to William Stirling of Wheal Grenville: 'Mr Fortescue feels strongly that no sooner does he make one concession than your Committee asks for something more' and the following year, Bevill wrote:

> I really think the Committee are absolutely unreasonable in trying still further to put the screw on me. If they can pay their merchants bills, I fail to see why I should be expected to continue to forego the dues – during 1897, I gave up the dues on three quarters and only took ½ the dues. On another quarter, giving up £1165 and receiving £215. In other words, tin was sold off the mine to at least the value of £30,000 and I only received £215.[6]

Further, Bevill Fortescue disputed William Stirling's contention that all the money received from the sale of the tin had been expended on developing the mine. He pointed out that, over the last twenty years, dividends of between eight shillings and nine shillings per share had been declared in each year. If the company, instead of distributing all of the receipts among the shareholders, had placed some money into a reserve fund, there would have been no necessity to make calls to raise additional capital.[7] Between 1 July 1900 and 30 June 1901, receipts from minerals and clay were, in total, £2,923.13s.2d.[8]

Requests to remit part of the dues continued through the early part of the twentieth century, although in 1903 matters had improved and Bevill Fortescue wrote that 'Wheal Grenville appears to be doing remarkably well, and I read in the Western Morning News that a 10/- dividend is expected'.[9] In 1905, Bevill Fortescue agreed to grant a new lease to the Wheal Grenville Company for twenty-one years,[10] although arguments continued about the amount of dues that were owed to him.[11]

In 1906, Wheal Grenville, South Condurrow and West Wheal Frances were amalgamated into a company that was called Grenville United Mines.[12] Profits were initially healthy as a result of excellent tin prices. A report dated 15 January 1910 written by William Hosking concluded that the Grenville United Mines during the year 1909, in spite of the lower price for the output per ton, had been able to carry out its work with commendable energy and as a result, would sell about 9 tons more than in the year 1908 and show an increase of just over £400 in receipts. In addition, conditions in the mine were improving.[13]

Despite this positive report, there was still criticism that the company was placing profit before long-term development. Blame had to be attributed to the directors and not to the mine captain, who could not carry out the improvements required without adequate funds. If more tin was raised, the price of the shares would increase pro tem, but would leave the mine in a worse position for the future because the richer portions would have been dug out and exhausted. In 1917, the directors suggested that Bevill Fortescue should advance a loan of £10,000 to the company, but he declined to offer them any financial assistance.[14]

The First World War created a demand for metals which drove prices up, but around 20 per cent of the workforce was conscripted into the armed forces, leaving a dearth of skilled workmen. In the post-war period, it was impossible to find the funds to work Wheal Grenville and, following a further crash in metal prices, a liquidator was appointed in 1920. The mine finally closed in 1921.

A draft agreement to allow John Jewell, a tin streamer, to work and extract ore from the dumps at Wheal Grenville, West Basset and West Wheal Frances mines was drawn up in March 1923 for a term of 21 years, but whether this agreement was ever executed and implemented is unclear.

West Wheal Frances mine

Situated to the west of Treskillard near Newton Moor and bounded on the west by the Red River, West Wheal Frances was a small sett worked from 1848 to 1896. Although it raised over 9,000 tons of black tin during this period, it did not prove to be profitable. The returns of £22,000 were far outweighed by the capital investment of just less than £100,000.

The mine was leased from Lady Grenville and a company was formed with 512 shares, with dues at 1/15th. Production ebbed and flowed throughout the 1850s, improving in late 1861 when additional deposits of ore were discovered. New plant and machinery was purchased late in the following year and in 1864, a lease was granted by George Fortescue, with the dues now payable at 1/18th.

The mining historian Thomas Spargo reported on the mine in the mid-1860s:

> West Wheal Frances is in Illogan, and adjoining South Frances and West Basset. Working commenced in 1848. The returns have been very small. The position of the sett – immediately west of South Frances – imparted a high estimation of its value; but, after fourteen years' operations, no discovery of importance has been made; but great confidence of good results is, notwithstanding, entertained and warranted by the "indications." Owner of the soil, Lady Grenville. Dues – 15th. Depth, 97 fathoms under adit. 36 men and 4 boys employed (1861). A pumping engine of about 45-inch cylinder, and a 22-inch steam whim, are the machinery employed. Two lodes worked on. Purser, R H Pike; manager, Charles Thomas.[15]

Sales of tin increased steadily from 2 tons in 1860 to 136 tons in 1866, but the slump in tin prices in the latter year severely affected West Wheal Frances. Although production increased to 222 tons in 1869, it did not clear the mine's debts. It recorded a small profit in 1868 and 1872, but even though prices rose, costs also increased and overall, production fell. The *Mining Journal* of 17 May 1873 reported the fall in production as being caused by a 'lack of men'.

As the price of tin fell once more in 1873–74, West Wheal Frances renegotiated the terms of its lease with George Fortescue, the 'mineral lord'. He agreed to allow the mine to pay dues at the lower rate of 1/30th but, as the price of tin continued to fall, so the company's financial position grew worse. Early in 1875, the bottom of the mine was flooded due to heavy rain and had to be pumped clear of water before extraction of the ore could continue.

Tin production increased in 1883 and 1884 and dividends were paid between 1887 and 1889. 'Tin has advanced in price considerably … our Mines in the west are all looking well especially West Frances which now I think will make a good mine',[16] but when tin prices slumped in 1893, West Wheal Frances struggled on for a few more years, but was finally abandoned in 1896. The company was wound up in 1898 by G.A. Jenkins, the Official Receiver in Bankruptcy.[17]

South Terras mine – Cornwall's premier uranium and radium mine

The mine was located on the upper reaches of the River Fal, near to Tolgarrick Mill, about one mile south-west of the village of St Stephens. Its active life spanned six decades, from 1870 to 1930, those years divided approximately equally between the production of iron, uranium and radium. Originally it was worked as an opencast pit, but as it grew deeper, it became unviable and more traditional underground mining methods had to be utilised. Crossing the sett, in addition to an ochre pit, were several tin lodes and one major uranium lode trending south-west to north-east.

The mine commenced work as South Terras Tin Mining Company in 1872, although initially the output was very modest. During the early years, the mine concentrated solely on extracting the iron and magnetite from the ochre. On Christmas Day 1887, a new twenty-one-year lease was granted to work the sett and the mine was acquired by Uranium Mines Limited. Public mention of the discovery of uranium, in the form of pitchblende, was reported in *The Mining Journal* in 1889. Uranium was widely distributed in Cornwall, but South Terras was the only mine in the county where uranium was the principal ore raised. In 1900, Captain W.R. Thomas reported that thirty-three persons were employed.

Work at the mine was suspended between 1903 and 1904. By 1905, South Terras was operating again, but was up for sale once more in 1911. On 16 November 1912, the mine was acquired by the Société Industrielle du Radium Limited. It had a capital of £200,000 and a new lease was negotiated for twenty-one years until March 1934. Radium had only been discovered in 1902 by Professor Pierre and Madame Marie Sklodowska Curie, who had found that the mineral called pitchblende contained polonium and radium.

In 1913, a prospectus was published by the Société Industrielle offering shares for sale in the company at £5 each. Reports were presented from the 'highest authorities' in the world on the subject: from Madam Sklodowska Curie, Chief of the Sorbonne in Paris, Professor Jacques Danne, Directeur, Laboratoire d'Essais des Substances Radio Actives, at Gif, France, Professor Jean Danysz, Chief of Staff of the Faculté les Sciences in Paris and Chief of Madame Curie's laboratory, and Professor John Joly, Department of Sciences, Dublin University.[18] In July 1912, Frank Sherwood Gray asked Marie Curie, Professor at the Paris Faculty of Sciences, to have an investigation made by her laboratory on the radioactivity of the pitchblende mine of South Terras. Marie Curie instructed Mr Jean Danysz, Preparator at her laboratory, to carry out the necessary experiments on the spot. He proceeded to the mine on 23 September 1912 and set up a small laboratory in St Austell. The investigation was based on the radioactivity of the water which had submerged the mine, the radioactivity in two dumps of earth which had been excavated from the shafts, and the radioactivity of some samples taken from the deep levels of the mine before it had flooded. As a result of the experiments the prospectus claimed that 'Madame Curie has discovered the world's greatest supply of uranium and pitchblende ores in which radium is found at Grampound Road in the South Terras mine'. The ore from the mine was shipped to Gif in France to be treated.

Operations at South Terras were suspended during the First World War and were restarted in 1922 when a new extraction plant was built. The mine did not pay the dues owing to the Boconnoc estate expeditiously: 'I went up to Terras Mine today and I find that some 97 tons of ore have been sent away, of which up to the present, we have received no report.'[19]

In 1924, South Terras Mine was amalgamated with the nearby Tolgarrick Mine to extract as much radium as possible. The following year the landlord, the Boconnoc estate, began action which aimed to receive a just rent from the mine owners. Protracted legal action took place over the following years, leading ultimately to the downfall of the mining company. The company had failed to comply with many of the clauses in its lease and breaches included not keeping proper sales records, leading the landlord to suspect that he was not being paid his just dues. The old dumps and the remnant ore had been worked, but no money had been spent to dewater the mine or on any exploration underground. In instructing solicitors to act, F.J.H. Somerset, the Boconnoc steward and agent, wrote that the company was 'hopeless to deal with'.

Statutory notice was given to the South Terras Company with a view to instituting action to terminate the lease.[20] Bevill Fortescue's solicitors wrote that the company had admitted breaches of covenant, which they attributed to want of working capital. They did not hold out any immediate prospects of their being able to obtain sufficient money to work and develop the mine in a proper manner. Bevill Fortescue gave the company three months to get the operation onto a proper financial basis.[21]

According to a letter from William Hosking to F.J.H. Somerset: 'It is like "beating the air" to discuss matters with these people – they do not carry out the conditions of the lease, either in spirit or actual working.'[22]

The mine was purchased in 1928 by the British & General Radium Corporation Limited, a German-owned syndicate. Pumping commenced and the mine was dewatered to the 40-fathom level. This venture was also short-lived as negotiations with the Boconnoc estate became strained and South Terras finally closed in March 1930.[23] A series of events aimed at exploring two of the most expensive elements to be mined at that time failed, largely due to under-funding.

The mine on the Boconnoc estate

In the early 1720s, Thomas 'Diamond' Pitt (I) had hopes that a mine on the Boconnoc estate would be of value. He told his son Robert: 'I would have you by no means forget to inquire into the Affaire of the Mine in ye Park. There is some roguery in that affaire, I believe they hope to tire me out & have ye working of it for nothing.'[24] Some ore was brought up, but nothing came of the assay tests.[25]

In 1763, a report made to Thomas Pitt (II) said that 'a very rich Silver and Tin work had been cut in Trowling the Kitchen Garden' (the old Hop Garden) at Boconnoc, but when John Bennett went to see it, he found that it was only a 'Bundle of Lead', which never made much in Cornwall, but he would get a small trial made of it.[26]

A lead mine in the park, possibly the one that had interested 'Diamond' Pitt (I), was opened in 1765, but men were only put to excavate when the weather would not permit them to do any other work.[27] When the Grenvilles inherited the estate, Lord Grenville employed miners to open up a shaft.[28] A man called Carne was employed as the engineer and a Mr Jones as the mine captain. The shaft was widened and the miners began driving along a lode northward. Once an assessment had been made of these workings, Grenville believed it would be possible to make some judgement about the long-term prospects and specimens were sent away to be examined. The mine had certainly been exploited at a previous date, but not within the last fifty years. The lode ran nearly north and south and had been worked to the south and there were traces all the way up the hill of shafts that had been opened in that direction. They had been filled up again with the rubbish or 'deads' that had been extracted from the workings, suggesting that the mine had been worked for profit at some former period, but that it had ultimately been abandoned, probably because of the lack of power in the area that could be utilised to enable water to be pumped out and drained from the shaft.[29]

Bowen wrote to Grenville about the problems he was experiencing with the mine and more particularly, with the workmen. Mr Carne had good practical judgement, but because he lived at St Austell and was so busy, he had only been to Boconnoc five times. A man had been appointed as a foreman who had worked in some of the best mines in the county. Other miners had been found, who from 'necessity and a spirit of adventure', had come to seek employment in areas other than those from where their labour had recently been required. This was owing to the failure of the great western mines and many similar men were now crowding into the area around Boconnoc.

The men initially said they would not undertake the work for less than £15 a fathom, but towards evening six men came and agreed to do the work for £7. They had commenced work, but then they all left again, some to go to Mr Glynn's new mine near Bodmin. A new group of men was now working at £12 a fathom. Bowen asked Grenville to ascertain the qualities of the ore by taking a piece to be assayed at the Royal Institution.[30]

Grenville had given the matter some thought and advised Lady Grenville that even if the mine proved to be of any worth, he would be unwilling to grant a sett, being concerned it would give the miners a degree of power over the park, which he was not disposed to give. Bowen pointed out:

> the inconvenience of having Mines near the mansion and in the midst of wood and pleasure grounds, could have an influence on the morals, and effect upon the farming interest which it may be said Miners are likely to have on the neighbourhood around them.[31]

In the end, the report from Carne was unfavourable, both as to the quality of the ore and the increasing amount of water which was threatening further progress.[32] There was some appearance of copper, but it was not enough to be of any importance and Grenville had an increasing conviction that the lead mine was 'not worth a button'. It was settled with Mr Jones, the mine captain, that all further work on the lode in the present shaft should be abandoned and the shaft filled in.[33]

THE CHINA-CLAY INDUSTRY

High-quality translucent porcelain was made for many thousands of years in China, using a combination of the material known as china-clay (kaolin) and a ground china-stone known as petuntse. The wares coming from the east were made of this mixture, which produced a 'hard paste'. The European china-makers could only produce 'soft paste' and once trade with China commenced in the seventeenth century, European manufacturers, particularly in Germany, started making attempts to discover the exact constituents of the Chinese porcelain.[34]

In the eighteenth and nineteenth centuries, the industry that developed after the discovery of substantial china-clay deposits in Cornwall became of significant importance to the economy of the county.

William Cookworthy (1705–80)

William Cookworthy, an apothecary, chemist and Quaker, was born in Devon in 1705. After reading an account written by Père D'Entrecolles, a French Jesuit missionary, of the methods employed by the Chinese in porcelain-making, Cookworthy began to seek a material in England that was comparable to the consistency and quality of the Chinese kaolin. In 1745, after many years of searching, Cookworthy discovered in Cornwall the material which was known locally as Moorstone, Growan and Growan Clay. 'I first discovered it', wrote Cookworthy, 'in the parish of Germo, in a hill called Tregonnin Hill.' Subsequently, he found the 'caulin' (kaolin) more commodiously in the parish of St Dennis and in two quarries, one in St Stephens and the other at Carloggas.

The land on which Cookworthy had found the materials belonged to Thomas Pitt (III), 1st Lord Camelford. In November 1766, George, Lord Edgcumbe of Mount Edgcumbe, acting as an intermediary, wrote to Pitt requesting that a sett of the area in which the materials had been found should be granted to Cookworthy.[35] In the Cornwall Record Office and the British Library there are forty-one letters dating from between 1766 and 1769.[36] These are written either by Cookworthy himself or by Pitt's agent, Dr John Mudge.[37]

The letters recount in great detail the experiments that Cookworthy had been conducting and the vicissitudes he experienced when trying to recreate the qualities of the Chinese porcelain. Cookworthy established a manufactory in Plymouth and after much experimentation, he developed a way of creating high-quality china ware. The Plymouth Porcelain Factory became the first English company to produce porcelain utilising a process similar to that of the Chinese.[38]

Cookworthy was happy that Pitt was going to participate in the enterprise and that he had agreed to grant a lease that incorporated rights to raise the china-clay, erect sheds and utilise the water courses.[39] In July 1767, a final agreement was reached between Cookworthy, who was then visiting Boconnoc, and Pitt, which was witnessed by John and Thomas Bennett, Pitt's steward and his steward's son.[40] The discovery of the china-clay and stone on Thomas Pitt's property proved fortunate because Pitt was able to provide capital for the burgeoning commercial enterprise and to assist in applying for a patent, granted to Cookworthy on 17 March 1768 as first discoverer.

Cookworthy wrote frequently to Pitt, reporting on the experiments he was carrying out and on the problems he was attempting to resolve: the glaze on the samples was too thick, the cassettes, the clay boxes into which the products were placed in the kiln to protect them from the fire and smoke, kept cracking and collapsing, a larger kiln was needed and they were trying to eliminate yellow spots that appeared on the surface of the porcelain.[41]

A company with a share capital of £420, fourteen shares at £30 each, was formed. The shares were taken by Pitt, Cookworthy and their business associates. Pitt took four shares, Cookworthy, three, his brother, Philip, one and the six remaining shares were taken by men from Bristol. At a later date, it was suggested that Pitt should offer one of his shares to John Mudge, his agent, an eminent doctor and 'a man of Genius in Mechanicks and of an Elegant taste in Arts'.[42] In January 1768, Cookworthy was again in Cornwall and was able to report that he had had some success in the experimental processes.[43] There was some suggestion that the Plymouth manufactory might be moved to Lostwithiel, close to the woods at Boconnoc, which could provide the fuel necessary to keep the kilns burning.[44]

Pitt himself was interested in how porcelain was manufactured and had a collection 'not to be equalled perhaps in the kingdom'. He was in Worcester in July 1768 and visited a porcelain factory in the town,[45] while the following month, he wrote from Scotland where he had visited another manufactory.[46] Although there is no direct evidence, it was possible that he was undertaking experiments at Boconnoc on his own behalf.[47]

The final letter from Cookworthy to Pitt was sent from Truro and dated 19 January 1769.[48] Four months later, the business at Plymouth was closed and moved to Bristol. Cookworthy remained a partner until 1773, but he then transferred the patent and the business to Richard Champion, who had been involved with the company from the early days. By 1770, Pitt had also sold his interest to Richard Champion.[49] In the end, none of the participants in the enterprise – Pitt, Cookworthy or Champion – received any great financial benefit from their efforts. Some of the technical problems were overcome, but neither Cookworthy nor Champion proved competent to master the commercial aspects of the business.

The china–clay business after Cookworthy

Champion applied for a renewal of Cookworthy's patent for a further fourteen years, but he encountered opposition from Josiah Wedgwood and some of the other Staffordshire potters who wanted to take supplies from Cornwall themselves. After legal action in 1775, Wedgwood succeeded in preventing the renewal of the patent. Champion no longer had a monopoly and landowners and potters were free to make bargains with anyone that they wished.

In June 1775, Wedgwood himself crossed the Tamar and wrote in his diary:

> June 3rd. Buconic, the seat of Mr Thomas Pitt – and he being at home, and a friend of mine as well as of Mr Champion, I wished to wait upon him to let him know what had been done respecting Mr Champion's patent. The lands are inclosed and in general good … We enter Buconic down, Mr Pitts property – several barrows are seen to the right, and to the left, this is a fine down, and at the entrance of it there is a delightful view to the right hand. There are several miles of these walks in this valley, and on the declivities of the banks, where we come to a fine old beech tree in the bottom, by the side of the brook, the roots of which were visible in various folds above the surface. Mr Pitt laid himself easily down, and repeated those fine lines in Greys [sic] Elegy written in a country church yard. 'There at the foot of yonder nodding beech …' After being entertained at this hospitable mansion for a few hours, with great hilarity, and classic elegance, we parted in high good humour, and proceeded on our journey.[50]

Wedgwood moved on to the St Austell area where they were 'now in the midst of mines, and hillocks thrown up from them … and they were extremely eager to examine their contents'. Wedgwood talked to the labourers, looked at the materials and collected some to take away for further inspection.

Pitt (III) wrote to Champion to advise him that Wedgwood had visited and had gone further into Cornwall to obtain samples in order that he could conduct experiments. Under the terms of the lease with Cookworthy, Pitt was unable to grant Wedgwood the rights to raise clay and stone on any property owned by the Boconnoc estate, so Wedgwood proceeded to Tregonning Hill and commissioned a farmer called Yelland to find out whether any land was available in the same area to lease or purchase.[51] Wedgwood wanted to obtain the grant of some land owned by Lord Falmouth, which adjoined Pitt's land for about 800 yards in length and contained similar high-quality materials.[52] Lord Falmouth wrote to Thomas Pitt, asking his advice: 'I have had an offer from Wedgwood to take my clay in the Parish of Gonvean. I will wait until I hear from you about what leases I should offer to Wedgwood.'[53]

In July 1785, Thomas Bennett refused to allow Richard Champion's agent to send off any more materials from the sett that had been granted originally to Cookworthy and subsequently acquired by Champion, because Bennett believed it had been forfeited as a result of breaches that had been committed contrary to clauses in the lease: dues amounting to £116.18s.9d were six months in arrears, the Adventurers had neglected the sett for four years, it was now unoccupied and all the lessees were dead or had absconded. A lease granted to Cookworthy and dated 12 December 1770 had specified that, if the rent was unpaid by a space of sixty days and if the sett was not worked for a period of two years, the grant would cease.[54]

In 1789, Thomas Pitt, by then Lord Camelford, took advice from Counsel, Mr W. Baldwin, barrister of the Temple who advised that the lease could be declared void.

Thomas Pitt, 2nd Lord Camelford

In January 1795, a man called Barker Chifney was commissioned to prepare a report for the 2nd Lord Camelford about property at Carloggas Moor. Chifney's report was studied and thereafter, a new lease was granted to a company called Bagnall & Co. from 4 March 1795 until Lord Camelford came of age, that is on 19 February 1796. It is possible that Bagnall & Co. were very closely associated with the New Hall Company, which had previously taken a lease from Richard Champion. The arrangement with Bagnall did not prove to be a success for the lease was available again in 1799. In that year, Thomas Bennett wrote to Charles Cowper (one of the 2nd Lord Camelford's legal advisors) to say that he had been out with Messrs Spode and Chifney at St Stephens, looking over the clay grounds. The land was granted to Chifney Spode & Co., although during the negotiations for the Carloggas sett, there was concern among Lord Camelford's representatives that potential lessees were attempting to organise the potters into a combination, an alliance, so that they could negotiate as a collective and secure better financial terms. Eventually, the areas leased were Carloggas Moor, the Quay Close, Trethosa Moor and Helland Moor, the lease running from 29 September 1799 for twenty-one years, expiring on 29 September 1820.[55]

Lord and Lady Grenville – the early nineteenth century

In October 1820, Josiah Spode II sent Grenville a draft for £900, the amount of one year's rent for the clay mines. This effectively terminated the lease he had taken from the Boconnoc estate.[56] In the same year, another giant of the china industry, Thomas Minton, was in Cornwall and secured an interest in Treloar Common. At the end of the year, he combined with Wedgwood, the New Hall potters and others to work Hendra Common.[57]

The Staffordshire potters were so remote geographically from Cornwall that ultimately they were unable to retain adequate control of their business. The vacuum created by their slow withdrawal allowed the industry to be taken over, organised and run by a plethora of small Cornish companies and local tradesmen who invested their savings in the china-clay pits. They began selling to a rapidly expanding market. Some families, for example the Stockers and Martyns, became very affluent. By the 1830s, demand for Staffordshire ware had declined significantly. In September 1842, John Bowen, as agent for Lady Grenville, advertised the lease of a number of clay works (eight lots, including Virginia, Hallew Moor, Trethosa Moor, Little Johns and part of Carloggas Moor) and Stone Quarries (four lots). Tenders were invited for rents and rates per ton of clay and stone respectively.[58] On 19 January 1843, a lease for twenty-one years was taken by a company, comprising china-clay merchants who called themselves The Cornwall China Stone and Clay Company.[59] The partners were Edward Bullman of Leeds, Charles Truscott of St Austell, John Martin, Elias Martyn, Thomas Broad and Richard Yelland of St Dennis. All the leases granted by Lady Grenville stipulated that, wherever possible, the carriage of the clay and stone should be undertaken by her own tenants.[60]

The Fortescues

The new company was only in business for five years. Early in 1848, it was in decline and the partners indicated that they wanted to bring their tenancy to an end on 25 December 1848.[61] An analysis of their accounts demonstrated that for the first three years, not enough clay or stone had been raised to equal the minimum rent of £1,300 per annum and a year later, 4,000 tons of china-clay and 6,000 tons of china-stone remained unsold.

Some of the leases relinquished by The Cornwall China Stone and Clay Company were taken by another company, the West of England Clay & Stone Company. The partners of this company were Elias Martyn, Edward Stocker, William Marshall Grose (a linen draper in St Austell), Thomas Whitford, Thomas Maynard and Thomas Theophilus Hawkey. Edward Stocker became one of the ablest of the china-clay producers and the founder of an important 'china-clay family'. William Pease attended the first meeting of the company on 7 January 1850, when the Adventurers 'fixed salaries and had for dinner haunch of venison, leg of mutton, salmon, roast goose, hare and pheasant'.[62] By 1852, Henry Medland Stocker, the grandson of Edward Stocker, employed 7,200 workers in the stone quarries and clay works of Hensbarrow.[63]

In the second half of the nineteenth century, there was a considerable increase in the number of new works and in 1858, for the first time, an official list was compiled of the works in operation, their estimated annual production and the type of clay raised in each.[64] Those belonging to Lady Grenville showed:

Name of clay work	Freeholder	Tenant	Type of clay	Tons
Little Johns	Grenville	W of England Co	Potting	800
Carloggas	Grenville	W of England Co	Potting	4,000
Hallew	Grenville	W of England Co	Potting	200
Victoria	Grenville	W of England Co	Bleaching and Potting	400

Owing to the inaccurate way in which the books of accounts were kept detailing the amount of clay that had been raised, William Pease retained a close interest in the figures and demonstrated to Messrs Stocker, Maynard, Elias Martyn and George Yelland Junior that they had paid too little in dues. They paid a further £500 without demur.[65] A month later, another meeting was held with Pease and members of the committee. A new system was instituted so that all clay raised would have a distinctive mark by which it could be identified in the company's books and another book would be kept that would contain particulars of all the clay sent off the works.[66]

In October 1864, Mr Stocker was anxious to know if the West of England Company would be granted a new twenty-one-year lease.[67] After much negotiation, George Fortescue acceded to the terms proposed and agreed to remit £1,000 out of the dues for the first year towards opening up the works, so that the terms were £4,000 for the first year, £5,000 a year for the next six years, £5,500 for the next seven years and £6,500 for the last seven years.[68]

Transport

The increasing amount of china-clay that was being produced necessitated improved methods of transport. In 1858, Lady Grenville, at the suggestion of William Pease, had considered a plan to build a narrow-gauge line to link her tenants' setts (held by the West of England Company) with the railway on Hendra Downs built by Joseph Treffry. Nothing came of this proposal.

In 1864, the Newquay & Cornwall Junction Railway Company was formed. Pease was appointed a member of the committee of this venture, together with Edward Stocker and George Yelland. George Fortescue agreed that the line could pass through his estates, but this scheme also came to nothing due to a lack of funding.[69]

The decline of the china-clay industry

In the third quarter of the nineteenth century, there was excessive output and overproduction.[70] The West of England Company lost markets for their products due to the disruption caused by a series of conflicts on the continent of Europe. Thousands of tons were sold below cost price, competition was increasing and losses were being made by many companies.[71]

Edward Stocker died in his seventy-sixth year and his business interests were taken over by his three sons, Francis, Edward and Thomas. The pits still active were Little Johns, Trethosa, Wheal Louisa, East, North and South Carloggas, Dubbers and Hallew, plus the twenty china-stone quarries in Quarry Close.

By 1910, Cornwall was producing 50 per cent of the world's china-clay, around 1,000,000 tonnes, of which 75 per cent was exported to Europe and America. During the First World War, pits closed as exports decreased.[72] In 1919, the three major producers merged, calling themselves English China Clays (ECC). Half of the productive capacity was now under the control of one company. ECC continued to dominate the market until it was bought by Imerys, a French company, in 1999 for £756 million. In the early part of the twenty-first century, Imerys relocated a substantial part of their business to Brazil and many of the pits in the St Austell area were abandoned, with a consequent reduction in the number of staff employed in Cornwall.[73] The sharp white peaks, known as the Cornish Alps, still dominate the landscape of the St Austell area and are a visible and prominent reminder of the long history of china-clay extraction in Cornwall.

SLATE QUARRYING

In the nineteenth century, the estate owned a number of slate quarries, on or near the north Cornish coast. As with other land owned by the estate, tenders were invited and offers made for leases for various of their quarries. In 1851, William Pease received a letter from John White of Medrose, near Delabole, asking Pease to ride out and meet him 'and his freands' from Tavistock at the 'Intend west Delabole slate quarry' in north Cornwall.

He begged that Pease would not give permission to 'Mr King nor Richards' to work the quarry as they would not manage it efficiently and he had 'a Party that will put it to work in a proper Manner'. A plan of the West Delabole quarries shows the blacksmith's shop, the whims and the counting house.[74]

A number of other quarries were leased such as The Tines Green Slate Company. In 1868, Sir William Williams, of Llandovery in South Wales, applied for the lease through the agency of a man called John Jenkin. Jenkin was prominent in slate quarrying circles, having worked at the Delabole quarry, about which he wrote a history in 1888, and the Prince of Wales quarry at Tintagel.[75]

In 1911, Bevill Fortescue exchanged lands with the directors of the Old Delabole Slate Quarry Company to allow the quarry to consolidate their property into one contiguous block of land holdings.[76]

AGRICULTURE

The bailiff's accounts dating from 29 September 1431 to 30 September 1432, prepared by the bailiff, Richard Menebryll, show that the lord of the manor, Thomas de Carminow, received rents for his land from tenants. Menebryll also accounted to de Carminow for timber, wood, bark and corn that he sold on behalf of the lord. Unfortunately, part of this set of accounts appears to be missing as there is no information about animals that were on the estate which it would have been expected would be included in the accounts.[77]

There is little evidence about matters agricultural until the time of Thomas 'Diamond' Pitt in the eighteenth century. Letters to his steward, John Phillips, give information about what was being grown. In 1721, Pitt gave orders that the gardener should keep attempting to grow 'aprycocks'.[78] The following month, he sent the gardener fifty fruit trees for the orchard 'together with Pease and Collyflower seed'. Fir trees would be sent during the following month.[79] Wheat and barley were grown and Pitt gave orders that the latter should be threshed, sold at seven shillings per bushel, near a third less than the market price and supplied to the labourers and the poor of Boconnoc and Braddock. In 1722, John Roberts, one of the employees, was about to begin ploughing Colts Hill and if Pitt wanted him to try growing vetches there (a plant with small flowers used to feed farm animals), seeds should be sent down to Cornwall.[80]

George B. Worgan

In 1911, George Worgan wrote a book about agriculture in the county of Cornwall. He reported that the agricultural labourers in Cornwall could be arranged in four classes – farm servants, parish apprentices, day labourers and a fourth class, who did not work for one employer but took work wherever it was offered. Women performed a large share of the rural labours, particularly the harvest work, weeding the corn, hoeing turnips and potatoes, and attending the threshing machines.[81]

Triggabrowne Farm

This farm provides a good exemplar of an agricultural enterprise, owned by the Boconnoc estate and leased to tenants. In 1815, the farm was in the hands of William Wyett. The family consisted of Wyett, his wife and five sons. The eldest son, John, was the tenant of Great Gelley Farm in the parish of St Pinnock. The second son, William, rented Trevithick Farm in Lansallos parish about a mile-and-a-half to the east of Triggabrowne. The next son, Thomas, was 'also brought up to Husbandry'. He lived with his father, who allowed him only meat, drink, lodging and a little spending money; he was nearly 30 years old and a hardworking, profitable servant – or rather assistant – to his father; the fourth son was called James. He was aged about 27 and was a husbandman and also a thatcher: his time was employed on Triggabrowne in the same way as Thomas, except that, when his work upon the farm permitted, he undertook thatching for the neighbouring farms. The fifth son, Henry, was a carpenter, also sometimes involved with husbandry. He was about 22 years of age and had recently married his first cousin, the daughter of his father's brother John. She was about the same age as Henry, but the marriage would probably be the occasion of Henry leaving the family home, where he too had been for some time past as useful as his brothers. Thomas and James were both single. Wyett wanted to have had his son Henry in some situation far distant from home, which might have prevented the marriage, but it had now taken place and he applied to Lord Grenville to procure a place for Henry in the Excise.

Animals on the farm at Triggabrowne were: forty head of bullocks, including ten working oxen and steers, five milch cows, including three with calves, and twenty-five improving bullocks of one, two and three years old; eighty sheep, mostly ewes with lambs, no wethers; fifty-five lambs; five working horses; 'four two-year old ponys' [sic]; one sow and nine farrows; eight young pigs and three geese. The crops cultivated were thirty acres of wheat, following turnips and barley with potatoes, twenty-six acres of barley and twelve acres of oats. The rent arrears amounted to £402.16s.9d and Bowen and Grenville were trying to decide what action to take and whether Wyett and his family should be given notice to quit and evicted.[82]

Lady Grenville and the Fortescues

George Fortescue wrote frequently to Lady Grenville, giving her news of the weather and in consequence, the progress of the harvest. During the period known as 'the Hungry Forties', the tenants at Boconnoc, in common with inhabitants of other parts of the country, lost many of their crops. George Fortescue wrote:

> We have had four or five fine and dry – tho' not warm days, and the harvest was begin-
> ning about us – but there is a return of rain, with westerly wind and a falling Barometer!
> The wheat in this neighbourhood is bad and the price is gone up; the barley and oats
> are good – but what is most sad and alarming is the failure of the potatoes – some dis-
> ease attacks them which in the course of a few days kills them – root and stalk – I hear

of hundreds of acres in this state – many of them belonging to the labourers, who will, I fear be grievously distressed by their loss during the winter.[83]

Even Lady Louisa was concerned about food for the servants, writing to her husband: 'I have spoken to Burt about limiting the bread … but I know not what the servants are to eat instead if their bread be curtailed, as vegetables are so scarce, no more cabbage, or turnips, only broccoli once a day.'[84]

The depression in farming counties continued into the early 1850s. At a court held for the tenants of Lady Grenville's manors in the neighbourhood of Boconnoc in December 1851, George Fortescue reported that an abatement of 15 per cent in rents had been made, and with other reductions, amounted to 20 per cent overall. He regretted that farming continued to be depressed and there was no doubt that great distress existed.

During a similar depression in agriculture in the 1880s, Simeon Truscott, acting as agent for the Boconnoc estate in St Stephens parish, wrote to Cyril Fortescue: 'Taking your tenants as a whole I believe it would be difficult to find a more industrious and thrifty lot, but regret to say that no lot of tenants within several miles have suffered more and they are obliged (almost without exception) to take money from their capital or other sources to meet their rents.'[85] The tenants were due to pay their rents in June 1885, but William Pease believed that some allowances would have to be made in view of the prevailing conditions.[86] It was an anxious time for everyone, landlord as well as tenant, and if they had more seasons as of late, few of the farmers would survive.[87]

There was no market for cattle, sheep or any farm produce in 1893 and the outlook for the coming winter was gloomy. Several acres of spring corn would never be cut and fields which had always been green even in the driest time in former years had not a green blade of grass. This was also the state of the farms in north Cornwall at St Minver and St Teath.[88]

Selling farms belonging to the Boconnoc estate

After the First World War, Bevill Fortescue sold off a considerable number of farms and other properties, mainly in north Cornwall.[89] A number of farms were offered for sale by auction: Tregildras in St Kew parish, 106 acres; Sawle in St Teath and St Endellion parishes, 198 acres, entirely a cliff farm and in a lonely place; Trefreesa in St Minver parish, 143 acres; Polroad Mills, 10½ acres in St Tudy parish, and Polroad and Foxhole, 59 acres, also in St Minver parish.[90] The following year, he found he had to sell as much of his landed property as possible.[91] Property sold in 1920 in St Teath parish included Delamere Downs, West Downs, Tregardock, Hockings Tenement, West and East Ribbys, Middle Hendra, Joses Tenement, Deer Park and Lower Hendra. Treligga was sold to Thomas Hill for £1,800, Knights Mill was sold to Mrs Bastard, Foxhole Tenement to Mr W.H. Long, Rough Park to the tenant, Harry Cottell, for £1,700 and other properties were sold in St Wenn, Troon and Camborne.[92] The total acreage of the Boconnoc estate overall shrank significantly.

NOTES AND REFERENCES

1. The National Archives (TNA): SC6/Henry VIII/6159, Ministers' Accounts, 1511–1512.
2. Cornwall Record Office (CRO): AP/M.141/1, will of Ann Mohun.
3. British Library (BL): Add MS 59489, Collon, Bennett to the 1st Lord Camelford, 9 December 1784, f. 23.
4. D.B. Barton, *A Guide to the Mines of West Cornwall*, 1963, pp. 24–27.
5. www.cornwallcalling.co.uk/mines/Camborne/grenville-united.htm; www.cornwallinfocus.co.uk/mining/genville.php
6. CRO: F/3/10/520, 39 Pont Street, London, SW, 6 April 1898, Bevill Fortescue to William Pease.
7. CRO: F/3/10/13, 744, Lostwithiel, 27 April 1898, William Pease to William Stirling.
8. CRO: F/3/10/16, 593.
9. CRO: F/3/10/498, 48 Berkeley Square, 8 May 1903, Bevill Fortescue to Peter Watson, Chairman, Wheal Grenville.
10. CRO: F/3/10/18, 128–132, William Pease to Wheal Grenville.
11. CRO: F/3/10/19, 966, Lostwithiel, 27 January 1905, William Pease to Peter Watson, Chairman, Wheal Grenville.
12. Kenneth Brown and Bob Acton, *Exploring Cornish Mines, Volume 2*, Truro, 1995, p. 117.
13. CRO: F/3/10/201, Report dated 15 January 1910.
14. CRO: F/3/10/22, 810–811, 29 April 1910, FJH Somerset to Peter Watson, Chairman of Wheal Grenville; CRO: F/3/10/26, 258, 29 October 1917, FJH Somerset to G Hadlee, Grenville House, Strand, London WC2; CRO: AD2337/9.
15. Thomas Spargo, *Statistics and Observations of the Mines of Cornwall and Devon*, 1864.
16. CRO: F/3/10/513, Lostwithiel, 15 June 1885, William Pease to Cyril Fortescue.
17. www.cornwallinfocus.co.uk; CRO: F/1/685, Lostwithiel, 28 March 1898 to W. Bailey.
18. CRO: CH/30/1/11/1-2.
19. CRO: F/3/10/28, 177, 24 March 1922, F.J.H. Somerset to Mr Fortescue.
20. CRO: F/3/10/369, 22 June 1925 from Fladgate & Co.
21. CRO: F/3/10/373, Pall Mall, SW1, 15 December 1925 from Fladgate & Co. to Messrs Waterhouse & Co., 10/12 Bishopsgate, EC.
22. CRO: F/3/10/375, Tehidy Office, Camborne, 21 April 1926, William Hosking to FJH Somerset.
23. www.cornwallinfocus.co.uk
24. BL: Add MS 59479, 29 August 1721, Thomas Pitt to Robert Pitt at Boconnoc, f. 217.
25. TNA: C108/424/no 9, Pall Mall, 11 November 1721, Thomas Pitt to John Phillips at Camelford, f. 519.
26. BL: Add MS 69320, Lostwithiel, 29 July 1763, John Bennett to Thomas Pitt, f. 51.
27. BL: Add MS 69322, Lostwithiel, 24 December 1765, John Bennett to Thomas Pitt, f. 43.
28. BL: Add MS 58873, Boconnoc, Monday morning, 6 September 1813, Lord Grenville to Lady Grenville.
29. BL: Add MS 58873, 14 September 1813, Lord Grenville to Lady Grenville, ff. 95–99.
30. BL: Add MS 59440, Boconnoc, 8 July 1813, John Bowen to Lord Grenville, ff. 17–22.
31. BL: Add MS 59440, Boconnoc, 24 July 1813, Bowen to Lord Grenville, f. 28; BL: Add MS 58873, Boconnoc, September 15 and 16 1813, Lord Grenville to Lady Grenville, ff. 100–114.
32. BL: Add MS 59440, 24 July 1813, John Bowen to Lord Grenville, f. 28.
33. BL: Add MS 58873, September to November 1813, Lord Grenville to Lady Grenville, ff. 108–199.
34. R.M. Barton, *A History of the Cornish China-Clay Industry*, Truro, 1966, p. 15.
35. CRO: F/4/80/2.
36. BL: Add MS 69323; CRO: F/4/80/1-30.

37. A. Douglas Selleck, *Cookworthy, 1705–80 and His Circle, 'A Man of No Common Clay'*, Plymouth, 1978, p. 159; Mudge was a respected physician and was already known to Pitt as he had visited Boconnoc in 1775, probably to attend Anne Pitt when she was giving birth to their son, Thomas, later 2nd Lord Camelford.

38. CRO: F/4/80/1-30, articles in *Apollo* magazine.

39. CRO: F/4/80/3.

40. BL: Add MS 69323, 28 July 1767, ff. 12–13.

41. BL: Add MS 69323, 6 October 1767, ff. 14–15.

42. CRO: F/4/80/12.

43. CRO: F/4/80/12.

44. CRO: F/4/80/13, 28 January 1768; BL: Add MS 69323, 2 February 1768, ff. 20–21.

45. CRO: F/4/80/20, 2 July 1768.

46. CRO: F/4/80/24/1, 21 September 1768.

47. CRO: F/4/80/25/1, 25 October 1768.

48. CRO: F/4/80/27.

49. Selleck, *op. cit.*, p. 62.

50. CRO: AD621/11, Josiah Wedgwood's diary.

51. Barton, *op. cit.*, pp. 24–25.

52. BL: Add MS 59489, 24 June 1782, f. 143.

53. BL: Add MS 69489, Tregothnan, 12 September 1782, Lord Falmouth to Thomas Pitt, ff. 144–146.

54. CRO: F/1/342.

55. BL: Add MS 59442, f. 51; opinion of Counsel, Mr Selleck, *op. cit.*, p. 57.

56. BL: Add MS 59468, Stoke, 19 October 1820, J Spode to Lord Grenville, f. 108.

57. Barton, *op. cit.*, p. 35.

58. *The West Briton*, 23 September 1842.

59. Barton, *op. cit.*, p. 84.

60. BL: Add MS 59442, Boconnoc, 19 April 1815, John Bowen to Lord Grenville, f. 51.

61. Barton, *op. cit.*, p. 86.

62. CRO: X715/12, William Pease's diary, 7 January and 11 February 1850.

63. Barton, *op. cit.*, p. 93.

64. Barton, *op. cit.*, pp. 96–98.

65. CRO: X715/21, William Pease's diary, Thursday, 24 March 1859.

66. CRO: X715/21, William Pease's diary, 12 April 1859.

67. CRO: X715/26, William Pease's diary, 8 October 1864.

68. CRO: X715/27, William Pease's diary, Tuesday, 31 January 1865; CRO: X715/28, William Pease's diary, Tuesday, 13 February 1866.

69. Barton, *op. cit.*, p. 113.

70. Barton, *op. cit.*, p. 127.

71. Barton, *op. cit.*, pp. 127–128.

72. Barton, *op. cit.*, p. 162.

73. www.imerys.com

74. CRO: F/3/10/43, October 1851; TF 894.

75. Catherine Lorigan, Delabole. The History of the Slate Quarry and the Making of its Village Community, Reading, 2007; CRO: F/1/351.

76. CRO: F/3/10/23.

77. CRO: F/4/3.

78. TNA: C108/424/No 9, Pall Mall, 11 November 1721, 519, Thomas Pitt to John Phillips.

79. TNA: C108/424/No 9, Pall Mall, 14 December 1721, 526, Thomas Pitt to John Phillips.

80. TNA: C108/424/No 9, Lostwithiel, 6 November 1766, John Bennett to Thomas Pitt, f. 59.

81. George B. Worgan, A general view of the agriculture of the county of Cornwall, London, 1811, p. 159.

82. BL: Add MS 59442, Boconnoc, 8 May 1815, John Bowen to Lord Grenville, ff. 59–60.
83. BL: Add MS 69052, Boconnoc, 19 August 1844, GM Fortescue to Lady Grenville, f. 82.
84. BL: Add MS 69363, Boconnoc, 16 May 1847, Lady Louisa to GM Fortescue, ff. 99–103.
85. CRO: F/3/10/505, Brannel, Grampound Road, 28 January 1885, Simeon Truscott to Cyril Fortescue.
86. CRO: F/3/10/513, Lostwithiel, 15 June 1885, William Pease to Bevill Fortescue.
87. CRO: F/3/10/513, 15 July 1885, William Pease to Cyril Fortescue.
88. CRO: F/3/10/9, Lostwithiel, 5 July 1893, William Pease to Bevill Fortescue, ff. 428–430.
89. CRO: F/3/10/26, 27 January 1919, FJH Somerset to Mr E Mutton, Helland Farm, f. 681.
90. CRO: F/3/10/26, 15 April 1919, FJH Somerset to J Wilson, the County Council Agent in Truro, f. 807.
91. CRO: F/3/10/27, 20 April 1920, FJH Somerset to John Button, Bareoak, f. 383.
92. CRO: F/3/10/27.

CHAPTER 10

A MISCELLANY:
EMIGRATION, EDUCATION, LAW AND ORDER, THE POOR LAW, FERRIES AND RAILWAYS

'This is a very nice little school. Miss Gunn keeps good
order and the instruction is sound and thorough.'
(Cornwall Record Office (CRO): P17/28/6/18, Boconnoc School Records, May 1878)

EMIGRATION

The movement of people from Cornwall known as 'The Great Emigration' continued for just over a century, from 1815 to the early 1930s. In the 1830s and 1840s, there was an economic depression in Cornwall, followed in the later nineteenth century by a crisis in the mining industry, when the market for copper and tin crashed. As a result of the decline in mining and the consequent lack of employment, there was a mass movement of men (and some women), predominantly miners, but also merchants, tradesmen, shop-keepers and slate quarry workers.[1] Emigration took place to many countries: North and South America, Mexico, Australia, New Zealand and South Africa, creating a network of Cornish emigrants scattered across the world.

From the Boconnoc estate, there was emigration to Mexico, the USA, New Zealand and Australia. One of their best labourers sailed for America in 1854.[2] In 1863, Harry Hawken wrote to G.M. Fortescue from Liskeard saying that 'if he could get the means to obtain an Assisted Passage for himself, his wife and seven children, he would go to New Zealand or Australia', while Cristina Pond of Nanpean left for New Zealand in 1878.[3]

In 1928, an application was made by Giles Frithey, lately returned from Mexico, the son of a former tenant at Boconnoc, for the grant of a part of Colvethick Wood and if he could 'not be suited in Cornwall', he would return to Mexico.[4]

Sometimes, wives were left behind in Cornwall, when husbands moved abroad. In 1921, Mabel Ruse could only pay £1 towards her rent as her husband, Thomas, was in America and had not been able to get work until two months previously. She intimated that she would try to pay the remaining £4 by March.[5] Five years later, in December 1926, Mrs A.J. Osborne wrote to say that her husband had had a serious accident in America three months previously, when two pieces of timber sixteen feet long fell on him and crushed both his legs and he could not do any business.[6] In 1928, he was in hospital, owing to his legs being 'busted up again' because of the accident he had sustained two years previously.[7]

There was some emigration by tenants from Boconnoc, but to nowhere near the level that was experienced 'down west' in the mining areas of Cornwall. In this aspect, Boconnoc was less of an exemplar of Cornish history. Although there were times of economic depression in agriculture, farmers were attached to their land which may have been handed down through many generations of the same family. They had less incentive to emigrate if they could still make their livelihood from a farm. In contrast, employment for miners in the west of the county had virtually disappeared.

EDUCATION AND THE SCHOOL

The eighteenth century

The first mention of a school at Boconnoc is in 1785 when Thomas Bennett, the steward, went to Mrs Alee to offer her money 'on account of the school'. The financial assistance was refused, since she had not spent all the money she had already received from Lady Camelford.[8]

In 1791, Joseph May, during an examination relating to his settlement for the purposes of the Poor Law, declared that he had been born in the parish of Boconnoc and lived with his parents there until he was 13 years of age. After working a year for a farmer, he returned to Boconnoc where he 'rented a cottage and kept a school for some years'. It is difficult to know what level of education May could have provided because, in the Poor Law records, he was listed as a 'labourer'.[9]

The earlier nineteenth century

In 1832, the rector of Boconnoc, Arthur Tatham, was concerned that, for some time, there had been no schools daily or weekly under the immediate charge of a clergyman in either of his parishes of Boconnoc or Braddock. In consequence, dissenters had become active in the education of the young and had succeeded in withdrawing from the church a very large portion of the parishioners. Tatham, with the agreement of the Grenvilles, intended to establish and superintend a daily school in both parishes where the children would learn reading and useful habits and the principles of the church. From the very real difficulty which the poor had in finding the weekly payments for the education of their children, he suggested that attendance at the schools should be free.[10] Lord Grenville agreed to Tatham's proposals and Lady Grenville sent books to Boconnoc for the scholars.[11]

A parochial school was built at Boconnoc in 1841, at Great Penvose, with a school house attached for the teacher. Schoolmistresses are enumerated in the decennial censuses of 1841, 1851 and 1861. In the 1841 census, Elizabeth Coad, aged 20, was listed as 'schoolmistress'. She was living with her father, Samuel, a blacksmith and her mother Elizabeth at Couch's Mill.[12]

Hard times

In 1847, during the decade known as 'The Hungry Forties', Lady Louisa provided porridge made of rice, barley and treacle for the 'starved looking children at the school'. It cost 1s.6d for about thirty pints and she continued to provide this sustenance until the weather became warmer in May of that year. The provision of the porridge 'made the school popular'.[13]

The later nineteenth century

Despite her youth, Elizabeth Coad must have proved an efficient teacher, for she was still employed at the school in 1851. She had remained resident at Couch's Mill, although now married to Thomas Hunking, an agricultural labourer and had two children of her own, a son and a daughter.[14] In the 1851 census, sixty-two children were listed as scholars.

In 1861, there were sixty-six scholars and two schoolmistresses were resident in the parish – Ann P. Scantlebury, aged 33, living at Couch's Mill with her parents, her father William Scantlebury, a tailor and her mother, Alice. Ann Furze, aged 40, was lodging in School Cottage with the family of John Minards, a labourer.[15]

The Education Act of 1870

The Education Act of 1870 made attendance at school compulsory for children up to the age of 11 or 13. Where buildings that were currently being used were not large enough for the numbers of children to be educated or were substandard, a school board had to be elected to take on the responsibility of erecting and maintaining new premises. Although the Act of 1870 made the provision of a school compulsory, many school boards were not formed immediately and in some cases, were not in place for many years after the Act came into force.[16]

In 1870, the schoolmistress Sarah Smith had had seventy-four children at the school on one day, nearly half of whom had come from the outskirts of the surrounding parishes. Lady Louisa was unsure what effect the Education Act would have: the school was large enough for their own parishioners, but in general was constantly overfull.[17] In order that they could decide what school provision would be required for the district, the Education Department wrote asking for information about the parish of Boconnoc. From 1874, an annual financial grant was paid for the school by the department and the school was inspected annually.[18]

The first report was made by Her Majesty's Inspector in 1873.[19] The Inspector commented that discipline was good and the instruction was given efficiently, but more reading books were required, especially for the younger children.[20] The room was crowded and William Pease forwarded a plan to the Education Department, showing the details of a proposed new and additional classroom which was to be built.[21] The enlargement of the premises was welcomed by the Inspector who said that, once the new desks and furniture arrived, it would be an excellent specimen of a country school.[22] A small gallery was added in 1882, although 'the seats in the gallery are too high for such small children, they should be furnished with a foot board and backs'.[23]

Although after 1870 school was compulsory for all children up to the age of 11 or 13, some parents avoided sending their children to be educated. Families already living on a limited income suffered a double financial penalty when their children were ordered to school, losing the benefit of any wages the children might have been earning and having to find the weekly fee to be paid to the school. Education must have seemed singularly irrelevant to working people when many of the boys would later be employed on the estate or on the surrounding farms, while the girls were destined for domestic service or to remain at home assisting their mothers until they themselves were married and were running their own households.

In 1876, the Education Department was worried about the poor attendance and wrote to a number of schools advising them that the parent of every child between 5 and 13 years of age had to ensure their children attended school, or they would be liable to a penalty not exceeding five shillings for each offence.[24]

The teachers and pupils

Sarah Smith was still the schoolmistress in 1874. Four years later, Miss Gunn had taken over and the Inspector reported: 'This is a very nice little school. Miss Gunn keeps good order without harshness and the instruction is sound and thorough …'[25]

In June 1881, the mistress needed assistance and it was decided to employ a Pupil Teacher, a senior pupil who taught the younger children.[26] These girls, coming from less affluent backgrounds, were financially unable to pay to attend a Teachers' College. A Pupil Teacher, Elizabeth D. Saunders was engaged in 1886.[27] In April 1890, Sarah E. Pearce was appointed, initially for three years, but she was still at the school in 1897 when the report said: 'the infants are pleasantly managed and satisfactorily taught by Miss Pearce'.[28]

The next teachers whose names are known are temporary head teacher, Florence Moon in 1898 and Mary Catherine Prisk from September 1890 until February 1900[29] who had been a Pupil Teacher at the National School in Camborne.[30] She was followed by Carrie Lanyon Oliver (née Tonkin), from 30 April 1900, who had trained at the Boconnoc school and then Mary Bailey from October 1900.[31] Miss Prisk's salary was £65 per annum and Mrs Oliver's £61 per annum.

The Inspectors' reports were mixed. Although discipline and order were generally satisfactory, the rapid turnover of staff was unsettling and meant that the teaching often needed improvement to induce the children to apply themselves with diligence to their lessons.[32] In 1888, the Inspector reported that the children were 'shewing very little intelligence'[33] and in the following year: 'the state of the school is at present below the mark, but it appears likely to improve under Miss Real, who has been here only two months …'[34] In 1892, 'the children are in excellent order. The results of Examination are generally satisfactory.'[35]

On occasion, the children were invited to the 'Big House' or the school was visited by one or more of the Fortescue ladies. At Christmas 1870, Lady Louisa was interrupted 'by the arrival of 64 school children to receive their Xmas gifts – they were so disappointed yesterday at being stopped from coming by heavy rain that Mrs Smith would delay no longer!'[36] In November 1897, Dorothy Fortescue visited the school to hear the children sing.[37]

The curriculum

The school syllabus was split into five standards, each of which the children were expected to attain by a specific age.[38] In addition to the '3 Rs', reading, writing and arithmetic, they were taught grammar, composition, singing by ear, geography and religious instruction. The boys were taught drawing three times a week. The older girls were taught cookery and laundry work and at Boconnoc school they were particularly proficient at needlework, receiving praise for being 'excellent' in 1879[39] and 'decidedly above average' in 1882.[40]

From time to time the school put on an 'Entertainment'. One was given on 26 April 1898 by the teachers and children, assisted by the Reverend R.H. Sowell, with the evening's events being chaired by the Reverend Canon V.H. Aldham. For the front seats the admission price was 6d and for the back seats 3d. The programme included songs such as 'Who killed Cock Robin?', performed by the teachers and children, and 'The Flower Girl', change-ringing on handbells and recitations such as 'The Village Blacksmith' and 'Seven Golden Keys'. Mr Sowell sang a song, there was a pianoforte solo and the teachers, the Misses Prisk and Moon, played a duet. The concert concluded with 'God Save the Queen'.[41]

The twentieth century

In the 1910 Valuation Records, the entry for Great Penvose listed the house, garden and school, the latter with two classrooms for sixty scholars.[42] In November 1908 and May 1914, the Education Department pointed out that the infants' room was unsatisfactory in that they only had the use of a very small area, not a 'classroom, more a gallery in a recess' approached through the main room and separated from it only by a curtain.[43] This deficiency was not remedied until 1928, when a sliding door was inserted so that the room could be divided into two discrete areas.[44]

A new head teacher who took charge in February 1921 worked hard and improved standards, but staffing at the school still did not satisfy the minimum conditions and was being addressed by the Local Education Authority. When Mr Dohman, the Inspector, visited in March 1923, the head teacher was responsible for thirty-six children in Standards II to VII; the remaining nineteen were taught by an unqualified and inexperienced teacher. Overall, the improvement mentioned in 1921 had been maintained.[45] As on many previous occasions, the children's progress was hampered by the headmistress moving on after the inspection and a new one not being appointed until 1925.

The reorganisation of the school

In 1930, it was agreed that the Boconnoc Parochial School would become a junior school, for scholars under the age of 11 years. The senior pupils would attend the Lerryn, Braddock or Lanreath Church of England senior schools.[46] A new headmistress was appointed in November 1933 and was assisted by a monitress, but there were only twenty-three children at Boconnoc.[47] The change proved to be unsuccessful. Many of the pupils came from large families, whose fathers, working as low-paid farm labourers, could not afford to provide adequate clothing for their children. Having to walk significant distances on foot, often without warm coats and boots in inclement weather, the pupils suffered considerable hardship just getting to school. At midday, lunch largely consisted of warmed-up inferior pastry and there was a long wait until they had their next meal. The parents were unhappy with the new arrangements and pressed for the school to revert to its previous status, providing for all children of school age.[48]

In 1935, the school reverted to an all-age school with twenty-four children on the books. In 1939, the Inspector complimented the children in the upper class on their friendliness and polite behaviour, although the management of the infants was 'unsatisfactory', being left entirely in the hands of the young monitress, who was not given adequate guidance.[49]

The final document in The National Archives dates from 1944 when, yet again, it was noted that there had been staffing difficulties. The condition of both the upper class and the infants, who were being taught by a supplementary teacher, formerly the monitress, was unsatisfactory.[50]

LAW AND ORDER

Offences and the Corn Laws

There were frequent reports about various minor offences in the area. These included hunting without permission, poaching, tenants removing items such as timber or corn from their farms, contrary to the terms of their leases, and one employee from the estate being intoxicated and arrested for committing an assault on a young woman.[51]

Several of the Fortescues, including George Matthew and Bevill, were appointed as Justices of the Peace. In 1857, at the Trecan Gate session, George Fortescue and the Reverend Arthur Tatham sat to hear a case (not at the top end of the criminal spectrum) between the Reverend J.B. Kitson, the complainant, and R. Waksham, defendant and others. The defendants were charged with shooting a duck belonging to the complainant. The complaint was withdrawn after the defendants had expressed their sorrow at what they had done and paid the costs of the case.[52]

The Corn Laws and riots

The Corn Laws were measures enforced in the United Kingdom between 1815 and 1846, which were designed to keep grain prices high to favour domestic producers. The laws raised food prices and became the focus of opposition and riots in many areas across the country. The Anti-Corn Law League was responsible for turning public opinion against the laws and they were finally repealed.

However, in the 1840s, which came to be known as 'The Hungry Forties', the country suffered from an economic depression which increased unemployment, while simultaneously bad harvests caused suffering to the poor as the price of bread – a staple of their diet – increased to hitherto unknown heights. In 1847, George Fortescue wrote to Lady Grenville that he and Lady Louisa had been trying soup from a recipe they had obtained from a French cook called Soger and they had distributed the recipe widely. He had also sent for a quantity of rice and Scotch barley, which they would sell at a reduced price to their tenants.[53]

Riots in Cornwall in 1847

With a dearth of corn in Cornwall and a shortage of food, particularly in the west of the county, Mr Tatham, the rector of Boconnoc and a magistrate, was called to Lerrin (Lerryn) by Elford Parkyn, son of a corn merchant, to speak to and disperse a mob of miners, their wives and children, almost 200 in number, who were armed with picks and sticks. They had assembled near Parkyn's granary, by the water's edge below Ethy, having been told that corn was about to be shipped out and being determined to stop it, saying that their children were starving from the high price of corn. An assurance was given by Mr Kendall, another magistrate, that the corn would not be shipped away that week and the mob dispersed.[54]

Lady Louisa arranged for corn to be sold to those in need on the Boconnoc estate for a price below market value and in May, she collected half a bushel of corn from Lostwithiel, to be shared with the tenants. Eventually, albeit slowly, the price of corn began to fall.[55]

THE POOR LAW

The Old Poor Law

Two Parliamentary Acts of 1598 and 1601, known jointly as The Old Poor Law, devolved responsibility for the financial maintenance of the poor to individual parish authorities, paid for by a levy imposed on rate payers. Those too old or unable to work through illness were given what was known as outdoor relief in the form of food and clothing, while some of the poor were accommodated in the almshouse or poor house within the parish. In 1597, the post of Overseer of the Poor was created to which two men were elected annually at Easter. They set the rate to be paid, organised its collection, reported to the vestry and maintained the account books.

Lawful settlement

In order to ensure that a pauper was eligible for relief in a particular parish, a system of settlement certificates and removal orders was instituted. To qualify, the person had to be born in the parish of legally settled parents, or be hired by a legally settled person for 365 days continuously, or serve an apprenticeship to a legally settled man for seven years, or rent property worth more than £10 per annum in the parish. Women changed their legal settlement on marriage and adopted their husband's settlement. Where there was a dispute between parishes, an examination would be held to determine in which parish the pauper could claim a settlement and then, if appropriate, an order would be applied for from a local Justice of the Peace to allow the pauper to be removed to the relevant parish.

Examinations as to settlement

Ann Lean, spinster: her examination was taken on 16 March 1763. She was born in the parish of St Tane (it is not clear which parish this was) and lived with her parents there until they had died five years before. She then moved to the parish of Warleggan and served for a year as a servant to Alexander Marks, a farmer. During the time she worked for Marks, he moved from Warleggan parish to Boconnoc parish, where she served the last three months of her employment. She served another year as a servant in the parish of St Neot, then moved to the parish of St Stephens near Saltash to work for William Westlake, a breeches maker. At the end of five months Westlake discharged her for 'sufficient reasons'. The sufficient reasons turned out to be that 'she was Big wth Child' and incapable of performing her duties. It is not known who the father of Ann Lean's child was and sadly, the final outcome is not known. This is the situation with all but one of the following cases.[56]

Robert Haly: while this man could claim a settlement in Boconnoc, if or when he was unable to support his family financially, they could be 'thrown' on the parish. In 1782, Haly was six months in arrears with his rent and had deserted Boconnoc. If Haly was to be prosecuted, he would be sent to prison and his family would have to rely on Boconnoc parish for relief.[57]

Joseph May: the decision about the parish in which an individual could claim settlement could be very complicated. May's case was heard on 16 May 1791. He was born in the parish of Boconnoc, moved to Lanreath, returned to Boconnoc, then resided consecutively in the parishes of St Veep, St Martyn near Looe, St Germans, East Looe, went back to St Germans and finally became a resident of the parish of Sheviock.[58]

Elizabeth Carne: in 1849, a complaint was brought by the Churchwardens and Overseers of the parish of Lostwithiel that Elizabeth and her daughter, Catherine, had come 'to inhabit the parish … not having gained a lawful settlement there'. The officers of Lostwithiel made an application for a warrant for the removal of Elizabeth and her daughter to the parish of Boconnoc.[59]

Elizabeth Carne stated that she was born in the parish of St Winnow. Many years ago she had attended with her mother, Ann Carne, at Trecan Gate to be bound a parish apprentice to Lord Grenville and went to reside with Mr Bowen, Lord Grenville's steward, in the parish of Boconnoc. She stayed with Mr Bowen until the death of Lord Grenville and for a short time thereafter. She had not resided in Lostwithiel for five years before this time.[60] As we have seen, she was living at the stewardry as a servant to John Bowen in 1832, when she was a candidate for confirmation.

The Justices sent an order to the Overseers of Boconnoc on 9 March 1849, ordering the removal of Elizabeth Carne and her daughter from Lostwithiel to Boconnoc. It was confirmed by James Phillips, one of the Overseers, that the 'within named pauper and her child' were received at Boconnoc on 30 March 1849.

The poor in Boconnoc parish

A poor house had been established in Boconnoc parish by the mid-eighteenth century. In the will of Mary Leach, widow of Philip Leach, the rector of Boconnoc, she bequeathed 'the sum of five pounds to the poorhouse keepers of the parishes of Broadoak and Boconnock to be severally divided between them …'[61] The Overseers' Accounts show that the location of the poor house was at Little Menaburle Cottage owned by a Mr Carson. At Easter 1812, the Overseers, James Roskilly and Thomas Hawken, paid out a total of £3.16s.6d for repairs to the poorhouse building, which included the cost and carriage of lime, stone, repairs to glass, the smith's bill and the rent of the house.[62] Between 1823 and 1826 amounts were paid for new flooring and for repairing the thatch.[63]

The property was 'rented for the use of the Poor and rent £1.1s.0d – for the period 26th February 1826 to 26th March 1826 – was paid to Mr Carson'.[64] In 1832–33, the amount of 7s.6d was paid for repairs to the cottage.

Clothes were made and distributed to the poor: 5s.0d for a hat; £1.12s.5½d for clothing; 7s.6d paid the taylor (sic) for making a coat and breeches and the shoemaker's bill, 10s.2d[65] and items given to 'John Powils Family' were: cash, 6s; a chimney croack, 3s.6d; a teakettle, 2s.6d; bedtie & bolster, 13s.6d and other goods such as a pair of blankets and barley.[66] Other monies were expended on bread, tea, wool, calico, beer, coals, wood, wheat, candles, soap, linens and medicines. The total paid out between 1833 and 1834 was £119.18s.9½d.

Those who were ill were supported with small amounts of cash: on 2 April 1824, Mary Freethey was given 2d, which she was paid 'in Sickness'.[67] The doctor, Mr Lanyon, was paid 3s.6d, by Jonathan Walcomb, one of the Overseers, for his 'attendance and certification of Insane persons in Boconnoc'.[68]

In 1822, payments were made for an unnamed pauper's funeral: 1s. as the fee to the Reverend Thomas Bennett for conducting the funeral, 2s. for the sexton's fee, £1.6s.0d for the coffin, 2s.8d for the shroud, 8s.9d for liquor for the funeral and 2s. for the attendance of the Overseer.[69]

The proposal to establish a workhouse

In 1829, a proposal was put forward by the clergymen of six parishes, including Boconnoc and Braddock, that a workhouse should be established for the use of the poor in their parishes. The clergymen believed that:

> Such a building in this District would be highly advantageous not only to reduce the Rates; but to improve the Morals, as well as to increase the Comforts of the Impotent Poor, by adopting a system of cleanliness and regularity, which is seldom, if ever to be found in Parish Workhouses. This would deter the Idle Poor from applying for parochial relief.[70]

In the end, nothing came of this suggestion and five years later, Boconnoc became part of the Liskeard Poor Law Union.

The New Poor Law

In 1834, the Poor Law was transformed by the Poor Law Amendment Act. The most important change was that, instead of each parish being responsible for their poor, a number of parishes were consolidated into a Poor Law Union to be jointly responsible for paupers, each union overseen by an elected Board of Guardians. There had been many complaints that individual parishes had been financing the poor to an unacceptable level and that employers could keep workers' wages at a low level, knowing that they would be supplemented from the poor rate. Under the new law, the able-bodied poor were no longer to be given 'outrelief' (except in exceptional circumstances), but could only receive help from the authorities if they were resident in a workhouse which each union had to build and maintain. The inmates were given food and clothes in exchange for manual labour, males and females were separated and the inmates had to wear a uniform. Portions of food were strictly regulated and consisted mainly of bread and soup. Meat was only served on rare occasions.

The Liskeard Poor Law Union

The Liskeard Poor Law Union, formed by the amalgamation of twenty-six parishes, including Boconnoc, was formed on 1 February 1837 with forty-six members on the Board of Guardians.[71] In 1839, George Fortescue was elected as Chairman of the Board. The Union Workhouse was built in 1837–39, on the west side of Station Road in Liskeard. It was designed by George Gilbert Scott and his partner William Bonyton Moffatt and could accommodate 350 inmates.

The Poor Law documents record the names of the paupers who were resident in the workhouse from 1837 to 1841. In that period, only one, a woman called Grace Bartlett, came from Boconnoc parish. She died on 14 August 1840, aged 51, of a diseased liver.[72] In 1847, another Bartlett from Boconnoc, Thomas, aged 63 was in the workhouse. It is not known if he was a relation of Grace's, but he was listed as an 'idiot from birth, not dangerous to himself or others and not of dirty habits'. The cost of his weekly maintenance and clothing was 2s.

G.M. Fortescue relinquished his position as Chairman of the Board of Guardians on 7 September 1849 and was succeeded in that office by Sir William Lewis J. Trelawney.

The County Lunatic Asylum

Pauper lunatics, sent to the asylum at Bodmin, were also listed in the Poor Law documents. John Mutton, chargeable to Boconnoc parish, a lunatic who was dangerous to himself and others, was sent to the asylum on 4 June 1834, aged 25. He was still there in 1859, when he had been of unsound mind for twenty-five years. He thereafter disappears from the records.

The only other inmate of the asylum chargeable to Boconnoc parish was Elizabeth Thomas, sent to the asylum on 8 December 1847. In 1850, her age was given as 23.

THE POLRUAN, BODINNICK AND FOWEY FERRIES

Polruan and Bodinnick

Polruan, the name dating back to 1292, is situated on the east bank of the River Fowey with a sheltered harbour. The quay was (and is) at the heart of Polruan and for many centuries the best access to the village was by water transport. Goods were loaded and unloaded at the quay and passengers travelled to and from Fowey on the ferry, which only accommodated foot passengers.

Bodinnick is also on the east bank of the River Fowey, north of both Pont Pill creek and Polruan. The ferry crossing at Bodinnick dates back to the fourteenth century and belonged to the manor of Bodinnick at Hall. Many of the cottages in the village were owned by the Boconnoc estate and rented by tenants. In contrast to Polruan, the Bodinnick ferry carried horses and carriages.

In 1468, Sir Henry Bodrugan, knight, granted to William Mohun 'a messuage and one acre of land with "le Kaye" to the same adjoining in Bodinnick, lying between the *rivulum maris* [the sea rivulet] on the West side and the toft of William Mohun, Lord of Bodinnick on the east and the common street on the North, and "Le Hillegh Park" on the South'. In 1478, a grant to ply the ferry was made to John Davy, yeoman.[73] The Inquisitions Post Mortem of John Mohun, Reginald Mohun and William Mohun show they were all 'seised of the manor of Bodinnick with the passage upon the water of Fowey'.[74] In 1567, the ferry was held by Reginald Mohun at a rent of 1d per year.

The Treffrys of Place in Fowey may once have had an equal right to the ferries as the Mohuns, but 'an act of outlawry pending a trial of the disputed rights left the passage in the undisputed possession of the Mohuns'.[75] The land on the Fowey side of the harbour where the ferry boats landed, belonged to Mr Austen (later Treffry). In consequence, he claimed that tradesmen and labourers working for him and any implements of husbandry owned by him should be carried free.

In 1661 and 1662, Willem Schellinks (1627–78), a Dutch landscape painter, was travelling around England, keeping a journal containing a record of his journeys. He visited Fowey describing it as 'situated in Cornwall, long famed for the naval battles fought thereabouts as well as for the good harbour which is deep and protected by the surrounding hills against all storm winds'.[76] One of his drawings shows the entrance to the river of Fowey and in the bottom right-hand corner, the ferry, loaded with a coach and four horses and being paddled from the back of the vessel by a ferryman [*Plate 29*].

There has been speculation that Schellinks was a spy and was working on commission for the Dutch government, for many of his drawings include strategic points that would have interested his government's intelligence service, but this has not been proved conclusively.[77]

In 1720, the deeds conferring Boconnoc and the rest of the Mohun lands, including Bodinnick, from Lady Mohun to Governor 'Diamond' Pitt (I) do not mention the ferries specifically, although they were held in the right of the manor of Bodinnick.[78] In an indenture dated 30 March 1772, 'Thomas Pitt [III] of Boconnock granted to Michael Dennison of the Burrough of Fowey Gardiner. All that Passage or Ferry called by the name of Fowey Passage and all that one other passage or Ferry called Polruan Passage … from 25th April next for five years'. In addition to paying a yearly rent of £70, Dennison was to keep and maintain all the ferry boats, oars, moorings and all other tackle and if damaged, to provide new equipment.[79]

The rents paid arising from the ownership of the ferries was, in theory, a useful additional source of income, but in practice the ferries caused numerous problems for the owners of the Boconnoc estate. There were endless arguments about the amount of dues that should be charged to passengers, where the landing places should be and whose responsibility it was to keep the slip at Fowey in repair, in addition to disputes with men who persistently challenged the right of Lady Grenville and her successors to run the ferries.

The challenges to Lady Grenville's right to run the ferry

By 1852, Richard and Sarah Pill, who had rented the right to run the Polruan ferry from Lady Grenville, were experiencing problems with men who were plying a ferry on their own behalf. In January, Richard Pill wrote to William Pease, 'John Palmer's son is taking passage to and from Polruan against my interests'[80] and two weeks later, Palmer said that he intended to continue to take passengers to and from Polruan in defiance of Lady Grenville.[81]

Four years later another man, Richard Scantlebury, had, in turn, started to take passengers.[82] Scantlebury said that all he did was to take three people over and back again on Saturdays to the Fowey Quay and 'the water is free for any Person'.[83] Further correspondence ensued, but no action was taken.[84]

Thomas Hill and Polruan

Thomas Hill was for some years employed by Sarah Pill as the ferryman, plying between Polruan and Fowey. He left her employment (he claimed) because she owed him nineteen shillings. Having no livelihood and wanting to avoid the workhouse or prison, Hill started to ply a ferry on his own account. Hill (being illiterate) arranged for a letter to be written by a friend to George Fortescue in which he claimed that a 'gentleman advised him to ply for myself saying I could not be hurt by so doing'. The letter ended with an X, 'the mark of Thomas Hill'.[85]

Pease wrote to Hill telling him to desist, but to no avail. A friend of Mrs Pill, Peter Tadd, visited Thomas Hill with a policeman 'and Tomy said he should not stop for you or aney one as the Ferrey was free for aney body …'[86]

Robert Childs, the Fortescues' solicitor, was instructed to take out an injunction against Hill[87] which the latter ignored and continued as before[88] 'in opposition'.[89] In May, a second injunction was served on him,[90] but when this was also ineffective, Hill was 'conveyed off' to prison in Bodmin.[91]

Dr A.A. Davis wrote to G.M. Fortescue saying, 'The poor man in question … was always regarded as being deficient in intellect and I am satisfied that had he been endowed with common sense he would not have been in his present situation but he had no friend to advise him …'[92]

Hill arranged for a letter to be written from the County Prison in Bodmin, saying he was sorry for the way he had acted in invading the right of ferry at Polruan, asking for forgiveness and for release from prison and promising that he would not interfere with the ferry again.[93] Now that Hill had (apparently) seen the error of his ways, George Fortescue undertook to see how the term of imprisonment could be shortened.

On 21 December, Peter Tadd reported that 'Tomy Hill is not home yet nor will he be out of Prison very quick. There is money to pay before he is released and none of his friends are dispos'd to do that good for him'.[94] Hill was still incarcerated in September 1864 and Commins & Son, Solicitors were predicting that 'Hill the Old Ferryman at Polruan would die in gaol unless some exertions are made to get him out. The Governor and Chaplain of the Gaol are most anxious for his discharge as he would otherwise end his days there very shortly'.[95] Ten days later, Hill signed a formal undertaking that, on his discharge from gaol, he would not commit any breach of the injunctions.[96] He was released on 23 September 1864.[97]

Within a month of his release, Hill had again 'commenced to interfere with the Ferry', notwithstanding that Peter Tadd, who was now renting the ferry, had proved himself to be almost the only friend that Hill had in Polruan and had exerted himself to the utmost to raise the sum required for Hill's liberation.[98] Tadd asked that Hill should be put 'in Prizon' again.[99] Hill must be 'either a fool or a rogue and is behaving infamously', wrote Thomas Commins to Pease.[100]

Hill claimed that he was entitled to take passengers to Fowey Quay, a different landing place from that which he had been using previously. After much correspondence, Hill was taken back to court. Mr Cole, counsel for Hill, said that his client was a poor old man and argued that the rights claimed by Mr Fortescue were much more extensive than could be legally sustained: not only did Mr Fortescue claim a right of ferry from Polruan across to the Whitehouse steps, but also to the Town Quay and all the waterway up to the town of Fowey, which effectively deprived the watermen from earning their livelihood. Together, Mr Karslake, barrister for G.M. Fortescue, and Mr Cole defined Mr Fortescue's rights and they agreed that Hill (and others) could ply up towards Fowey, to earn a living there, which would not interfere with the ancient right of ferry, claimed by Mr Fortescue.[101] Sir Arthur Quiller Couch, pen name 'Q' (1863–1944), used the dispute between G.M. Fortescue and Thomas Hill as an incident in his book called *Shining Ferry*.[102]

The landing slip at Whitehouse in Fowey

The slip was built about the year 1793 by public subscription. Prior to that, the passengers had been landed on the natural beach and rock. Lord Grenville had consented to pay half the annual expense of putting and keeping the slip in repair, but no work had been carried out for many years and the stone work had gradually fallen away and had been swept out by the tides. This prevented carriages from coming over as the horses could not get over the landing place. In 1816, Lord Grenville's agent and steward John Bowen had observed the slip was decaying and proposed that the costs of the repairs should be paid for by the inhabitants of Fowey, because the damage was being caused by the Fowey boatmen who were fastening their boats to the slip and knocking out some of the side stones. Joseph Treffry proposed a change to the place where the ferry landed, believing it would be more convenient for the public and would enable a larger subscription to be raised from the locality towards the costs.[103]

In 1817, George Isbell, surveyor, advised William Pease that an indictment was about to be issued in consequence of the dangerous state of the landing place at Fowey, believing that, as Lord Grenville was receiving profits from the ferry, he should pay for the repairs.[104] The question of whose responsibility it was to keep the slip in repair was referred to a barrister, Mr S. Gaselee of the Temple in 1821. His opinion was that the owner of the ferry was not bound to repair the slip and landing place, but as both the owner of the ferry and the inhabitants derived advantage from them, some agreement should be reached so that each side made some financial contribution.[105]

The matter was still under discussion over fifty years later. A meeting was held of the inhabitants of Fowey and Polruan in September 1874, when the subject of the state of the landing place at Fowey was raised again. William Pease put forward an offer that, although Mr Fortescue would not accept responsibility for the slip, if a subscription was taken up, he would subscribe the amount of three years' rent, that is, £36.[106] In 1896, Bevill Fortescue agreed to contribute a third of any sum not exceeding £100 for repairs or alterations to the slip.[107]

Complaints about the ferry services

There were frequent complaints about various aspects of the services provided by the ferries. William Pease complained to Nicholas Butson at Bodinnick that the ferry had been left in charge of two children, aged 11 and 8, and ordered that an experienced man must be in constant attendance. Butson replied that there had been problems with the ferry and that it had been running in snow and hail, although why this meant an adult had not been in charge is unclear.[108]

On another occasion, the Bodinnick ferry was being run by an unlicensed man called James Medlin and Pease indicated to John Gay, lessee of the ferry at the Ferry Inn in Bodinnick, that this practice should cease.[109]

Percy Whiting wrote in 1891 to Bevill Fortescue complaining about the way that the ferryman at Polruan, Mr Ede, was conducting himself. On one occasion, he had been kept waiting at Fowey for sixteen minutes. On another night, a lady residing in Polruan was kept waiting thirty minutes at Fowey for the ferry.[110]

The Harbour Commissioners drew notice to the fact that there was frequent over-crowding on the ferry from Whitehouse to Polruan and they feared that a serious incident might occur.[111] The number of people using the ferry caused inconvenience for some who had to cross the water to Fowey daily to get to their place of employment at set hours, such as working men and shop girls. Many of them wanted to go back to Polruan for dinner (lunch), but it often happened that there were more passengers than the boat could accommodate and some were left at Fowey until the boat returned. It was suggested that a special boat should be sent at these times.[112]

Landing dues at Bodinnick and Sir Arthur Quiller Couch ('Q')

A well-known name in Cornwall was involved in a dispute about landing dues: Sir Arthur Quiller Couch, 'Q', who lived in Fowey, wrote to F.J.H. Somerset, the steward and agent at Boconnoc, asking if Mr Powell, the new lessee of the ferry, had a right to demand a toll from anyone landing or leaving the slip at Bodinnick. Powell was now insisting on reimposing a toll that had not been charged for many years.[113] Somerset replied that Bevill Fortescue was the owner of the ferry rights between Bodinnick and Fowey and the slipway at the former was his private property and kept in repair at his sole cost. Everyone who landed or left the Bodinnick slipway should be charged and tolls were also levied on goods that were landed or embarked. Legally, the lessee was bound to enforce the toll under the terms of his lease.[114]

The sudden reimposition of this charge caused much consternation. The clerk to the Liskeard Rural District Council, A. Glubb, maintained that, as far as living memory went, no tolls had been charged, except to those using the ferry boats, and all other persons had always landed or embarked free.[115]

A previous holder of the ferry, Nicholas Butson, had been notoriously lax in demanding the landing charges and they had effectively been allowed to lapse. As there seemed little chance that Powell, the new lessee, would be able to reintroduce them, Bevill Fortescue agreed with Mr W.J. Graham, the clerk to the Harbour Commissioners, that no one would be charged for landing or embarking, except by the ferry.[116]

Bevill Fortescue sells the rights to Polruan Ferry

In 1911, the inhabitants of Lanteglos-by-Fowey requested that Bevill Fortescue provide an improved ferry service between Polruan and Fowey, saying that they had for many years endured the hardship of a ferry worked with rowing boats with its attendant disadvantages of delay and exposure to inclement weather. They asked that a ferry service worked by steam or other mechanical motive power, which would make the passage across the harbour more comfortable and expeditious, should replace the rowing boats.[117] By the time this request reached Bevill Fortescue, he had already sold his rights to the ferry to Mr A.E. Skentelbury, of Lostwithiel, who had worked for the Boconnoc estate for a number of years. The price was £450, to include the rowing boats, and Skentelbury took control at Michaelmas 1911.[118]

Figure 20 The Fowey ferry in the 1950s. (Photograph courtesy of Jim Matthews)

The ferry at Bodinnick

A similar request for a new ferry came from the lessee at Bodinnick, Mr E. Jackson. Bevill Fortescue was willing to build a new ferry boat to carry large motors if Jackson would pay 5 per cent on the outlay and undertake to keep the boat in thorough repair.[119]

The present

Both ferries still run today. Cars crossing from Fowey to Bodinnick land near the Old Ferry Inn. The two car ferries, *Jenack* and *Gellan*, both licensed to carry fifteen cars, were built down the river at the boatyard of C. Toms & Sons.

The Polruan passenger ferry operates a continuous daily service (except on Christmas Day) between Polruan and Fowey, departing each side of the harbour approximately every ten to fifteen minutes.[120]

THE RAILWAYS

The Cornwall Railway

The Cornwall Railway was built in the second half of the nineteenth century and became one of the key routes improving communications, opening up Cornwall to holidaymakers and allowing Cornish produce to reach London and elsewhere so much more quickly than previously that it contributed significantly to Cornwall's increasing economic prosperity.

A proposal for the Cornwall Railway was first made in 1839. The final scheme was given royal assent on 3 August 1846, one of the stipulations being that the ferry at Saltash should be replaced by a railway bridge linking Cornwall to the rest of the United Kingdom. Isambard Kingdom Brunel was appointed chief designer and engineer and construction started in May 1854.

The first test train crossed the bridge on 11 April 1859. Prince Albert, the Prince Consort, gave his consent to calling it the Royal Albert Bridge and opened it officially on 2 May 1859. The line was opened from Plymouth to Truro on 4 May for passenger trains and for goods trains on 3 October 1859. George Fortescue wrote to Lady Grenville to tell her that the railway and bridge had opened and when they accompanied Cyril to school at Malvern on 6 May, 'we may in safety trust our persons upon its airy viaduct'.[121]

He commented on how the railway had affected their lives: 'It seems strange to one used to the old ways of travelling – but we left home after lunch at 1 – stayed near 3 hours in Plymouth and got home to a 7 o'clock dinner.'[122]

The station at Lostwithiel which served the Boconnoc estate, opened with the Cornwall Railway on 4 May 1859. A report at the time claimed that it 'is generally admitted to be the handsomest station on the line and looks as gay and bright as fresh paint can make it'.

NOTES AND REFERENCES

1. Philip Payton, *The Cornish Overseas,* Fowey, 1999.
2. British Library (BL): Add MS 69056, Boconnoc, 15 April 1854, GM Fortescue to Lady Grenville, ff. 48–49.
3. Cornwall Record Office (CRO): F/3/10/502, Liskeard, 5 May 1863, Harry Hawken to GM Fortescue; F/3/10/147, 20 May 1878, Simeon Truscott to William Pease.
4. BL: Add MS 69178, Boconnoc, 28 January 1928, ff. 46–49.
5. CRO: F/3/10/352, South View, Goverseth Hill, Foxhole, near St Austell, 6 December 1921, Mabel Ruse to Bevill Fortescue.
6. CRO: F/3/10/377, James Lane End, High Street, near St Austell, 7 December 1926, Mrs AJ Osborne to Bevill Fortescue.
7. CRO: F/3/10/382, James Lane End, High Street, near St Austell, 15 February 1928, Mrs AJ Osborne to Bevill Fortescue.
8. BL: Add MS 59489, Collon, 15 March 1785, Thomas Bennett to 1st Lord Camelford, f. 33.
9. CRO: P208/13/4/2.
10. BL: Add MS 58997, Boconnoc, 12 December 1832, Arthur Tatham to Lord Grenville, ff. 128–129.
11. BL: Add MS 58997, Dropmore, 29 January 1833, Lord Grenville to Arthur Tatham, ff. 130–131.
12. HO107/153, 1841 census.
13. BL: Add MS 69052, Boconnoc, 14 February 1847, GM Fortescue to Lady Grenville, f. 165; Add MS 69053, March 1847, ff. 5–6; Add MS 69364, Boconnoc, 12 May 1847, Lady Louisa to GM Fortescue, ff. 87–92.
14. HO107/1903, 1851 census.
15. RG9/1532, 1861 census.
16. Catherine Lorigan, Delabole. *The History of the Slate Quarry and the Making of its Village Community,* Reading, 2007, p. 182.
17. Hampshire Record Office (HRO): 115M88/C10/3/50/18-19, Boconnoc, 14 December 1879, Lady Louisa to GM Fortescue.
18. CRO: P17/28/6/1-2.
19. CRO: P17/28/6/6.
20. CRO: P17/28/6/6.
21. The National Archives (TNA): ED21/2224; CRO: F/3/9/5/11, plan dated 22 November 1873.
22. CRO: P17/28/6/15; P17/28/6/7.
23. CRO: P17/28/6/25.
24. Lorigan, *op. cit.,* p. 184.
25. CRO: P17/28/6/18, May 1878; HRO: C10/3/89/10/1-2, Lady Louisa to Harriet Phillimore (née Fortescue).
26. CRO: P17/28/6/32.
27. CRO: P17/28/6/31.
28. CRO: P17/28/6/44.
29. CRO: P17/28/6/56 & 58.
30. CRO: P17/28/6/50.
31. CRO: P17/28/6/50.
32. CRO: P17/28/6/27.
33. CRO: P17/28/6/32-33, 7 April 1888.
34. CRO: P17/28/6/34, 4 April 1889.
35. CRO: F/3/23/14/14.
36. HRO: 115M88/C10/3/50/18-19, 14 December 1870, Lady Louisa to Harriet Phillimore.
37. CRO: F/3/10/457.
38. Lorigan, *op. cit.,* p. 184.

39. CRO: P17/28/6/20.

40. CRO: P17/28/6/25, 4 May 1882.

41. CRO: F/3/10/459.

42. The National Archives (TNA): IR58/71649, 1910 Valuation Records.

43. TNA: ED21/24972; ED21/2224.

44. TNA: ED21/24972.

45. TNA: ED21/24972.

46. TNA: ED21/24972.

47. TNA: ED21/24972.

48. TNA: ED21/24972.

49. TNA: ED21/48432.

50. TNA: ED21/48432, inspected on 3 March 1944.

51. BL: Add MS 69322, Lostwithiel, 26 April 1765, John Bennett to Thomas Pitt, f. 14; BL: Add 71594, June to August 1811, John Bowen to Lord Grenville, ff. 101, 117, 141, 152, 169 and 173; BL: Add MS 59440, Boconnoc, August 15 1813, John Bowen to Lord Grenville, f. 46.

52. *Royal Cornwall Gazette*, 7 January 1857.

53. BL: Add MS 69053, Boconnoc, 4 March 1847, GM Fortescue to Lady Grenville, ff. 5–6.

54. BL: Add MS 69363, Boconnoc, 12 May 1847, Lady Louisa to GM Fortescue, ff. 87–92.

55. BL: Add MS 69363, Boconnoc, 25 May 1847, Lady Louisa to GM Fortescue, ff. 143–146.

56. CRO: P214/13/4/5.

57. BL: Add MS 59489, Collon, 29 April 1782, Thomas Bennett to Lord Camelford, f. 14.

58. CRO: P208/13/4/2.

59. CRO: P128/13/2/189 and 182.

60. CRO: P128/13/2/189-190.

61. TNA: PROB11/1055/65, dated 1761, probate, 1779.

62. CRO: P12/12/1-2.

63. CRO: P12/12/2.

64. CRO: P12/12/1.

65. CRO: P12/12/1.

66. CRO: P12/12/1.

67. CRO: P12/12/1.

68. CRO: P12/12/2, year ending at Lady Day, 1830.

69. CRO: P12/12/2.

70. BL: Add MS 69178, Boconnoc, 22 April 1829, John Bennett to Lord Grenville, ff. 93–94.

71. www.workhouses.org.uk/liskeard

72. TNA: MH12/1430.

73. Valerie R. Belsey, *British Roads*, Peterborough, 1994, p. 85.

74. Inquisitions Post Mortem (IPMs): John Mohun, 8 Henry VIII, 21 October 1516, Series II, Vol. 78, No. 116; Reginald Mohun, 17 January 1567, Series II, Vol. 150, No. 186; Royal Institution of Cornwall (RIC), Henderson Catalogue XVIII, William Mohun, 30 Elizabeth, 1 June 1587.

75. BL: Add MS 59443, 8 January 1817, John Bowen to Lord Grenville, f. 80.

76. Willem Schellinks, Maurice Exwood and H.L. Lehmann (eds), *The Journal of William Schellinks' Travels in England, 1661–1663*, London, Royal Historical Society, 1993, pp. 117–118.

77. www.getty.edu/art/collection/artists/479/willem-schellinks

78. CRO: F/3/7/2/2, 12 August 1720.

79. CRO: F/3/7/2/79.

80. CRO: F/3/10/44, Polruan, 7 January 1852, Richard Pill to William Pease.

81. CRO: F/3/7/2/67, 19 January 1852, Richard Pill to William Pease.

82. CRO: F/3/7/2/66, Boconnoc, 21 October 1856, William Pease to Richard Scantlebury.

83. CRO: F/3/7/2/52, Polruan, 24 October 1856, Richard Scantlebury to William Pease.

84. CRO: F/3/7/2/65, Boconnoc, 27 October 1856, William Pease to Richard Scantlebury; CRO: F/3/7/2/69, Boconnoc, 27 October 1856, William Pease to Sarah Pill.

85. CRO: F/3/7/2/31, Polruan, 4 February 1863, Thomas Hill to G.M. Fortescue; CRO: F/1/295, 19 February 1863, Sarah Pill to William Pease; CRO: F/1/295, 19 February 1863, Peter Tadd to William Pease.

86. CRO: F/3/10/95, Polruan, 25 February 1863, Peter Tadd to William Pease.

87. CRO: F/1/295, 25 Coleman Street, London, EC, 25 February 1863, Robert Childs to William Pease; CRO: X715/25, Thursday, 26 February 1863, William Pease's diary.

88. CRO: F/1/295, Polruan, 7 March 1863, Sarah Pill to William Pease.

89. CRO: F/1/295, Polruan, 19 March 1863, Sarah Pill to William Pease.

90. CRO: X715/25, Saturday, 23 May 1863, William Pease's diary.

91. CRO: F/1/295, Polruan, 28 July 1863, Sarah Pill to William Pease.

92. CRO: F/3/7/2/31, Fowey, 14 October 1863, A[rthur] A Davis to William Pease and GM Fortescue.

93. CRO: F/3/7/2/31, Thomas Hill to GM Fortescue.

94. CRO: F/3/7/41, Polruan, 21 December 1863, Peter Tadd to William Pease.

95. F/1/295, 14 September 1864, Commins & Sons to RW Childs.

96. CRO: F/3/7/2/29, 23 September 1864.

97. CRO: F/1/295, Coleman Street, London, 28 September 1864, RW Childs to William Pease.

98. CRO: F/3/7/2/31, Boconnoc, 12 October 1864, William Pease to Thomas Commins at Bodmin.

99. CRO: F/1/295, 13 October 1864, Peter Tadd to William Pease.

100. CRO: F/3/7/2/31, Bodmin, 14 October 1864, Thomas Commins to William Pease; F/3/7/2/31, Bodmin, 22 October 1864, Thomas Commins to William Pease.

101. CRO: F/3/7/2/26; The Western Morning News, 26 March 1866.

102. 'Q' (Sir Arthur Quiller Couch), Shining Ferry, 1928, Chapter VIII, 'Right of Ferry'.

103. BL: Add MS 59443, 8 January 1817, John Bowen to Lord Grenville, f. 80.

104. CRO: F/3/7/2/108. Fowey, 2 January 1817.

105. CRO: F/4/200/5, Temple, 26 January 1821; CRO: F/3/7/2/2, January 1821, Draft case for the Opinion of Mr Gaselee.

106. CRO: F/1/295, 29 September 1874.

107. CRO: F/3/10/11, 970, Lostwithiel, 31 July 1896 to Albertus Dingle, Bodinnick Passage.

108. CRO: F/3/10/2, 590, 28 March 1883, William Pease to Nicholas Butson; CRO: F/3/10/185, Bodinnick, 29 March 1883, Nicholas Butson to William Pease.

109. CRO: F/3/10/19, 849, Lostwithiel, 13 December 1904, William Pease to John Gay.

110. CRO: F/3/10/218, Hill House, Polruan, 8 February 1891, Percy Whiting to Bevill Fortescue.

111. CRO: F/3/10/222, Fowey Harbour Board, 14 January 1892.

112. CRO: F/3/10/248, 30 May 1898, Samuel Slade to William Pease.

113. CRO: F/3/10/21, 171, Bodinnick, 'Q' Arthur T Quiller Couch to FJH Somerset, 14 August 1906.

114. CRO: F/3/10/21, 16 August 1906, FJH Somerset to 'Q' Arthur T Quiller Couch, The Haven, Fowey.

115. CRO: F/3/7/78/2, Liskeard RDC, A Glubb, Clerk to Fladgate & Co., 5 December 1906.

116. CRO: F/3/7/78/13, Without Prejudice letter from Bevill Fortescue to WJ Graham, Fowey, clerk to the Harbour Commissioners, 15 February 1907.

117. CRO: F/1/519, Polruan Ferry, 1911.

118. CRO: F/3/10/23, 293, FJH Somerset to FD Williams, 31 July 1911.

119. CRO: F/3/10/24, 219, 17 May 1913, FJH Somerset to Mr E Jackson, Ferry House, Bodinnick.

120. ctomsandson.co.uk

121. BL: Add MS 69060, Boconnoc, 19 April 1859, GM Fortescue to Lady Grenville, ff. 96–97.

122. BL: Add MS 69060, Boconnoc, 23 March 1863, GM Fortescue to Lady Grenville, ff. 195–198.

CONCLUSION
BOCONNOC: THE EPITOME OF CORNISH HISTORY?

'Boconnoc – it is the paradise of Cornwall.'
(BL: Add MS 69314, 19 September 1799, James Wallis to Lady Camelford, ff. 103–104)

This conclusion will draw together various strands that have been explored in this book and will return to the question of whether it can be argued that Boconnoc is an exemplar of Cornish history, a way in which Cornwall can be observed through the experiences of one house and estate. As intimated in the Introduction, the answer is both yes and no.

Figure 21 Detail of the engraving of the ferry of Fowey by Willem Schellinks, 1662.
(© Österreichische Nationalbibliothek, Vienna)

In the fifteenth century, there was chronic disorder in the counties of south-west England. The unrest created in 1381 by the Peasants' Revolt during the reign of Richard II and, later, the vacuum of physical power and the absence of a local magnate to control Cornwall in the reigns of Henry IV and Henry V, allowed lawless activity and clashes between landowners to spread. The violence was exacerbated because the distance of the western counties from the centre of royal administration meant that no help was sent by the Crown to maintain order. In some areas, there was a 'culture of violence' and open warfare broke out which became a normal part of everyday life. The 'leading members of the county establishment frequently used violence in promoting their own interests and indeed relied on its use as a means of social and political control'.[1] This has been seen in the aggression shown between the Carminow and Sergeaux families, local power going backwards and forwards between them when they were respectively the sheriff of Cornwall or holding another office of local government.

No battles were fought on Cornish soil during the Wars of the Roses, but during that conflict the Courtenay family, supporting the Lancastrian faction, was involved in revolt and insurrection in Devon and Cornwall, fighting in particular against the Bonville family, who supported the Yorkists.

In 1506, a Venetian ambassador described Cornwall as 'a very wild place … in the midst of a most barbarous race, so different in language and customs from the inhabitants of England that they understood each other as little as we do', and 'a wild spot where no human being ever comes, save the few boors who inhabit it'.[2] There were many documented reports of violent disorder and in the mid-sixteenth century polemicist Andrew Borde claimed that Cornishmen were ready to go to law 'for waggyng a straw'.[3]

Before the commencement of the Civil War in the mid-seventeenth century, many Cornish MPs were initially hopeful that some agreement could be reached between the Crown and Parliament, despite the increasing level of animosity between the two factions. It had become obvious by 1642 that no agreement could be reached and the vast majority of the Cornish gentry and the commoners positioned themselves firmly in support of the king during the ensuing Civil War, including Warwick, Lord Mohun. The royalist journal *Mercurius Aulicus* opined: 'Cornwall (which is little Wales beyond England) proved themselves true Brittaines, when no English county stood intirely for his Majestie.'[4]

The battles that took place in Cornwall have been described, involving the regiment founded by Lord Mohun and culminating in what has been called the 'Cornish Mousetrap' when Essex's Parliamentary forces were trapped in a pincer movement, surrounded by the king's troops between Fowey and Lostwithiel. Boconnoc, as with other Cornish estates, suffered from the severe financial penalties that were imposed by the Parliamentarians at the end of the Civil War, which affected the estate for many years.

Owners of Boconnoc, from the time of the Carminows, were appointed to local government offices, particularly that of the Sheriff and Commissioners, to enforce the edicts of central government.

For many estates, including Boconnoc, Heligan and Lanhydrock, the First World War marked the beginning of the slow demise of a way of life that had prevailed for many hundreds of years. The story of the Lost Gardens of Heligan is well known. Tim Smit and John Nelson made a chance discovery of a number of signatures scrawled on the wall of a building. It was found that the names were those of the gardeners who had gone to fight in the Great War, most never to return. The gardens had gradually become overgrown and disappeared before being reclaimed from the wilderness in the 1990s.

At Lanhydrock, the staff was reduced to sixteen men and one apprentice.[5] Similarly, at Boconnoc, fewer men were employed after the war and Bevill Fortescue sold many of the farms situated on the north Cornwall coast. Gradually, workforce numbers on the respective estates were reduced. The Second World War had a similar effect: there were eight gardeners employed at Boconnoc before the war, but only two after.

In contrast, there were several aspects where Boconnoc did not epitomise Cornwall and its history. In the eighteenth century, John Wesley (1703–91) founded a movement known as Methodism which was originally intended to revitalise the Church of England from within. Over time, the ideals of the new movement gradually started to move away from those of the established church. Anglicanism was perceived to be for the rich and for gentry families, while the simple doctrines of the Methodist movement, deriving inspiration from the teachings of John Wesley and stressing personal accountability, appealed to those lower down the social scale, miners, farmers, fishermen and the like. New communities composed of like-minded people who subscribed to Wesley's tenets established their own churches and schools. The Cornish took to Methodism like no other part of the country and by 1851 Cornwall was the only area (apart from North Wales) where the majority of the population attended services at Methodist chapels. The vicar of Crowan was forced to admit 'the religion of the mass is become *Wesleyan Methodism*'.[6]

There are few references to Methodism, or indeed any other forms of religious dissent, in the Boconnoc documentation except that, on occasion, pieces of land were leased to Methodists to build or enlarge a chapel. The inhabitants of the 'Big House' were immune to the attractions of this new denomination.

In 1799, Benjamin Forster informed the Bishop of Exeter that there were no dissenters in Boconnoc or Braddock parishes. This situation had changed by 1832, when Arthur Tatham was rector. He was concerned that there were no schools in his parishes under the charge of a clergyman and as a result, dissenters had become very active in the education of the young. They had succeeded in drawing a large number of parishioners away from the parish church and, to counteract this, he wanted to take the initiative and to start schools that would be run under his guidance and bring the children back to traditional Anglicanism.

Finally, Lady Louisa wrote to Harriet remarking on the large number of dissenters that had come into Cornwall, but made no further comment. The owners of Boconnoc were all staunch members of the Church of England and preferred that their servants should also be adherents of the established church and thus, there was no interest or engagement with any of the dissenting sects.

'Cornwall is quintessentially a maritime region' and made a significant contribution to the rich sea-trading and naval traditions of the nation.[7] In the 1850s, William Pease, the steward, owned a quarter share in a sailing ship called the *Par* while Joseph Treffry owned the other three-quarters. The vessel, which undertook home and coastal voyages, was sold in December 1860 when Pease received the sum of £75.15s for his interest.[8] This was the only association that there was with any maritime matters. The Boconnoc estate received cargos of coal and other goods from ships that sailed up the River Fowey and owned a substantial number of houses and other property in Polruan and Bodinnick, in addition to owning the rights to run the ferries, but it took no part in ship-building, ship-owning and the like or the fishing industry.

Finally, as we have seen, emigration, an aspect that strongly typified the Cornish, had only minimal effect on the working population of Boconnoc who, for the most part, did not stray far from the environs of the estate.

THE PAST, THE PRESENT AND THE FUTURE

The past

In the later nineteenth century, as a result of the industrial decline, particularly in the western mining areas, Cornwall fell into economic depression. In 1898, 'Q' (Sir Arthur Quiller Couch) was already thinking about how Cornwall could be revitalised. One possible way was by encouraging tourists to come and enjoy the beauties of the county:

> On the one hand I see Cornwall impoverished by the evil days on which mining and (to a lesser degree) agriculture have fallen. I see her population diminishing and her able-bodied sons forced to emigrate by the thousand, the ruined engine-houses, the roofless cottage, the cold hearthstone are not cheerful sights to one who would fain to see a race so passionately attached to home as ours is still drawing vigour from its soil. In the presence of destitution and actual famine (for in the mining district it came even to this, a little while ago) one is bound, if he cares for his countrymen, to consider any cure thoughtfully suggested.
> The suggestion is that Cornwall should turn her natural beauty to account, and by making it more widely known, at once benefit thousands and honestly enrich herself.[9]

Yet, by the 1960s, there had been little respite. Ron Perry summarised the situation:

> At the beginning of the 1960s, after a hundred years of more or less uninterrupted decline, what had Cornwall to offer? Some valuable raw materials, almost unique as far as the UK was concerned, like tin and china-clay, together with potential for new energy sources – wave, wind, tide, geothermal – and a climate and terrain suitable for dairy-farming and horticulture. A strong sense of identity, a positive attitude to

industrial redevelopment and a distinctive semi-urban settlement pattern with larger labour catchment areas than many other rural areas. On the other it lay at the end of a long and narrow peninsula, much farther away in travel-time and travel-cost than the rest of England or Wales, or indeed much of Scotland, from the main centres of industry and commerce. Unemployment was double the national rate, per capita incomes were 30 per cent below and earnings 20 per cent below the national level and employment both in the primary and in the manufacturing sector was falling. On balance it hardly seemed set for rapid expansion.[10]

There was still little employment in the county during the 1970s. Only a few manufacturing industries remained and even those companies that had survived like Holman & Co., a 'symbol of Cornwall's lost industrious prowess', and English China Clays, were eventually taken over by larger (and sometimes foreign) companies, with control passing to those residing across the Tamar or abroad and a consequent reduction in potential employment opportunities for local workers.[11] What was left was tourism and service industries. These started to provide jobs for more and more people, but mainly at low wages and often of a seasonal nature.

Cornwall has a unique and individual identity, distinct from the rest of England, with its own customs, language and institutions. As the number of tourists grew, there was a revival in interest in the social, economic and industrial history of the county. Visitors have become 'invested' in what might be called 'brand Cornwall', which encompasses not only its beautiful countryside, coastline and inland moorland areas, but aspects of Cornish life, past and present.

The present

While this was all to the good, in 2016 the *Western Morning News* initiated a campaign aimed at 'building an economy to match the beauty, sparkling seas and fresh air' of the West Country. While the natural beauty of the region was incomparable, its economy too often still lagged behind other parts of the country.[12]

Boconnoc, in common with other estates in Cornwall, suffered as the result of depredations on their staff numbers caused by the two world wars and the subsequent decline in the fortunes of the house and estate. Anthony and Elizabeth Fortescue took many years to complete the restoration, planning to take full advantage of the setting of the house, grounds and gardens. The estate is now a popular venue for wedding receptions, for parties and lunches and the stunning location is enjoyed by many visitors. In addition to the events already mentioned, other ingenious activities have been devised, for example, 'The Glow in the Park Night Run', a 5-kilometre evening dance/walk/run through the parkland with Glow Zone areas for partying – 'the ultimate night time running experience', with the monies raised donated to charity. Open-air performances of plays, given by the Miracle Theatre, are a further innovation. According to Bill Scott, the Artistic Director, 'open air performances are a real joy … a genuine shared experience'.[13]

This desire to allow others to enjoy Boconnoc has been balanced with careful, thoughtful and sympathetic changes that ensure that nothing disturbs the serenity of the estate. Still family-owned and run, Boconnoc retains the qualities that give it its magical and timeless ambience, while simultaneously, it has become a dynamic and successful business [*Plate 30*].

Following the tradition of several of his predecessors, Anthony Fortescue was appointed High Sheriff for the year 2015–2016, but sadly, he died on 9 November 2015. Sir Simon Jenkins, former Chairman of the National Trust, paid tribute to him:

> Anthony was one of our country house saints, one of a precious few who sacrificed much to love, rescue and restore a great work of art. Under his care, Boconnoc is once again among the magic houses without which Cornwall and England would be immeasurably impoverished. It is his memorial.[14]

The admiration and affection in which Anthony Fortescue was held in Cornwall and beyond the Tamar was demonstrated on 9 May 2016, when Truro Cathedral was full to capacity for a Service of Thanksgiving for his Life.

The future

Elizabeth Fortescue and her daughters, Clare and Sarah, are determined that Anthony's work will be carried on, ensuring Boconnoc's future not only for the family, but for all 'who love its beauty, peace and space'. Their stated aim is to be good custodians and to maintain the estate for the generations to come.[15]

It was through Anthony Fortescue's 'imagination, will power and creative skill' that the house and gardens were brought back to life and his legacy and plans for the future will continue.[16] Boconnoc has been subject to many vicissitudes, trials and tribulations during its long history, but in the competent hands of Elizabeth, Clare and Sarah, it will flourish and develop as it has for many centuries past.

NOTES AND REFERENCES

1. Hannes Kleineke in Linda Clark (ed.), 'Why the west was wild: law and disorder in fifteenth-century Cornwall and Devon', in *The Fifteenth Century: 3. Authority and Subversion*, Woodbridge, 2003, pp. 75–93.
2. PRO: 31/14/1, p. 184; Kleineke, *ibid.*, p. 93.
3. F.J. Furnivall (ed.), The Fyrst Boke of the Introduction of Knowledge made by Andrew Borde, EETS, 1870, p. 122.
4. As cited in Mark Stoyle, *Loyalty and Locality: Popular Allegiance in Devon in the English Revolution*, Exeter, 1996, p. 241.
5. Ray Hingston, 'Home front at Lanhydrock and Wimpole', *Lanhydrock Journal*, 2013, No. 12.
6. Cornwall.co.uk.
7. Philip Payton, Alston Kennerley and Helen Doe (eds), *The Maritime History of Cornwall*, Exeter, 2014, p. 1.

8. Cornwall Record Office (CRO): TF/2874; MSR/597.
9. *The Cornish Magazine*, Vol. 1, 1895, p. 236.
10. Gareth Shaw and Allan M. Williams (eds), *Industrial Change in Cornwall: Proceedings of a Seminar on the Collection and Analysis of Data*, South Western Paper in Geography, Plymouth Polytechnic, Plymouth, 1981, pp. 10–11.
11. Philip Payton, *The Making of Modern Cornwall*, Redruth, 1992, pp. 176–177.
12. *The Western Morning News*, Monday, 3 October 2016.
13. Boconnoc.com: Bill Scott, Artistic Director of the Miracle Theatre.
14. Boconnoc website.
15. The *Plymouth Herald*, 24 March 2016.
16. Boconnoc website.

APPENDIX

THE RECTORS OF BOCONNOC: 1266–2016

Sources: RIC: Henderson East Cornwall Book; CRO: AD409/27; The Clerical Guide; www.theclergydatabase.org.uk; The Clergy List; Crockford's Clerical Directory; Truro Diocesan Kalendar, later Yearbook.

1266	Walter Peveral
1268	Robert de Wyke
1275	Thomas de Kent
1301	Walter de Kent
1318	Richard Barri
1320	Richard Lovecock
1325	Peter de Castro
1333	Ralph de Lancarrow
1349	Walter de Kelly
1362	Bartholomew Waleis
	John Philippe
1382	Roger Piers
1394	Walter Coke
c. 1403	John Bundene
	Walter Raynald
1418	John Kouper
1445	Thomas Olertone
1454	Walter Colle
	John Tyrell
1461	John Pawton
1495	Henry Tredennek
1529	David Hensley
1533	William Smyth
1537	Roger Prior, curate to William Smyth

1561	Niottus Woodwarde
1574	Alexander Fitzgeffrye
1588	William Parker
1602	Robert Hardinge
1635	John Hardinge
1677	Ambrose Triggs
1706	Thomas Triggs
1708	Albert le Blanc
1708/9	John Pomeroy, curate to le Blanc
1710	Edward Dennis, curate to le Blanc
1714	Charles Peters
1714	Thomas Whitford, curate
1723	Henry Sutton
1730	John Gilbert, curate
1731	George Lesly, curate
1731	Francis Ayscough
1731	Philip Leach, curate
1742	Boconnoc was united with Braddock. Philip Leach was the first vicar of the united parishes of Boconnoc and Braddock
1773	Benjamin Forster
1773/4	Henry Dixon, curate to Forster
1775/7	Joseph Pomeroy, curate to Forster at Braddock
1777	Francis Dixon, curate to Forster at Boconnoc
1806	Thomas Bennett
1832	Arthur Tatham
1874	Vernon Harcourt Aldham
1877	Hugh St Aubyn Rogers, curate
1891	R.J. Morgan, curate
1900	Lewis Wilkinson, curate
1902	G.W. Hunt, curate
1903	Montague James Case, curate
1907	James Herbert Norton Knight, curate
1913	Frederick John Pickard, curate
1916	Francis Ellington Leslie, curate and rector from 1917
1925	Bernard Steele Lowe
1932	Albert William Pender
1936	Charles Percival Triplett
1943	Evan Thomas
1944	Vacant
1945	Harold Dalton Streatfield
1952	Percy Austin Openshaw

1957	George Robert Owen Jones
1961	Laurence William Day, incumbent and curate
1967	Vacant
1968	Canon Alfred Edwin Peaston, incumbent and curate
1972	Mark Bevan Kennaway, curate in charge
1975	Geoffrey Gilbert Pinnock
1981	Vacant
1982	Canon Deryck Harry Percival Davey
1987	Alexander Erwin Allardice, curate of Boconnoc with Bradoc, 1987–1990, rector of Lostwithiel, St Winnow with St Nectan's Chapel from 1990
1991	Frank Edward Stubbings, honorary curate until 2015
1998	Frederick Crichton Stevens, rector of Lostwithiel
2002	Elizabeth Ann Heaton, curate
2008	Philip James Conway, rector of Lostwithiel
2008	Samuel Denyer, curate
2015	Vacant
2016	Paul Benyon, rector of Lostwithiel

BIBLIOGRAPHY

PRIMARY ARCHIVAL SOURCES

The National Archives (TNA) (formerly the Public Record Office)

ADM1/1624 and 1626	Admiralty records, 2nd Lord Camelford
C108/422/21	Thomas Pitt (I) to son, 1719–20
C108/424	Thomas Pitt (I) letters and notebooks
E178/5199	Depositions – shipments of cloth by Lord Mohun, 1633
IR58	Valuation Office records, 1910
JUST1/117A membrane 4 & 46v	Cornwall Eyre of 1302
JUST1/1285, membrane 16r	Case against Thomas de Cancia, 1290
MH12	Poor Law records
SC6/Henry VIII	Ministers' accounts
SC8/22/1097	William and Alice Bonville, 1402
SC8/38/1867-1869	Petition to King and council, 1377–1378
SC8/277/13836-38	Botreaux v. Carminow, 1381

British Library (BL)

Add MS 11314	Mohun documents
Dropmore Papers	Pitt, Grenville and Fortescue families
Egerton 1969	Thomas Pitt to John Strange
Egerton 3880	Richard Symonds's commonplace book
Harley 6804	List of sick soldiers at Boconnoc
MS Cotton, Augustus I.i.38	Henry VIII's map of coastal fortifications

Royal Institution of Cornwall (RIC)

Charles Henderson calendars	
MS.BV 1/4	Cornish Enquiry, 3 December 1483

Berkshire Record Office (BRO)

D/EN/F7	Trelawny papers

Cornwall Record Office (CRO)

AD409/22-26	Index of clergy
AD621/11	Diary of Josiah Wedgwood, 1775
AD644	Map of Boconnoc, sixteenth century
AD806/1-2	Mohun family tree
AD1930/1/1	Tywardreath Priory
B/LISK/281	Mayor's accounts, Liskeard
BC/24/2	Antony MS
B35/15-84	Accounts and Civil War papers – seventeenth century
BY 34	China-clay and Boconnoc estate
CH/30/1/11/1-2	South Terras Mine
ED21	School records
EL 542	Warrant to arrest William Mayowe
EL 564	Lord Mohun's Vice-wardenship of the Stannaries
EN2003	Sermons by Benjamin Forster
F1-F4	Fortescue catalogue
FS/2/51	Antony MS
FS/3/1120	Biography of William Pease by CR Clinker
FS/3/1220	Trelawny family
FP12/1/1	Boconnoc Parish Registers
ME/771	Warwick, Lord Mohun
PB8/9/101-103	Mohun documents
P12	Church records
P17	School records
P128	Poor Law records
TA/TM 12	Boconnoc Tithe map and apportionment
X415/8	Sale of Boconnoc properties
X415/131	Boconnoc obelisk and other information
X715/1-44	Diaries of William Pease
X839	Building plans at Boconnoc
X847/RL/2	Plans by Richard Coad, nineteenth century

Cornwall Historic Environment Service (HES)

MCO 2263-64	Aerial photographs of the Boconnoc estate

Oxford

Bodleian, Weston Library	MS.Eng.lett.d.84. Letters between Thomas Pitt, 1st Lord Camelford, and Mr Justice (George) Hardinge
Christ Church	Letters – Fortescue and Phillimore

Devon Record Office (DRO)

ECA Book 51	Hooker's commonplace book
4088M	Meyrick Carey papers
W1258/M/E17 and E19	Ashwater papers

Hampshire Record Office (HRO)

115M88	Phillimore catalogue

Huntingdon Library, San Marino, California, USA

ST Vol. 7, 1764–1769	George Grenville's diary

Keele University Library

SC10-103-104	Sneyd Manuscript

Sir John Soane's Museum, London

Sketch for an entrance arch for Boconnoc, *c.* 1780, by Thomas Pitt (III)

Letters from Thomas Pitt (III) to John Soane

PRINTED PRIMARY SOURCES

Bishops' Registers

Census 1841–1891

Close Rolls

Feet of Fines, Devon and Cornwall Record Society, Vol. II, Richard II to Henry VI, 1377–1461, Devon, 1950

Fine Rolls

HMC Twelfth Report, The Manuscripts of SH le Fleming of Rydal Hall

HMC Twelfth Report, The Manuscripts of the Duke of Rutland

HMC Twelfth Report, The Manuscripts of the Duke of Portland

Inquisitions Post Mortem

Mercurius Aulicus, 1644

Mercurius Britanicus, 1644

Patent Rolls

Pleas before the King or his Justices, 1198–1201, DM Stenton (ed.), Selden Society, London, 1952

Red Book of the Exchequer, Hubert Hall (ed.), 3 vols, 1896

Thomason Tract, EEBO, E.102.17, A true Relation of the proceedings of the Cornish Forces under the command of the Lord Mohune and Sir Ralph Hopton, London, 1643

Thomason Tract, EEBO, E.100.20, A Full Relation of the great defeat given to the Cornish Cavalliers, by Sergeant Major Generall Chudley, London, May 3 1643

Thomason Tract, EEBO, E.103.12, The Truth of our bad News from Exeter, London, May 24 1643

Thomason Tract, EEBO, E.37.20, A Declaration published in the County of Devon by that Grand Ambo-dexter, Sir George Chudleigh, Baronet, London, 1644

William of Worcester

Newspapers and periodicals

Cornish Guardian

Daily Mirror, 30 July 2013

Daily News

Devon and Cornwall Notes and Queries

Devon and Cornwall Post

London Courant

The Morning Post

The New Annual Register

Plymouth Herald

Royal Cornwall Gazette

Sherborne Mercury

The Astrologer's Magazine & Philosophical Miscellany

The West Briton

Trewman's *Exeter Flying Post* and *Plymouth* and *Cornish Advertiser*

Western Morning News

Internet sources

Carminow Family History on Pat Patterson's Pages

Dictionary of National Biography

History of Parliament: www.historyofparliamentonline.org

English Heritage: Images of England

www.tudorplace.com.ar

www.loosemore.co.uk

www.domesdaybook.co.uk/cornwall

www.girders.net/index

www.icmacentre.ac.uk/soldier/database/search

www.historical-cornwall.org.uk

www.cornwallheritagetrust.org/page-history-cornwall-bronze-age

www.info.sjc.ox.ac.uk/forests/glossary

www.heraldry.sca.org

www.louvre.fr/en/oeuvre-notices/diamond-known-regent

www.etoncollege.com

www.highsheriffs.com

www.lancaster.ac.uk/fass/projects/manorialrecords/manors

www.paleo.anglo-norman.org/account2.html

www.savinggeorgianbuildings.blogspot.co.uk

www.cornishstainedglass.org.uk

www.cornwallcalling.co.uk/mines/Camborne/grenville-united

www.cornwallinfocus.co.uk/mining/grenville

www.imerys.com

www.workhouses.org.uk/liskeard

www.getty.edu.art/collection/artists/479/willem-schellinks

www.ctomsandson.co.uk

SECONDARY SOURCES

Books

Ackland, N.A. and Druce, R.M., *Lanteglos-by-Fowey with Bodinnick*, Fowey, 1978.

Airs, Malcolm, *The Making of the English Country House 1500–1640,* Chichester, 1975.

Banks, Stephen, *A Polite Exchange of Bullets. The Duel and the English Gentleman, 1750–1850,* Woodbridge, 2010.

Barratt, John, *The Civil War in the South-West,* Barnsley, 2005.

Bartley, Paula, *Prostitution: Prevention and Reform in England, 1860–1914,* Abingdon, 2000.

Barton, D.B., *A Guide to the Mines of West Cornwall,* 1963.

Barton, R.M., *A History of the Cornish China-Clay Industry,* Truro, 1966.

Beacham, P. and Pevsner, N., *The Buildings of England: Cornwall,* New Haven, CT and London, 2014.

Belsey, Valerie R., *British Roads,* Peterborough, 1994.

Berg, Maxine, *Luxury & Pleasure in Eighteenth-Century Britain,* Oxford, 2005.

Birdwood, Vere (ed.), *So Dearly Loved, So Much Admired. Letters to Hester Pitt, Lady Chatham from her relations and friends, 1744–1801,* London, 1994.

Bladenburg, John Ross, *A History of the Coldstream Guards, 1815–1896,* (private publication)

Brown, Kenneth and Acton, Bob, *Exploring Cornish Mines. Volume 2,* Truro, 1995.

Brown, Peter Douglas, *William Pitt, Earl of Chatham, The Great Commoner,* London, 1978.

Carew, Richard, *The Survey of Cornwall,* ed. F.E. Halliday, London, reissued 1969.

Clabburn, Pamela, *The National Trust Book of Furnishing Textiles,* London, 1988.

Clarendon, Earl (Edward Hyde), Lockyer, Roger (ed.), *The History of the Great Rebellion*, OUP for the Folio Society, London, MCMLXVIII (1968).

Coate, Mary, *Cornwall in the Great Civil War and Interregnum, 1642–1660*, Truro, 1963.

Cockain, Aston, *Small Poems of divers sorts written by Sir Aston Cockain (1658)*, Early English Books Online (EEBO) Editions, 1658.

Croft-Murray, E.C., *Decorative Painting in England, 1537–1837*, Vol. 2, 1970.

Crook, David, *Records of the General Eyre*, Public Record Office Handbooks Number 20, London, 1982.

Darley, Gillian, *John Soane. An Accidental Romantic*, New Haven, CT and London, 1999.

Dean, Ptolemy, *Sir John Soane and the Country Estate*, Aldershot, 1999.

Doe, Helen, *Jane Slade of Polruan*, Penryn, 2002.

Duffin, Anne, *Faction & Faith. Politics and Religion of the Cornish Gentry before the Civil War*, Exeter, 1996.

Dugdale, James, *The New British Traveller*, London, 1819.

du Maurier, Daphne, *The House on the Strand*, London, 2003.

Dunkin, E.H.W., *The Monumental Brasses of Cornwall*, London, 1882.

Ede-Borrett, Stephen, *Lostwithiel 1644. The Campaign and the Battles*, Farnham, 2004.

English Heritage, Boconnoc House and Boconnoc Park report, 77/2007, tree-ring analysis.

Fox, H.S.A. and Padel, O.J., *The Cornish Lands of the Arundells of Lanherne, Fourteenth to Sixteenth Centuries*, Exeter, 2000.

Friar, Stephen, *The Local History Companion*, Stroud, 2001.

Gambier-Perry, E., *Suakin 1885 being a sketch of the campaign of this year, by An Officer who was there*, London, 1885.

Gardener, S.R. (ed.), *The Fortescue Papers*, Camden Society, London, 1871.

Gibbs, V., *The Complete Peerage of England, Scotland, Ireland, GB and the UK*, London, 1916.

Gilbert, C.S., *An Historical Survey of the County of Cornwall*, Congdon, 1820.

Girouard, Mark, *Life in the English Country House*, Harmondsworth, 1980.

Glencross, R.M., Douch, H.L. and Stoate, T.L. (eds), *The Cornwall Protestation Returns, 1641*, Bristol, 1974.

Gray, Todd (ed.), *Harvest Failure in Cornwall and Devon. The Book of Orders and the Corn Surveys of 1623 and 1630–1*, Plymouth, 1992.

Hardyment, Christina, *Behind the Scenes. Domestic Arrangements in Historic Houses*, London, 1997.

Hatcher, John, *Rural Economy and Society in the Duchy of Cornwall. 1300–1500*, Cambridge, 1970.

Hatcher, John, *English Tin Production and Trade before 1550*, Oxford, 1973.

Henderson, Charles, Rowse, A.L. and Henderson, M.I. (eds), *Essays in Cornish History*, Oxford, 1935.

Henwood, George, *Cornwall's Mines and Miners*, Truro, 1972.

Hext, Jean (ed.), *The Staniforth Diary, A Visit to Cornwall in 1800*, Truro, 1965.

Higham, Robert (ed.), *Security & Defence in South-West England before 1800*, Exeter, 1987.

Hollowell, Steven, *Enclosure Records for Historians*, Chichester, 2000.

Holmes, Richard, *Civil War Battles in Cornwall, 1642–1646*, Keele, 1989.

Hopton, Ralph, Chadwyck-Healey, C.E.H. (ed.), *Bellum Civile*, Somerset Record Office, 1902.

Horrox, Rosemary, *Richard III. A Study in Service*, Cambridge, 1989.

Hudson, Kenneth, *The History of English China Clays. Fifty Years of Pioneering and Growth*, Newton Abbot, 1969.

Hyde, Edward, Earl of Clarendon, *The History of the Great Rebellion*, Lockyer, Roger (ed.), OUP for the Folio Society, London, MCMLXVIII (1968).

Jupp, Peter, *Lord Grenville. 1759–1834*, Oxford, 1985.

Kain, Roger J.P. and Prince, Hugh C., *Tithe Surveys for Historians*, Chichester, 2000.

Keast, John, *'The King of Mid-Cornwall.' The Life of Joseph Thomas Treffry (1782–1850)*, Redruth, 1982.

Kennedy, Róisín, *Dublin Castle Art. The Historical and Contemporary Collection*, Dublin, 2010.

Langdon, Andrew, *Stone Crosses in Mid Cornwall*, 1994.

Langdon, Arthur G., *Old Cornish Crosses*, Cornwall Books, 1988.

Lever, Tresham, *The House of Pitt. A Family Chronicle*, London. 1947.

Lorigan, Catherine, Delabole. *The History of the Slate Quarry and the Making of its Village Community*, Reading, 2007.

Loosemore, W.R., Loosemore of Devon, An Outline Family History, loosemore.co.uk.

Lyte, Maxwell H.C., *History of Dunster and of the Families of Mohun and Luttrell*, London, 1909.

Maclean, John, *The Parochial and Family History of the Deanery of Trigg Minor in the County of Cornwall*, 3 vols, 1811–1895.

Mowl, Timothy, Horace Walpole. The Great Outsider, London, 1996.

Murray, Edward Croft, *Decorative Painting in England, 1537–1837*, 2 vols, Country Life, London, 1970.

Neal, Larry, *'I am not master of events'. The Speculations of John Law and Lord Londonderry in the Mississippi and South Sea Bubbles*, New Haven, CT and London, 2012.

Orme, Nicholas (ed.), *Unity and Variety. A History of the Church in Devon and Cornwall*, Exeter, 1991.

Orme, Nicholas, *English Church Dedications*, Exeter, 1996.

Orme, Nicholas, *Cornish Wills. 1342–1540*, Exeter, 2007.

Orme, Nicholas, *Cornwall and the Cross. Christianity 500–1560*, London, 2007.

Orme, Nicholas, *The Minor Clergy of Exeter Cathedral. Biographies: 1250–1548*, Exeter, 2013.

Payton, Philip, *The Making of Modern Cornwall. Historical Experience and the Persistence of 'Difference'*, Redruth, 1992.

Payton, Philip, *The Cornish Overseas*, Fowey, 1999.

Payton, Philip, Kennerley, Alston and Doe, Helen (eds), *The Maritime History of Cornwall*, Exeter, 2014.

Peachey, Stuart, *The Battles of Launceston and Sourton Down*, Bristol, 1993.

Peachey, Stuart, *The Battle of Braddock Down*, English Civil War Battles, Bristol, 1993.

Penderill-Church, John, *William Cookworthy. 1705–1780. A Study of the Pioneer of True Porcelain Manufacture in England*, Truro, 1972.

Polsue, Joseph, *Lake's Parochial History of the County of Cornwall*, Truro, 1867.

Quiller Couch, Arthur ('Q'), *Shining Ferry*, London, 1928.

Radcliffe, George, *The Earl of Strafforde's Letters and Dispatches*, Dublin, 1740.

Rees, Siân, *The Floating Brothel,* London, 2001.

Robertson, R. and Gilbert, G., *Some Aspects of the Domestic Architecture of Cornwall,* 1979.

Rowse, A.L., *Tudor Cornwall*, London, 1969.

Schellinks, Willem, Exwood, Maurice and Lehmann, H.L. (eds), *The Journal of William Schellinks' Travels in England. 1661–1663*, Royal Historical Society, London, 1993.

Selleck, A. Douglas, *Cookworthy, 1705–80 and his circle, 'a man of no common clay'*, Plymouth, 1978.

Sparrow, Elizabeth, *Secret Service. British Agents in France 1792–1815*, Woodbridge, 1999.

Sprigge, Joshua, *Anglia Rediviva, England's Recovery: being the History of the Motions, Actions and Successes of the Army under the Immediate Conduct of His Excellency Sir Thomas Fairfax, Knight, Captain-General of all the Parliaments Force in England*, London, 1647.

Staniforth, Thomas, Hext, Jean (ed.), *The Staniforth Diary. A Visit to Cornwall in 1800*, Truro, 1965.

Stater, Victor, *High Life, Low Morals. The Duel that Shook Stuart Society*, London, 1999.

Stoate, T.L. (ed.), *Cornwall Subsidies in the Reign of Henry VIII, 1524 and 1543 and the Benevolence of 1545*, Bristol, 1985.

Stoate, T.L. (ed.), *Cornwall Hearth and Poll Taxes 1660–1664. Direct Taxation in Cornwall in the Reign of Charles II*, Bristol, 1981.

Stoyle, Mark, *Soldiers & Strangers. An Ethnic History of the English Civil War*, Bury St Edmunds, 2005.

Stoyle, Mark, *West Britons. Cornish Identities and the Early Modern British State*, Exeter, 2002.

Stuart, D., *Manorial Records*, Chichester, 2010.

Sutton, Anne and Hammond, Rodney W. (eds), *The Coronation of Richard III: The Extant Documents*, London, 1984.

Symonds, Richard, *Diary of the Marches of the Royal Army*, Long, C.E. (ed.), Cambridge, 1997.

Thompson, Edward Maunde, *Hatton Correspondence*, Camden Society, London, 1878.

Thorn, Caroline and Frank, *Domesday Book. Cornwall*, Chichester, 1979.

Tolstoy, Nikolai, *The Half-Mad Lord, Thomas Pitt, 2nd Baron Camelford (1775–1804)*, London, 1978.

Valdrè, Ugo and Lynch, Camille, *Vincenzo Valdrè (Faenza 1740–Dublino 1814): Un Artista Versatile in Inghilterra ed Irlanda*, Società Torricelliana di Scienze e Lettere Faenza, Faenza, 2009.

Valdrè, Ugo, Lynch, Brian and Lynch, Camille, *Vincenzo Valdrè (Faenza 1740–Dublino 1814). Pittore, Decoratore ed Architetto a Parma (?1766), a Roma (1767–1772), con Richard Norris (1771–72), a Parigi (1773), a Londra (1774–1778), a Stowe (1779–1789) e a Dublino (1790–1814)*, Società Torricelliana di Scienze e Lettere Faenza, Faenza, 2014.

Vivian, J.L., *The Visitation of Cornwall comprising The Heralds Visitations of 1530, 1573 and 1620*, Exeter, 1887.

Walker, Edward, *Historical Discourses upon Severall Occasions, viz. The Happy Progress and Success of the Arms of K. Charles I*, London, 1705.

Wallis, John, *The Cornwall Register*, Bodmin, 1847.

Westland, Ella (ed.), *Cornwall. The Cultural Construction of Place*, Penzance, 1997.

Whetter, James, *The Bodrugans. A Study of a Cornish Medieval Knightly Family*, St Austell, 1995.

Worgan, George B., *A general view of the agriculture of the county of Cornwall*, London, 1811.

Worthy, Charles, *The History of the Suburbs of Exeter*, London, 1892.

Wrottesley, Major-General the Hon. George, *Crecy and Calais from the Original Records in the Public Record Office*, London, 1898.

Wyndham, Maud, *Chronicles of the Eighteenth Century*, 2 volumes, London, 1924.

Articles and chapters

Adams, J.H., 'The medieval chapels of Cornwall', *Journal of the Royal Institution of Cornwall*, Vol. III, New Series, Part 1, 1957, pp. 48–65.

Arthurson, I. and Kingwell, N., 'The proclamation of Henry VII as King of England, 3 November 1483', *Bulletin of the Institute of Historical Research*, 63, 1990, pp. 100–106.

Beal, Mary, 'The royalist Richard Symonds and an unclaimed portrait by Sir Peter Lely', *British Art Journal*, Spring 2016, pp. 16–21.

Betjeman, John, 'Two Cornish houses', *Architectural Review*, LXXIII, April 1933, pp. 153–158.

Binney, Marcus, 'A restoration inspired by history', *Country Life*, 19 November 2008.

Chesney, H.E., 'The transference of lands in England, 1640–1660', *Transactions of the Royal Historical Society*, Fourth series, 15, 1932, pp. 181–210.

Churchill, Penny, 'An exceptional country estate in Norfolk', *Country Life*, Thursday, 2 June 2011, pp. 1–3.

Clarke, Kate M., 'The Carew-Mohun chimneypiece', *Devon and Cornwall Notes and Queries*, Volume IX, from January 1916 to October 1917, No. 194, pp. 233–239.

Curry, Anne and Bell, Adrian R., 'Waging war in the fourteenth century', *Journal of Medieval History*, 37, 2011, pp. 231–232.

de Alcazar, Dom Pedro, The Law of Arms in Medieval England, © Craig Levin.

de Faria, Tiago Viũla, 'Tracing the chemyn de Portyngale: English service and servicemen in fourteenth-century Portugal', *Journal of Medieval History*, xxx, 2011, pp. 1–12.

Drake, S.J., 'Politics and society in Richard II's Cornwall: a study in relations between centre and locality', *Journal of the Royal Institution of Cornwall*, 2013, pp. 23–48.

Duffin, Anne, 'The defence of Cornwall in the early seventeenth century', in R. Higham (ed.), *Security & Defence in South-West England before 1800*, Exeter, 1987, pp. 69–77.

Gibbon, M.L., 'The history of Stowe, XXIII, Lord Buckingham and the completion of the interior', *The Stoic*, December 1875.

Goodway, Keith, 'Landscapes and gardens at Keele. 1700–1900', *Essays on the History of Keele*, 1986.

Habakkuk, H.J., 'Landowners and the Civil War', *The Economic History Review*, New Series, 18(1), pp. 130–151.

Hatcher, John, 'Non-manorialism in medieval Cornwall', *Agricultural History Review*, 18, Part 1, 1970, pp. 1–16.

Kleineke, Hannes, 'Why the west was wild: law and disorder in fifteenth-century Cornwall and Devon', in Linda Clark (ed.), *Authority and Subversion*, Woodbridge, 2003, pp. 75–93.

Mace, Frances A., 'Devonshire ports in the fourteenth and fifteenth centuries', *Transactions of the Royal Historical Society*, Fourth Series, 8, 1925, pp. 98–126.

Orme, Nicholas, 'Visitations of Cornish churches, 1281–1331', in P. Payton (ed.), *Cornish Studies: Twenty-One*, Exeter, 2013, pp. 76–103.

Pool, P.A.S., 'The tithings of Cornwall', *Journal of the Royal Institution of Cornwall*, New Series, VIII, Part 4, 1981, pp. 275–337.

Rawle, Carole, 'The politics of marriage in later medieval England: William Lord Botreaux, and the Hungerfords', *Huntingdon Library Quarterly*, 51(3), Summer 1988, pp. 161–175.

Spring, David, 'Ralph Sneyd: Tory country gentleman', *Bulletin of the John Rylands Library, Manchester*, 38(2), March 1956, pp. 535–555.

Staal, C., 'William Cookworthy and his Plymouth porcelain factory', *Journal of the Royal Institution of Cornwall*, New Series, VIII, Part 4, 1981, pp. 267–274.

Stansfield, R.E., 'The Duchy of Cornwall and the Wars of the Roses: patronage, politics and power, 1453–1502', in P. Payton (ed.), *Cornish Studies: Twenty-One*, Exeter, 2013, pp. 104–150.

Stoyle, Mark, 'Afterlife of an army: the old Cornish regiments, 1643–44', in P. Payton (ed.), *Cornish Studies: Sixteen*, Exeter, 2008, pp. 26–47.

Thomson, J.A.F., 'The Courtenay family in the Yorkist period', *Historical Research*, 45(112), November 1972, pp. 230–246.

Wentersdorf, Karl P., 'The clandestine marriages of the Fair Maid of Kent', *Journal of Medieval History*, 5(3), September 1979, pp. 203–231.

Whitley, H. Michell, 'The church goods of Cornwall at the time of the Reformation', *Journal of the Royal Institution of Cornwall*, VII(xxv), 1882, pp. 92–135.

Wills and inventories

CRO:

AP/M/141/1-7	Mohun, Ann, 1608

TNA:

PROB11/16/1509	Courtenay, Edward, Earl of Devonshire,
PROB11/1436	Forster, Benjamin, Rector, 1806
PROB11/70/340	Harvye, Richard, 1587
PROB11/1055/65	Leach, Mary, Wife, 1779
PROB11/984/207	Leach, Philip, Rector Clerk, 1773
PROB11/13	Mauleverer, Halnath, 1502
PROB11/182/593	Mohun, Raynold, 1640
PROB11/317	Mohun, Warwick, Lord Mohun, 1665
PROB11/72	Mohun, William, 1588
PROB11/1228/202	Pitt, Thomas, 1st Lord Camelford, Baron of Boconnoc, 1793
PROB11/1412/202	Pitt, Thomas, 2nd Lord Camelford, Baron of Boconnoc, 1804

Other documents

Catalogue from the Weiss Gallery, *A fashionable likeness, a catalogue of early portraiture 1550–1710*, www.weissgallery.com

Pam Dodds and Joy Wilson, Cornwall Gardens Trust report, 2007.

Vincent Waldre's [Valdrè] ceiling paintings in Dublin Castle, *Apollo*, January 1872.

A Cambridge Alumni Database.

Dictionary of Land Surveyors and Local Mapmakers of Great Britain and Ireland, 1530–1850, British Library, 1997.

Unpublished theses, dissertations and articles

Bourke-Borrowes, Kildare Hubert, 'Hon Algernon Henry 'Algy' Bourke, a short biography', 2012.

Palmer, Susan, 'The adventures of a Regency architect in the West Country', 2008.

Troup, Cynthia K., 'Lady Anne Grenville: an unsung heroine in garden history', dissertation submitted for the degree of MA in Garden History, 2004, History of Art Department, University of Bristol.

Trowbridge, Benjamin, 'English intervention in Iberia during the Hundred Years War: the English army and expedition to Portugal in 1381–2', dissertation submitted for the degree of MA(Res) in Medieval Studies, University of Reading, 2007–08; 2009 Amended and Updated Version.

Tyldesley, C.J., 'The Crown and the local communities in Devon and Cornwall from 1377–1422', PhD thesis, University of Exeter, 1978.

Vernon, Joanna Elizabeth, 'Thomas Pitt, Lord Camelford, amateur architect, connoisseur and patron of the arts: a case study in the history of taste 1760–93', presented for the degree of Master of Philosophy, Royal Holloway and Bedford New College, University of London, 1993.

Wood, Min, 'Parks and lawns. The making of the Boconnoc landscape', 21 January 2015.

INDEX

Italics indicate an illustration

The destination for history
www.thehistorypress.co.uk